Literary Generations
A Festschrift in Honor of Edward D. Sullivan
by His Friends, Colleagues, and Former Students

FRENCH FORUM MONOGRAPHS

78

Editors R.C. LA CHARITÉ and V.A. LA CHARITÉ

For complete listing, see page 254

Literary Generations

A Festschrift in Honor of
Edward D. Sullivan
by His Friends, Colleagues,
and Former Students

Edited by
Alain Toumayan

FRENCH FORUM, PUBLISHERS
LEXINGTON, KENTUCKY

The volumes in this series are printed on acid-free,
long-life paper and meet the requirements of the
American National Standard for Permanence of Paper
for Printed Materials
Z 39.48-1984.

Library of Congress Catalog Card Number 91-73986

ISBN 0-917058-82-8

Printed in the United States of America

Contents

Preface

As one can see in Edward Sullivan's essay in *Literary Generations*, the subject of generations is one which animated his thinking and his reflections on literature through his teaching. For this reason, as well as for the subject's intrinsic richness, it seemed an appropriate topic for a volume paying tribute— albeit in a very limited way—to Ed Sullivan. The subject of literary generations was proposed to the authors in this collection as an invitation, not as a limitation, and authors were enjoined to interpret it each in his or her own manner. Thus the questions of relations between parents and children in the literal sense as well as in a broad range of figural senses, between literary periods and movements, and the more general questions of literary influence and the various issues involved in the engendering of literary texts represented possible avenues for reflection on the subject.

In an even broader manner, however, the subject of generations seemed an appropriate one to evoke in a volume honoring Ed Sullivan, for such a subject assumes that seeking connections, that establishing and nurturing relationships across all boundaries, be they the boundaries of periods, of national literatures, of disciplines, of cultural practices, of genre or gender would enrich one in unsuspected and surprising ways. The tributes paid to Ed Sullivan in this volume by Robert Goheen and Sara Vagliano will attest to Ed Sullivan's embracing and championing of these connections in such concrete ways as creating a department of comparative literature, bringing coeducation to Princeton, creating the Princeton-in-France program, and encouraging the cooperation between the business and academic sectors. And I think that the assumptions involved in such enterprises inform the individual essays in this collection and inform the collection as a whole.

Yet the inspiration for this volume and for the subject of generations involved more than Ed Sullivan's remarkable professional achievements and institutional contributions which, in themselves, would warrant a greater tribute than can be paid in a *Festschrift*. Since I joined Princeton's department of Romance Languages and Literatures at the time of Ed Sullivan's retirement in 1982, I can certainly attest to his continued involvement in the department and in the university as a counsellor, advisor, and sage and, like so many others, I felt fortunate to be one of the beneficiaries of his immense reservoir of expertise, knowledge, and experience, all generously shared. It is his interest in and dedication to the people at all levels of the profession and his energetic and avid desire to serve which represent achievements which I wish to evoke and acknowledge most gratefully in this tribute to which, I hope, the idea of generations lends some form.

This volume would not have been possible without the help, advice and support of many friends and colleagues. First and foremost, I wish to express my deep gratitude to François Rigolot whose active and enthusiastic support of this project from its inception in 1989 was crucial in bringing it to completion. Albert Sonnenfeld provided me with some very useful information concerning the early days of Princeton's Department of Romance Languages and Literatures and for this, I am very grateful. Louis MacKenzie provided some very helpful editorial advice as did John Logan on whose limitless knowledge I often relied for advice and help. I wish also to thank my friend Tom Trezise for his insightful comments on my own essay which have substantially improved it. I am very grateful also to Raymond C. La Charité for his expert assistance with this manuscript. Special thanks are also due to the members of the Decio Steno Pool at the University of Notre Dame for their assistance in typing substantial portions of this manuscript. Finally, my warm thanks to my wife Vicki for her expert help in every aspect of this project and her patience.

Funding for the publication of this volume has been provided by the President's fund of Princeton University, and, for his generous assistance, I am grateful to President Harold Shapiro. I wish also to thank Nancy W. Malkiel, Dean of the College, and Aaron Lemonick, Dean of the Faculty emeritus, for their generous joint contribution through the J. Douglas Brown Dean's fund. My sincere thanks are also due to the Council of the Humanities, and to the Department of Romance Languages and Literatures at Princeton for their generous financial support of this volume. Finally, my sincere thanks to the Cultural Services of the French Embassy for its contribution.

Alain Toumayan

Robert F. Goheen

Edward D. Sullivan in the Service of Princeton University

To join in this tribute to Edward D. Sullivan is a distinct pleasure, and I appreciate the opportunity to record my admiration and my gratitude for his manifold and invaluable services to Princeton University as a teacher, scholar, and academic administrator extending over thirty-six years.

A native of Boston, Edward Sullivan came to New Jersey in 1946 from Harvard, where he had taken both his undergraduate and graduate degrees, to join Princeton's Department of Modern Languages (as it was then known). He rapidly established himself as a well-liked teacher, a popular and engaged member of the University community, and a respected scholar and critic of modern French and European literature. His rise through the faculty ranks was steady and even relatively fast for those pre-Sputnik days. He attained tenure as an associate professor four years after his arrival and, despite recall to military service during the Korean War, became a full professor just twelve years after joining the Princeton faculty.

His active service as, first, a professor of French and then, after 1975, of French and Comparative Literature extended to the time of mandatory retirement in 1982, when he was in his sixty-ninth year. Along the way he had brought singular vision and skill to bear when called upon to shoulder the duties of Departmental Chairman (1958-1966), Dean of the College (1966-1972), and Chairman of the Council of the Humanities (1974-1982).

Others writing in this volume can speak more authoritatively than I to Edward Sullivan's achievements in the classroom and lecture hall, to the international reputation gained by his writings on nineteenth-century French literature, and to the recognition conferred by the French government on his contributions to Americans' understanding of France. I shall direct my observations to the telling service he rendered Princeton in the three major administrative positions that he held while an active member of the Princeton faculty. The first two were on my watch. The third fell in the presidency of my successor, William Bowen, but ties of friendship and shared endeavor bound us, and I could still observe from a distance—and applaud—Edward Sullivan's sure handling of those latter day responsibilities as leader of the University's Humanities Council.

Chairman of the Department

The fall of 1958, when Edward Sullivan assumed the chairmanship of the Department of Romance Languages, marked the first year following the split of the former Department of Modern Languages into separate German and Romance Languages Departments. Thus one of his first tasks was to work out new housing, scheduling, and secretarial arrangements at more or less the nuts-and-bolts level. He swiftly accomplished that and moved beyond it to display in the job a splendid combination of energy, thoughtful concern for the fit between curriculum and students, a fine and judicious eye for faculty talent, and a strong organizational sense.

Under his leadership, for example, the departmental faculty early in the second year undertook a careful review of the program of instruction in French, which led to considerable revisions in its offerings and a more integrated course of study for departmental majors. Similar curricular reviews and revisions were carried out over the following years with the undergraduate offerings in Spanish and Italian. A major overhaul of the Department's graduate program was then undertaken to make it both more effective and attractive. Meantime, as Chairman of Romance Languages Edward Sullivan was also responsible for helping nurse toward autonomy a section of Russian Languages and Literature that had remained appended to his Department. At the same time he was a leading advocate for, and contributor to, the creation of an interdepartmental Program in Comparative Literature. Established during 1962-63, under the auspices initially of the Council of the Humanities, Comparative Literature subsequently became a full fledged, free standing department. Early in the 1960s before its establishment as an academic entity at Princeton, Edward Sullivan presciently argued that it would not only be a valuable addition to the University's intellectual bill of fare but that it also would attract more and better students to the language departments. The prediction was quickly proved right.

But the Chairman's interests and activity were by no means focused only on such curricular matters. The prime determinant of any department's vitality and influence is, of course, its faculty, and this was very much toward the forefront of his attention. Indeed, the years of his chairmanship were truly formative years for Princeton's present Department of Romance Languages, as also for the current Department of Comparative Literature. Major appointments made then included, for example, Léon-François Hoffmann, Karl Uitti, Alban Forcione, Albert Sonnenfeld, Clarence Brown, and André Maman to name a few. (Parenthetically, it may be noted that the Sullivan net for a few years also contained a dynamic young comparatist from Yale, the late A. Bartlett Giamatti, who, it was expected, would revitalize Italian studies at Princeton. However, he proved unable to resist a call to return to his alma mater, where at a still young age he soon became President.)

Not to be omitted from this phase of Edward Sullivan's career was the leading and highly effective role that he played in developing and directing the Princeton Program for Summer Work Abroad. Initiated on a small scale by his predecessor as department chairman, Professor Ira Wade, this program puts American college students (mainly but not solely from Princeton) into working situations for the course of the summer in France, Germany, and other non-English-speaking countries. A requirement is that the student have a good working grasp of the language of the country in which he or she is to work. A wide variety of employers overseas has been enlisted, and the nature of the employment experienced by student participants can range from work in banks, to hospitals, to government offices, to summer camps, and as beach attendants.

While Chairman of Romance Languages, Edward Sullivan developed the contacts and organization, and also raised the funding, that enabled the program to jump from a level of 10 student placements when he took it over in 1958 to a high of 88 in the summer of 1963, when the students involved came from 15 American campuses. What the experience has meant to its student participants may perhaps be epitomized in the words of one who commented, "Working in another language, fending for yourself, you learn patience, courage, perseverance. It gives you a very confident feeling." By 1988 the Princeton Program for Summer Work Abroad could boast more than 1000 alumni who had returned from their summers in Europe or South America with enhanced language skills, an enriching cultural experience, and "the sense," as one said, "that they can do anything."

Dean of the College

The latter half of the 1960s and first year of the next decade were years fraught with an unusually high degree of strain and of demands for change in America's institutions of higher education, as also in the society at large. There were many reasons for this. Among them, on the intellectual side, was the intensification of specialization, the explosion of knowledge, and the burgeoning of new fields of inquiry in the post-World War II years. The inquisitive student was likely to find himself pulled in many directions. Any given subject was vast and not easily mastered, and there were many subjects to be dealt with. Then there was the restlessness—the often mingled sense of moral inadequacy and indignation—arising from the civil rights movement and the belated, spreading recognition of the injustices so long suffered by America's black population. Many students became active workers in the movement. Many others were touched emotionally by it. But of even greater influence on the campuses was the Vietnam War, which not only became increasingly hard to accept as a just war but which also kept many restless students penned up on college campuses avoiding the military draft.

Prior to 1966-67, the Princeton campus had been a relatively calm one, and occasional grumbling about the form and efficacy of the undergraduate curriculum, except for the foreign language requirement, came more often from members of the faculty than the undergraduate body. By then, however, the times were beginning to change. Princeton was entering a period in which undergraduate education, together with other aspects of student life and the relation of students to the institution, would demand intense scrutiny and adjustments where appropriate.

It was at this time and in these conditions that Professor Sullivan agreed to my request that he surrender the chairmanship of his department and take on the much broader responsibilities of Dean of the College. As Dean, he assumed oversight of all undergraduate studies and of all campus services and agencies concerned with the educational life of the undergraduates.

Part of the job was managerial, and here Dean Sullivan's understanding of people and his organizational sense stood the University in good stead as over the next six years he guided the manning and oversaw the operations of a dozen varied student services. They included, for example, Admissions, the (Faculty) Board of Advisers, Counselling Services, Career Services, Teacher Preparation and Placement, and the Registrar.

More central to his office and to his interests was oversight and development of the undergraduate curriculum. To these duties, he brought sensitive human understanding, a clear educational vision, and much effective energy. Among the curricular innovations and adjustments during his Deanship— accomplished in collaboration with the faculty Committee on the Course of Study, which he chaired—were a reduction in the required course-load for underclassmen to relieve what had clearly become an overload and to open to students added opportunities either to dig more deeply into their studies or to venture out intellectually more on their own; establishment of Latin American Studies, African Studies, and Afro-American Studies as organized programs; the development of additional courses in the Creative Arts; reexamination and revision of Princeton's then aged grading system that paralleled no other; student-initiated seminars and opportunities for selected students to develop independent majors, working with faculty advisers, where the students' interests did not fit existing departments or programs; a semester-in-the-city program for credit supervised by faculty and related to the students' departmental work; and expanded opportunities for a term or year of study abroad.

The thrust of all this was not to lower standards nor to overturn the basic structure of the existing undergraduate course of study, which appeared sound; it was to introduce greater flexibility adapted to individual needs and so, within the general structure, gain greater student engagement in their learning. As the Dean wrote in his annual report to the President for 1971-72:

> We have not abandoned requirements but we do exercise judgment as to when they may be counter-productive in individual cases and at that point provide some kind of constructive alternative. . . . It has seemed to me that flexibility should be possible within it (an overall structure) but without permitting avoidance of educational responsibilities or catering to mere whims.

Special mention must be made of the traumatic days and weeks of early 1970 following the "incursion" of U.S. military forces into Cambodia. For a time there the good sense and purposeful intent of the Dean as just expressed, and indeed the University's whole educational enterprise, were deeply shaken. Students were in turmoil. Radicals thought the revolution had come. The faint-hearted despaired. Steadier souls were hard pressed. Meeting after lengthy meeting of the faculty led finally to a resolution to permit end-of-the-year procedures to be waived. Students could elect to postpone to the fall the completion of the year's academic requirements without prejudice to their standing. Through all this strain, toil, and debate, Edward Sullivan was a deeply engaged and steady figure. Characteristically, he wrote in his Dean's report to the President that summer, "It was an extraordinary period, and extraordinary measures had to be taken to deal with events in coherent fashion." He pointed out that the measures taken "all served to put the burden of choice on the individual student," and that, finally, the number of postponed courses, papers, and examinations amounted to only about 13.5 percent of what the students might have opted.

By the fall of 1970, the turmoil on the campuses had subsided for reasons not yet entirely clear. Students returned from the summer prepared to study. Faculties could again devote themselves to teaching and scholarship. At Princeton, deans, departmental chairmen, and the Committee on the Course of Study could again look to the fine-tuning of the curriculum. But I would particularly like to share a few more of Dean Sullivan's observations about students from an earlier point in those troubled years. They show well, I think, the range and depth of his understanding and his steadiness of purpose:

> Clearly, what is happening is not just the result of spring fever (though that helps) nor is it the result of a world-wide conspiracy (though there are conspirators). There is simply too much dissatisfaction about for there to be any simple explanation of it—except to say—inadequately—that a very large number of young people, here and abroad, for a multitude of different reasons find the world they live in a sham and a mockery. Given *any* occasion they rebel. Their strength is that they have no program and can join in one band all who feel any kind of dissatisfaction. Some are frankly

anarchists or nihilists, but their exhortations would be wholly ineffective were it not for the underground reservoir of undifferentiated discontent to which I have referred. . . .

Why *is* there so much discontent? Rightly or wrongly, young people in different countries and for different reasons feel hemmed in, circumscribed, limited. They see themselves in current terms as an oppressed minority and take their analogies from the struggle of tiny North Vietnam against the United States colossus and the struggle of the black minority against the dominant white culture. They take their analogy in action from the techniques of guerilla warfare and street-fighting, further identifying with the oppressed minorities.

All one can do is seek out the sources of dissatisfaction and keep communications open. As long as there is some sense that one can be heard, that one will be taken seriously, then there is hope that the normal rational modes of discourse will prevail. This means too that it behooves us to continue to examine all that we do, review our structures and procedures in advance of any complaint or confrontation, and revise what needs to be altered to fit a rapidly changing society. This we have been trying to do, as most of this report suggests, and this we shall continue to do. It will require wisdom, foresight, and luck. (*Annual Report to the President by the Dean of the College, July 1968*)

As I have already confessed, just what lanced the boil of youthful discontent and rage that came to a head in the spring of 1970 remains to me largely a mystery. With it behind us, however, we can look with greater appreciation on what was surely the largest single innovation in undergraduate education in Princeton's history since Woodrow Wilson's presidency (1902-1910) if not since Witherspoon's (1767-1794).

It was the introduction of coeducation in 1969, and it occupied much of the attention of the Dean of the College and his associates during the final four years of Edward Sullivan's service in that office. He himself was involved in it to the hilt all the way: in the initial study committee, in the operational planning, in travelling the country to help persuade alumni groups of the essential merits of the step, in putting the plans into effect, and finally in viewing with delight "the education of women as undergraduates at Princeton becoming a substantial reality" and then the positive contributions which the young women almost immediately began to make to both the educational and social life of the place. The germination, nurture, and blooming of coeducation at Princeton during his deanship were not of course Edward Sullivan's sole doing, but he contributed much to them, and indeed, they made a fitting climax to his service as Dean of the College.

Chairman of the Council of the Humanities

With the advent of a new President of the University in 1972, Edward Sullivan relinquished administrative duties and returned to full-time teaching and scholarship as Avalon Foundation Professor of the Humanities, one of the University's few endowed chairs not tied to a single department. Just two years later, however, he was again called on to share in the University's academic administration as Chairman of Princeton's Council of the Humanities.

The role of the Council is to be concerned with every level of humanistic teaching and scholarship in the University from courses for undergraduates to graduate work, the scholarly development of younger faculty, the recognition of older scholars, and the infusion of the insights and experience of visiting thinkers and writers into the mix and interplay of on-campus humanistic endeavor. The Council encourages cooperation among the University's humanistic departments, focuses attention on issues and problems common to their disciplines, and administers the income from gifts and endowment so as to foster particularly interesting lines of inquiry and the development of the humanities as a whole.

Thus the Chairman of the Council is required to oversee and help advance a variety of undertakings. Prominent among them from the start has been a program of Visiting Fellows bringing to the University, originally for a semester, "people of vigor and distinction to infuse new ideas by their presence." Too often, unfortunately, people whom Princeton wanted proved unable to get free from other obligations to give Princeton a full semester. Edward Sullivan early seized on this problem, and his very successful answer was to trade off one budgeted term-long slot for as many as eight visitors on shorter tenure. The roster of Visiting Fellows for the late 1970s reads as a galaxy of academic stars, or persons soon to become so, drawn from across this country, Europe, Latin America and occasionally East Asia. Among them were such names as Noam Chomsky, Michel Foucault, and Bernard Williams in Philosophy; Carlos Fuentes in Romance Languages and Literature; E. L. Doctorow, Robert Fitzgerald, and Stanley Kunitz in Creative Writing; C. Vann Woodward and Carlo Ginzberg in History; Alasdair MacIntyre and Masao Abe in Religion; and others no less stimulating in Classics, Comparative Literature, and English.

Inherited subsidiaries of the Council requiring oversight included at this time American Studies, European Cultural Studies, the Gauss Seminars in Criticism, Comparative Literature (soon to become independent), Classical Philosophy, Political Philosophy, Linguistics, the Committee on Humanistic Studies (responsible for undergraduate courses), the Ferris Professor of Journalism (a sequence of visiting appointments), and the E. L. Faber Class of 1915 Memorial Lectures (bringing in annually 15 or so visiting speakers in humanistic fields). New undertakings that drew the Chairman's encouragement and came to be lodged under his tent were the Program of Modern Greek Language and Literature, the Theater and Dance Program, the Women's Studies Committee, and the Committee for Medieval Studies. Altogether this array of new and continuing enterprises clearly required of its overseer great intellectual range and an empathetic responsiveness to diverse manifestations of humanistic aspiration and endeavor. In Edward Sullivan they found that, and it can be said that humanistic learning was nurtured well and the capabilities of Princeton's Council of the Humanities well exercised during his eight years as its Chairman.

Had not "man for all seasons" become so shop-worn a metaphor, it would have been a fit characterization of the Edward Sullivan I have known as colleague and friend for over forty years. But there never has been anything shop-worn or trite about Edward Sullivan. His was and is a vital spirit, in which seriousness of purpose is twinned with zest, even joyousness, whenever engaged in a cause or task of importance. Over the thirty-eight years prior to his retirement, these qualities were abundantly manifest in his teaching, in his writing, and in his ready and varied administrative undertakings aimed to help make the teaching and learning of students and of colleagues as fruitful as possible.

I salute him, then, as a three-dimensional academic of much more than ordinary substance and stature. Teacher, Scholar, Academic Administrator. In each dimension his contributions to Princeton have been great.

Sara Vagliano

Edward Daniel Sullivan:
A Biographical Essay

Some years ago in Princeton a not-so-young Assistant Professor of Romance Languages leaped from the ivory tower—and survived to write this biographical essay because Ed Sullivan broke her fall. He seems to think that his intervention—in the form of a human recycling project he had helped invent—was, as the French say, "parfaitement normal."

Ed has had this same view of all the prodigious investments of energy, imagination, intelligence and generosity he has made in the long career which we honor in this volume. However, even the most inexperienced biographer knows that she cannot resist or avoid turning up the modestly proffered fabric to see where and how the threads of the pattern are knotted. "Where" will follow shortly; "how" merits an observation based upon what I have understood about Ed after nearly 20 years of collegial friendship and particularly upon the long conversations we have had recently in preparation for this essay. It is simply this: the same Edward D. Sullivan who has open-handedly given himself to being at once teacher, administrator and intellectual bridge-builder for more than 50 years is in fact the most economical of men.

Oikonomos: "manager of a household"; *economy*, "the administration of the concerns and resources of any community or establishment with a view to orderly conduct and productiveness." Fundamentally conservative and thus unwilling to countenance waste or loss in any form, Ed has always provided generous and exemplary management of the resources of his extended household—this family of colleagues, friends and students. His communities have been several: Harvard College, the Middlebury French Summer School, the United States Navy, and most of all Princeton University. But they have included, at every point, groups and individuals not ordinarily associated with the academic community. For Ed, the university is not an enclosure, it is a forum, an agora through which all manner of passages should lead. Or if it is more modestly a large multi-generational household, it is one in which the doors and windows must be kept open. These notions clearly underlie the approach Ed has taken to every task, every assignment, every course he has devised.

Boston-born (December 9, 1913), Ed Sullivan stayed close to home throughout his student years. Following his graduation from the Boston Latin School in 1931, he graduated from the Phillips Exeter Academy in 1932, then *summa cum laude* from Harvard College in 1936, where he was elected to Phi Beta Kappa. Having concentrated in French language and literature, he used his Sheldon Traveling Fellowship from Harvard in 1936 to cross the Atlantic for a year of study and travel. Already determined not to waste resources or opportunities, Ed also served during that year as a special European correspondent for the *Boston Evening Transcript*. One can imagine the adventures of the burly young Boston Irishman armed with what he describes as his "abominable" French accent—actually learning to speak the language not having been a Harvard priority at the time.

That was soon to change, however, when André Morize, Ed's former tutor at Harvard, took him on in the summer of 1936 as his assistant at the Middlebury Summer French School of which Morize was the Director. The School featured a remarkable collection of guest lecturers, writers and actors from France, who shared in teaching the seminars and courses. Because Morize believed that theater is an important point of cultural access for students, faculty and staff members also produced and performed a French play every week. And thus it was that Ed Sullivan learned both to build scenery and to perform Molière with Béatrice Dussane and Jean Moulineau of the Comédie Française. He returned to Middlebury every year until 1941. The last two years he was accompanied by his wife, the former Eleanor Harrold, whom he met on a Boston school car and whom he remembers first as "that pretty young girl with a violin case." Music was Eleanor Sullivan's incentive to learn French, and she began to know the language through French art songs.

The doctoral thesis Ed completed at Harvard in 1941 concerned "The Interpretation of Molière's Alceste from 1666 to the Present." The literary critic and historian who confronts a script has a particular problem, one not shared by analysts and historians of prose fiction and poetry: like music, theater exists in part on the printed page and in part in the perceptions of its performers and its audience. To write intelligently about theater, therefore, demands an understanding of the triangle of text-interpretation-reaction that is the living reality of the medium. Sullivan's experiences as literary scholar, set-builder and performer provided the point of view from which he explored the evolution of the meaning of *Le Misanthrope* through 300 years of readings by actors who functioned, in Sullivan's thesis, both as critics and interpreters.

The word, however, is always the beginning, and the text itself is primary to every effort of analysis and criticism. Sullivan remembers his mentor André Morize, himself a student of Gustave Lanson, as a precursor of the American

New Critics in his insistence upon the solidity and primacy of the text, of words richly encrusted with the accrued crystals of their cultural evolution. Indeed, Sullivan's doctoral degree from Harvard is in Romance Philology; "literature," he remembers ruefully, "you had to bootleg in by yourself." And when he did just that, developing over time a critical approach to prose fiction which came to include modes of analysis derived from the social sciences, he continued to insist upon the primacy and the density of the text itself.

When Sullivan became, upon completion of his doctorate in 1941, an instructor in French language at Harvard, he found a fellow instructor sympathetic to his notion that words have power in the world of events. With William T. Locke, later librarian at the Massachusetts Institute of Technology, Sullivan decided that military language should be included in the otherwise literary-historical context of the undergraduate language courses the two were teaching. The two instructors created a collection of articles in French on military subjects. Produced on an electric typewriter and photocopied by the Boston Blueprint Company, *La Guerre moderne* was integrated into the undergraduate language program, and the original edition was sold through the Harvard Coop. It includes a series of texts on the conduct of war, a glossary, and a Comparative Table of Ranks. Subsequently The Harvard University Press, which had had considerable success in World War I with *French for Soldiers*, reprinted the collection in a letterpress edition.

At the same time that he produced *La Guerre moderne*, Sullivan became involved with a Boston-based foundation which owned a short-wave radio station, WRUL. Its mission was to broadcast news from the United States in foreign languages all over the world. The broadcasts by Sullivan and his fellow teachers of French Civilization at Harvard ultimately became the basic source and model for the Voice of America.

In 1942 Ed Sullivan was called to military service. He served until 1946 as a Lieutenant (j.g.) in the United States Navy, on assignment which was and remains classified. He will say, however, that he was part of a group of young PhDs recruited by the Navy "from all over the lot," on the assumption that well-trained minds can quickly assimilate and analyze new information and apply it effectively. His own memories are of intense work, wonderful conversations, and excellent games of chess and bridge. "From that group one could have formed a first-class university," he remembers. My own reaction upon hearing the description of the group was that it must surely have served Sullivan as a model in theory and administration for the "Careers in Business" program he later created. That effort aimed at identifying and training in a graduate business school program young PhDs in the humanities who could then find useful work in business. In both instances the basic assumption was that a good mind is a terrible thing to waste; its powers can always be applied in more than one area of activity.

Following this first, important experience of "curriculum interruptus," Ed Sullivan spent a year as an Associate in French at George Washington University, then accepted the offer of a teaching post at Princeton tendered by Christian Gauss, then Dean of the College and Chairman of the Department of Modern Languages. Among the distinguished senior colleagues who welcomed Sullivan to the University were Maurice Coindreau, Gilbert Chinard, and Alfred Foulet. However, Sullivan had been offered only a one-semester contract. He complained to Gauss, who answered, "Have you no confidence in yourself?" To which Sullivan replied, "I have confidence in myself; it's you I'm worried about!"

Clearly, mutual confidence was warranted. Ed Sullivan completed one year as Instructor in French, three as Assistant Professor of French, and in 1950 was granted tenure as Associate Professor. Eight years later—including another year of interrupted career during which he served again in the Navy during the Korean conflict—he became Professor of French and Chairman of the Department of Romance Languages, a service he rendered until 1966 when he was named Dean of the College by President Robert Goheen. In 1960 he was named Advisory Editor, then General Editor of the Scribner French Series, a responsibility he relinquished in 1974. He was also a Correspondent of the Société d'Histoire littéraire de la France from 1963 until 1980. President Goheen's essay on those years and the ones beyond, when Sullivan in 1972 became Avalon Professor of the Humanities and later Chairman of the Council of the Humanities, is a separate part of this volume. I shall therefore concentrate this part of my essay upon the aspects of Sullivan's career I knew best throughout the Seventies—those concerning a senior colleague and a friend. I find in reading President Goheen's essay that he and I share a perception of Ed Sullivan as a man who is at once generous and economical in all he undertakes. I cannot therefore do other than amplify those views from another perspective.

Having spent the turbulent years of the late sixties and early seventies in France, I arrived at Princeton rather innocent of all the strains that venerable institution had recently undergone, and ignorant of the significant role Ed Sullivan had played in guiding the university community through them. I did know that he was a distinguished Maupassant scholar: his *Maupassant the Novelist* is a standard work in the field of late nineteenth-century literary history and criticism, as is the later *Maupassant: The Short Stories*. Significantly, the work on Maupassant as a novelist originated in Sullivan's interest in the relationship between the author's journalistic *essais* and *chroniques* and his fiction. Having unearthed some 300 pieces published by Maupassant in *Le Gil Blas* and *Le Gaulois*, on subjects ranging from North Africa to the Eiffel Tower and from literature to politics, Sullivan integrated his reading of them into his analysis of Maupassant's novels and short stories. Those large works have been refined and expanded through the years in a series of analytical and bibliographical essays, articles and reviews on Maupassant and other subjects, some literary, others addressing problems of language learning and teaching, all distinguished by their clarity and thoughtfulness. (A bibliography of Sullivan's work follows this essay.)

Ed Sullivan was from the beginning kindness itself to his very junior colleague who at times was not at all certain that Princeton really liked what it had become—a coeducational institution further altered by the presence of a slowly increasing number of women faculty members. He somehow never lacked the time and patience to chat, to tell a bit of local lore, to make one feel part of a common endeavor. I first understood his extraordinary energy and capacity for paying real attention to every question, every student, when we worked together on the Summer Work Abroad Program ("Princeton in France") that he had helped to found. The Program arranges for summer jobs in France for selected Princeton undergraduates fluent in French and eager to work in banks, business offices, summer camps, as laborers for the French gas company, or even as beach attendants (at Deauville!). For most students this is a powerful experience of being completely on their own, learning to cope with a wholly new undertaking, a different culture, and in a foreign language. For the faculty members on the selection committee there were endless rounds of interviews and meetings, the inevitable Saturday morning ones made less dreary by the bottle of Rémy Martin contributed by Blanchard Bates to counter the effects of too much departmental coffee in paper cups. Ed Sullivan was at every point patient, perceptive, and best of all, cheerful.

His gift for inclusion was again demonstrated in the times I was a preceptor for Ed's course on the theme of parent-child relationships in the novel. It was his course—and one of the most heavily subscribed throughout the years he taught it—but we junior colleagues could critique it, discuss it, and even argue about it with him, confident that we were doing just what he believed was important for us to do.

Later, when the undergraduate interdisciplinary program first known as Western Cultural and Historical Studies (later European Cultural Studies) was created by Professor of History Carl Schorske and Professor of Architecture Anthony Vidler, Ed Sullivan as Chairman of the Council of the Humanities once again exercised the qualities of imagination, sensitivity and effective energy of which President Goheen writes. He was an advocate of what became one of Princeton's most highly regarded undergraduate programs, but which at its inception was fraught with all the difficulties inherent in crossing departmental lines, team-teaching by faculty members representing both the humanities and the social sciences, and just plain trying to resolve conflicts of temperament. Again I enjoyed the benefit of Ed's encouragement and counsel when I joined the program which became for me the greatest single source of intellectual pleasure I have known.

That program was, of course, the embodiment of Ed Sullivan's own notion that, as he puts it, "literature contains information about life." That notion did not, however, reign unchallenged in the years of structuralist fever and beyond, so there was a certain degree of tension between those of us who caught it and those who did not, or who had only a mild case. Sullivan never was drawn, however; with the confident equanimity he always displays, he simply went on teaching and writing about literary texts—constructed objects, surely, with their own linguistic building codes and structures, but objects imbued with meaning which can be teased out and incorporated into our broader understanding of human experience. But his own essay in this volume, "Surveying the Generation Gap: Parents and Children as Seen in the Novel and in the Social Sciences," develops this point of view far more eloquently than I or anyone else could do.

Generational change, anxieties of influence, intellectual killings of the father, the priest and the king are of course the stuff universities are made of. Ed Sullivan is probably more aware of this than most, given the nature of the many aspects of university life he has actively known, and given his own nature. In talking with me about his forty-plus years of association with Princeton students, faculty, administrators and alumni, he observed that at every difficult juncture along the way, "people's insecurity is always the most troublesome thing." That explains in part, as Sullivan sees it, the romantic creation *ex post facto* of a Princeton that never existed by the classes of '43 and '44 whose studies were interrupted by World War II and who, returning, willingly suspended disbelief and imagined the place as the preserver of all the innocent security they felt they had lost. It is also, he believes, part of what exploded in universities around the world in the sixties, as well as a source of the tensions that arose at Princeton as the student body became the multi-ethnic, multi-cultural coeducational mix it is today.

During that time of profound social change in the United States now designated simply as "The Sixties," Ed Sullivan was Dean of the College at Princeton, and fully occupied with the university's efforts to understand, analyze, and respond to the combined internal and external pressures being felt by the entire community. The composition of the student body, the shape and aims of the undergraduate curriculum, the university's relationship to policies of the U.S. government (crystallized for Princeton students and faculty in R.O.T.C. and the Princeton-based Institute for Defense Analysis), were only some of the items on the agenda. Ed Sullivan nevertheless found it possible at that same time to participate in a project sponsored by the American Council of Life Insurance, whose University Advisory Council he then chaired. Blake Newton, executive director of the ACLI, saw the importance of growing student unrest across the country and looked for ways to interpret it to his associates; Ed Sullivan joined him in organizing a series of regional meetings where students, faculty, administrators and CEOs of American businesses met together to explore the nature of student concerns. He also developed the Business Executive in Residence Program which placed senior executives on college campuses for two to four weeks as teacher-consultants and resource persons. Additionally, Sullivan organized and chaired the Arden House conferences of ACLI, which at five-year intervals dealt with long-range societal questions engaging both the business and academic worlds. These experiences gave Sullivan a privileged vantage point for observing the multiplying tensions and miscommunications between the university and the worlds of business and government with which the university had to connect—indeed, *was* connected, like it or not. The integrity of the university had to be preserved, but in Sullivan's view this could best be achieved by turning outward to meet the problems, not by practicing "ostrich politics."

Ten or so years later, when Ed Sullivan was Chairman of the Council of the Humanities, another kind of tension began to manifest itself, this time among junior faculty members at universities and colleges all over the United States. The extraordinary expansion of post-secondary education since the immediate post-war years had peaked, leaving thousands of younger faculty members, particularly in the humanistic disciplines, without reasonable hope of a life-long career in scholarly research and teaching. Who was responsible for this unfortunate situation? What could be done with or for these men and women with highly specialized training, a somewhat diseconomic passion for their present pursuit, and a well-developed preference for working on their own?

In 1977, Ed Sullivan published a brief paper called "Alternative Careers" in the *Association of Departments of Foreign Languages Bulletin*. Two years earlier, he had become a consultant to the New York State Regents Doctoral Evaluation Project, and had met Dr. Dorothy G. Harrison, Assistant Commissioner for Postsecondary Policy Analysis of the New York State Education Department. Sympathetic to the notion that a variety of career choices were indeed available to people holding the PhD in a humanistic discipline, Sullivan joined with Dorothy Harrison; Ernest May, chairman of the Department of History at Harvard; Germaine Brée, Kenan Professor of French at Wake Forest University; Maurice Mandelbaum, Mellon Professor of Philosophy at Johns Hopkins; and William Dill, Dean of the Graduate School of Business at NYU, to design a program aimed at preparing interested members of that junior faculty group for jobs in the corporate world. Jointly funded by the National Endowment for the Humanities and a number of major American corporations, and based in the Graduate Business School of New York University, "Careers in Business" was open for business in 1977.

The success of that initial program, which served only 50 carefully chosen participants in its first year (1978), can be measured in two ways: first, that it was replicated well into the eighties by The Wharton School of the University of Pennsylvania, by Northwestern University, by the University of Virginia, and by several other distinguished research universities; second—and far more telling, I believe—that such programs no longer exist. The notion that one can well have more than one career, that a scholar of the humanities can usefully and happily perform other work, is now part of our culture. It seems entirely consonant with the rest of Ed Sullivan's career that he should have been one of the first advocates and planners of a program which opened yet another door between the university and the world around it.

Still other opportunities of reaching beyond his own environment awaited Ed Sullivan in 1980, when he became Princeton University's representative to the ten-member American consortium of advisers to Saudi Arabia's University of Petroleum and Minerals. U.P.M. was the creation of the Saudi government in the seventies, when it recognized the need for an indigenous engineering university. For five years Sullivan served as a consultant on language teaching (U.P.M. having decided to operate in English) and on administrative structure and implementation. His years of experience as an evaluator of language and doctoral programs in a dozen American universities, as well as his work as the language coordinator of Princeton's Peace Corps Training Program (1964) were now brought to bear on familiar problems in a somewhat unfamiliar setting.

In 1982, Ed Sullivan became Professor Emeritus of French and Comparative Literature at Princeton. In theory, Ed was thus free to *cultiver son jardin*. In reality, he continued to write, to consult (most notably as Senior Adviser for Academic Appeals to the President of Princeton University, 1987-1989), and of course to enjoy the activities he refers to as "applied things," a handsome and very real garden in Princeton not least among them.

When we talked most recently, I asked Ed if he thought a young academic could now have the kind of career he himself has had in a major research university, somehow maintaining a balance between the intellectual and the practical, between working alone and working to bring others together, guided as he has been by a clear sense of *oikonomos*. Characteristically, the answer came from the quintessential optimistic realist. The generation gap between today's university faculties and students is focused upon what Sullivan perceives as the students' broad notions of useful human service as against a bias toward the exclusivity of intellectual pursuit on the part of their professors. Yet Sullivan feels that "the island" will never again be without bridges, and that teaching and learning now take place in a far more expansive context than the one he knew as a young student.

This essay was not conceived as a narrative listing of all the honors and distinctions earned by Ed Sullivan in the course of his career. Yet it is not possible to end it without mention of the most significant among them. In addition to having been named a Fulbright Research Scholar attached to the Collège de France in 1956-57, Ed has been honored on three separate occasions by the French government for his service to French-American scholarly relations. In 1960 he was named *Chevalier* of the Ordre des Palmes Académiques and was promoted to *Commandeur* of the Order in 1978. In 1968 he became a *Chevalier* of France's most prestigious order, the Légion d'Honneur. Princeton honored Sullivan in 1972 by naming him to a distinguished University Professorship, as Avalon Foundation University Professor of the Humanities.

There is also a more recent acknowledgement of Ed's value to the community he has so long served; this one without a title but with a very particular significance. In the summer of 1988, Ed Sullivan and his wife Eleanor traveled to Colmar, France, where Ed planned to explore the possibility of additional summer jobs in France for students of the Princeton in France Program. He was significantly aided in this by Maurice Amiel, head of The Timken Company's European operations, whose headquarters are in Colmar. Shortly after his arrival in Colmar, Ed suffered a stroke, with additional complications, and was hospitalized for five weeks in grave condition. New friends in Colmar, particularly the Amiels, Ed's doctors and their wives, rallied around to support Eleanor and to insure the best possible care for Ed. When it became apparent that Ed needed to return to the United States for extended treatment, senior officials of Princeton University undertook to arrange a special military transport direct from Colmar to its sister city of Princeton, working through former students and associates of Sullivan in the Department of Defense. "I have never been more moved," Ed remembers, "than when I saw, with my wife and two sons, who had flown to Colmar, the insignia of the United States of America on the plane that would bring me home to Princeton."

If anyone has understood and lived out the imperative expressed in Woodrow Wilson's conception of "Princeton in the nation's service," it is Edward Daniel Sullivan. Like the medals, the titles, and even the airlift, this Festschrift seems a modest attempt to express the admiration and affection of many for a remarkable man; we hope only that it gives him pleasure.

A Bibliography of Works by Edward D. Sullivan

Books

La Guerre moderne. Ed. with W.N. Locke. Cambridge, MA: Harvard UP, 1942.

Maupassant the Novelist. Princeton: Princeton UP, 1954.

Maupassant: The Short Stories. London: Edward Arnold, 1962. (Reprinted by Barron's.)

Témoins de l'homme. Nouvelles et Récits. Ed. with Albert Sonnenfeld. New York: Charles Scribner's Sons, 1965.

Change or Revolution. An Analysis of Interacting Social Forces. Ed. New York: Institute of Life Insurance, 1971.

Articles

"The Actors' Alceste: Evolution of the Misanthrope." *Modern Language Quarterly* 9.1 (1948): 74-79.

"Molé's Interpretation of Molière's Misanthrope." *Modern Language Quarterly* 9.4 (1948): 492-96.

"Portrait of the Artist: Maupassant and *Notre Cœur.*" *French Review* 22.2 (1948): 136-41.

"Sur l'eau, a Maupassant Scrapbook." *Romanic Review* 40.3 (1949): 173-79.

"Supplément à la bibliographie de Guy de Maupassant." With Francis Steegmuller. *Revue d'Histoire Littéraire de la France* 49.4 (1949): 370-75.

"Constraint and Expansion in Benjamin Constant's *Adolphe.*" *French Review* 32.4 (1959): 293-99.

"Maupassant and the Motif of the Mask." *Symposium* 10.1 (1956): 34-41.

"Introduction." *César Birotteau.* By Honoré de Balzac. Trans. Frances Frenaye. Juniper Press, 1965.

"Foreword." *Boule de Suif and Other Stories.* By Guy de Maupassant. Trans. Andrew R. MacAndrew. New York: New American Library, 1964.

"Research and Language Learning." *Language Teaching: Broader Contexts.* Ed. Robert G. Mead. New York: Northeast Conference Reports, 1966.

"Beyond Anger." *Princeton Alumni Weekly* 68.1 (30 April 1968): 14 and 18.

"The Colby College Conference on the Undergraduate Major in French." With others. *French Review* 42.1 (1968): 66-73.

"Discussion of Perspectives on the Language Laboratory and Language Learning." *Dimension: Language 67. Proceedings of The Third Southern Conference on Language Teaching.* 1969. 20-23.

"Problèmes actuels de l'université américaine." *Annales du Centre Universitaire Méditerranéen* 22 (1968-69): 9-23.

"The Relevance of Fiction." *Virginia Quarterly* 46.3 (1970): 411-32.

"The Meaning of Literature." *The Bulletin of the Pennsylvania State Modern Language Association* 52.1 (1973): 3-10.

"Maupassant et la nouvelle." *Cahiers de l'Association Internationale des Etudes Françaises* 27 (1975): 223-36.

"Alternative Careers." *Association of Departments of Foreign Languages Bulletin* 9.1 (1977) 27-29.

"Maupassant: The Short Stories. The 'Contes': 'The eternal benefits of constraint.'" *Die Romanische Novelle.* Ed. Wolfgang Eitel. Darmstadt: Wissenschaftliche Buchgesellschaft, 1977. 254-276.

Reviews

Maupassant: A Lion in the Path. By Francis Steegmuller. *French Review* 23.4 (1950): 329-31.

Gérard de Nerval, 1805-55: Poet, Traveler, Dreamer. The New York Times Book Review (15 July 1951).

French Review Grammar. By Mathurin Dondo and Frederick Ernst. *The Modern Language Forum* (September-December 1951).

Correspondance inédite. By Guy de Maupassant. Collected and presented by Artine Artinian with Edouard Maynial. *Romanic Review* (December 1952).

Pour et contre Maupassant: Enquête internationale. 147 Témoignages inédits. Ed. by Artine Artinian. *Romanic Review* 47.4 (1956): 308-09.

Lélia. By George Sand. Ed. by Pierre Reboul. *Consuela* and *La Comtesse de Rudolstadt.* By George Sand. Ed. by Léon Cellier and Léon Guichard. *Modern Philology* 59.2 (1961): 141-43.

The Gates of Horn: A Study of Five French Realists. By Harry Levin. *Thought*
38.151 (1963): 462-64.

The Career of Alphonse Daudet. A Critical Study. By Murray Sachs. *French
Review* 40.2 (1961): 298-99.

Artists and Writers in Paris: The Bohemian Idea, 1807-1867. By Malcolm
Easter. *Modern Language Journal* 51.2 (1967): 127.

Guy de Maupassant, scrittore moderno. By Antonio and Mario Fratangelo.
Revue d'Histoire Littéraire de la France (July-August 1979) 699-700.

Edward D. Sullivan

Surveying the Generation Gap: Parents and Children as Seen in the Novel and in the Social Sciences

Do you know what I was reminded of, brother? I once had a dispute with our poor mother; she stormed, and wouldn't listen to me. At last I said to her "Of course you can't understand me; we belong," I said, "to two different generations." She was dreadfully offended, while I thought, "There's no help for it. It's a bitter pill, but she has to swallow it." You see, now our turn has come and our successors can say to us, "You are not of our generation: swallow your pill."

Turgenev, *Fathers and Sons* ch. X (trans. Constance Garnett)

In a period like the present, in which "communication" is one of the most frequently used buzz-words, invoked repeatedly to explain the difficulties in relationships as "failure of communication" (when, in fact, the people involved actually have little to say to each other), it may seem unsporting to call attention to the persistent difficulty many people have in speaking to those of a different generation across the "generation gap." Yet, that is what the present essay sets out to do, examining particularly the factors that separate parents and children, mainly as developed by a number of novelists in their fictions and as supplemented by work in the social sciences.

The tensions inherent in the parent-child relationship have attracted novelists in search of readily recognizable conflicts. I was led to explore some of this area while giving courses on the European novel over many years at Princeton University and then by developing a special course on novels which deal with parent-child problems. While giving the European novel course at a time when Princeton was still an all-male institution, I was struck by the reactions of the students to the various novels which ranged from *Don Quixote* to *Madame Bovary* and *Anna Karenina*. The young men responded eagerly and articulately to most of the novels, but reacted rather strangely to Turgenev's *Fathers and Sons*, which seemed to make them uneasy and less articulate. It was evident that this penetrating exposition of the gap between generations hit close to home for many of the students. Perhaps it was only troubled self-recognition, as in the scene which depicts the awkwardness of bringing a college friend home to meet one's parents, and one's embarrassment in respect to both friend and parents.

Turgenev's was the only novel in the course which had this effect; Balzac's *Eugénie Grandet*, for all its somber detail and excruciatingly intense relationships, did not disturb them in the same way. Nor could one explain it by noting that *Eugénie Grandet* is about a father-daughter relationship, and one could expect that a group of young men could believe it didn't apply to them. The situation was not, however, any different after coeducation came to Princeton and young women, daughters all, participated in the course, and they too seemed to find Balzac less troubling than Turgenev.

All of this led me to propose and give an experimental course, using a group of novels (with some variations from year to year) all of which emphasized and dramatized a parent-child conflict. To them I added appropriate supplementary readings in history, sociology and psychology which dealt with similar problems but in very different terms. (See below for the syllabus of the course, as it was given for the last time in the fall of 1979.) It includes variants used in other years. For the novels the date given is the date of first publication in the original language:

Week 1. Supplementary Readings (henceforth SP): Bruno Bettleheim, "The Problem of Generations," in *The Challenge of Youth*, ed. Erik Erickson (Doubleday Anchor, 1965) 76-109.

Week 2. Novels (henceforth N): Balzac, *Eugénie Grandet* (1833) (Modern Library or Penguin). SP: Philippe Ariès, *Centuries of Childhood* (Vintage, 1962) 365-407.

Week 3. N: Turgenev, *Fathers and Sons* (1862) (Penguin). SP: Lewis Feuer, *The Conflict of Generations* (Basic Books, 1969) 88-119, 126-29, 146-54.

Week 4. N: Dostoevsky, *Netochka Nezvanova* (1849) (Prentice Hall) or Dostoevsky, *The Adolescent* (1875) (Doubleday Anchor) or Colette, *My Mother's House* (1922) and *Sido* (1930) (Farrar, Strauss and Giroux) or Henry James, *Washington Square* (1880) (New American Library). SP: Freud, "Dostoevsky and Parricide," in *Dostoevsky, A Collection of Critical Essays*, ed. René Wellek (Prentice Hall, 1962) and C. G. Jung, "Psychology and Literature," in *Modern Man in Search of a Soul* (Harvest, 1933) 152-72 or R.D. Laing, *The Politics of the Family* (Vintage, 1972) 65-124.

Week 5. N: Joyce, *Portrait of the Artist as a Young Man* (1917) (Viking, Compass) or Maupassant, *Pierre et Jean* (1888) (Penguin). SP: Erik Erickson, *Identity, Youth and Crisis* (Norton, 1968) 208-31.

Week 6. N: Lawrence, *Sons and Lovers* (1913) (Viking). SP: Freud, *An Outline of Psychoanalysis* (Norton, 1969) and Freud, "The Transformation of Puberty."

Week 7. N: Hesse, *Rosshalde* (1914) (Farrar, Strauss and Giroux). SP: C.G. Jung, "The Psychology of the Child Archetype," in *Psyche and Symbol* (Doubleday Anchor) 113-31.

Week 8. N: Machado de Assis, *Dom Casmurro* (1900) (U of California P). SP: Claude Lévi-Strauss, "The Family," in Harvey L. Shapiro, *Man, Culture and Society*

(Oxford) 142-70. Also *Family in Transition*, eds. Skolnick and Skolnick (Little Brown) 50-72.

Week 9. N: Gide, *The Counterfeiters* (1925). SP: R.D. Laing, *The Politics of the Family* (Vintage) 65-124.

Week 10. N: Mauriac, *Génétrix* (1923) in *A Mauriac Reader* (Farrar, Strauss and Giroux). SP: J.P. Sartre, *The Words* (1964).

Week 11. N: V. Woolf, *To the Lighthouse* (1927) (Harvest) or Geoffrey Wolff, *The Duke of Deception* (1979) (Berkeley). SP: Karen Horney, *New Ways in Psychoanalysis* (Norton) 7-87, 133-53.

Week 12. N: Thomas Wolfe, *Look Homeward Angel* (1929) (Scribner's) or Flannery O'Connor, *Everything that Rises Must Converge* (1965) (Farrar, Strauss and Giroux) or Mary Gordon, *Final Payments* (1978) (Ballantine). SP: Margaret Mead, *Culture and Commitment. A Study of the Generation Gap in the 1970's* (1978) (Anchor Press, Doubleday).

As the course developed it was not enough simply to set forth what novelists (or a particular selection of novelists) have to say about relations between parents and children; other questions arise, such as the conflict between the search for universal laws or general prescriptions and a respect for individual variations. Balzac, for example, was avowedly eager to seek out general laws that govern human conduct and human society, but he had a passion for the particular which kept his focus on individuals in specifically detailed situations who refuse to be either abstract or typical in spite of Balzac's own claims.

That the relations of parents and children are troublesome (or potentially so) is not doubted by anyone, and they have proved to be a rich terrain for novelists of many countries as well as for historians, philosophers and sociologists. The historians have been particularly active in recent years in re-examining the history of childhood, most notably Lawrence Stone and Philippe Ariès.

As one reviews the whole historical spectrum of parent-child relations, we are struck by the fact that these relations have a particular intensity in our time—indeed they seem to be a specialty of contemporary western civilization. In other cultures and in other times, matters were seen rather differently. Sociologists are led to wonder why there is so much parent-adolescent conflict in our culture when there are so many other contemporary cultures where youth is docile rather than rebellious, and they therefore set about to analyze the differences.[1]

In the last three decades the historians have been examining closely the concept of childhood and how it has varied in different periods in western Europe. The pioneer in this important development, the French historian, Philippe Ariès, whose seminal work, *L'Enfant et la vie familiale sous l'ancien régime*, appeared in 1960 (translated in 1962 as *Centuries of Childhood*), traces the changes that took place in parent-child relations from the Middle Ages to early modern times, noting that in the early period there was no notion of childhood as a special concept. In the Middle Ages and into the sixteenth century in France children were treated more or less as adults as soon as they could get along without the help of a nurse or mother, that is, from about the age of seven, or only a few years after being weaned, which was generally very late. At that point they joined the general community and shared the work to the extent of their capabilities. Life was collective, involving in one house all ages and conditions; what was conspicuously lacking was privacy—there was little opportunity for solitude or intimacy. Medieval civilization had forgotten the ancient Greeks' emphasis on the education of children, the *paideia*, and had nothing resembling our contemporary preoccupation with education. They simply did not have the idea of education, says Ariès. There were no "rites of passage" which marked the transition from childhood to adulthood such as are found in so-called primitive societies.[2]

As time went on, there was gradual but significant change and a history of childhood can be traced. The stages on the road can be marked out reasonably well before the child comes clearly to the fore in mid-eighteenth century. Rousseau had, of course, great impact, but the ground had been prepared. Thus emphasis on childhood coincides with the development of an urban mode of life, where the bourgeois class becomes vigorous and distinct (Ariès 474-75).

Ariès's concepts set off a great deal of discussion and have been questioned for various details, but in fact he opened up a whole area of historical investigation which had not been seriously worked. At the same time other historians were exploring similar fields, not just the great public events and political movements, but the basic conditions of life: birth, marriage, death, disease—often employing quantitative techniques—and focusing on "collective mentalities": systems of belief, basic perceptions and assumptions which determine how life is viewed—and lived (cf. interview with Ariès in *Psychology Today*, August 1975).

Thus, instead of a universal problem, we appear to be dealing with a situation which is localized in our own culture and in our own time. The range is more limited than one might think and, given this historical perspective, one can understand why childhood and adolescence have not been at all times a prime subject for literature. The treatment of the parent-child relationship in literature is sporadic, uneven, and one might usefully examine what it means when there is more interest in such subjects in some periods than in others, and why some literary forms are more concerned with it than others.

The novel, which is of relatively recent origin, is concerned seriously with family relationships, but it does so chiefly in terms of the young man's conflict with society as a whole, his effort to break old patterns, and create his own individuality. The novel develops at the same time as bourgeois society and describes the forces at work in that society which is trying to will itself into existence and create its own identity. Yet, as we move toward the twentieth century, we become aware of how intensively the novel is beginning to treat—and take seriously—the adolescent and his revolt not only against society, but now even more specifically against his parents. In the eighteenth century, Werther's indictment is against the stolid bourgeois society which stifles the artist and the poet, but one knows very little about his parents. They are referred to briefly and respectfully, but whatever contributions they have made to his problems are not recorded. The emphasis begins to change in the nineteenth century.

Novels dealing principally with an adolescent were rare in France before the end of the nineteenth century, but in the period between 1890 and 1930 there was in France a veritable deluge of such books. These novels are not so much concerned with family relations as with the physical, intellectual and spiritual awakening of the individual young person. Yet there are some novels in which the relations of parents and children are crucial, with Gide and Mauriac heading the list (*Les Faux-monnayeurs, Génétrix*). There are few female adolescents; the novels are almost all by men and are largely autobiographical. Justin O'Brien's study, *The Novel of Adolescence in France* (1937), makes these points, and in the opening pages also cites the role of George Sand: "The first person to recognize that there existed a problem of the adolescent and that literature had ignored it was George Sand, who wrote in 1854-1855 'that poets and novelists had failed to see the potential in this subject, this unique period in a man's life.'"

There has been, of course, in the present century an extraordinary amount of discussion on a theoretical or social-psychological level of how parents and children relate to one another, although this is frequently simply a subdivision under more general theories of adolescence.

When one examines the innumerable theories of adolescence which were developed in the twentieth century, it is curious to note that while they discuss the young person in his various forms and stages, they tend to assume that the parents are invariable, a fixed point, a constant, as if all adolescents had the same kind of parents. There is a curious blankness on one side of the equation, however rich and complex the stages of adolescence on the other side may be. Even when the adolescent is dealt with as a part of general theory of human behavior, the discussion takes place with the parents as a constant, which makes it hard to have a real sense of existential, day-to-day interaction between parents and children in terms of the theory being developed.

Current tendencies in theories of parent-child relationships (as seen in a number of sociology textbooks, for example)[3] like Skolnick and Skolnick, *Family in Transition*, attack the nuclear family, looking nostalgically to the large, "extended" family group composed of relatives of all sorts, a larger community offering support of various kinds. Some of the communes which have sprung up in recent years are a specific manifestation of this dissatisfaction with the restricted family. Old theories on the role of the child and of child-rearing are being challenged, particularly what is called "socialization," that is, the process whereby the child is controlled, trained and brought up to continue the values and traditions of society, as defined by the parents, so that society will survive. Those who quarrel with the essentially conservative nature of socialization are less concerned with how this contributes to the child's knowledge of his cultural heritage and to his own self-development, and they look upon it rather as an unfortunate mechanism for providing society with useful, well-adjusted, non-rebellious manpower. They speak of the "politics of child-rearing," and overlook to a great extent the creative part played by the child himself, for example in learning his own language (as Chomsky views the process) or in discovering the nature of the physical world.

Jean Piaget, whose ideas have had repercussions in many fields, emphasizes the child's "natural will to learn" and believes that children's seriousness and competence have been underestimated.[4]

R. D. Laing, on the other hand, gives the most desperate, despairing view imaginable of parent-child relations, more somber even than Joseph Heller's account of such matters in his recent novel *Something Happened*. Laing argues for universal schizophrenia, asserting that all parents drive their children crazy by making them conform to demands which are absurd, although socially acceptable. He calls this process a "mystification" and equates it with the rhetoric of imperialism and colonialism. In any case, he believes that family life inevitably involves conflicts of interest and impulse, hence the titles of Laing's books, such as *The Politics of Experience* and *The Politics of the Family*.[5] Young people rebelling against their parents find a very handy ally in R. D. Laing and his somber texts.

Erik Erikson, in spite of occasional quirkiness, provides along with Karen Horney useful insights as he goes about modifying Freud's theories to take account of the continuous development of the human being over the whole course of his life as he passes through an explicit series of stages. Erikson gives more emphasis than Freud to the cultural context, marking its importance along with the psycho-sexual dimension as the child works toward the acquisition of a strong, healthy ego-identity. Erikson, in emphasizing the ways in which parents and children act together, shifts us away from Freud's tragic image of child-rearing in which parents and children are bound to clash in irreconcilable, unavoidable conflict.[6]

One may well ask: what insights do our novelists bring to the discussion? A rapid review of the novels read in the course may be helpful.

Balzac made as good a starting point as one could desire: he wrote in and about a period when new forces were emerging after a great revolution and in which family relationships were changing significantly with the emergence of the bourgeois class. Throughout the *Human Comedy* there is an obsession with paternity, with family relationships of all sorts, with the importance of marriage (especially its social and financial aspects), and with the ways in which parents and children treat one another. The best known are the novels of Père Goriot and his daughters and of Eugénie Grandet and her parents. In addition, those ubiquitous young men whose activities fill many pages of a dozen or more novels of the *Human Comedy*, Eugène de Rastignac and Lucien de Rubempré, are sons closely attached to their families, although family sentiment more often than not yields to selfishness when the going is rough. Both reflect on the family as an institution and Lucien even has a "theory of the family."[7]

In terms of family relationships, *Eugénie Grandet* is particularly instructive: in a novel which appears to be more concerned with money than with anything else, the theme of parents and children underlies everything, and a concentration on it helps us see more intensely what this novel brings to light.[8]

It is clear from the beginning that this is no abstract exercise in defining family relationships—or kinship customs—but it is rooted in a very particular situation. *Eugénie Grandet* is specifically located in time, in place, and at a particular conjunction of historical forces: 1819, the town of Saumur, a provincial town in a post-revolutionary period, when, after the upheavals of the Revolution and Napoleon's Empire, the Restoration sought to stem the tide of change. In terms of family life, as with everything else in this small town, one is struck by the paradox that there is both an obsession with secrecy and a lack of privacy. However eager each person is to keep his own affairs to himself, there is plenty of time for each to observe and spy on the others. "A housewife can't buy a partridge without the neighbors asking her husband if it was done to a turn" and Blazac comments: "Nothing can be hidden there, just as those impenetrable, dark, silent houses are completely lacking in secrecy" (Penguin 36). Impenetrable, yet without secrets: this paradoxical combination is at the heart of the problem of finding workable sociological and psychological laws. The study of literature may help us to discover insights and provide guidelines for analysis—if only to warn us of the complexity of what we have before us. The point was made some time ago by the Swiss observer, Herbert Luthy, who declared flatly that, as far as France is concerned, literature "is the only possible social science in a society composed of individual relationships, organized in such small private groups which are perfectly knowable from the inside but perfectly impenetrable from the outside." Luthy cites Balzac as the prime example, although one need not share Luthy's dismissal of the social sciences: "Even today," he asserts (in 1955) "one can learn more in Balzac than in the publications of the Office of Statistics. A difficult time is in store for anyone who wants to set up new norms. Here any statement is debatable, any rule works only half the time, any law is mere form, any principle is only theoretical: everything in moderation."[9]

What sense, then, does one get in *Eugénie Grandet* of family relationships, of the behavior of parents and children, and of the family as an institution? We see families in this novel with strong internal bonds which have little to do with love or affection, but which present firm defenses to the society around them. Money dominates: marriages are arranged to unite fortunes and land; children are pawns in the game and owe obedience to their parents. Women play a paradoxical role: subservient, self-effacing and simple, like Madame Grandet; but also sharp, clearheaded, dominating from behind the scenes like Madame des Grassins. Charles's letter to Eugénie, telling her he will marry someone else in order to assure for his children an advantageous social situation, illuminates still another paradox: children are expected to be wholly subservient to their parents' wishes, but the parents do everything for the sake of the children—or at least so justify their actions. As Charles puts it with fraudulent piety: We owe ourselves to our children ("Nous nous devons à nos enfants," *Eugénie Grandet* 260).

Yet, who can say that affection is totally lacking here? Surely there is something between Eugénie and her mother, and, indeed, between father and daughter once you get beyond the commercial vocabulary and the gold-laden metaphors of the old miser.

One can profitably look beyond Balzac to the work of scholars, especially the historians who have been so active recently delving into the "mentalities" of each period, using even greater quantities of detail than Balzac, and in fact testing the abundant imaginative hypotheses he set forth.

When we turn to psychologists and sociologists for help, we gain certain insights, but it is not at all clear that any particular sociological, psychological system can be applied comfortably to *Eugénie Grandet*, *Père Goriot*, or any of Balzac's novels and make them more meaningful. Nor can one say that these novels illuminate or illustrate any particular system. Balzac seemed to think that *Le Père Goriot* illustrated the phrenology of Gall—the old man, says Balzac, has "la bosse de la paternité," but this is hopelessly inadequate to deal with the complexities of life as Balzac knew them, and the "paternal bump" functions only as a brief metaphor in the dense context of the Balzacian novel.

Later, Turgenev's novel, *Fathers and Sons*, written in the mid-nineteenth century, provides insight into a student generation in revolt against its elders and at the same time reveals something about the student activism of the 1960s in our own country and elsewhere. In fact it is the recurring pattern that is so striking, the fact that student or generational revolts have been remarkably similar in form and expression in widely different countries and in widely separated periods.

These similarities have been pointed out in a massive study by Lewis S. Feuer, *The Conflict of Generations*,[10] and his work helps put Turgenev's perceptions into a broader perspective. Feuer's is a rather obsessional study, concentrating single-mindedly on student movements everywhere and was no doubt marked by the fact that he was a Berkeley professor when the movement of the sixties began. Yet for all his obsessions, he does point out some interesting patterns which have recurred time and again. He states that "What was true of the Russian student movement [the one that underlies Turgenev's novel] was likewise true of the German student movement of 1815 to 1819, and the Bosnian student movement as well in the years before the First World War." In addition to these, he explores similar revolts in Africa, Asia, Europe and the United States. The pattern he describes is the following and we can see for ourselves how it fits the conditions of Turgenev's *Fathers and Sons* as well as how it squares with our own memories of the student activism of the 60s here: "The distinctive character of student movements arises from the union in them of motives of youthful love, on the one hand, and those springing from the conflict of generations on the other." He thus sees both an altruistic, generous side, an urge for social reconstruction, and then an inevitable movement toward violence, the end justifying the means, toward terrorism and self-destruction (Feuer 3).

The varied elements of the pattern form a progression: "beginning with unconscious, generational revolt, then the search for a cause, the joy of comradeship and fraternity, the sense that the older generation had made a mess of things, combined with a sense of guilt in revolting against the fathers, the search for allies in the proletariat, the peasants, the workers, and followed by a rejection of the students by the masses. Other distinguishing marks were a style of dress and hair, and, usually, an appeal to 'science.' The downward movement was toward violence—the peace movement had trouble avoiding the use of violence—and some form of self-destruction or liquidation of the movement" (Feuer 5).

The student revolts recently experienced in China, East Germany, and elsewhere in Europe fit Feuer's pattern reasonably well, but it is by no means certain at this point how they will ultimately turn out. In any case they will provide a splendid test of Feuer's theory.

Whenever the fathers as a group are ineffectual and indecisive, the basis for a generalized revolt is present. As Feuer puts it: "Each generation of elders was regarded as having been a moral failure, as having betrayed its ideals, as having proved itself unmanly, as having allowed itself to become emasculated. The family might be generous and permissive, but the sons loathed the notion that they would become amiable liberals like their fathers" (152). Feuer, of course, was writing out of his personal and immediate reactions to the Berkeley student movement as it developed from 1964 on, but he used it as a model for an analysis of student movements generally, looking for the common elements, and the basic pattern.

In Turgenev's *Fathers and Sons* the fathers are associated with the "liberals of the forties"; the conflict is explicit in terms of ideas and is bound up in the word "nihilism," newly coined to express a total rejection of the past and a desire to push out in new directions. The rhetoric that accompanies this desire frequently becomes extreme and often ends in violence, as it does in the novel in the duel of Bazarov, the "nihilist" and Pavel Petrovich, the defender of the old order.

Bazarov helps us understand some of his present-day counterparts who respond in similar terms to the problems of our own times. For all his energy and truculence he turns out to be a "superfluous man," a common figure of 19th-century Russian life and literature, a man unable to find a way of expressing his energy fruitfully and meaningfully. Like so many others in other times, he is a heroic character who lives in a world where heroism has been devalued—a latter day Don Quixote. It is not that the world lacks heroes; it is simply that, in such times, heroism lacks meaning.

The basic motif was well expressed by Bruno Bettelheim in "The Problem of Generations" in *The Challenge of Youth*:[11] ". . . the problem of the generations, when it goes wrong, may be characterized by saying that, whenever the older generation has lost its bearings, the younger generation is lost with it. The positive alternatives of emulation or revolt are replaced by the lost quality of neither" (105-06).

Turgenev's essay "Hamlet and Don Quixote" is an insightful analysis of the basic situation. This essay is summarized by Feuer as follows:

. . . the double-edged choice which confronts student movements is perhaps best expressed in an essay by Ivan Turgenev, 'Hamlet and Don Quixote,' written as the Russian student movement was being born. For Hamlet, with his negation, destructive doubt, and intellect turned against himself, was indeed the suicidal pole of the Russian student character, whereas Don Quixote, with his undoubting devotion to an ideal, his readiness to fight for the oppressed and to pit himself against all social institutions, represented the messianic, back-to-the-people component. The Russian student activist, like his later successors, oscillated between these polar impulses; rejected by the people, he would often find in terrorism a sort of synthesis, for thereby he could assail a social institution in a personalized form and hurl against it all the aggressive passions which menaced himself. Don Quixote thus becomes a student terrorist. When his ventures in terror miscarried, his passions turned against himself; in the last act he was Hamlet destroying himself. Yet Turgenev believed that if there were no more Don Quixotes the book of history would be closed. (6)

Arguments between members of different generations are difficult enough, and in Russia, one is led to believe, more difficult than anywhere else. V. S. Pritchett remarked acutely that "the idea of 'convictions' haunts every Russian quarrel of the period; no one has opinions, they have absolute convictions."[12]

In *Fathers and Sons* Arkady's father, Nikolai, is wise enough to see the eternal context of the discussion, to see it as part of the age-old, constantly repeated conflict of generations. (See the passage quoted earlier.)

One finds many expressions in literature and elsewhere of exasperation with children, indeed of despair, but Tolstoy provides balance in the famous opening sentence of *Anna Karenina*: "All happy families resemble one another, but each unhappy family is unhappy in its own way."

George Eliot contributed a summary of family tensions and problems in *Adam Bede* when she probed the awkwardness of family resemblances: "Family likeness has often a deep sadness in it. Nature, that great tragic dramatist, knits us together by bone and muscle, and divides us by the subtler web of our brains; blends yearning and repulsion, and ties us by our heartstrings to beings that jar us at every moment. We hear a voice with the very cadence of our own, uttering the thoughts we despise."[13]

Dostoevsky's preoccupation with family relationships and with children is abundantly evident, culminating in the powerful exploration of the depths in *The Brothers Karamazov*. Some of his less frequently read novels provide many suggestive insights as well, and two of these, *Netochka Nezvanova* and *The Adolescent*, (also translated as *A Raw Youth*) are worth pausing over.

Dostoevsky began *Netochka Nezvanova* in 1846 after the overwhelmingly enthusiastic reception of *Poor Folk* in 1845, and he intended it as a major work that would repeat his initial success. But he kept interrupting this effort to write *The Landlady* and *The Double*, and so *Netochka* remained unfinished. The main character, Netochka, is a little girl who hates her mother because she believes that the mother is thwarting the artistic fulfillment of the father who is a musician. Joseph Frank, in his very rich study of Dostoevsky, sees this novel as a "confession," as a barely disguised transposition of Dostoevsky's own resentment against his father for having insisted that he become a military engineer and for refusing to consider the possibility of a writing career for the son. "Netochka's terrible sense of guilt for having hated her poor, long-suffering and hard-working mother, whom she even cheats out of money to aid her miscreant artist-father, can also be interpreted as a reflection of Dostoevsky's own guilt-feelings connected with his father's murder."[14]

The Adolescent, a much more elaborate work, was written in 1875, between *The Possessed* (1871) and *The Brothers Karamazov* (1880). This is a complex and difficult—not to say bewildering—book, not only because of the wealth of incident and the tangle of plot lines, but because it is all filtered through an awkward, muddle-headed youth, a singularly imperceptive narrator. The novel finds its unity in the theme of the family, the role of the family in society, the relations of a father and son, their involvement with a woman, and the search for the father by the son—and all of this at the center of a web of ideological and philosophical preoccupations.

Dostoevsky is deliberately depicting what he calls a "haphazard" or "accidental" family—not the ordinary or traditional family, and not the unhappy but conventional family of which Tolstoy wrote. Dostoevsky is pushing off into darker waters and using this haphazard family as a means of analyzing contemporary society. The adolescent, Arkady, is an illegitimate son who suffers from never having had a father's continuing presence, and he longs for his father to come and save him when he is at school, and later he sets out in quest of the father.

Above all, the adolescent longs for order and beauty in a world from which, according to Dostoevsky's firm belief, these qualities had disappeared. The family is no longer a place of order and security; families are broken up and become accidental groupings, "all merging into the general disorder and chaos" (565). Dostoevsky, again aiming a barb at Tolstoy, declared that the old "landowner literature" was finished and that *he* was writing of humbler folk, the majority, and revealing their "distorted and tragic side" (from his notebook, quoted in Konstantin Mochulsky, *Dostoevski*).[15] The disintegration of the family, the "unsightliness" of the fathers, which offends the young generation, is deeply felt by Dostoevsky, who pursues the theme in *The Brothers Karamazov.* As Mochulsky puts it: "Versilov's 'haphazard household' (in *The Adolescent*) in the process of its decomposition must generate the household of the Karamazovs" (517).

Joyce's *Portrait of the Artist as a Young Man* is not uniquely about a young man's relations with his parents, although this theme pervades the *Portrait* and is extensively developed in *Ulysses* and in *Finnegan's Wake*. The *Portrait of the Artist* is most frequently studied as a treatise on literary esthetics, but it has many other elements which an emphasis on *The Young Man* brings out: school and religion as shaping forces, language, adolescence, sex, and politics.

The father-son relationship was certainly important for Joyce as well as for Stephen, but it was no simple sentiment—it was a mixture of affection and exasperation, even of love and hate, a sense of belonging and yet a desire to break the ties. Parents, country and church were all symbols of authority from which he sought to free himself, while at the same time recognizing the strong bonds of affection and tradition that made total escape impossible. There is much about Stephen's mother, but she is more dimly seen than the father, and she is a much less powerful figure, certainly, than Mrs. Morel in *Sons and Lovers*.

D. H. Lawrence's novel is a massive exploration of mother-son relations and their consequences. There is the dominant mother with her tight hold on her son's affections, while the father is a conspicuous disappointment, for whose deficiencies the son is expected to compensate.

Sean O'Faolain, pointing to the difficulty of knowing when and how children turn into adults, used this as a metaphor for describing the Irish people.

Referring to children in a family who reach "that tiresome age when they can no longer be treated quite as children and cannot yet be treated as adults," he went on to develop his theme: "One alternatively thinks fondly of them as they were when they were dependent, biddable, wishes to heaven they would grow up quickly, and wonders why the devil one ever had them. One is by turn patient with them and furious with them, sympathizes with them and loathes the sight of them. (Parents do not always admit this, but parents do not always tell the truth.) There they are; and we must put up with them, and they will never know what beasts they were in their teens. . . ."[16] O'Faolain, at considerable risk to himself, lets this description serve as the proper attitude to take to the Irish peasant who has moved to the towns.

With the nineteenth-century Brazilian novelist, Machado de Assis, author of *Dom Casmurro* and *Epitaph of a Small Winner*, we have nothing but ambiguities. A childless man, Machado had an obsession with paternity (like Balzac and Maupassant) which runs through his stories and novels. *Dom Casmurro* poses problems of interpretation, dealing with the puzzle of paternity—how a man knows who his children are in a society where marriages are arranged and infidelities abound. A witty, disillusioned book which skips lightly over very deep waters, it provides a fascinating study of family relationships in a particular society with its own peculiar sets of assumptions about institutions and ideas.

Maupassant in *Pierre et Jean* raises some profound questions, not merely about the identity of the actual father of Jean, but how to deal with an almost abstract problem—a situation out of the distant past which explodes like a time bomb in the present. What is involved are linkages, the threads that connect events, and the novel defines the consequences of tracing one of those threads—out of the past into the present and what all this does to presumably stable family relationships.

Hesse's *Rosshalde*, written early in Hesse's career, is similarly concerned with failed relationships but contrasts sharply with *Dom Casmurro*. Removed from history and society, isolated on a lovely estate, without money problems, cared for by servants, the characters (and readers) are able to concentrate entirely on the algebra of relationships without any distractions. The only outside force which intervenes is art and the question is posed: are marriage and family life compatible with the total dedication required of the artist?

Gide's hatred of the family, often expressed and often quoted reminds us of R. D. Laing's similar views. *The Counterfeiters* (*Les Faux-monnayeurs*) is a complex novel in which the accent is on family relationships, most of which are bad. People in general have great difficulty in communicating with each other in Gide's world, but parents and children more than most. In addition there are a number of *false* family relationships: Bernard is not the son of his presumed father; Boris is illegitimate; Laura has a child by her lover, not by her husband. These false relationships are discovered, the subterfuges revealed and sometimes patched up, but the basic themes are the falsity of appearances and the constricting nature of family life, "l'égoisme familial." *The Counterfeiters* has echoes of Dostoevsky's *Adolescent* and is enriched as well by comparison with Machado's rather different view of the same themes, and with Mauriac's *Génétrix*, where the intensity of hatred is brought to bear on a daughter-in-law.

Colette provides us with a mother-daughter relationship full of love and admiration on the part of the daughter, Colette, who learned so much from her mother—a deep understanding of nature, and serviceable, if quirky, wisdom about life in general. It is only when we see Colette in relation to her own daughter that we sense some of the hostility—well concealed—that can lie beneath the surface in such relationships. This is the same question that we raise about Paul Morel in *Sons and Lovers* and his mother.

In Virginia Woolf's *To the Lighthouse*, what one of the children (Nancy) calls "the horror of family life" is sensitively perceived and beautifully rendered. Far more than in the uncompromising expressions of Gide ("familles je vous hais") one sees the deep hostility of children toward their parents—here the father—yet coupled with love. But love finds expression sometimes in tyranny, "that crass blindness and tyranny of his which had poisoned her childhood and raised bitter storms," as Cam put it (252-53). The insights to be found in the book are not great philosophical revelations, but "little daily miracles, illuminations, matches struck unexpectedly in the dark" (240), and it is around Mrs. Ramsay that the epiphanies occur.

Flannery O'Connor, too, in *Everything that Rises Must Converge,* deals in revelations, and epiphanies, but not in a strictly religious sense, though her own religious beliefs are firm and evident. She looks intently at the odd bits of life around her, but is continually looking beyond them into mystery—another dimension.

The last books in the course introduce contemporary authors who have written insightful works on the theme we have been dealing with: Mary Gordon's *Final Payments* and Geoffrey Wolff's *The Duke of Deception.*

Geoffrey Wolff writes his novel in the first person and describes his father, the "Duke of Deception" who is a notable trickster; the search for the father when the latter is a consummate confidence man adds piquancy to the quest. Geoffrey's relations with his father, the Duke, are comparable to Joyce's (or Stephen's) with his father: there is the same feeling of affection even while seeing clearly the imperfections of the father. He writes about his father, as he puts it, "with no want of astonishment and love."[17] Geoff speaks of himself "as a child, in love with my father, as with no one else" (290-91), and then, reviewing it all he writes: "I had been estranged from my father by my apprehension of other people's opinions of him, and by a compulsion to be free

of his chaos and destructions. I had forgotten I loved him, mostly, and mostly
how I missed him. I miss him " (291).

The Duke of Deception is a picaresque novel—an old form—but this time
told from the point of view of the picaro's son, and the essential subject is not
the Duke's deceptions but the nature of love between him and his son, and the
very nature of truth.

Novels are full of climbers—social climbers upwardly mobile—Balzac
has them in plenty—Charles Grandet, Rastignac, and others—but Geoffrey
Wolff's father set his mind to refusing to join the establishment—to deceive it
is to not join it.

In short, Duke wouldn't climb aboard the train: "my father was capable of
violent anger when he was faced with someone's cruelty, or what he perceived
as cruelty. But his deepest rebellion was quiet, a Bartleby-like refusal to play
ball, a preference for the declined gambit. So untroubled was he by negation
that he could afford his amiable manners which came not from an eagerness to
please but from a cooling, in early age, of those fevers that provoke young men
to run fast to mount that very train my father had no wish to ride" (37).

Religion is a factor in many of these novels, but it is dealt with usually
obliquely. Wolff's belated discovery that among his father's deceptions was the
concealment of his Jewish origins, thus presenting for Geoffrey an additional
factor in the usual problem of identity. Catholicism appears in our novels in
various forms. Flannery O'Connor's stories in *Everything That Rises Must
Converge* are suffused with Catholicism—a particular kind of Catholicism—
southern American, which is different from Joyce's Irish Catholicism, which
is also not the same thing as Mary Gordon's Irish-American Catholicism, and
still more removed from Machado's Brazilian variety. Mary Gordon does write
about Catholics, but Flannery O'Connor treats the subject differently—she
writes from the sense of the southern Catholic as being distinctly in a minority
position, and looks beyond the particularities of sect, worship, and personality
to the larger questions of good and evil.

Final Payments is ostensibly about a young woman's life *after* the death
of her father, an invalid to whom she has devoted 11 years of her life caring for
him. His death releases her and she sets about creating a life for herself, but it
is quite clear that the character and personality of the father dominate her life
and the book. He is present even after his death, and intensely so. There is the
sharpness of a barely submerged hatred of her father in the first pages, tautly
written, quite brilliant. Yet she admires him,[18] loves him, has that mixture that
we saw in other proportions in Geoffrey Wolff's relations with *his* father.

Her problem at first is to cease to be simply her father's daughter, to be
someone herself. She wants to join the others, be like the rest of humanity, end
her separation and uniqueness. After she meets Hugh Slade, she says: "I felt I
had finally joined the company of other ordinary humans" (168).

But she herself has a thirst for the absolute much like her father. After the long period of caring for him and after her release from this confining task, she wants to make up for lost time and is impatient with the imperfections of the present and thirsts for some kind of absolute relationship.

What she is after is love—not charity—that is, something unique, individual, rather than undifferentiated, impersonal concern. Commenting on Auden's poem, she notes: "We will all come to grief because it is love we want, love for our differentness, love for our uniqueness, rather than charity, universal love, love because we simply *are*, as everyone else *is*, the kind of love that is plentiful, that is possible" (232).

After the confrontation with Hugh Slade's wife, she breaks down, wonders if she is or can be a "good person." She accuses herself of selfishness and inflicts a terrible punishment on herself—a kind of martyrdom—by devising her own penance: a life caring for Margaret Casey.

But after the visit of Father Mulcahey there is a reversal. She discovers the pride, the arrogance of loving the unlovable: "a charade one plays for one's own benefit." It involves another kind of selfishness, the avoidance of risk. If you love someone you risk the loss of that love, but it is simply cowardly and selfish to refuse to love for that reason: "It came to me," she says, "that life was monstrous: what you loved you were always in danger of losing. The greatest love meant only, finally the greatest danger. That was life; life was monstrous."

She finds too that charity is "small and tactical," not an absolute, not even a government program. It is closely related to Virginia Woolf's "little daily miracles, illuminations, matches struck unexpectedly in the dark." We can only be "small winners" in Machado de Assis's phrase, the English title of one of his books.

Where Flannery O'Connor's older characters cling to the belief that they "know who they are," the younger ones are trying to discover who they are, like Geoffrey Wolff who is intent upon "knowing who I was, being who I was" (203). We have been following these meandering trails: identity is still the key word.

There are, all in all, a good many novels which deal with children and how they relate to their parents, but these novels tend to cluster at certain times and in certain countries, and are obviously related to prevailing cultural conditions. It is odd, however, to note how few American novels make this subject a major theme. Philip Roth's *Portnoy's Complaint* (1969) inevitably comes to mind. We have had John Cheever's *Bullet Park* (1969) and Joseph Heller's *Something Happened* (1974), and the conjunction of these two sad, suburban works set off a discussion of the subject by John Leonard in *The New York Times Book Review* (January 26, 1975), which received a detailed and thoughtful comment from a reader, Dennis Morgan (March 9, 1975). Leonard's quick survey raises some interesting questions:

A few of our established male novelists, those who are principally concerned with manners and morals, instead of the inadequacy of language and the cunning of the Id, have begun at last to write about their children. Updike tries to do so. At a distance, always a chilly distance, Bellow toys with it. Mailer, Vonnegut, Malamud have so far avoided the subject. Henry James did amid subterfuges. Hemingway and Fitzgerald were their own bright little boys to the end, with wooden swords: there's room in the nursery for just one of us. Faulkner violently engaged the generations, but his children were flowering curses, clocks wired to bombs: they proved a thesis. The male American novelist has usually been too busy killing his father to contemplate being one.

In a discussion like this it is easy to point out omissions—and there are many interesting novels and many aspects of the problem that I have not even mentioned—but one needs to strive less for completeness than for a sense of what the various phenomena mean. That is what I have been working toward. The greatest benefit from assembling so disparate a group of novels and confronting them with social and psychological theories is that they all interact in strange and unpredictable ways, yielding new insights. It is a complex and hazardous task to put together novels that are joined only by their common theme across differences of language, culture, and time. But one result can be a freshness of view, a new approach to familiar works, the discovery of novels which would otherwise remain unknown to you. There is no simple conclusion, no neat set of propositions to be derived even from the limited sample we have been exploring. The single theme is rich and has many variations: fathers and daughters in Balzac, Dostoevsky and Virginia Woolf; mothers and sons in Lawrence, Machado, and O'Connor; mother and daughter-in-law in Mauriac and Lawrence; grandparents and grandchildren in O'Connor, the artist as son in Joyce and the artist as father in Hesse; the whole complex web of entangling family relations in Gide, Virginia Woolf, Flannery O'Connor; and some appreciation is gained of how hazardous those relationships are—how various are the forces which shape and break them.

Our novelists show quite clearly that what flows across the generation gap between parents and children is a mixture of love and hostility, and it is the part of wisdom to recognize that both exist and to learn to accept both. This is rather different from the more frequently encountered sentimental view that the essence of the relationship is either all gentle love or all hostility or resentment. A clear perception of the complexity of the generation gap is essential since it is a basic part of the fundamental theme: the discovery of the self and the acceptance of ambiguity.

Notes

[1] Cf. Kingsley Davis, "The Sociology of Parent-Youth Conflict," in *The Family: Its Structures and Functions*, ed. Rose L. Coser (1963; rept. New York: St. Martin's Press, 1974) 446-59.

[2] Philippe Ariès, *L'Enfant et la vie familiale sous l'ancien régime* (Paris: Plon, 1960) 462-63.

[3] For example: Arlene S. Skolnick and Jerome H. Skolnick, *Family in Transition: Rethinking Marriage, Sexuality, Child Rearing and Family Organization* (Boston: Little Brown, 1971).

[4] For a detailed discussion of the differing views of Piaget and Chomsky see *Language and Learning: The Debate between Jean Piaget and Noam Chomsky*, ed. Massimo Piattelli-Palmarini (London: Routledge and Kegan Paul, 1980). This is based on the discussions at a meeting held at the Abbaye de Royaumont in October 1975 and includes the papers prepared for the conference by Piaget and Chomsky and distributed to the participants before the colloquium. The French edition, *Théories du langage, théories de l'apprentissage*, was published by Seuil in 1979.

[5] Ronald David Laing, *The Politics of Experience* (New York: Ballantine Books, 1967); Ronald David Laing, *The Politics of the Family* (New York: Pantheon Books, 1971).

[6] Cf. David Hunt, *Parents and Children in History* (New York and London: Basic Books, 1970) 25.

[7] Balzac, *Les Illusions perdues*, in *La Comédie humaine*, Bibliothèque de la Pléiade (Paris: Gallimard, 1952) 10: 1010.

[8] Balzac, *Eugénie Grandet*, in *La Comédie humaine*, Bibliothèque de la Pléiade (Paris: Gallimard, 1952) 3: 260.

[9] Herbert Luthy, *A l'heure de son clocher, essai sur la France* (Paris: Calman-Lévy, 1955) 58-59 (my translation).

[10] Lewis S. Feuer, *The Conflict of Generations, the Character and Significance of Student Movements* (New York and London: Basic Books, 1969).

[11] Bruno Bettelheim, "The Problem of Generations," in *The Challenge of Youth*, ed. Erik Erikson (New York: Doubleday Anchor Books, 1965).

[12] Victor Sawdon Pritchett, *Turgenev, the Gentle Barbarian, the Life of Turgenev* (New York: Random House, 1977) 139.

[13] George Eliot, *Adam Bede*, Book I, Ch. 4.

[14] Joseph N. Frank, *Dostoevsky* (Princeton: Princeton UP) from the typescript of Vol. 4, not yet published.

[15] Konstantin Mochulsky, *Dostoevski* (Princeton: Princeton UP, 1971) 496.

[16] Sean O'Faolain, *The Irish: A Character Study* (New York: Devin-Adair Company, 1949) 169-70.

[17] Geoffrey Wolff, *The Duke of Deception* (New York: Random House, 1979) 8.

[18] Mary Gordon, *Final Payments* (New York: Random House, 1978) 40-41.

Victor Brombert

Meanings and Indeterminacy in Gogol's *The Overcoat*

Akaky Akakyevich is the central character of Gogol's story *The Overcoat*. Although Dostoevsky gave common currency to the term "anti-hero" in *Notes from Underground*, it is Gogol's Akaky Akakyevich who is the genuine, unmitigated, and seemingly unredeemable anti-hero. For Dostoevsky's anti-heroic paradoxalist, afflicted with hypertrophia of the consciousness, is well-read, cerebral, incurably bookish, and talkative. Akaky Akakyevich is hardly aware, and almost inarticulate. Gogol's artistic wager was to try to articulate this inarticulateness.

The story, in its plot line, is simple. A most unremarkable copying clerk in a St. Petersburg ministry—bald, pockmarked, short-sighted, and the scapegoat of his colleagues who invent cruel ways of mocking him—discovers one day that his pathetically threadbare coat no longer protects him against the fierce winter wind. The tailor he consults categorically refuses to repair the coat which is now beyond repair, and tempts Akaky Akakyevich into having a new overcoat made, one totally beyond his means, but which by dint of enormous sacrifices, he manages to acquire and wear with a newly discovered sense of pride. But his happiness lasts only one short day. Crossing a deserted quarter at night, he is attacked by two thieves who knock him to the ground and steal his coat. Drenched, frozen, deeply upset, brutally reprimanded by a superior whose help he dared seek, Akaky develops a fever, becomes delirious, and dies.

One can hardly speak of an interesting plot line. Yet this simple story lends itself to orgies of interpretations. In fact, there may be as many interpretations as there are readers. *The Overcoat* can be read as a parable, a hermeneutic puzzle, an exercise in meaninglessness. But to begin with, there is the temptation to read it seriously as satire with a social and moral message. In *The Nose*, Gogol had already made fun of the rank-consciousness and venality of civil servants. In *The Overcoat*, he seems to deride systematically the parasitical, lazy, phony, world of Russian officialdom, whose members are the impotent mediators of a hierarchic and ineffectual power structure in which every subordinate fears and apes his superior. Early Russian critics, convinced that literature must have a moral message, read such a denunciatory and corrective satirical intention into the story even though it is clear that Gogol constantly shifts his tone, defends no apparent norm, and systematically ironizes any possible "serious" message.

There is of course the temptation to read *The Overcoat* as a tale of compassion, as a plea for brotherhood. The pathetically defenseless little clerk, taunted and persecuted by the group, remains blissfully oblivious to the cruel pranks of which he is the butt, intent on his humble copying activity. Only when the jokes become too outrageous, or interfere with his work, does he protest ever so mildly. But here the tone of the story seems to change. For Gogol introduces a young man, recently appointed to the same office, who is on the point of sharing in the general fun, and who is suddenly struck by the strange notes in Akaky's voice which touch his heart with pity and make him suddenly see everything in a very different light. A true revelation emanating from an "unnatural" ("*neestestvennyi*") power allows him to hear other words behind Akaky's banal entreaty to be left alone. What he hears are the deeply penetrating, unspoken words echoing with poignant significance: "I am thy brother."

And with this voice from behind the voice comes the shocked awareness of how much "inhumanity" there is in human beings, how much brutality lurks in what goes as civilized society and civilized behavior. The apparent lesson in humanity given by the scapegoat victim seems, in the immediate context, to have an almost religious character, especially if one relates it to the narrator's comments, after Akaky's death, on how a man of meekness who bore the sneers and insults of his fellow human beings disappeared from this world, but who, before his agony, had a vision of the bright visitant ("*svetluy gost*"). The man of meekness, the man of sorrows, like the unspoken but clearly heard "I am thy brother," seems to have a Christian if not Christological, resonance.

But we forget Akaky's name, and that we are now allowed to do. For the patronymic appellation not only stresses the principle of repetition (Akaky's first name being exactly the same as his father's), but the funny sound repetition is even funnier because the syllable *kak* = like (*tak kak* = just as) embeds the principle of sameness in Akaky's name, determining, it would seem, his single-minded, life-long activity of copying and implicit condemnation to sameness. Regarding the many years Akaky served in the same department, Gogol observes that he "remained in exactly the same place, in exactly the same position, in exactly the same job, doing exactly the same kind of work, to wit copying official documents." But there is better (or worse) especially to Russian ears, for *kakatj* (from the Greek *cacos* = bad, evil) is children's talk for defecate, and *caca* in many languages refers to human excrement. To be afflicted with such a name clearly relates to the garbage being regularly dumped on Akaky as he walks in the street, and to his being treated with no more respect by the caretakers than a common fly. The cruel verbal fun around the syllable

kak extends beyond the character's name, and contaminates Gogol's text.
Gogol indulges in seemingly endless variations of the words *tak, kak, kakoi,
kakoi-to, kakikh-to, vot-kak, neekak, takoi, takaya, kaknibut,* (just so, that's
how, in no way, somehow, and so on) which in the translation disappear
altogether. The exploitations of sound effects or sound meanings clearly
correspond to a poet's fascination with the prestigious cacophonic resources of
ordinary speech.[1]

One last point about the choice of Akaky's name, specifically the Christian
act of "christening": according to custom, the calendar was opened at random
and several saints' names (Mokkia, Sossia) including the name of the martyr
Khozdazat, were considered, only to be rejected by the mother because they
sounded so strange. Akaky was chosen because that was the name of the father.
But Acacius, a holy monk of Sinai, was also a saint and martyr, and we find
ourselves—especially since the Greek prefix *a* (Acacius) signifies not bad,
therefore good, meek, humble, obedient—back to the religious motif. If Akaky
continues to copy for his own pleasure at home, this is in large part because the
bliss of copying has a specifically monastic resonance. Gogol does indeed refer
to his copying as a "labor of love."

Here a new temptation assails the reader. Should *The Overcoat* not be read
as hagiography in a banal modern context, or at the very least as a parody of
hagiography? A number of elements seem to lend support to such a reading of
the story in or against the perspective of the traditional lives of the saints: the
humble task of copying documents, reference to the theme of the martyr
("*muchenik*"), salvational terminology, sacrificial motifs of communion ("I am
thy brother"), Akaky's visions and ecstasies, his own apparitions from beyond
the grave. But the most telling analogy with hagiographic lore is the conver-
sion-effect on others, first on the young man who has a revelation of a voice that
is not of this world ("*svet*"), and toward the end the self-admiring, domineering,
Very Important Person on whom Akaky's ghost-like apparition makes a never-
to-be-forgotten impression.[2]

The overcoat itself can take on religious connotations because clothing, in
the symbology of the Bible and orthodox liturgy, often represents righteousness
and salvation. The only trouble with such an interpretation—and Gogol has
written *Meditations on the Divine Liturgy* which refer to the priest's robe of
righteousness as a garment of salvation[3]—is that the coat can have an opposite
symbolic significance, that of hiding the truth. Hence the traditional image of
disrobing to reveal the naked self. In addition, there are many other possible
meanings quite remote from the religious sphere: the metonymic displacement
of the libido (the Russian word for overcoat—*shinel*—is appropriately feminine), the effects of virilization (in his new coat, Akaky surprises himself in the
act of running after some woman in the street!), loss of innocence and loss of
"original celibacy."[4] The coat itself thus turns out to be a form of temptation

(material acquisition, vanity, pride), and the devilish tailor is the agent of this temptation just as the writer or narrator (who in fact is he?) "tempts" the reader into a succession of vacuous and mutually canceling interpretations.

This provocative writer-reader relationship, sustained throughout the narration, casts a special light on Akaky's fundamental activity of copying— the act of writing in its purest form. It does not take much imagination (our modern critics discover self-referentiality everywhere) to see in Akaky's copying an analogue of the writer's activity. And like the proverbially absorbed writer or scholar, he is obsessed by his writing to the point of finding himself in the middle of the street while thinking that he is in the middle of a sentence. This self-absorbed and self-referential nature of Gogol's act of writing might be seen to imply a negative attitude toward the referential world, toward all that which is not writing. Much like Flaubert, who dreamt of composing a "book about nothing," and whom contemporary critics like to view as an apostle of self-referential, intransitive literature, Gogol yearns for monastic withdrawal. Flaubert was haunted by the figures of the monk and the saint. Similarly, Gogol explained in a letter: "It is not the poet's business to worm his way into the world's marketplace. Like a silent monk, he lives in the world without belonging to it. . . ."[5]

Pushed to a logical extreme, this sense of the radical deceptiveness of life calls into question worldly authority, and leads to a destabilizing stance that challenges the principle of authority, a subversive *gesta* of which the real hero is the artist himself. There is indeed something devilish about Gogol's narrative voice. It has already been suggested that the devil makes an appearance in the figure of the tailor who tempts Akaky into buying the coat. This caricature of the sartorial artist who quite literally is the creator of the overcoat, this ex-serf sitting with his legs crossed under him like a Turkish pasha, has diabolical earmarks: he is a "one-eyed devil" living at the end of a black staircase; he has a deformed big toenail, hard and thick as a tortoise shell; he handles a thrice referred to snuff box on which the face of a general has been effaced (the devil is faceless); he seems to be nudged by the devil and charges "the devil knows what prices."[6]

This verbal playfulness seems to extend to the narrator himself, who undercuts his own narration in truly diabolical fashion by means of grotesque hyperbolizing, mixtures of realistic and parodistic elements, sudden shifts from the rational to the irrational, and elliptical displacements from epic triviality to unrestrained fantasy. Indulging in a game of mirages and fog-like uncertainties, the narrator subverts the logical progression of his story. Ultimately, even the ghost is debunked, and we are back in the blackness of quotidian reality. In the Russian text, these shifts in tone and textual instabilities are even more insidious, since everything seems to blur into the undifferentiated flow of seemingly endless paragraphs.

This merging of discontinuities undermines any sense of plot, undercuts the notion of subject, and suggests at every point that what is told is *another* story, thereby teasing the reader into endless interpretations that can neither be stabilized nor stopped. Some of this is the inevitable result of a mimesis of inarticulateness, a narrative style that is the imitative substitute for Akaky's manner of communicating mostly through prepositions, adverbs, and "such parts of speech as have no meaning whatsoever." But the strategy of destabilization and fragmented diction also has a deeper subversive purpose. The non sequiturs and hesitations reveal the arbitrariness of any fictional structure, and in the last analysis subvert any auctorial authority. The concluding page of *The Nose* represents an authorial critique of the story as incomprehensible and useless. The mediating self-negator is the fictionalized narrator identified in *The Overcoat* as the "*raskazyvaiushyi*"—the narrating one. And this narrator, occasionally pretending to be ignorant or semi-ignorant (like Cervantes's narrative voice as of the very first sentence of *Don Quixote*) does not know in what town, on what day, on what street the action takes place—in fact, complains of loss of memory. All this, however, only accentuates the possible importance of the unknowable and the unsayable, while protecting the protagonist's sacred privacy. The narrator clumsily speculates on what Akaky might or might not have said to himself as he stares at an erotic window display in the elegant quarter of St. Petersburg, and he concludes: "But perhaps he never even said anything at all to himself. For it is impossible to delve into a person's mind" (in Russian, literally: to creep into a person's soul).

The Overcoat is thus marked by conflicting and enigmatic signals, pointing to oxymoronic textures of meanings. Inversions hint at conversions. What is seemingly up is in fact seen to be down, while the reverse is equally true. The downtrodden creature turns out to be capable of heroic sacrifices, while the powerfully constituted VIP with the appearance of a "*bogatyr*" (hero) is cut down to human size by fright. On the other hand, when Akaky's fall is likened to a disaster such as destroys the czars and other great ones of this earth, one may well feel that Gogol is ironic about all heroic poses, heroic values, and heroic figures. When Akaky wears the new coat, his pulse beats faster, his bearing seems to indicate a newly discovered sense of purpose ("*tzel*"), his eyes have an audacious gleam, he appears somehow to have almost become virile. Yet the overcoat is also the emblem of false values, of trivial passion, of a silly reason for a human downfall. One might wish therefore to read a deeper significance into these mutually canceling interpretations. In English, the word *passion* is fraught with a multiple significance: in the ordinary sense, it denotes intense and even overwhelming emotion, especially of love; yet etymologically, it signifies suffering. Love and suffering are of course linked in a grotesque manner in *The Overcoat*. Whether such love and such suffering are commensurate with any objective reality remains unresolved in this story which seems to say that any love is great no matter what its object, that love is all-powerful; and conversely, that any passion can drag one down, that the more intense it seems, the emptier it is. Gogol's style is in itself an admirable instrument of ambivalence: enlarging trivia, and thereby trivializing what we may for a moment be tempted to take as significant.[7]

What complicates Gogol's text for the reader is that it is not a case of simple ambivalence. It will not do to praise Gogol as a compassionate realist with an ethical message or to see him as a playful anti-realist indulging in overwrought imagery and in the reflections of distorting mirrors. The hard fact is that Gogol is a protean writer whose simultaneity of possible meanings allows for no respite and no comfortable univocal message. If the narrator is center stage, it is because ultimately he becomes a performer, a buffoonish actor mimicking incoherence itself. Intelligent readers of Gogol—Boris Eichenbaum, Vladimir Nabokov, Victor Erlich, Charles Bernheimer, Donald Fanger[8]—have in varying degrees and with different emphases, understood that rather than indulging in a feast of ideas to be taken seriously, Gogol delighted in verbal acts as a game—a game that implied the autonomy of narrative style, a declaration of artistic independence, and a thorough deflation of l'esprit de sérieux.

Perhaps there is an underlying autobiographic urge in *The Overcoat*, and the verbal clowning and narrative pirouettes are telling a story in which the irrational takes on an exorcising and liberating virtue—much as the idiosyncrasies of Dostoevsky's *Notes from Underground* present a vehement protest against spiritually deadening rationality. What is certain is that Gogol needs to wear a mask. Haunted by the monsters born of his imagination, afraid to be unmasked, Gogol literally disappears in his writing by becoming a multiplicity of voices.[9]

But there is a danger in depicting Gogol as an escape artist struggling against his own demons at the same time as he struggles against the repressive reality he wishes to deny. Similarly, there is the risk of considerable distortion in the determination of formalist and post-structuralist critics to draw Gogol to the camp of radical modernity by seeing him exclusively concerned with speech acts and sheer rhetoricity. Polyvalence does not mean the absence of meaning. The real problem, much as in the case of Flaubert, who complained of the plethora of subjects and inflationary overfill of meanings, is that overabundance and multiplicity become principles of indeterminacy. Excess is related to emptiness. Similarly, Gogol seems torn between the futility of experience and the futility of writing about it, between the conviction that writing is the only salvation, yet that it is powerless to say the unsayable— aware at all points of the gulf between signifier and signified.

Nabokov may have come closest to the heart of Gogol's dark playfulness when he wrote: "The gaps and black holes in the texture of Gogol's style imply flaws in the texture of life itself. . . ."[10] To this one might add, however, that the hollowness of the gaps, the terrifying absence, is also an absence/presence: a void that asks to be filled by the interpretive act. The dialectics of negativity, so dependent on the antiheroic mode embodied by Akaky, displace the production of meaning from the almost non-existent character and undecidable text to the creative reader.[11]

Notes

[1] Boris Eichenbaum speaks of Gogol's "phonic inscriptions" and "sound-semantics" in "How 'The Overcoat' Is Made," in *Gogol from the Twentieth Century*, ed. Robert A. Maguire (Princeton: Princeton UP, 1974) 280.

[2] See John Schillinger, "Gogol's 'The Overcoat' as a Travesty of Hagiography," *Slavic and East European Journal* 16.1 (1972) 36-41.

[3] See Anthony Hippisley, "Gogol's 'The Overcoat': A further Interpretation," *Slavic and East European Journal* 20.2 (1976) 121-29. Hippisley points out (123) that Gogol, in his *Meditations on the Divine Liturgy* quotes Psalms 132:9: "Let thy priests be clothed with righteousness. . . ."

[4] The expression is Charles Bernheimer's, in his fine essay "Cloaking the Self: The Literary Space of Gogol's 'Overcoat,'" *PMLA* 90.1 (1975) 53-61.

[5] Letter to Pogodin, quoted by Charles Bernheimer (53), and Donald Fanger, *The Creation of Nikolai Gogol* (Cambridge: Harvard UP, 1979).

[6] Dmitry Chizhevsky, who stresses the presence of the Devil in "The Overcoat" writes: "As someone who was well read in religious literature, as a connoisseur and collector of folklore materials—from popular songs and legends—Gogol of course knew about the Christian and folk tradition that the Devil is faceless." "About Gogol's 'Overcoat,'" in *Gogol from the Twentieth Century* 320.

[7] I am largely indebted to Dmitry Chizhevsky who has admirably shown in "About Gogol's 'Overcoat'" (295-322) how the repeated and incongruous use of the adverb "even" ("*daje*") breaks up the logical train of thought, enlarges trivia, and frustrates the reader by making the insignificant seem significant, and vice versa. Such a narrative strategy is related by Chizhevsky to the semantic oscillations of the text.

[8] Boris Eichenbaum, "How 'The Overcoat' Is Made"; Vladimir Nabokov, *Nikolai Gogol* (New York: New Directions, 1944); Victor Erlich, *Gogol* (New Haven: Yale UP, 1969); Charles Bernheimer, "Cloaking the Self"; Donald Fanger, *The Creation of Nikolai Gogol*.

[9] Victor Erlich has very convincingly discussed Gogol's motif of the mask and tendency to "speak in somebody else's voice" in his chapter "The Great Impersonator" in *Gogol* 210-23. Gogol himself writes: "If anyone had seen the monsters that issued from my pen, at first for my own purposes alone—he would certainly have shuddered" (quoted by Valery Bzyusov in his essay "Burnt to Ashes," reproduced in *Gogol from the Twentieth Century* 111).

[10] Vladimir Nabokov, *Nikolai Gogol* 143.

[11] The substance of this paper was presented to the American Philosophical Society on November 9, 1990.

Suzanne Keller

Christina of Sweden, the Queen-King: Life Prefigures Revolution

Genealogies take many forms, from the tracing of biological linkages over the generations back to some illustrious or pioneering forbears to linkages based on elective social or psychological affinities (that may make one feel more at home with the ancient Minoans than with one's contemporaries). In the latter, the concept of generation transcends its biological connotations to include ancestries united by cultural preferences thereby enlarging potential arenas of identity and belonging.

For those who break new ground by challenging conventions, political, moral, or social, the discovery of precursors in times past can be curiously elating. Not only can it reduce the sense of isolation and vulnerability that accompanies innovation but it can provide a ballast against the social turmoil created by departures from social expectations.

It is in this spirit that the present essay is offered as a contribution to the theme of this volume. It proposes as an unclaimed ancestor for the feminist discourse of our time an extraordinary historic personage: Queen Christina of Sweden, woman, ruler, and exile.

It may come as a surprise to contemporary observers for whom the feminist movement originated in the 1960s to realize that history contains many forerunners of contemporary developments in the form of women rebels, pioneers, and iconoclasts who defied the destinies their societies had decreed for them. To them surely belongs that strange rebel Queen, Christina of Sweden. This remarkable woman defied the family and gender norms of her time in a way that would even now be considered daring but must then have seemed incomprehensible. To this day she has managed to arouse intense historical curiosity about her person, her actions, and her motives. She was both vilified and idolized, and, from the earliest years, rumor, gossip, and mystery draped themselves around her image. Much of the fascination she has inspired is due not so much to her grand deeds or her even grander misdeeds but to her resplendent personality and her courage to claim freedom as her birthright.

Her modes of defiance were many. In an age where marriage and procreation were women's prime destiny, she refused to marry. As sole heir to her father's kingdom, she abdicated her throne. And in a country steeped in Lutheranism that had fought a bitter 30-year war for the faith, she became a convert to Roman Catholicism. Finally, she chose permanent exile in Italy where she engaged in spirited exchanges with the Pope and established an international center for art and thought.

How, one must ask, given the customs and preferences of the times, was such a historic personage generated? By what forces—generational, cultural, political—is human clay shaped into such a special destiny?

The year is 1626. Sweden had barely recovered from her defeat in the war with Denmark (1611-13) and was engaged in the protracted conflict known as the Thirty Years' War. The great Gustavus Adolphus II, Christina's father, had made this small peasant country—one-half million strong—something of an international force in the councils of Europe, and was soon to give his life for Sweden's championing of the Protestant cause.

Consider this in light of Christina's later rejection of both her throne and the religion for which her countrymen had fought and her father had died. But, then, she was always a defiant spirit, determined, undaunted, a woman of strong will and independent mind, a rebel virtually from the moment of her appearance in this world. Indeed this created quite a drama in its own right, given the fact that Christina started her worldly existence as something of an impostor. This had less to do with Christina, however, than with her parents, the illustrious young king and his pretty, neurasthenic young wife, who had put all their hopes on this blessed event. After three miscarriages and the death of an infant, all during the first five years of their marriage, they were most anxious about the succession and eager to welcome what they were sure would be the long-awaited male heir. But, against prediction and plan she arrived on December 8, 1626.

Perhaps because the birth was a difficult one, or because the desire for a male heir was so strong, or because the astrologers had adamantly divined it, or, as most historians seem to feel, because the baby was born with a caul from head to toe—the newborn was announced to the eager monarch as the boy he had longed for.[1] When *la petite différence* was, as it inevitably had to be, discovered by the midwives, they were terrified and dared not tell the King. It was his sister Catherine who took the infant to the King's chamber and without a word had the King see the corporeal truth for himself.

Instead of the feared wrath, however, the King with only the barest hesitation took the infant in his arms and ordered the full complement of salutes and festivities due a male heir, noting, in words that charm us to this day that "She will undoubtedly be a clever woman for even at her birth she has succeeded in deceiving us all."[2]

By all accounts, her father adored her and proceeded to treat her as the son he had desired. As early as age two, Christina accompanied him on military reviews and, perhaps in a premonition of his premature death, he hastened to devise a comprehensive program for her royal education. She was to be brought up as a prince, be given a boy's training, and learn everything a young prince should know including military tactics, science, high finance, and statecraft. Above all, he explicitly forbade the inculcation of any feminine ideals and pursuits, except for those of "virtue and modesty."[3]

It was an extraordinary idea for that time and that place. And Christina proved an outstanding pupil—becoming as adept a "boy" as he could have wished. That it might also create a permanent confusion of gender identity never occurred to the great man.

Thus early in life, Christina was trained to ride (and did so superbly) to hunt, to shoot and as she was later to put it so well, my "inclinations agreed wonderfully with his designs," for from an early age, also, she disliked conventional femininity with a passion. In this she was encouraged by her unfortunate fate to have a mother who rejected her only child because she was, "a girl and ugly." These words were to be imprinted on that child forever—as recorded in all their starkness decades later in the autobiography she left for posterity. Rejected and wounded in the emotional sphere, she found bliss in the life of the mind. She adored learning and spent hours at her studies. "I was delighted when my studies called me. . . . I went there with an inconceivable joy . . ." (Masson 35).

This brilliant and precocious child, who could do everything well as her startled teachers announced again and again, was in that sense, too, her father's child. Himself a great soldier and statesman, a gifted linguist and orator, a musician and a world-class charmer, he transmitted to his daughter a thirst for knowledge that proved a leitmotif throughout her life.

Spurred on by an insatiable curiosity, she loved to reason things out for herself and to plumb the depths of art and thought. That this passion for discovering the truth may have had its roots in the brutal maternal rejection and the early loss of her father does not diminish her astonishing achievements. She excelled at everything except the one thing she could not learn from great books or great men—trust in human relationships.

Rule and Abdication

When Christina was less than three weeks old, her father had her officially declared his successor to the Swedish throne. At age four she made a little speech to the Estates—a speech she had learned by heart, whereupon she was cheered by the Assemblage as their future ruler.

And then when she was six years old, her beloved father was killed, far away in the Battle of Lutzen (1632). He was then 39 years old. She had been disconsolate at being parted from him by the war and his death devastated her. A year later, in 1633, the Riksdag convened to proclaim Christina King of Sweden. (Sweden, as was true of Hungary, called reigning Queens, *Kings*. A Queen was the wife of the King. Thus social status superseded gender [Goldsmith 24].) She was then seven years old and already aware of the seductions of power. "I do remember" she was to write later, "my delight at seeing people at my feet and kissing my hand" (Masson 27). Henceforth, of course, her life was not her own. All emphasis was on her becoming a ruler able to fulfill her royal destiny. A normal childhood was thus not available to her but there were additional anomalies: Christina, though a woman, was brought up like a man, she was a lonely child yet always surrounded by people; she had neither sister nor brother and the only parents available were old or older men who instructed, tutored, judged, and counselled, but did not warm her heart.

Crowned at 19, Christina threw herself seriously into matters of statecraft, domestic and international affairs, and political theory. She impressed all with her abilities as a ruler; but then on August 7, 1651, six years into her reign, when she was 25 years old, Christina informed her aghast royal Council that she wished to abdicate in favor of her chosen heir, for whom she had previously maneuvered the political way: her cousin Karl Gustav. She gave three ostensible reasons for this step: 1) the welfare of the nation required it, 2) the readiness of the heir supported it, and 3) she yearned for tranquility. She assured them that she had thought about this for years and that her decision was irrevocable.[4]

What were her real reasons for laying down the Crown and a destiny for which she had been preparing all of her life? The full answer will never be known, but deep-rooted conflicts about identity and intimacy seem to have played their part. Despite a youthful fancy for her cousin which came to an abrupt end upon adolescence, she was adamant about her refusal ever to marry. When the resident French diplomat who had become her confidant once alluded to a possible future marriage, she rebuked him with these words: marriage, never. "The truth of the matter is that for a long time I felt that for me marriage was 'une violence nécessaire' but now I am cured of this fear."[5]

Her next step therefore was to arrange for the succession, which she did, simultaneously freeing herself from the demands of future matrimony and maternity. Indeed these were the words that finally convinced the strongly opposed Council to do her bidding: "I declare quite definitely that it is impossible for me to marry."

Her abdication was followed by another dramatic step—namely, her conversion to Roman Catholicism, which led to her permanent self-exile in Italy. For a monarch to become a Roman Catholic in the Sweden of that day is akin to an American President joining the communist party in our time. Sweden was in a state of shock, yet she was adamant, negotiating both her abdication and her subsequent conversion with patience and strategic skill. What force of will it must have taken to defy her court, her country and her councilors! And so, not yet 30 years old she left her throne, her country, and her faith and made her way to the Italy she adored.

By this time she was the talk of Europe and the center of attention wherever she went. In Paris, for example, one stop in her journey, she was splendidly received, with guns booming and crowds estimated at more than 200,000 people. She rode through the city on a gray horse, named Unicorn, escorted by 15,000 troops. The 18-year-old Louis XIV was so curious to see this extraordinary visitor that he rode to Chantilly with his brother to have a look at her incognito (Masson 295).

Despite her casual disregard of rules of dress and appearance, she seems to have captivated the French court. Madame de Motteville, recording her first impressions in her diary, admitted to being shocked by her bizarre appearance and her disregard for proper attire, noting her "absolutely extraordinary dress, more like a man's than a woman's with skirts so short her feet showed . . . [and] . . . her man's shirt only fastened at the neck with a pin" (Mason 276-77). Nonetheless she adds that she was soon captivated by her talk, by her beautiful eyes, her dignity and a certain gentleness. It was by sheer force of personality and presence that Christina triumphed again and again.

Even at the most sophisticated Court of Europe, moreover, she stood out by her knowledge of French art collections and the inside gossip of the Royal world. And at the earliest opportunity on that visit she escaped to see some of the people congenial to her such as the Duc de La Rochefoucauld and Saint-Amant.

Henceforth also she would negotiate with Kings and Popes, consult with scholars and poets, and stand her ground in the pursuit of truth. In effect, she had renounced power in one realm only to harness it in another. Henceforth, when she was not stirring the political pot and fomenting alliances—and she was a master intriguer—(one of her many causes was to become Queen of Naples)—she would devote herself to art, science, and the higher learning. She made notable use of her brilliant gifts, spoke eight languages fluently, read Dante and Boccacio, Virgil and Cicero in the original. She wrote essays on Cesar and Alexander the Great in impeccable French (as though she were born in the Louvre said one French diplomat). Corelli dedicated his first work to her (in 1681) and she recognized Scarlatti's genius from the first. Later in life, political passions subdued, she founded a renowned academy at her small Palace in Rome that "became a magnet for artists and scholars, both male and female, of every land" (Lewis 266-67).

In her fifties, she became a student of astronomy with the most distinguished astronomer of the time (one Giovanni Cassini who discovered a comet) who at first was most reluctant to accept this neophyte. But he soon discovered her to be an enthusiastic and highly gifted pupil which challenged his masculine prejudices. As he was to note in his memoirs: "it is a pity that so fine a mind should have been wasted on a woman. Had her majesty been born a man she would have become one of the greatest scientists of this or any age" (Lewis 267). Patronizing though the compliment is, it is nonetheless an astonishing tribute. "There was no author, artist, or scientist in Italy who did not know and respect her" (Lewis 274). The famous Bishop Burret considered her one of the most interesting people he had ever met, "the chief of all the living rarities that one sees in Rome." And Europe agreed with him.

She also had a sense of humor and a felicitous use of language. Of a distinguished but boorish French classical scholar at her Court, who tried in vain to act the polished courtier, she was to comment: "He knows the name of a chair in dozens of languages but he does not know how to *sit* on even one" (Goldsmith 104). And to Cardinal Mazarin: "I will willingly do anything to please you—except be afraid of you."

She continued in exile what she had begun in her twenties in Sweden when she had made her Court a mecca for creative and distinguished minds, and was known as the Pallas Athena of the north. No less a philosopher than the great Descartes was attracted to that court and to the young Queen who tantalized him with such questions as "Which is worse, the abuse of love or of hate?" A dissertation later he assured her that the abuse of love was worse. Alas, their fateful encounter at Court proved disappointing to both, but when Descartes died a few months after arriving at Court—from a congestion of the lungs aggravated by the Arctic winter and their pre-dawn discourses—she was devastated and would always have a gnawing sense of responsibility for it. He had made an immense impact on the young Queen and she on him.

Christina the Woman

The contradictions inherent in Christina's status as Queen-King seem not to have struck her contemporaries as they do us. But they were striking. For, as a ruler she had the power to command her country and her people and to occupy the center of the national stage. As a woman, on the other hand, she was stereotypically defined as weak, emotional, indecisive, dependent, and "naturally" disposed to obey. These antithetical expectations were bound to create a schism of the soul.

Christina sought to resolve this by taking on male trappings as to dress, masculine displays of temper, and a stance of independence. Very early in life, she had decided that she liked power, and power in her world was masculine. As a result, and hardly unusual in a gender-polarized world, she could not choose the male role without at the same time denigrating the female one. Then, too, her nature was rooted in a desire for independence. This proved extremely awkward in seventeenth-century Sweden and later in Rome where women were expected to be silent in the churches and the squares. Independence of mind and conduct was hardly accepted for either sex at that time—but for a woman it seemed totally unnatural.

Yet on every occasion, Christina made clear that no one would dictate to her how she should live. She always reserved the right to express her own opinion on any question. Self-willed, provocative, and, yes, at times, exasperating, her independence could prove irritating to authorities of whatever stripe—Popes, Kings, or public opinion.

For example, when the Pope, in a fit of prudery common to aging men, issued strict orders that no woman in Rome was to wear a low-necked gown, Christina appeared before him wearing a particularly high man's cravat (Goldsmith 290). And this when she depended on his good will for a pension!

And then there was her appearance. In patriarchal societies, appearance is for a woman what power is for a man—part of their gender capital. Alas, sparked by the earliest judgment of herself as ugly, she flaunted her indifference to looks and dress, but it was a pretense. Youthful portraits show her as quite arresting, with large, luminous eyes, a sensuous mouth, and exquisite hands. But she was preoccupied with her inadequacies, a notable one stemming from an accident in early infancy when a nurse dropped her—deliberately in her view to express her disdain of her sex. Henceforth, one shoulder would be markedly lower than the other, a defect she attributed to maternal neglect and hid through skillful dress. This, plus the memory of her mother's disparagement ever raw in her mind, led her to dismiss beauty and sensual appeal as irrelevant, though she could resort to finery when she chose to do so.

Given her masculine upbringing and style of dress, Christina had later to learn to dress as a woman. She did this by grafting female apparel on to the masculine base as she did also in regard to her personal and social conduct. She was perhaps the first public female figure to be explicitly androgynous in appearance, blending selected characteristics from each sex into a unique amalgam. She would meet diplomats and distinguished visitors attired in dress "such as men wear and a woman's skirt put on for the occasion on top of the man's trousers . . . her hair . . . [hanging] free cut like a man's" (Masson, 219). Not surprisingly, her defiance of the sartorial code made the proper Swedish Burghers bristle with indignation and led to a horde of rumors about her virtue, her sex, and her normalcy, not in the least, in matters of love.

Christina and Love

Love is second only to beauty in the traditional historic image of woman. And rumors about Christina's amorous liaisons, though unproven, circulated widely, from her imputed passion for an Italian nun to her avid pursuit of lovers young and old. Nonetheless, the weight of scholarly opinion suggests that Christina, though not immune to the promptings of the flesh, seems to have sublimated the passions without, however, relinquishing intense emotional attachments to chosen favorites. Much has been made of fervent letters addressed to women but here again, one needs to be cautious in not viewing seventeenth-century rituals through twentieth-century eyes. Under the influence of *Les Précieuses* literary declarations of love and admiration without regard for gender prevailed in the salons of the day. *Les Précieuses* were well-born women who rejected what they considered the tyranny of marriage and men and sought love on a pure plane. Powerless to reform the institution of marriage, they chose instead to withdraw from the condition of dependence it imposed and aspired to a love among equals, one of dignity and refinement, freed from baseness and force. Christina, a keen follower of these ideas, spent hours dissecting the passions and ascertaining the nuances of love and friendship with like-minded devotees. This is why she would later be able to declare both that she had no experience of love and yet had much to say on the matter. Certainly the topic always intrigued her intensely.

What is undisputed is her fear and rejection of marriage. Even in our divorce-prone society, her words are chilling. "Marriage" she wrote "is the sovereign remedy against love and the marriage bed its tomb" (Masson 283). And more graphically, "I do not wish at any price to be a field for a man to plough."

Her repugnance for pregnancy, childbirth, and the male-female union generally seems to have reflected a deep-rooted terror of intimacy. The roots of this terror must surely have had some connection to the absence of a loving union in her own family and to the devastation caused by her father's early death and her mother's ambivalent treatment, alternately hostile and rejecting or overpossessive and stifling.

Then, too, there was her struggle to define herself within the curious framework available to her that posed profound contradictions between an idealized—and unattainable—masculinity and a pervasive denigration of femininity. This left her, in gender terms, in a psychic no man's land which she proceeded to fill in with a self-created androgyny of style, of intellect, and of ambition.

If she was never to form a permanent union with another it was not, however, for a lack of feeling—all describe her as of an ardent temperament—but because of a conviction that love meant imprisonment. It was the consequences of passion not the emotions from which she fled. Throughout her life she struggled with sexual impulses she found hard to control, worried about sexual temptation, and turned towards religion to help her contain her carnal nature. What she feared above all was the subjection of woman to man and this fear shaped her fiction of love throughout her life.

To be sure, there had once been an irresistible *homme fatal*, at the Court of her youth, but their dalliance did not transgress important limits, whether because of her or his reluctance is not clear. This unrequited passion was to cause her much anguish and eventually the favorite would be toppled from his high place and be as much despised by the young Queen as he had once been adored (Stolpe 75). Overall, her life seems to have been more a spiritual than a sensual odyssey, a search for the *moi profond*, the primary self, that had in a sense been stolen from her.

Touchingly, like the innocent and neglected child she had been, she tried to be good, and to love honor and duty while grappling with the acute anxieties and physical infirmities that were the permanent legacies of early torments and emotional dislocations. With the exception of her very last years, she was never to be truly at peace, ever at pains to perfect herself and to banish pride, imperiousness, and prejudice. In a letter to a friend, late in her life, she wrote "I have in no way become more beautiful; all my good and my bad qualities remain the same and as vital as ever. And I am now quite dissatisfied with my person as I always was" (Goldsmith 292). As astute an observer of her own character as she was of that of others, she knew, in the depth of her being, that the ardently longed for union of heart and soul, body and mind, with another mortal would be denied her forever. She knew also that her lifelong quest for the great truth of life was a quest as well for the smaller truth of herself. Fated to remain alone, as the six year old had once been, she sought in the life of the mind a passionate commitment and meaning, and in religion, a union with a very personal and loving God.

Toward the end of her life, with the defiance of her youth muted by the respect and affection the world now offered her, young and old flocked to her residence for the wit and wisdom she dispensed with undiminished flair. She lived on a modest pension, supporting other people's children and artists as finances permitted. Every so often there were flurries of the old drama and agitation, most notably a violent dispute with Pope Innocent XI; she lost and was forced to capitulate in writing. The Pope in a magnanimous gesture of all is forgiven sent her a huge basket of out-of-season peaches, a rare treat, whose receipt prompted this oft-quoted remark: "the Pope needn't think that his gift will lull my suspicions . . . on the contrary I shall be more on my guard than ever" (Lewis 288). But she ate the peaches.

At the last, the emotional storms having largely subsided, Christina did manage to create a world in which she felt at home. Surrounded by a few faithful friends, several protégés, her beloved books, her antiques (now in the Prado), and letters exchanged with luminaries throughout Europe, she achieved a measure of tranquility.

Perhaps a fitting epitaph for this brilliant, restless, searching soul who saw herself as of "violent and ardent temperament with a slight tendency to melancholy" would have been the very words she used on one political occasion when she was young: "I love the storm and fear the calm." When she died on the 19th of April 1689, the dying Pope sent his blessings and church bells tolled in Rome for 24 hours to mark her passing. In Sweden, by contrast, few remembered her and and no one mourned. She was laid to rest in St. Peter's, one of only five women ever to have been buried there. A small monument graces the spot despite her explicit instructions to have but a simple gravestone with these words: VIXIT Christina, Annos 63. Christina has lived.

Viewing her life at a distance of three centuries, what does one make of it? Certainly she had an unenviable childhood in significant respects—notably her mother's rejection, her father's early death, and the isolation imposed by her exalted station. Then, too, the psychic costs of becoming her father's "son" threw a shadow on an otherwise exuberant life force. It estranged her from herself and preceded her subsequent estrangement from her country culminating in exile in search of a spiritual home. At the same time, I also see her as triumphant. After all the turmoil and torment, the constant worries about money, the scandals, and the disorderly passions, she held her ground. She managed to live independently, she was famous, she was esteemed as a patron of the arts and higher learning, and she was respected as a person of distinction.

True, she had abandoned a position of worldly power so as to be a free spirit—a choice not everyone would make or understand—but for her this had been the main quest: freedom from the tyranny of convention and freedom of the individual against any establishment—and this for a woman and in a religious age! In short, she had succeeded in creating her own unique place in the sun. How many of us can say as much and be remembered for 300 years?

A final comment on Christina as an unwitting precursor of modern feminism. Given the exaltation of masculinity and the denigration of women prevalent in her surroundings, Christina confronted some familiar modern problems. The resultant self-rejection led to her profound opposition to what she perceived to be the subjugation of women in marriage and romance. In fact, some have attributed her abdication as Queen to her refusal to marry and procreate. Yet, unable to reconcile the contradiction between womanhood and personhood, she found a creative—and daring—solution: to be independent, to be a person ever in process of development rather than a gender bound to a preordained destiny. Of course this exchange exacted its price—loneliness and permanent exile among them—a price she valiantly and defiantly paid as she made her way forward. By showing later generations that there are alternative ways of charting a meaningful life course, Christina may be seen as a forerunner of a very modern spirit.

Notes

[1] Paul Lewis, *Queen of Caprice* (New York: Holt, Rinehart and Winston, 1962) 20.

[2] Margaret Goldsmith, *Christina of Sweden* (New York: Doubleday, Doran and Company, 1933) 8.

[3] Georgina Masson, *Queen Christina* (London: Secher and Warburg, 1968) 38.

[4] Curt Weibull, *Christina of Sweden* (Bonniers: Svenska Bokforlaget, 1966) 82.

[5] Sven Stolpe, *Christina of Sweden* (New York: MacMillan, 1966) 62.

Brian J. Dendle

Spanish Intellectuals and World War I

I wish to preface this brief essay by expressing my deep gratitude to and admiration for Edward D. Sullivan. I arrived in Princeton in the fall of 1963, a young immigrant bewildered by the seeming complexities of the American educational system. Princeton offered good graduate teaching and the resources of a fine library. Comparisons are, of course, invidious. However, among the excellent teachers who introduced me to American academic life, the one who most stands out in my memory is Edward Sullivan. I will always remember the highly professional manner in which Edward Sullivan conducted his seminar on Flaubert. I recall his warmth and wisdom, his insistence on high standards, the encouragement which he readily volunteered, and his willingness to share his time and knowledege with students. Much later, I was deeply honored when Edward Sullivan consented to serve on the editorial board of *Romance Quarterly*. His thorough evaluation of manuscripts, his promptness, and the generous advice that he offers to younger scholars are a blessing to an editor. At a recent international conference in Toulouse, French academics told me of the high esteem in which Edward Sullivan's scholarship is held in France. I also wish to acknowledge the courage shown by Edward Sullivan during his recent illness, during which he cheerfully and willingly continued to fulfill his editorial responsibilities. Thank you, Ed, for all you have given to your students and colleagues.

At the time of the Spanish-American War (1898), Spain found herself in diplomatic isolation. Resentment at British support for the United States, as well as the long-standing irritant of British possession of Gibraltar, led to strong Spanish popular sympathy for the South African republics during the Boer War. Although the political instability of Spanish governments between 1898 and 1914 prevented Spain from having any clearcut foreign policy, fears of continued isolation amid the newly-forged European alliances of this period brought Spain within the orbit of the *entente cordiale*. Alfonso XIII married a granddaughter of Queen Victoria in 1906. Two French presidents—Loubet in 1905 and Poincaré in 1913—made successful official visits to Madrid.

One of the most enthusiastic supporters of a Spanish *rapprochement* with Great Britain and France was Benito Pérez Galdós, Spain's leading novelist who became head of the republican party in 1907.[1] Prominent Spanish intellectuals (Manuel Machado, *Azorín*, Emilia Pardo Bazán, Alberto Insúa, Vicente Blasco Ibáñez, Pérez Galdós, et al.) contributed to the journal *L'Espagne* ("Organe de l'Entente franco-espagnole"), which, no doubt with a subvention from the Spanish government, began publication in Paris in August 1913, with as editor the Guatemalan journalist Enrique Gómez Carrillo. In the first numbers of *L'Espagne*, members of the liberal cabinet (Romanones, García Prieto) called for a Spanish alliance with France; Eduardo Dato, who headed the conservative government of October 1913, made a similar plea.[2]

At the outbreak of the World War, the great majority of Spaniards were relieved to learn that Spain was not committed by a secret pact to any of the warring powers. Spain was economically weak; her small army was fully engaged in Morocco. The declared governmental policy of neutrality was therefore highly popular. The only prominent Spaniard to wish for Spanish intervention was the Radical Republican Alejandro Lerroux, whose political fiefdom was Francophile Barcelona. Another leading dissident was the liberal statesman the Conde de Romanones who argued, to the indignation of his compatriots, that Spain was geographically and economically linked to the allies; failure to intervene would have harmful consequences for Spain when the war ended ("Neutralidades que matan," *Diario Universal* 19-VIII-1914).[3]

Spanish intellectuals, although favoring neutrality, were strongly partisan in their sympathies. Liberals and republicans for the most part supported the allied nations, i.e., *neutralidad con benevolencia*. Authoritarians (right-wing politicians and Catholics) defended the Central Powers.[4] The most prominent organs of Germanophile propaganda were the influential newspaper *ABC* and the Catholic *El Correo Español*. Other newspapers to support the Central Powers in 1914 were *La Tribuna, El Debate, El Parlamentario, El Universo, El Siglo Futuro*, and *La Mañana*. By 1917, the Federal Republican Rodrigo Soriano's *España Nueva* also defended the German cause. Although the Catholic press had before the war condemned the harmful influence of German philosophy, Catholics feared "republican, atheistic, and immoral" France; their hostility was no doubt bolstered by the Spanish belief that the French despised Spain (an opinion still current in the Spain of the 1980s). The Carlist leader, Vázquez de Mella, had a pathological hatred for the British. The republican and liberal newspapers *El Liberal, El Imparcial*, and *Heraldo de Madrid*, on the other hand, sympathized from the outset of war with the allies, Great Britain and France allegedly being the representatives of freedom and progress.[5]

In the early months of the war, the views of the *germanófilos* predominated in the press. The situation began to change in 1915. The weekly *España*, founded at the beginning of the year and to which the flower of Spain's

intellectual élite contributed, was strongly *aliadófilo*. From early 1916, when
the socialist Luis Araquistain became editor, *España* received subsidies from
the British Secret War Propaganda Bureau ("Wellington House"). In mid 1917,
when the British government became alarmed at revolutionary sentiment in
Spain, the French government assumed the subsidies to the journal. The official
organ of Spanish conservatives, *La Epoca*, was also subsidized by the British
propaganda services.[6]

The World War had almost as devastating an effect on Spain as on the
belligerent nations. By 1917, political instability had led to the collapse of even
the pretense of representative parliamentary rule and to insurrection. Although
certain sectors of the Spanish economy prospered by supplying raw materials
to the warring powers, the excessive demands on Spain's railroad system, the
loss of markets in central and eastern Europe, the torpedoeing of Spanish
vessels by German submarines, and a clumsily enforced allied war embargo
created considerable economic distress. Furthermore, its strategic importance
made Spain a center of foreign intrigue. Allied and German subsidies to the
press and to individual writers and cartoonists led to justifiable fears for the
integrity of Spanish institutions.[7]

The propaganda campaigns went beyond the detailing of German atrocities in Belgium or proclamations of the superiority of German *Kultur* over that
of frivolous and immoral Latins. British and French publicists emphasized their
nations' traditions of democracy and cultural freedom. On July 9, 1915, *España*
published the important "Manifiesto de adhesión a las naciones aliadas,"
signed by Spain's intellectual élite.[8] From December 1915 to March 1916,
Corpus Varga published in *España* a series of interviews with French intellectuals ("Los personajes de Francia hablan de España"). In April 1916, as part of
the propaganda battle, leading English writers issued a manifesto expressing
admiration for and gratitude to Spain. The following month, prominent French
scholars, including Henri Bergson, lectured in Madrid. In the summer of 1916,
España published extracts from Rudyard Kipling's *Sea Warfare* (London:
Macmillan, 1916) ("Historias de submarinos").

With the war, Spanish newspapers and journals suffered considerable
financial difficulties, the consequence of greatly increased prices and shortages
of newsprint (which before the war had been supplied by the Baltic provinces
of Russia), the disappearance of foreign advertising, and the high cost of
reporting from the war zones. Nevertheless, despite the expense involved,
prominent writers contributed commentaries on the war.

1. The *aliadófilos*

The Spanish foreign correspondent most known outside of Spain was Vicente Blasco Ibáñez, who in 1914 reported from France for the expensive cultural journal *La Esfera*.[9] Blasco Ibáñez also contributed to allied war propaganda (as well as to his own self-promotion), with his handsomely-illustrated nine-volume *Historia de la guerra europea* (Valencia: Prometeo, 1914-1919). In *Los cuatro jinetes del Apocalipsis* (Valencia: Prometeo, 1916), his best-selling novel which enjoyed enormous success in English translation, Blasco Ibáñez portrays the conflict as a defense of western civilization against the barbaric followers of Wotan. In the potboiler *Mare nostrum* (Valencia: Prometeo, 1918), Blasco Ibáñez depicts the sinister seductions of a *femme fatale* in the pay of German espionage and the horrors of German submarine warfare in the Mediterranean, the cradle of Latin civilization.

The most readable Spanish war-reporting was that of the Guatemalan journalist Enrique Gómez Carrillo (who was for a while reputedly amorously involved with Mata Hari). Gómez Carrillo, a Francophile who had lived many years in the French capital, reported from Paris, Bordeaux, and the Western Front with a series of lively dispatches for the prominent republican daily *El Liberal*; he became editor of *El Liberal* in November 1916. His articles, covering the first three months of the war, attest to the high morale and nobility of spirit of the French, while regretting the loss of "la Alemania pensadora, noble, estudiosa y poética" (266); the articles were published as a book, *Crónica de la guerra* (Madrid: Sucesores de Hernando, 1915). Later articles, based on interviews with civilians in the Marne region and with soldiers at Verdun and in Lorraine, document atrocities committed by German occupying forces and demonstrate the gallantry and courage of the French army. These articles were published, with a eulogistic preface by Benito Pérez Galdós, in *Campos de batalla y campos de ruinas* (Madrid: Sucesores de Hernando, 1915).[10] In both collections, the Bohemian Gómez Carrillo scathingly contrasts the ferocious discipline of the German army with the democratic spirit and *joie de vivre* of French and British troops.

Gómez Carrillo continued his eulogy of the French in *En las trincheras* (Madrid: Sucesores de Hernando, 1916). This work, written in 1915, describes visits to the front line in Alsace, to Amiens, and to Flanders; the French are good-humored and courageous. Gómez Carrillo also interviews German prisoners (well-treated) and French generals (heroic and wise).[11] The Guatemalan journalist's account of the contradictory qualities of the "childlike" Germans bears repetition:

Es una raza misteriosa, extraña, a la vez primitiva y complicada. Hay en ella algo de salvajismo infantil, algo de gravedad mística, algo de melancolía enigmática. Es una raza de contrastes y de sorpresas. Es pesada, y, sin embargo, lleva a cabo una labor inverosímil de asimilación y de invención. Es orgullosa hasta el delirio, y, no obstante, sabe, cuando se encuentra ante una fuerza superior, inclinarse sin sufrir y humillarse sin llorar. Es de una energía innovadora que sólo los yanquis superan, y a la par es de un fatalismo resignado igual al de los árabes. Es poética, sin duda; tiene siempre un fondo de ensueño y de quimera; y también es positiva, de un positivismo sin entrañas. Es cruel de un modo feroz, y es bondadosa. Es, en suma, algo que compendia, entre oposiciones desconcertantes, la extrema civilización y la extrema barbarie. (198-99)

In *En el corazón de la tragedia* (Madrid: Sucesores de Hernando, 1916),[12] Gómez Carrillo praises the "fair play" ("caballerosidad"), tenacity, sense of humor, and courage of the British at war. *La gesta de la Legión* (Madrid: Sucesores de Hernando, 1918) portrays the heroism and *insouciance* of members of the Foreign Legion, paying particular attention to the contribution of Spaniards and Spanish Americans. Spaniards give their lives for France because France incarnates the ideals of mankind: "Porque Francia, en su compleja constitución moral e ideológica, encarna al mismo tiempo todos los grandes anhelos del espíritu moderno: los de la democracia y los de la disciplina espiritual, los de la tradición y los de la utopía" (106). In a supplement to *La gesta de la Legión*, "El alma de los curas-soldados," Gómez Carrillo portrays the role of priests who serve in the French army, emphasizing their spirituality, self-sacrifice, humility, and tolerance of other beliefs, qualities sadly lacking in Spanish religious fanatics.

In the summer of 1916, the journalist Ramiro de Maeztu (who in the 1930s was to eulogize Hitler and was executed by the Republicans in late 1936), wrote from London and the Western front a series of articles highly laudatory of the English war effort. The articles were published in *La Prensa* of Buenos Aires and *La Correspondencia de España* of Madrid; they were reprinted (at the expense of the British propaganda services?) in the book *Inglaterra en armas* (London: Darling and Son, 1916). Despite their constant extolling of British efficiency and morale, the essays, which give details of life in the trenches and of the popular songs of the English troops, may be read today with interest.

Further praise of the British can be found in the sympathetic articles on British customs and policies that Salvador de Madariaga published in 1916 and 1917 in *España, El Imparcial*, and *La Publicidad*; the essays were reprinted in *La guerra desde Londres* (Madrid: Editorial Monclus, 1918). Madariaga is impressed by the Christian spirit that inspires western democracies, by English common sense, courtesy, energy, and "fair play," and by the excellent military organization of the British army in France. Madariaga contrasts the moral failures of Spain (silence with regard to Belgium, failure to provide leadership for Spanish-speaking nations) with the success of the British Empire, "esta hermosa comunión de la raza británica en una empresa de justicia y libertad."

José Martinez Ruiz (*Azorín*), journalist, man of letters, and, depsite his conservatism, a strong Francophile ("Nosotros, apasionados de Francia, entusiastas de España"), published two collections of war-time articles. The first, *Entre España y Francia (páginas de un francófilo)* (Barcelona: Bloud y Gay, 1916),[13] is a series of scholarly expositions of the cultural ties between the two nations. The bookish *Azorín* details Saavedra Fajardo's seventeenth-century vision of the French (favorable) and of the Germans (unfavorable), lauds the contribution of French authors (Constant, Descartes, Brunetière, and Renan) to civilization, and discusses the work of French Hispanophiles (Mérimée, Stendhal, Gautier, Hugo, Vigny, Musset). Despite *Azorín*'s frequent visits to war-time France, the only direct treatment of the war effort is that of the first chapter, a description of the organization of the French miliary hospital in Hendaye. A later volume, *París bombardeado, mayo y junio, 1918* (Madrid: Renacimiento, 1919), offers *Azorín*'s impressions, when sent to Paris in the spring of 1918 as a correspondent for *ABC*, of the calm of the Parisians under aerial and artillery bombardment; the essays are slight in content.

Miguel de Unamuno, the novelist and rector of the University of Salamanca, showed no sympathy for the *germanófilos*. Unamuno lashed out at the hypo critical defenders of a Spanish "neutrality" that suited German interests: "La beocia troglodita atudescada, la de los fariseos que se santiguan por rutina, pero tienen puesto el corazón en el neopaganismo imperial y militarista germánico, anda suelta" (*Iberia* 26-VI-1915).

The urbane essayist and novelist Ramón Pérez de Ayala, the instigator of the "Manifiesto de adhesión a las naciones aliadas," avoided strident partisanship, although his support for the allies was well known. He wittily satirized German claims to have triumphed at the Battle of Jutland ("Apostillas a la batalla naval," *España* 15-VI-1916). Discussing Spanish volunteers in the French Foreign Legion, Pérez de Ayala declared the morality of the allied cause: "Francia defiende, junto con su vida, la justicia eterna y la libertad del mundo. Sin dejar de ser nacional, su causa es, sobre todo, genéricamente humana. . . . Los aliados hacen la guerra por amor a la paz. Es un militarismo antimilitarista, civilista, pacifista; una paradoja profundamente lógica" ("La paradoja militarista contra el sofisma pacifista," *Espana* 11-I-1917). In *Herman encadenado* (Madrid, 1917), Pérez de Ayala described his visit to the Italian front. England is "el más poderoso país latino de la hora presente" (13) and the most civilized country in Europe; Germany is "la nacíon más corrompida de costumbres y materialista de toda la tierra" (21); the Italians are civilized, heroic, hospitable, hard-working, and lucid. Pérez de Ayala's esthetic vision is at times as grotesque as Valle-Inclán's; thus, the intoxicating odor of corpses can explain "la voluptuosidad bélico-macabra de los soldados que asaltan una trinchera, con obstinación de días y de meses, sin rendirse ante el horror continuo de la muerte y de la descomposición orgánica" (78).

The aging novelists Benito Pérez Galdós (1843-1920) and Armando Palacio Valdés (1853-1938) also commented on the war. In 1915, the now blind Galdós published in *La Esfera* four articles highly sympathetic to the allies and scornful of the Central Powers and their Spanish sympathizers.[14] The articles consist of stereotypical and romanticized descriptions of national characteristics, hazy strategical speculations, and rhetorical questions on the meaning of the war. For Galdós, Divine Providence and reason are on the side of the allies. Of greater interest is Galdós's denunciation of the "Spanish sickness," the resurrection of a mindless religious fanaticism that extols the German cause and the power of brute force.

From the outset of the war, the liberal Catholic writer Armando Palacio Valdés sympathized with the allies.[15] In March 1915, Palacio Valdés contrasted the Latin ideals of morality, virtue, and Christian charity with Germany's cult of force and the state ("Después de la paz," *España* 5-III-1915). In 1916, the sexagenarian Palacio Valdés, suffering from ill health, agreed, for reasons of conscience, to write from Paris a series of articles for *El Imparcial*. These fourteen articles were also published as a book, *La guerra injusta* (Barcelona and Paris: Bloud & Gay, 1917). A French translation of this work—*La guerre injuste, lettres d'un Espagnol*, trans. Albert Glorget (Paris: Bloud et Gay, 1917)—was published in the war propaganda series "Pages Actuelles (1914-1917)."

In *La guerra injusta*, Palacio Valdés offers the wide-ranging moral and religious reflections of a well-read and thoughtful liberal Catholic; the essays were intended to create a sympathetic view of the French, especially among Spanish Catholics. Palacio Valdés expatiates on original sin, the nature of optimism, the moral dimensions of Christianity, the primacy of reason over feeling, and the designs of Divine Providence. Despite his marked Anglophilia, Palacio Valdés's admiration for French culture—its literature and science, its civilizing influence—is manifest.

Palacio Valdés supports the allied cause as being that of reason and justice. He acknowledges the many virtues of the French. The French possess the soldierly qualities of "la astucia, la alegría, la habilidad manual, la improvisación" (26). Palacio Valdés corrects many Spanish misconceptions about the French. The French are neither overoptimistic nor frivolous but are, rather, an ambitious, calculating nation. They are not immoral and are for the most part devoutly Catholic. (Spanish women, on the other hand, are superstitious; few Spanish men attend mass.) French women of all social classes are fascinating, refined, courteous, and dignified.

The Germans, despite their solid virtues (tenacity, capacity for hard work, courage) lack a critical spirit and are therefore over-impressionable. They are not Christian, but worship scientific truth and justify cruelty. Nevertheless, Palacio Valdés charitably hopes that Germany will again become "la nación tranquila de filósofos, poetas y músicos que tanto hemos admirado siempre" (149).

Although *La guerra injusta* is ostensibly concerned with the World War, Palacio Valdés harshly castigates, with a moral indignation akin to that of the so-called "Generation of 1898," the backwardness and stagnation of contemporary Spain:

> Campos desecados, hombres hambrientos, el nepotismo dictando órdenes, la injusticia erigida en sistema, la frivolidad soltando carcajadas estúpidas, una política mezquina envenenando las inteligencias más altas y los más nobles caracteres . . .
>   ¡Duerme, pueblo español, duerme! Vale más vivir dormido que despierto y desesperado. (126)

In the final chapter ("¿Y Después?"), Palacio Valdés looks hopefully to the future. The belligerent nations will repent their wartime madness. France will see a new sense of fraternity and a moral cleansing in politics. Germany will lose its pride and seek refuge "en la moderación, en la sobriedad, en la tranquilla vida de familia, en las bibliotecas y en las salas de concierto" (192). England, whose literature, politics, customs, self-confidence, generosity, and spirit of freedom Palacio Valdés so greatly admires, will not change. The Czar, in contact with England and France, will grant greater freedom to his people. Italy will regain Trieste, Christians the Holy Land.

The most original Spanish treatment of the war is that of the novelist, poet, and dramatist Ramón del Valle-Inclán. Before leaving for France in the summer of 1916 to write a series of articles for *El Imparcial*, Valle-Inclán declared to Cipriano Rivas Cherif that the war was between the solar races of the Mediterranean (whose heirs would be the United States and Japan as England declined) and Germany, the representative of patriarchal Jehova (*España* 11-V-1916).[16] Valle-Inclán's "articles" in *El Imparcial* of late 1916 (published in book form as *La media noche. Visión estelar de un momento de guerra* [Madrid, 1917]) offer in 40 brief episodes a total, "astral" vision of one day of war. Valle-Inclán, employing an alliterative, impressionistic prose in the present tense (an obvious preparation for the historical series *El ruedo ibérico*), presents the war as a grotesque nightmare, a "barbarie atávica" of mutilation, rape, and stinking corpses. The following sentence typifies Valle-Inclán's surrealistic style: "Entre nubes de humo y turbonadas de tierra, vuelan los cuerpos deshechos: Brazos arrancados de los hombros, negros garabatos que son piernas, cascos puntiagudos sosteniendo las cabezas en la carrillera, redaños y mondongos que caen sobre los vivos llenándolos de sangre y de inmundicias" (99). A further group of articles, published in *El Imparcial* in January and February 1917 and consisting of short dramatic scenes illustrating French hatred of the German barbarians ("En la luz del día"), is of less literary interest.

Gabriel Alomar, in *La guerra a través de un alma* (1917), offers a mythical vision of the conflict akin to that of Valle-Inclán. Queen Elisabeth of Belgium possesses the virtues of a medieval saint: ". . . dulcemente femenina, incorpórea y esbelta, tiene la aureola de las legendarias santas coronadas (¡oh memoria de la otra Isabel, la de Turingia!), y parece poseer una facultad de 'imposición de manos' apostólica, que cura las llagas del herido y le vierte un óleo de consuelo y fortaleza." (9) The communion of the Belgian monarch with his people is a "verdadera Eucaristía" (12). Belgium is "como una concreción nueva de Mujer, idealizadora de la Esposa, suavemente burguesa, jovial y fuerte, aromada de trabajo como de una lustración"; Flanders is "El Eterno Femenino" (18). England and France represent solar and lunar principles: "Inglaterra y Francia, las dos naciones de la Revolución europea, representan algo así como el principio solar y el principio lunar el sistema de nuestra civilización. Hay algo de teogónico en ese dualismo, como el principio masculino y el femenino de nuestra progenie ideal; como un Osiris y una Isis, como un Apolo y una Diana" (22). Russia is expressed in the image of a Slavic virgin mother: "¿No recordáis con un atractivo de pureza 'sideral' la figura de la joven estudiante eslava, enigmática Sonia, Olga suavísima, que tenía, en la penumbra de su rincón de aula, transfiguraciones de virgen madre, madre espiritual de una sociedad todavía informe que surgiría de sus flancos castísimos?" (32). France is Woman: "Gallia, Gallia mujer, Gallia diosa, arcana y sibilina en los bosques druídicos de Bretaña, bella de primitivo gesto familiar cuando enjugaste el cuerpo sudoroso de los que venían de sojuzgar a Roma con Breno . . ." (40). British colonial troops are evoked in *modernista* terms: "númidas negros, oceánicos misteriosos, indostánicos decorativos" (94).

2. The *germanófilos*

The novelist Ricardo León, a Catholic nationalist who was later to extol Hitler as the savior of Europe, traveled, as a correspondent for *El Imparcial*, to France, Switzerland, and Germany in 1916. León claims that he writes without hatred, not even for "la fría y calculadora Inglaterra." Like *Azorín*, he views France (as also Switzerland and Germany) through its literature and history. As a Catholic, he notes with surprise that France is patriotic, full of religious faith, and suffering with "heroísmo cristiano." France is far from the corrupt and moribund nation he had formerly believed it to be: "¡Qué sorpresa más conmovedora para cuantos creíamos a Francia moribunda, sin raíces morales, corrompida hasta los tuétanos! ¡Cuán torpemente la juzgábamos al través de París, del París cosmopolita y licencioso; al través de sus ardientes bacanales, de sus vicios políticos, de sus instituciones degradadas!"[17]

In Germany, despite certain difficulties of adjustment to Teutonic ways, Ricardo León admires German discipline and organization and its national hero Frederick the Great. The secret of German organization, which Spaniards must learn, lies in the Will ("el querer") (257). León reproduces a Saxon lawyer's denunciation of French exclusiveness, self-satisfaction, and pride:

> Económico, hasta ponerle tasas al amor; localista y sedentario, le place, a la manera de príncipes, señorear el mundo sin salir de su casa, en donde vive, como Narciso, enamorado de su persona, muy satisfecho de la vida, mirándose a sí propio como al espejo más puro de la humanidad. A nadie reconoce ventaja; el universo, para él se reduce a París, a sus héroes, a sus poetas, sus artistas, sus críticos, sus pensadores, sus parlamentarios, sus mujeres del mundo y de la moda: fuera de esto, lo demás le parece inferior, lo desconoce y lo desdeña. (117-18)

Lengthy sections of *Europa trágica* reproduce tedious justifications by German Foreign Office officials of their cause. In other passages, of a Romantic impressionism, León admires the industrial might of Germany and the organization of the Western Front; he extols the prowess of the German navy and the heroism of German submarine crews. As a Spanish Catholic nationalist, however, León criticizes aspects of modern German (and French) life: the loss of the chivalric concept of woman as wife and mother; the demoralization that results from materialism and the loss of traditional values.

Between October 1914 and October 1915, José María Salaverría published, to the chagrin of *aliadófilos*, a series of essays written in London, Paris, and Germany; the essays were reprinted in *Cuadros europeos* (Madrid: Pueyo, 1916). Salaverría found life in London and Paris drab; he found much greater human warmth in Germany. He has only admiration for the Germans who, surrounded by enemies, are struggling successfully for survival. The Germans are heroic, intelligent, energetic, and virile; above all, they are a joyful nation. France itself owes its energy to its German neighbor:

> Sobre el país de Francia, en su hermosa mitad del Norte, la marea germánica viene actuando desde los tiempos prehistóricos por sucesivas y casi regulares invasiones. La marea germánica ha dejado siempre su limo fecundo y revividor. Del choque germánico le viene a Francia su energía. La savia germánica, en invasiones guerreras o pacíficas, infunde a Francia continuas renovaciones. Francia, amenazada o nutrida por Alemania, no podrá perder jamás su civilización, gracias al contacto de Alemania . . . La mejor suerte de Francia es tener a Alemania en un costado. (205)

The odd-man-out among Spanish Germanophiles was the anticlerical Basque novelist Pío Baroja. Baroja wished Spaniards to imitate "la Alemania científica, organizadora, industrial." For Baroja, the protest by colonial powers at the invasion of Belgium was arrant hypocrisy. Many Spanish women supported Germany because women admire force and favor order. Baroja was disgusted by the rhetorical commonplaces employed by intransigent *aliadófilos* and *germanófilos*. In the final lines of *Nuevo Tablado de Arlequín* (1917),

Baroja exposed the error of Spanish leftists. Germany, he approvingly claimed, would smash ("aplastar") the Catholic Church, Parliamentary democracy, and the trappings of Spanish traditionalism:

> Yo creo firmemente que todos los republicanos, todos los liberales, todos los revolucionarios españoles germanófobos están en un error. Es decir, no lo están, porque la mayoría no tiene en la cabeza más que palabrería huera.
>
> Yo creo que si hay algún país que pueda aplastar a la Iglesia católica definitivamente es Alemania.
>
> Si hay algún país que pueda arrinconar para siempre al viejo Jehová, con su séquito de profetas de nariz ganchuda y de grandes barbas de farsantes, con sus descendientes los frailucos puercos y ordinarios y los curitas pedantuelos y mentecatos, es Alemania.
>
> Si hay algún país que pueda desacreditar esta camama del parlamentarismo, es Alemania.
>
> Si hay algún pais que pueda acabar con la vieja retórica, con el viejo tradicionalismo español, soez y grosero, con toda la sarna semítica y latina, es Alemania.
>
> Si hay algún país que pueda substituir los mitos de la religión, de la democracia, de la farsa de la caridad cristiana por la ciencia, por el orden y la técnica, es Alemania.

The ardent debate between *aliadófilos* and *germanófilos* corresponded, as Altamira suggested, to the psychological needs of individuals rather than to any objective judgment of the belligerent powers. The partisan divisions of Spanish society presaged the political polarization of the 1930s. The support of the Central Powers by conservative Catholics falsified the terms of the polemic. Liberals felt obliged to defend France against charges of immorality and atheism. Liberals also claimed that there were two Germanies, one of poets and thinkers, the other of militarists. A similar duality is evident in the liberal division of Germans into rigid Prussians and more human Bavarians. A pseudo-racist mysticism is evident in the theory that a Latin, Christian civilization (which included French atheists and the British) was fighting for its existence against savage, Teutonic pagans. Most Spanish writers were Francophiles. The most imaginative treatment of the war was Valle-Inclán's impressionistic *La media noche*. Worthy of recall also are the urbane essays of the Anglophiles Salvador de Madariaga and Ramón Pérez de Ayala and the jaundiced, if perceptive, comments of Baroja who saw, better than liberal *aliadófilos* and clerical *germanófilos*, the destructive (or, for Baroja, cleansing) nature of German power.

Notes

[1] For a succinct discussion of Spanish foreign policy in the early years of the twentieth century and of the views of Galdós, see Brian J. Dendle, "Galdós, Morote, and the Foreign Policy Question of 1903," *Revista Canadiense de Estudios Hispánicos* 12 (1988) 308-16.

[2] See Brian J. Dendle, "Galdós, *L'Espagne*, et *Notre Roman réaliste*," *Bulletin Hispanique* 89 (1987) 267-74.

[3] For an intelligent discussion of Spanish neutrality, see Rafael Altamira, *La guerra actual* (Barcelona: Araluce, 1915). Altamira explores the psychological and intellectual factors involved in Spaniards' partisanship. His pleas for a strengthening of international organizations, a blunting of nationalism, and freedom of trade in a post-War Europe would find realization only a half century later.

[4] Among those intellectuals, none of the first rank, to support the German cause were: Jacinto Benavente, Carlos Arniches, Pedro Muñoz Seca, Julio Casares, Luis Bonafoux, José María Carretero, Francisco Villaespesa, José María Salaverría, Linares Rivas, and Pedro de Répide. For a scornful portrayal of Spanish Germanophiles, see Luis Antón del Olmet, *Los bocheros* (Madrid: Imprenta de Juan Pueyo, 1917). Antón del Olmet had supported the German cause in 1914.

[5] For a comprehensive discussion of Spanish partisanship in the First World War, see Fernando Díaz-Plaja, *Francófilos y germanófilos* (Barcelona: Dopesa, 1973). Díaz-Plaja treats, among other topics, the Germanophile views of Vicente Gay y Forner, and the reaction of Catalan intellectuals. Limitations of space prevent my discussing these topics here. See also J.-Félicien Court, *Chez les neutres. En Espagne* (Paris: M. Giard & E. Brière, 1916). Court reproduces (116-23) an interview with Valle-Inclán highly favorable to the allies; the interview has not been published elsewhere.

[6] Luis Araquistain, who became editor of *España* in February 1915, had been in contact with British propaganda services since the outbreak of war. For a useful discussion of foreign wartime subsidies to the Spanish press, see Enrique Montero, "La financiación de *España* y la propaganda aliada durante la Primera Guerra Mundial," *España* 1 (1915) (rpt.; Liechtenstein: Topos, 1982) xix-xxi. Montero claims that *El Liberal* and *El Imparcial* modified their support for the allies, following receipt of German subsidies. Frank J. Marion, the head of American propaganda services in Spain, claimed that by controlling supplies of newsprint he could change the Germanophile policies of *ABC*. See James R. Mock and Cedric Larson, *Words that Won the War* (Princeton: Princeton UP, 1939) 267-68.

[7] The cartoonist Luis Bagaría, who received British subsidies for his superb caricatures of the Germans in *España*, also worked for the Germanophile *La Tribuna*. For his justification of his position (his horror of war), see Díaz-Plaja 28-29.

[8] The Manifesto was originally published in Paris and was reputedly organized by Ramón Pérez de Ayala. Among other writers and intellectuals to sign were: Gabriel Alomar, Manuel Azaña, "Azorín," Américo Castro, Manuel B. Cossío, Antonio Machado, Ramiro de Maeztu, Gregorio Marañón, Gregorio Martínez Sierra, Ramón Menéndez Pidal, José Ortega Gasset, Armando Palacio Valdés, Benito Pérez Galdós, Miguel de Unamuno, and Ramón del Valle-Inclán.

[9] "Los dos soldados," *La Esfera* No. 43, 24-X-1914; "Ecos de la guerra: La casa del artista," No. 49, 5-XII-1914; "Los españoles en la guerra," No. 50, 12-XII-1914; "Un héroe," No. 53, 2-I-1915; "Visiones de la guerra," No 76, 12-VI-1915. See also the interview with Blasco Ibáñez by "El Caballero Audaz," No. 79, 3-VII-1915.

[10] Translated into French by J.N. Champeaux, *Parmi les ruines de la Marne au Grand Couronné* (Paris: Berger-Levrault, 1915), and into English by Florence Simmons, *Among the Ruins* (London: William Heinemann, 1915).

[11] The interviews with wartime leaders were reprinted in *Hombres y superhombres. El segundo libro de las crónicas* (Madrid: Renacimiento, 1923).

[12] Gómez Carrillo reprints certain of the essays, together with his interview with Gabriele d'Annunzio, in *El quinto libro de las crónicas* (Madrid: Mundo Latino, 1922). *En el corazón de la tragedia* appeared in English translation, *In the Heart of the Tragedy* (London and New York: Hodder and Stoughton, 1917).

[13] Translated into French by Albert Glorget, *Entre l'Espagne et la France: pages d'un francophile* (Paris: Bloud & Gay, 1918).

[14] "Pesadilla sin fin," No. 81, 17-VII-1915; "Pesadilla sin fin," No. 83, 31-VII-1915.; "La guerra europea * Pesadilla sin fin," No. 91, 25-IX-1915; "La guerra europea. Pesadilla sin fin," No 94, 16-X-1915. The articles are reprinted and commented in Brian J. Dendle, *Galdós y "La Esfera"* (Murcia: Universidad de Murcia, 1989).

[15] He was one of four Spanish writers—the others were Blasco Ibáñez and the poets Ramón Perés y Perés and Juan Ramón Jiménez—to contribute to *King Albert's Book*. *King Albert's Book* (London: Hodder and Stoughton, 1914) was the lavishly produced "Tribute to the Belgian King and People from Representative Men and Women Throughout the World," which the English novelist Thomas Hall Caine assembled in the interests of British propaganda. For the texts of the Spanish contributions, see Brian J. Dendle, "Les Ecrivains espagnols et *King Albert's Book*, 1914," *Les Lettres Romanes* 42 (1988) 211-17.

[16] The article has been reprinted by Dru Dougherty, *Un Valle-Inclán olvidado: Entrevistas y conferencias* (Madrid: Editorial Fundamentos, 1983) 78-82. For the background to *La media noche*, see José Caamaño Bournacell, "Los dos escenarios de *La media noche*," *Papeles de Son Armadans* No. 127 (1966) 135-50.

[17] Ricardo León, *Europa trágica* (Madrid: Renacimiento, 1917) 37. The only one-volume complete text of *Europa trágica* is that of Editorial Pueyo, 1919. The version given in the *Obras completas* (Madrid: Biblioteca Nueva, 1956) has numerous omissions.

Karl D. Uitti

The Lady and Her Place
in Twelfth-Century France

For Ed and Ellie

The two-hundred-year period running from about the year 1050 to 1250—the twelfth century, flanked by five decades or so on either side of its chronological limits—constitutes one of the very rare, truly seminal ages in the history of Western Europe and, consequently, in the formation of our present-day modernity. We still live off much of the capital raised then; sometimes, even without knowing it, we define ourselves with respect to this period. Let me add also that in its own right it is a fascinating, absorbing object of study.

This was the time during which what came to be known as the nation-state in fact came into existence, particularly in France and in England. It was also the time when a new kind of introspection and sense of selfhood were deemed essential, a judgment that led in 1214 to the sort of lucid examination of conscience which received sacramental value in the establishment, by a Church Council that year, of obligatory Confession. What we today understand as the integrity of the self would be incomprehensible without the twelfth-century formulations culminating in this new sacrament.

At the start of this period, and for reasons we are only now beginning to fathom, a new notion concerning the vocation of certain young men—adolescents, "teenagers"—began to be articulated. One form of this notion—the most important form—took the name, *miles Christi* or "soldier of Christ." The young man, usually of noble birth, but not necessarily because of his family or other genealogical roots, was defined in terms of a mission confided in him and freely—even joyfully—accepted by him: the defense of Christendom. Individual merit and youthful energy were valorized. (Christian Europe at this time was prepared to pass over to the offensive in its struggle against "pagans"—Muslims to the South and East, Saxons and still-unbaptized Slavs to the Northeast.) The personage we now know as the knightly hero, or *chevalier*, was born.[1] Grave ceremonies attended society's recognition of the youth's vocation, some of them modelled on those attending a young monk's taking final vows. By the end of the century even kings aspired to this knightly status, and dreamed of their sons' attaining it. The young man's life was thus invested with the possibility of transcendence, in terms that are quite with us still today: the valorization of individual merit and calling, it is claimed, inform the admissions policies of our finest universities and colleges, as well as those of our national service academies. Moreover, prowess and valor, then as now, hardly consisted exclusively in sheer physical strength or merely in the esteem of others, in fact they were not even essentially those things; they were invested with an intelligence of their own and a morality that rose above that of "society" and "society"'s unregenerate tendency to give into appearances for appearances' sake. The pertinent term here is *honor*. Thus, in deciding (against the "better judgment" of "wise," or "reasonable" Olivier) to fight it out against an overwhelmingly numerous enemy, even though the battle would cost the death of the entire rearguard which he commanded, Roland's rationale for doing so— his fear that were he to summon Charlemagne for reinforcements "sweet France" would be shamed—bespeaks his authentic prowess and understanding of honor. To paraphrase Pascal, "prowess has its reasons that reason itself cannot know." God Himself sends angels to bear Roland's soul to Paradise.

The chivalric spirit was at times to inform the very course of history. Thus, it is surely no simple coincidence that the process, in Spain, that culminated in the defeat of the last Moorish kingdom on the Iberian peninsula, in 1492, continued, with no interruption, into an extension of itself: the discovery, in that same year, of America, and the subsequent "adventurous" colonization of this newly discovered "world." The very name *California*, we might remind ourselves, derives from a medieval Spanish romance of chivalry.[2]

Since, alongside fighting for the justest of causes (e.g., the reconquest of the Holy Land), love and learning—love for the most beautiful and meritorious of women, learning in the pursuit (and defense) of truth—something of this same spirit of chivalric, even combative, transcendence begins to pervade the newly founded schools and early universities. (These, of course, were the prototypes of our present-day institutions of higher learning, as were the "liberal arts" so favored then—indeed, devised—as the basis for the human quest for truth.) Disputes and debates between masters and scholars, argumentation and wit, take on characteristics we can rightly associate with chivalric tournaments. We still use some of the words: our students "defend" a thesis, for example. One "wins" a debate. The young man earned his academic spurs through a series of "steps," or "degrees." As a "bachelor" (i.e., as "a young man" or *bacheler*) he acted as the squire of his "master(s)" until, one day, he too became a "master of arts," "licensed" to teach, and, perhaps, eventually, a "doctor." Informing all this, however, is the transcendence I referred to. Thinking things through constitutes an act of courage (*courage* "heart"), that is, something related to, but distinct from, mere rationality, just as Roland's "prowess" differed from Olivier's "wisdom." The great twelfth-century thinker and teacher (and lover-husband of the incomparable Heloise), Peter Abelard, who denounced superstition and traditions honored merely because they were old, can be seen as the still-relevant model of the new student-master of knightly values. The witty, often ribald, frequently deeply moving Latin poems we call Goliard verse (or song) also express this spirit extraordinarily well.

The period we are talking about was one of the most interestingly hopeful ages I know of. This was the time the so-called "Gothic" architecture was "invented." One marvels at Abbot Suger and others who worked out the principles of this architecture! After all, what they ostensibly sought to do was no less than to replicate the formally perfect beauty, the harmony, and the transcendant meaning of the long-destroyed Holy Temple of Jerusalem, and they wished to accomplish this in France! What they eventually came up with, we see, standing amidst the wheat fields of the French Beauce, was the cathedral of Our Lady of Chartres. Formally (and virtually in every other way) no two structures could possibly be more unalike than that cathedral and whatever the Holy Temple must have looked like. How naïvely "medieval" this is, we are tempted to conclude! It is something like all those thirteenth-century manuscripts that purport to tell the momentous stories of Troy and of Rome, but whose illuminated illustrations instead depict twelfth-century knights and their ladies. Clearly, we are led rashly to assert, our twelfth century had no idea of historical time and distance—as we do, nowadays.

The question that begs to be put, however, is this one: What, in reality, does our idea of historical time and distance attempt to account for? Does not, at least in some ways, what our historians and philologists do, for those of us who are not historians and philologists, tend to trivialize the past—to render it irrelevant and distant? Do we not turn the past into something "objective" that is absorbed, and then regurgitated during the academic exercises we call final examinations?

The past was vital, alive, for the twelfth century. Even the verb *invent* preserved, then, its old sense of "to find, to uncover." Thus, as one writer put it, *knightliness* and *learning* (*chevalerie* and *clergie*) were born in Greece; thence they passed to Rome. Now they are in France, and God grant them a long sojourn there![3] These values first took form in one place; they took a second form in another place; now they take place, and shape, here. The Ancients are dead and gone; but, or so said Bernard of Chartres, the great master of the cathedral school located in that city, they were giants, and we are but dwarfs. However, perched on their gigantic shoulders, we stand taller than they, and we see further than they did. Consequently, we are in a position to articulate the values of the past better than our greatest predecessors were, and to reveal the deepest meanings present, but only obscurely so, in their constructs.[4] Abbot Suger's "Gothic" thus, also in terms of transcendence, constitutes the only truly genuine twelfth-century formulation possible of what the Holy Temple of Jerusalem meant.

Let me pause in order to ask two simple questions: they are particularly relevant in the present-day political context of Europe: (1) Is not Moscow—even the Moscow of the former Soviet Union—still, in the Russian view, the "Third Rome" (i.e., following upon the "Western" Rome on the Tiber and the "Eastern" Rome on the Bosphorus), the true heir to historical process? (2) Is not the West Europe which our friends are at present building a more or less conscious "restoration" of Charlemagne's Empire, a worthy successor to (Western) Rome, and the successful, though then upstart, rival to the "Rome" of Constantinople?

What do these considerations of male transcendence, of history—of knighthood, of self-examination, of learning, and so forth—have to do with Ladies, with women and/or with Woman? I should like here to contend that, far from being merely incidental to these matters, Woman is central to them, that in an essential way twelfth-century Man came to the sort of understanding of himself that I have been talking about through a process of revelation, and that this process of revelation, far from causing him to revise an older "masculine" way of "looking at" Woman, derived from Woman and from his understanding of the significance of his relationship to—and with—her. Woman taught Man; and he realized that she was his mistress (*magistra*).

I have a number of reasons for believing strongly that what I have just said is accurate. Limitations of space allow me to cite only a few of these. The illustrations that follow will constitute the remainder of the present essay.

As was mentioned above, the twelfth century saw not so much the emergence as the creation of "Gothic" art, which it viewed as the restoration of the true Temple, in turn understood—however much it may have differed in external apperance from the new "Gothic" structures—as the faithful embodiment of the authentic place of spiritual Truth. Great edifices were erected in places whose names all of us know—Paris, Bourges, Chartres, Amiens—and their style spread far and wide, even to distant lands and times (Princeton University Chapel is a case in point). Overwhelmingly these buildings were consecrated in dedications to "Our Lady," to *Notre Dame*. In fact, according to Henry Adams's *Mont-Saint-Michel and Chartres*, if one were to add up the total purely economic cost of all the scores of cathedrals and churches built during this extended twelfth-century period and dedicated to "Our Lady," the money involved would be the greatest sum ever spent on any "civil," or public, project—that is, excepting wars—in the history of Europe, at least since the Egyptian pyramids of Antiquity. And, as Henry Adams pointed out in his magnificent book, these edifices were to be understood as Mary's—as the Lady's—place, as her home, where she would be revered and loved.[5] It was in the transcendent service of Mary—of the spouse and mother of God, as His sister and daughter, as our human sister and daughter and mother—that these buildings were erected, in deference to her power and to her glory: "Hail, Mary, full of Grace [pregnant with Grace]; blessed art thou among women." She would there receive the clothing of the greatest empress, of the woman whose beauty and authority were supreme. Loved and feared, and considered to be a hope of last resort—for what could a Father-Son-Spouse do but respond affirmatively to what was demanded of Him by His Daughter-Mother-Spouse? Over and over again in the copious miracle literature devoted to Mary we find examples of her interventions interrupting the "normal," "business-as-usual" process of Divine Justice.[6]

Mary's power was her own. It was hers because of her very special relationship to God—a relationship of God's choosing, to be sure, but corresponding nonetheless to a reality, an historical factuality that no exercise in abstraction could easily undo. For without Mary—and here Mary is at once symbolic and real—the human-ness that she represents in Humanity's relationship to God would be deprived of any hope whatsoever. Mary—Woman—is us, as Humanity, as Church, in our coupling with God. He is our Bridegroom; we are His Bride. Our story together is our history. This is the relationship that is depicted, as the twelfth century (for example, in the writings of Saint Bernard of Clairvaux) described it, in the biblical Song of Songs. Here is a sample from that beautiful text; it illustrates perfectly what I am driving at:

SPONSA: Vox dilecti mei; ecce iste venit, / Saliens in montibus, transiliens colles . . . En dilectus meus loquitur mihi.

SPONSUS: Surge, propera, amica mea, / Columba mea, formosa mea, et veni. / Iam enim hiems transiit; / Imber abiit, et recessit. / Flores apparuerunt in terra nostra. / Tempus putationis advenit; / Vox turturis audita est in terra nostra; / Ficus protulit grossos suos; / Vineae florentes dederunt odorem suum. / Surge, amica mea, speciosa mea, et veni: / Columba mea, in foraminibus petrae, in caverna maceriae, / Ostende mihi faciem tuam, / Sonet vox tua in auribus meis; / Vox enim tua dulcis, et facies tua decora.

SPONSA: Capite nobis vulpes parvulas / Quae demoliuntur vineas; / Nam vinea nostra floruit. / Dilectus meus mihi, et ego illi, / Qui pascitur inter lilia . . . (*Canticum Canticorum* 2:8-16)[7]
[The voice of my beloved! behold, he cometh leaping upon the mountains, skipping upon the hills . . . My beloved spake, and said unto me, Rise up, my love, my fair one, and come away.

For, lo, the winter is past, the rain is over and gone;

The flowers appear on the earth; the time of the singing of birds is come, and the voice of the turtle is heard in our land;

The fig tree putteth forth her green figs, and the vines with the tender grape give a good smell. Arise, my love, my fair one, and come away.

O my lover, that art in the clefts of the rock, in the secret places of the stairs, let me see thy countenance, let me hear thy voice; for sweet is thy voice, and thy countenance is comely.

Take us the foxes, the little foxes, that spoil the vines; for our vines have tender grapes.

My beloved is mine, and I am his: he feedeth among the lilies . . .][8]

The voice here of the Shulamite bride is yours and mine: it is our human voice; it is in no uncertain terms that of Woman.

The Couple of Man and Woman, in its Fall from Grace and in respect of its eventual redemption, brought about by God's love for humankind as His essentially feminine partner in the most fundamental historical narrative of all, pervades the thought, the sense of form, and, I believe, the most deeply ingrained beliefs of the French twelfth century. This is confirmed, let me contend, in the following illustration. The theme of the human Couple, and the extraordinary status accorded to Woman within it, informs the entire first century of vernacular Romance literature, and constitutes the basis of further literary development in the spoken languages of Romance Europe throughout the twelfth century and even beyond. Much of this still floats about in our individual memories. Who has not heard of Tristan and Iseut, of Lancelot and Guenevere, of "courtly love," of the *Belle Dame sans merci*, of the troubadours and the mysteriously beautiful ladies for whom, in the trauma of their love, they pined? We can all at least now begin to understand what the late General de Gaulle might have had in mind when he wrote down on the first page of his memoirs his idea of France—the "Madonna of the frescoes" whom he worshipped as a boy, while dreaming of one day serving her as her loyal soldier.

All this is very touching—it pertains to the world of Camelot, a never-never land of fairy tales, perhaps to something not quite grown up. Or does it so pertain, exclusively?

For those of us who have not forgotten Dante or Petrarch this never-never land is something other than a mere fairy tale. Dante's Beatrice is to be taken quite seriously indeed; without her *The Divine Comedy* would make no sense at all. And when Dante speaks of ladies who possess the "intellect of love," we must—at least as literary scholars—take notice. Meanwhile, Petrarch's Laura is poetically still real to us, as she was to countless poets over many centuries. Nevertheless, it is not easy for us genuinely to grasp that for both Dante and Petrarch a man's very existence—like that of a woman—depends for its verbal and historical meaning on the incorporation of that existence into a couple that it forms with Woman. Furthermore, neither Petrarch nor Dante stem from nothingness; behind them both lies a two-century span of thought and of poetic articulation from which they derive and which they perpetuate—in the service of which, as poets, they enlist and inscribe themselves. God's love for humankind is that of the Groom for His Bride; our love of Him is that of the Spouse for her Husband. The only terms available to us for understanding in any true way the depth and breadth of this love are the terms of necessary love that govern the relationship of Man and Woman—of the human Couple.

A sentence or two by the great twelfth-century Abbot of Cluny, Peter the Venerable, will exemplify what I mean. Peter is writing to the nun Heloise, the beloved and passionately loving widow of Abelard and Abbess of the Convent of the Paraclete, in order to console her upon the death of her former husband and lover:

Hunc ergo venerabilis et carissima in domino soror, cui post carnalem copulam tanto validiore, quanto meliore divinae caritatis vinculo adhesisti, cum quo et sub quo diu domino deservisti, hunc inquam loco tui, vel ut te alteram in gremio suo confovet, et in adventu domini, in voce archangeli, et in tuba dei descendentis de caelo, tibi per ipsius gratiam restituendum reservat.[9]

"Dear Sister in Christ," he adds, "your grief is inevitable, for in this way all earthly love must end." In no way has Peter embarked upon a sermon chastising Heloise for her unrepented carnal passion. The love of Abelard and Heloise, which began with the wildest and most shameless kind of lust on Abelard's part and which she, who taught him to love her, never for one moment regretted, is to be truly consummated in heaven—transcended there, by being rendered eternal and no longer subject to the vicissitudes of time and death. The line of demarcation between the fleshly and the spiritual is, to put it mildly, fuzzy; rather, it would seem, the two exist, in the case of Abelard and Heloise (and largely thanks to her), in a necessary correlation.

Surprising as this may at first glance appear, however, in eleventh- and twelfth-century vernacular literature "love," or amor, as such is seldom, if ever, talked about. The common meaning of the word, which derives from Latin AMOR(EM), is "sexual, or reproductive, desire affecting all natural creatures, including plants." (In many langue d'oïl dialects today, ameur signifies "in heat, rutting.") This element of physical, i.e., "natural" desire, subject to the corruption brought about by Original Sin, nevertheless lies at the core of what, in the relationship of the Couple, Man and Woman, endowed with immortal souls, seek to realize, understand, and truly fulfill. It was in the Provençal, or troubadour, term fin' amor ("refined love") that amor, applied to Man and Woman in its transcendental scene, gained currency as signifying something noble—something other, more than mere libido.

Meanwhile, in the romances of Chrétien de Troyes, for instance, Amors "Love" is usually a personification—male in, say, Cligés, female in the Lancelot story, either male or female in Yvain—who causes anguish, shoots arrows, utters commands. A German-language dictionary of Chrétien's vocabulary defines the word Amors of Yvain v. 20 as "Minne" ("love-service") but surely the term, like the Amors used a few lines earlier, means something like the "Goddess of Love," who has a covant ("covenant") and "disciples" of this covant. What, conversely, is in fact talked about is the Couple formed by Man and Woman: Erec and Enide, Tristan and Iseut, Lancelot and the Queen, or the lover and his/her beloved. Textually speaking, what love is is the manifestation of relationships having to do with the creation of a Couple by a male and a female—like that of Heloise and Abelard—as well as the effects of these manifestations upon the members of the couple as discrete individuals and upon others within the ambit of a specific text or of a group of significantly related texts. "To love," consequently, invariably means "to love someone," more exactly "to love someone in a story," and "love" is something that one seeks to merit. Meanwhile, in and of itself, the Couple is something more, and other, than the sum of its two constituent parts. Thus, what happens to Erec (or Tristan) when he falls in love is meaningful and interesting to the degree that the couple formed by him and Enide (or Iseut), and their conjoined truth, are affected. Authentic participation in the human Coupling constitutes a validation of one's life as a human being; that, precisely, is why stories about couples are so interesting. In the mid-twelfth-century *Jeu d'Adam*, one of the earliest dramas in Romance-speaking Europe, Adam eats of the apple given to him by Eve because she has asked him to do so. He decides to eat of it, or so he says, "because *tu es ma per*" ("you are my peer"): *that* is his only, and very sufficient, "reason."

For the twelfth century, the foundation of human existence rests on the bedrock of the human Couple; this construct is, historically and textually, a fact, and, as such, it is of the highest poetic and historical relevance. Chapter 1:27 of Genesis—a story—puts the matter unequivocally: "Et creavit Deus hominem ad imaginem suam: ad imaginem Dei creavit *illum*, masculum et feminam creavit *eos*" (emphasis mine; "So God created man in his own image, in the image of God created he *him*; male and female created he *them*"). *Homo* in God's image is "male" and "female" in their conjunction (*illum*) and in their natural individualities (*eos*). In this prelapsarian age, "Erat [singular subject: *homo*] autem uterque [plurality] nudus [singular adjective], Adam scilicet et uxor eius: et non erebusce*bant* [plural verb]" (2:25; "And they were both naked, the man and his wife, and were not ashamed"). They were "*duo* in carne *una*" (2:24; "and they shall be one flesh") once upon a time, in a past of perfection.

Through their sin, separation and death were visited upon the Couple, and, of course, shame. Human history, i.e., the masculine history of Adam's "begetting" and sweat-producing toil—and the feminine condition of suffering in childbirth commenced. That which previously had been innocence and joy reverted to shame, corruption, pain and death. To be sure, life continues—humanity is not obliterated—but sin has enveloped it within a new, and precarious, context.

Through God's love and the sacrifice of His Son (I John 4:9: "In hoc apparuit charitas Dei in nobis, quoniam Filium suum unigenitum misit Deus in mundum, ut vivamus per eum" ["In this was manifested the love of God toward us, because that God sent his only begotten son into the world, that we might live through him"]) the effects of sin are blotted out, and the Couple restored.

And, very interestingly for our purposes, our understanding and learning of this act of divine love are provided for by the coupling of God/Man with Woman: Christ is born of the Virgin Mary; the Good News of the Resurrection is first revealed (according to the majority of the Gospels) by Woman (to incredulous male disciples). *Dominus* and *Ecclesia* (God and Church) are understood—grasped—as constituting a—*the*—Couple.

Without a shadow of a doubt what I have been referring to suffuses the *bele conjointure*, or "beautiful conjoining," which Chrétien celebrates in the Prologue to *Erec et Enide* (ca. 1170), his first romance narrative (and the oldest vernacular Arthurian romance known to us). It also does much to explain the fascination the twelfth century felt for Martianus Capella's *De Nuptiis Mercurii et Philologiae* ("On the Marriage of Mercury and Philology," ca. 410), with the stress that strange work places on connubial harmony (i.e., music, the last and, one suspects, the culmination of the Seven Liberal Arts), and with these words of invocation spoken at the start of its verse Prologue by an ancient and wise narrator:[10]

> Tu quem psallentem thalamis, quem matre Camena
>   progenitum perhibent, copula sacra deum,
> semina qui arcanis stringens pugnantia uinclis
>   complexuque sacro dissona nexa foues
> (namque elementa ligas uicibus mundumque maritas
>   atque auram mentis corporibus socias,
> foedere complacito sub quo natura iugatur,
>   sexus concilians et sub amore fidem) . . .

[Sacred principle of unity amongst the Gods, on you I call; you are said to grace weddings with your song; it is said that a Muse was your mother. You bind the warring seeds of the world with secret bonds and encourage the union of opposites by your sacred embrace. You cause the elements to interact reciprocally, you make the world fertile; through you, Mind is breathed into bodies by a union of concord which rules over Nature, as you bring harmony between the sexes and foster loyalty by love.][11]

It is within the Couple that the very identity—the self—of its members resides and is given sense. Loving another within the Couple revolutionizes the self; by serving the Couple one is freed from the tyranny of the singularity of one's self, or ego, and one can know the Other. Only in this way do men and women avoid the pathetic fate of Narcissus. *Erec et Enide* offers a case in point. At the start of the marvelous scene during which Erec looks for the first time upon Enide who, as he puts it, "tant est bele et bien senee" ("she is so beautiful and of such good sense"), the maiden is described as of the sort that "an se poïst li mirer / *ausi com an un mireor*" ("one can look intently upon her as though into a mirror"); Erec "d'autre part s'esbahi, / quant an li si grant biauté vit" ("Erec stood gazing as though in a stupor because he saw so much beauty in her"). The identity of one's authentic self is located in the relationship established by the gaze (in love) which the Lover projects upon the *mirror-like*, "encyclopedic," and beloved Other.

Not surprisingly, then, a large number of the very earliest Old Provençal (= OPr) and Old French (= OFr) vernacular texts—the *Eulalia* sequence (late ninth century), the *Song of Saint Fides* (second third of the eleventh century), the *Life of Saint Alexis* (ca. 1050? 1100?)—are quite specifically based on the construct of the Couple. It is within the context of the story devoted to recounting the life of the Occitanian Fides that the Christian daughter of the pagan emperor Diocletian convinces her husband, the Roman governor of Marseilles, to convert and to defy her own father; this reflects Christ's injunction to couples (following word for word that of Genesis) to forswear all allegiance to mother and father, and to "cleave to one's spouse." The husband defeats the pagan Roman army, brings about the downfall of Diocletian and the instauration of a new, Christian era of history: the husband's name is, of course, Constantine. Here all History is shown to have been transformed through the revolutionary intervention of a woman within the framework of the couplehood of marriage. This couplehood *in the world of History* refracts, so to speak, the conjoining in Paradise, after her martyrdom, of Saint Fides (literally, "Holy Faith"), the poem's heroine, and her beloved "Adonaï" (the name of God for Moses). The saint's martyrdom—she is beheaded after refusing to accede to the desires of the pagan lord Maximian—is depicted as a sort of marriage ceremony: a winged angel, "whiter than a dove," covers the girl's naked, but "chaste and untouched," body with a golden sheet, and places a gold crown upon her head; her soul is borne to heavenly bliss (joy); a violent storm breaks out, a river of blood forms. The marriage is, so to speak, cosmically consummated. The bridal status conferred upon Fides—on Woman—extends also to the wife of Constantine, through whose agency Constantine, the *chevalier*, becomes enabled to serve God in human History.

The Couple pervades also the OFr *Life of Saint Alexis*. Alexis never renounces his Bride (the Dominus/Ecclesia relationship is evoked here); he tells this beautiful girl to take for her spouse Him who has redeemed us with His precious blood, because there is no lasting joy on earth. Their perfect couplehood—even coupling—takes place in Heaven after death, in their salvation: "Together are their souls, their joy is immense," says the narrator. But, without their earthly marriage and Alexis's overwhelming desire for his bride on earth, their reunion in Heaven would have no meaning. In a very profound sense, Alexis takes leave of his spouse on their wedding night in order to "save" their marriage, that is, to preserve—or create—the conditions of their true—unending—joy. One is inevitably reminded of Saint Bernard's *Commentary on the Song of Songs* and of his writings, in general, on love and charity. Let me add also that, to my mind, a closer examination of, and deeper reflection upon, the relationship within their coupling of Roland and his fiancée, Aude, in the above-mentioned *Song of Roland* would be very much to the point in precisely this context.[12]

Regrettably, I have not been able to prepare a set of plates depicting iconographically what I have been referring to in these pages—examples of statuary, stained glass, and manuscript illumination would have been enlightening beyond what words alone can convey.[13] Before closing with the quotation of a few bits of texts, however, I should like to mention an extraordinary twelfth-century institution, the Royal Abbey of Fontevraud, which is located on the left bank of the Loire River, at the point where the provinces of Anjou, Touraine, and Poitou meet—the juncture of France and Occitania, also the heart of the Continental domains of the Plantagenet ruling house in England: a very important, and geographically significant, place in twelfth-century Europe.

Founded around the year 1100 by a passionate Breton priest named Pierre d'Arbrissel who believed, and preached, that the salvation of mankind would be effected by the intercession of Woman and in no other way, Fontevraud was conceived as an authentic "City of Ladies." A massive set of very beautiful—even luxurious—structures, designed to accommodate a large number of noble religious ladies, the abbey was entirely governed by women. Its lands and wealth corresponded (easily) to those of several rich present-day New Jersey counties. It inspired the creation of a fair number of daughter communities; its influence on religious life was very great throughout the Middle Ages, and it became a great educational center for women. Its abbesses frequently came from the French Royal House; daughters of kings and of the highest nobility of France were educated there. It was of course closed down during the French Revolution, and Napoleon converted it into a prison, which it remained until the 1960s. It has now been restored and refurbished to serve as the French Cultural Center of the West.

At Fontevraud and its dependencies men served only as priests or as physical laborers. Governance was entirely feminine. Donations of money flowed to Fontevraud; its endowment can be compared today only to that of such modern educational institutions as the American private university. The King of France himself was named Fontevraud's protector. It was the place of predilection of Queen Eleanor of Aquitaine, former Queen of France and wife to Henry II Plantagenet, King of England. She and her husband are buried there, as is their son, Richard Lion-Heart, beside them.

Why did the vision of Pierre d'Arbrissel have so tremendous an appeal to the rich and powerful of his time? And why did the institution created to fulfill the prophecy of this vision last for so many centuries?

I submit that the answer to these questions is to be found in what we have been reviewing here. The powerful knights of the twelfth century recognized and loved, as well as feared, Woman in her transcendence, just as the people loved (and feared) Mary, the Mother of God. They understood their salvation to lie in a formalized relationship of couplehood with a community of noble religious women who would pray and intercede for them, gently, and with the special voice that was theirs and which God would hear. They wanted their daughters to be educated in this sense of themselves, in this dignity, which was, for the powerful knights, a very great dignity indeed. The transcendance they associated with Woman would, they believed, liberate them too from the sinful bonds of merely animal *ameur*, or "libido," and help them to accede to *fin' amor*, perhaps even, in this way (as outlined by Saint Bernard), to respond to Divine Charity; their faith would be strengthened. Fontevraud constituted a means of touching Woman without brutalizing Her (and themselves, in the process): it is a monument to loving respect.[14] Far from being merely undone, or forgotten, the physical—the real, the touchable—regains (or suggests) a prelapsarian state from which sinful shame is banished. This is the specific sense and function assigned to feminine transcendence.

Fontevraud thus contitutes a monument to the power of Woman, and it is a marvelous place—an ideal place, to be sure, but also a *real* place. One can be there; it is, please believe me, instructive to visit, and study, it.

Let me end by citing portions of three short texts, two by women, one by a man.

The first is very much a secular love song, by a *trobairitz* from the mid-twelfth century, who addresses her lover and who explains, I believe, the nature of her extraordinary power. The singer is known as the Countess of Dia:

> Estat ai en greu cossirier
> per un cavallier q'ai agut
> e voill sia totz temps sabut
> cum eu l'ai amat a sobrier
> ara vei q'ieu sui trahida
> car eu non li donei m'amor
> don ai estat en gran error
> en lieig e qand sui vestida.
>
> Ben volria mon cavallier
> tener un ser e mos bratz nut
> q'el sen tengra per ereubut
> sol q'a lui fezes cosseillier
> car plus m'en sui abellida
> no fetz Floris de Blanchaflor
> lui eu l'austrei mon cor e m'amor
> mon sen mos huoills e ma vida.
>
> Bel amics avinens e bos
> cora-us tenrai e mon poder
> e que jagues ab vos un ser
> e qe-us des un bais amoros
> sapchatz gran talan n'auria

qe-us tengues en luoc del marit
ab so que m'aguessetz plevit
de far tot so qu'eu volria.[15]

[I have suffered cruel pain because of a knight who was mine. I want it to be known forever that I loved him above all else, but I see that I am betrayed, for I did not give him my entire love and this has placed me in a state of error. In bed and when I am clothed I would so much wish to hold my knight, naked, within my arms, and that he would consider himself utterly satisfied, since I would serve him as a pillow. I am more desirous of him than Floire of Blanchefleur. I give him my heart, my love, my sense of everything, my eyes, and my life.

Handsome lover, most attractive and good, when shall I hold you in my power? When will I go to bed with you one evening, give you a wild kiss? Understand the great desire I have to hold you in the place of a husband, provided that you pledge to me to do whatever I might wish.]

Like Heloise in her letters to Abelard, the Countess of Dia despises the conventional, business-like institution she sees marriage to be in her time. The enslavement embodied by "traditional" marriage impedes the exercise of the kind of womanly power required in any authentic—that is, free and desired—coupling, and is destructive of the overwhelming joy such coupling is designed to bring about. Note also how she assumes the role of teacher here. Hers is the feminine voice that knows about love. It is she who directs her voice and her self to the knight, the only free man, one suspects—the man who by definition is free, or at least amenable to "liberation" through her good offices.

My second text reproduces part of a song written by a Northern French knight, Conon de Béthune, a great nobleman, who takes leave of his Beloved before departing on the Fourth Crusade (1202) to the Holy Land. (This crusade would involve the taking of Constantinople and the establishment of a "Latin" Empire there; Conon would serve in a very high official capacity. He died without returning to France):

Pour li m'en vois souspirant en Surie,
car je ne doi faillir mon creatour.
Qui li faudra a ces besoing d'aïe,
sachiez que il li faudra a greignour.
et sachent bien li grant et li menour
que la doit on faire chevalerie,
qu'on i conquiert paradis et honour
et pris et los et l'amour de s'amie.

Deus! tant avons esté preu par oiseuse:
ore i parra qui a certes iert preus,
s'irons vengier la honte doloreuse,
dont chascuns doit estre iriez et honteus;
car a no tans est perduz li sains leus,
u Deus soufri pour nous mort angoisseuse;
s'ore i laissons nos anemis morteus,
a tous jours mais iert no vie honteuse . . .

Tous li clergiés et li home d'eage,
ki en aumosne et en biens faiz manront,
partiront tuit a cest perlerinage,
et les dames qui chastement vivront,
se loiauté font a ceus qui i vont;
et s'eles font par mal conseil folage,
a lasches genz et mauvais le feront,
car tuit li bon iront en cest voiage.

Deus est assis en son saint iretage:
ore i parra con cil le secorront,
cui il jeta de la prison ombrage,
quant il fu mors en la crois que Turc ont.
sachiez, cil sont trop honi qui n'iront,
s'il n'ont poverte ou vieillece ou malage;
et cil qui sain et joene et riche sont
ne pueent pas demourer sans hontage.

Las! je m'en vois plorant des ieus del front
la u Deus veut amender mon corage,
et sachiez bien qu'a la meillour del mont
penserai plus que ne faz au voyage.

[For her I go off, sighing, to Syria, for I must not fail my Creator. Whoever fails Him in this hour of need will indeed fail Him in even greater need. And may both the highest and less-than-highest born know that there one must perform as knights, for thus one wins Paradise and honor, as well as praise and esteem, and the love of one's beloved.

God! we have merely played at being valorous. Now we shall see who is truly brave, and we will go to avenge the painful ignominy which surely must anger and shame us all, for in our time the Holy Places have been lost where God suffered the anguish of death. If now we permit our enemies to remain there, for all time our lives will be exemplary of shame . . .

All clergy and men of proper age who wish to dwell in good deeds and alms will depart on this pilgrimage, and ladies who live chastely will behave faithfully to those who depart. But if through bad counsel they do something foolish, they will do it only with cowards and dishonorable men, for all good men will have left on this voyage.

God is besieged in His holy fief. Let us see how those whom, by dying on the Cross—now in the hands of the Turks—He freed from the dark prison of death, will come to His aid. Let it be known that shame awaits those who stay, unless they are too poor, too old or too sick.

Alas! I take my leave with tears flowing from my eyes in order to go where God will strengthen my heart. And may it be known that I shall think more about the finest lady in the world than I do about this voyage.][16]

It is in the proper order of things—it is right—that for (or because of) her I depart upon this solemn crusade, declares Conon. Moreover, should the ladies left behind do something foolish while the rest of us have gone, it will not count, for "all good men will have departed." Such misbehavior has nothing to do with the true Couple—with a man and a woman whose merit is such that they deserve to be together. The source and inspiration of the knight's strength are the lady whom he loves and to whom, in the midst of the fighting, he will devote his thoughts. It is their presence together that imparts sense, or value, to everything he stands for. Conon de Béthune, love-poet and knight, has learned his lesson well!

My last text is taken from the Prologue to a collection of short, almost lyrical verse narratives attributed to a woman now known as Marie de France. This work, which is usually dated around 1175[17] and of which the author is justifiably very proud, she dedicates to a "noble king" who must have been Henry II Plantagenet, husband of Eleanor of Aquitaine; this is what she says, first of her work, then, as we shall see, in her dedication proper:

> Ki Deus ad duné escïence
> E de parler bone eloquence
> Ne s'en deit taisir ne celer,
> Ainz se deit voluntiers mustrer.
> Quant uns granz biens est mult oïz,
> Dunc a primes est il fluriz,
> Et quant loëz est de plusurs,
> Dunc ad espandues ses flurs . . .
> Ki de vice se voelt defendre
> Estudïer deit et entendre
> A grevose ovre comencier:
> Par ceo s'en puet plus esloignier
> E de grant dolur delivrer.
> Pur ceo començai a penser
> D'aucune bone estoire faire
> E de latin en romaunz traire;
> Mais ne me fust guaires de pris:
> Itant s'en sunt altre entremis!
> Des lais pensai, k'oïz aveie.
> Ne dutai pas, bien le saveie,
> Ke pur remambrance les firent
> Des aventures k'il oïrent
> Cil ki primes les comencierent
> E ki avant les enveierent.
> Plusurs en ai oï conter,
> Nes voil laissier ne oblier.
> Rimé en ai e fait ditié,
> Soventes fiez en ai veillié!

[Anyone who has received from God the gift of knowledge and true eloquence has a duty not to remain silent: rather should one be happy to reveal such talents. When a truly beneficial thing is heard by many people, it then enjoys its first blossom, but if it is widely praised its flowers are in full bloom . . .

Anyone wishing to guard against vice should study intently and undertake a demanding task, whereby one can ward off and rid oneself of great suffering. For this reason I began to think of working on some good story [history] and translating a Latin text into French, but this would scarcely have been worthwhile, for others [all of them men, professional clerics] have undertaken a similar task. So I thought of ancient Breton songs, now known as lays, which I had heard and did not doubt, for I knew it full well that they were composed by those who first began them and put them into circulation, to perpetuate the memory of adventures they had heard. I myself have heard a number of them and do not wish to overlook or neglect them. I have put them into verse, made poems from them and labored on them often very late into the night.][18]

The production of Marie's late-night labor is a good thing, a flower, or fruit, of her God-given natural eloquence. Her tales differ from the production of her male contemporaries, specialists in lengthy, chronicle-like romance historical narratives concerning cities of Antiquity, like Thebes, Troy, and Rome. Marie's poems are short; they all have to do with love. Each of them explores ramifications of the Man/Woman Couple, especially the woman's function, or malfunction, within the Couple. She presents this clerkly work of hers—which she compares favorably with the literary production of the best of her contemporaries and predecessors—to the "noble king," in his honor: namely, to the knight in whom all joy culminates and to whom joy pays rightful homage. Marie as a woman and as a writer (*clergie*) sets herself up as a member of a couple whose other member is the king himself, fount and wellspring of manly knightliness (*chevalerie*). Underlying this magnificent, and beautiful, conceit is, of course, the idea of Marie's book—her creation—as being the product of the marriage of (feminine) *clergie* and (masculine) *chevalerie*, as being the infant, and immortal, child only their transcendent couplehood could have engendered, conceived, and brought to delivery. She, moreover, invented this couplehood; it was *her* invention.

Here is the translated text of Marie's dedication:

In your honor, noble king, you who are so worthy and courtly, you to whom all joy pays homage and in whose heart all true virtue has taken root, did I set myself to assemble lays, to compose and to relate them in rhyme. In my heart, lord [OFr *seignor* means both "lord" and, of course, "husband"], I thought and decided that I should present them to you, so if it pleased you to accept them, you would bring me great joy and I should rejoice evermore. Do not consider me presumptuous if I make so bold as to offer you this gift. Now hear the beginning.[19]

The present article has barely scratched the surface of what it has been alluding to. I mean nevertheless to have at least suggested here the interest of looking at what the period we have briefly examined together did with these human realities that are still so very much with us. This interest is dual. It is, first of all, intrinsic. Secondly, it has relevance for our own time as we continue to question the foundations of the relationship of Man and Woman. We have observed some oddities, to be sure, but there is also a good deal that is not so strange or that is even recognizable to us today. For the twelfth century, it is clear, Woman—and women—knew a kind of transcendence that she, and they, would be deprived of in later centuries,[20] no matter how much in other ways, with respect to us and our own biases, the Middle Ages appear "backward," "obscurantist." This deprivation is a very serious matter indeed; we have only recently begun to address it now in programs of varying degrees of efficacy and by taking more or less adequate legal measures. I hope, therefore, that readers will have found this confrontation with our twelfth-century past intellectually provocative and potentially rewarding.

Notes

[1] For a handy and informative set of essays on the notion of knighthood, see Georges Duby, *The Chivalrous Society*, trans. Cynthia Postan (Berkeley and Los Angeles: U of California P, 1977).

[2] I refer to the fascinating fourteenth-century *Libro del Caballero Zifar*, the object of no less than three recent critical editions. See Michael Harney's detailed review article in *Romance Philology* 43 (1990) 569-601.

[3] Here is the earliest relevant Old French articulation of this idea, as expressed in the Prologue to the *Cligés* of Chrétien de Troyes (ca. 1176): "Ce nos ont nostre livre apris / Qu'an Grece ot de chevalerie / Le premier los et de clergie. / Puis vint chevalerie a Rome / Et de clergie la some, / Qui or est an France venue. / Dex doint qu'ele i soit maintenue / Et que li leus li abelisse / Tant que ja mes de France n'isse / L'enors qui s'i est arestee." *Les Romans de Chrétien de Troyes édités d'après la copie de Guiot (Bibl. nat. fr. 794), II: Cligés*, ed. Alexandre Micha, Classiques Français du Moyen Age 84 (Paris: Champion, 1970) lines 28-37.

[4] This idea was given forceful vernacular expression by Marie de France in the "Prologue" to her *Lais* (lines 9-16): "Custume fu as ancïens, / Ceo testimoine Precïens, / Es livres ke jadis feseient, / Assez oscurement diseient / Pur ceus ki a venir esteient / E ki aprendre les deveient, / K'i peüssent gloser la lettre / E de lur sen le surplus mettre" [The Ancients had the custom, so testifies Priscian, in the books which they composed, of speaking quite obscurely for those who were to come after them and were to learn them so that they—the Moderns—might gloss the letter and add what was necessary to complete their—the Ancients'—meaning]; in *Les Lais de Marie de France*, ed. Jean Rychner, Classiques Français du Moyen Age 93 (Paris: Champion, 1968), English version mine. For a close analysis of these lines see Alfred Foulet and Karl D. Uitti, "The Prologue to the *Lais* of Marie de France: A Reconsideration," *Romance Philology* 35 (1981) 242-49.

[5] Henry Adams, *Mont Saint Michel and Chartres*, Introduction and Notes by Raymond Carney (New York: Penguin, 1986); see, in particular, Chs. 6 and 7: "The Virgin of Chartres" and "Roses and Apses."

[6] Adams recounts the story, taken from the *Miracles de la sainte Vierge*, by Gauthier de Coinci, of a bad priest who in all ways neglected his pastoral duties, but who was restored to his parish, after having been removed from it by his bishop, thanks to the intervention of the Virgin to whom the priest, despite his many other imperfections, maintained a devotion. The bishop is powerless to "do his duty."

[7] Biblical texts in Latin are taken from *Biblia Sacra iuxta Vulgatem Clementinam*, Nova editio, Sexta editio (Madrid: Biblioteca de Autores Cristianos, 1982).

[8] Biblical texts in English translation are taken from the *Holy Bible* (Authorized King James Version) (Oxford UP, n.d.).

[9] Letter 115, ed. Giles Constable, *The Letters of Peter the Venerable*, 1 (Cambridge, MA, 1967) 307-08 (quoted by Peter Dronke, *Abelard and Heloise in Medieval Testimonies* [Glasgow UP, 1976] 37). Dronke's English version: "My illustrious and dearest sister in God: this man to whom you have cleaved after the sexual oneness, with the stronger and finer bond of divine love, he with whom and under whom you have long served God—I tell you, God is now cherishing him in his lap, in place of you, or like a replica of you. And at the second coming, at the sound of the

archangel and the trumpet heralding God descending from the heavens, God will restore him to you through his grace, having preserved him for you" (23).

[10] Martianus Capella's *prosimetrum*, as Dronke points out (16-18), is linked to allusions to the story of Heloise and Abelard in various twelfth-century works, e.g., the anonymous *Metamorphosis Golye episcopi* (c. 1142) "whose central allegory derives from Martianus." The importance to subsequent Old French romance narrative of the connections established between the well-known contemporary story of their couplehood and the authoritative Latin, i.e., clerkly, work is incalculable. These connections help one better to understand the groundings of Chrétien de Troyes's reworking of Martianus in terms of Arthurian legend in his trailblazing *Erec et Enide* (ca. 1165).

[11] The Latin text derives from *Martianus Capella*, ed. Adolf Dick (rev. by Jean Préaux), Bibliotheca Scriptorum Graecorum et Romanorum Tevbneriana (Stuttgart: Teubner, 1925 [1978]) 3. The English version is that of William Harris Stahl and Richard Johnson, with E.L. Birge, *Martianus Capella and the Seven Liberal Arts*, II: *The Marriage of Philology and Mercury* (New York: Columbia UP, 1977) 3.

[12] The *Song of Roland* (along with most other *chansons de geste*) is frequently, but to my mind superficially, characterized generically as according little importance to Woman. To be sure, the OFr epic seldom thematizes love as do most romance narratives. However, the Couple construct is fundamental to the *Roland*. Not only is the Roland/Aude pairing of great importance, it is symbolic, I believe, of the French/*douce France* binome which pervades the poem. *France* is much more than a mere geographical entity. *France* is what is served by Charlemagne and his host; and the service is chivalric—as chivalric and as total as that provided by Lancelot to Guenevere. In their service to *France* Charles and the twelve peers serve God. Roland's refusal to blow the oliphant is due largely to his desire that *France* not be shamed by such an act.

[13] For instance, the presence, in Chartres cathedral, of the beautiful Roland window, i.e., in an edifice dedicated to Our Lady, speaks volumes concerning the points raised in the present essay.

[14] Thus, it has been reported—somewhat to the consternation of certain modern commentators—that Pierre himself practiced "bundling," i.e., spending the night, in bed and unclothed (as was the custom in the twelfth century), with a girl or woman, also unclothed, but without sex. (A reflection of this custom is to be found in the Blanchefleur episode of Chrétien's *Conte du Graal [Perceval]*.) The practice is not without Catharistic overtones.

[15] The text given is that provided by Jacques Roubaud, ed., *Les Troubadours. Anthologie bilingue* (Paris: Seghers, 1971); I have chosen not to punctuate it.

[16] The OFr text is taken from *Chrestomathie de l'ancien français (VIIe-XVe siècles)*, eds. Karl Bartsch and Leo Wiese, 12th ed. (New York: Hafner, 1951), Pièce 42b; the English version is mine.

[17] Although this is not the place to examine the question in proper detail, there are, I believe, cogent reasons favoring an earlier dating, possibly in the early 1160s.

[18] The OFr text is that provided by Jean Rychner, ed., *Les Lais de Marie de France*, "Prologue," lines 1-8, 23-42; the English version is taken from *The Lais of Marie de France*, trans. with an Introduction by Glyn S. Burgess and Keith Busby (New York: Penguin Books, 1986).

[19] Marie's OFr text, as edited by Rychner ("Prologue," lines 43-56): "En l'honur de vus, nobles reis, / Ki tant estes pruz e curteis, / A ki tute joie s'encline / E en ki quoer tuz biens racine, / M'entremis des lais assembler, / Par rime faire e reconter. / En mun quoer pensoe e diseie, / Sire, kes vos presentereie. / Si vos les plaist a recevoir, / Mult me feez grant joie aveir, / A tuz jurz mais en serai liee. / Ne me tenez a surquidiee / Si vos os faire icest present. / Ore oëz le comencement!"

[20] A sense of this deprivation may be felt in women's writings already in the fifteenth century (e.g., Christine de Pizan), but it is especially with the advent of Humanism and the Reformation ("pre-Modernity") that matters become acute. One thinks, for France, of Marguerite de Navarre and, especially, of Louise Labé (who was referred to alternatively as "harlot" and "blue-stocking" by Calvin and others, in part for expressing sentiments not unlike those we find in many *trobairitz* songs). One recalls a famous sonnet by Louise Labé, the tone of which is at once passionate and elegiac (*Penguin Book of French Verse*, ed. Geoffrey Brereton [Baltimore: Penguin, 1967] 50):

Baise-m'encore, rebaise-moi et baise:
Donne-m'en un de tes plus savoureux,
Donne-m'en un de tes plus amoureux:
Je t'en rendrai quatre plus chauds que braise.

Las, te plains-tu? ça, que ce mal j'apaise
En t'en donnant dix autres doucereux.
Ainsi, mêlant nos baisers tant heureux,
Jouissons-nous l'un de l'autre à notre aise.

Lors double vie à chacun ensuivra.
Chacun en soi et son ami vivra.
Permets-m'Amour penser quelque folie:

Toujours suis mal, vivant discrètement,
Et ne me puis donner contentement,
Si hors de moi ne fais quelque saillie.

Louis A. MacKenzie, Jr.

Three Literary Visions
of Seventeenth-Century Paris

In his most celebrated and anthologized poem, "La Solitude," Saint-Amant has his narrator protest a keenly felt attraction for isolation, for what he calls "la nativité du temps." Especially intriguing in this poem is the fact that solitude, all the while associated with the formation of the poetic voice, would at the same time represent a threat to that voice.

> O que j'ayme la solitude!
> C'est l'élément des bons esprits,
> C'est par elle que j'ay compris
> L'art d'Apollon sans nulle estude.
> Je l'ayme par l'amour de toy,
> Connoissant que ton humeur l'ayme;
> Mais, quand je pense bien à moy,
> Je la hay pour la raison mesme:
> Car elle pourroit me ravir
> L'heur de te voir et te servir.[1]

Isolation and the meditative reverie it induces are understood to be subversive; they are apt to induce the kind of self-absorption that ends up working against the esthetic and psychic urge to seek solitude in the first place.

This negative side of self-imposed seclusion is handled much more brashly in "Les Cabarets," one of Saint-Amant's so-called bacchic poems that some critics have tended to dismiss as superficial. In celebrating dionysian prerogatives and pleasures, in singing the joys of camaraderie and good cheer, the narrator of "Les Cabarets" will ironize the appeal of solitude by advising his friend, Faret, to seek it no where else than in the poem of that name:

> Ne cherche point la solitude,
> Si ce n'est par fois dans ces vers
> Que j'ay donnez à l'univers. (61)

He also tries to persuade Faret, who has gone off to Fontainebleau, to rejoin him in Paris and to taste the joys that the city alone can offer. Faret, prominent member of the group of happy revelers, has, we are told, been lead astray by some demon who has intruded upon and infected the happiness of the group. What is more, the pleasures to be found and savored in Paris are linked intimately to a sense of group. In this regard, the narrator, referring both to the importunate devil and to "ce vain esclat de la fortune," asks accusingly:

> Auroit-il bien tant de puissance
> Que de t'oster la jouyssance
> Des plaisirs qu'on gouste à Paris
> Sans nul soucy des favoris? (58)

In the charming middle section of the poem, the narrator speculates on his friend's motives for leaving Paris. Could it be some "désir champêtre," an itch to contemplate the breadth and beauty of nature? Or is this absence due to a bout of melancholy that would move Faret to seek out the evening in order to write poetry worthy of the daylight?

> Ou tantost morne et solitaire,
> Revant à quelque haut mystère,
> Que les Muses, ces belles soeurs
> Montrent avec tant de douceurs,
> S'en aller en quelques lieux sombres
> Loger Phoebus entre les ombres,
> Et faire en cette obscurité
> Un vers digne de la clarté? (59)

The narrator calls for a response from his truant friend, urging him either to explain his absence or to risk jeopardizing the good-natured intimacy between his name and the good life in Paris. ("Parle, cher amy, je t'en prie, / Si tu ne veux que je m'escrie: / On fait à sçavoir que Faret / Ne rime plus à cabaret"). With a view towards luring his friend back to the friends and city he had unexpectedly and inexplicably forsaken, the narrator launches into a long and vivid portrait of Paris:

> Paris, où ce grand dicu préside
> Paris, où la Coiffier réside,
> Paris, où fleurit un Cormier,
> Qui des arbres est le premier;
> Paris qui prend pour son Helaine
> Une petite Magdelaine;
> Paris, qui présente à nos yeux
> La Pomme de pin, qui vaut mieux
> Que celle d'or, dont fut troublée
> Toute la divine assemblée;
> Paris, qui croissant tous les jours,
> Contient dans un de ses fauxbourgs

Mainte autre ville toute entière;
Paris, où dans un cimetière,
Fait pour enterrer les ennuis,
Nous avons tant passé de nuicts;
Paris, enfin, ce petit monde,
Où tout contentement abonde,
Et dans qui les plus grands désirs
Se peuvent saouller de plaisirs.(60)

Of capital importance to the narrator and to the line of his argument is the fact that Bacchus, "ce grand dieu," rules over the city. That he is characterized as "nostre puissant roy" suggests that his dominion is felt generally (by all Parisians) and specifically (by the group of friends of which Faret is a "compagnon d'office"). To live in Paris is to live under the bacchic sign and to participate in the bacchic liturgy. It is also significant that the poet puts specific Parisian cabarets on equal rhetorical footing with his expression of Bacchus's dominion over the city. In so doing, he effects a seamless coupling of Paris and mythological models. Allusions to Helen and the golden apple, all the while designed to underscore the notion of the mythic allure of the city and its cabarets, tend also to contaminate that vision with a potentially negative component. Exemplarily desirable, both Helen and the golden apple were to become motives for monumental jealousy and discord; and although it would surely be a mistake to gloss these allusions with much more than a mock-heroic patina, the poet's choice of mythological analogues does all the same seem curious. Among the possible explanations for this would be one that situates these allusions to potential disorder in the broader context of Saint-Amant's bacchic vision, one that he invokes on occasion in an apparent urge to counterbalance the more introspective, lyrical and orderly inflections of his poetry. At the very minimum, the narrator wants to convince his readers, among whom Faret, that Paris and her cabarets offer the possibility of memorable, even monumental revelry.

More explicit is the sense the narrator wants to give of the physical monumentality of the city itself. When he asserts that Paris, ever growing, contains in one of its *faubourgs* the equivalent of most other full-sized cities, he is also suggesting that the capital can itself be defined in terms of appetite: the city consumes, literally incorporating all the qualities and assets of less dominant localities. The growth factor distinguishing Paris from what would come to be known as the "desert" would, in the narrator's eyes and argument, seem to be not only an analogue to, but also a guarantor of, his own appetite for good cheer and his desire for satisfaction. What is more, the putative intent of the poem being to convince Faret to return to Paris, this description also implies that, in his absence, Faret will miss out on something as the city continues to advance along the path of its urban destiny.

The sense that Paris is by nature associated with appetite, nurturing, and hence, with life, is underscored even more compellingly when the narrator refers to one of the cabarets as a cemetery designed to lay all *ennuis* to rest. In transforming the ordinarily negative image of the place of death into an affirming place of life, this characterization also invites the reader, internal and external, to consider Paris as a magical place, as "ce petit monde où tout contentement abonde." The expression is especially rich, almost over-determined: its three principal terms, "monde," "contentement" and "abonde," convey the notion of plenitude. Paris would be the place of contentment, a term that does not simply mean happiness, but also satiety. The city is the receptacle; it is itself the larger manifestation of the cup from which the narrator and his "compagnons d'office" take their pleasure and make their liturgy. This is further enhanced by the fact that Paris is referred to as the place in which all desire is sated with pleasure. In Paris pleasure flows like wine; the drink is pleasure itself; which is to suggest that Paris is systemically ingestible, that it enters directly into the system. If, as the expression has it, you are what you eat or drink, you are also the place where you live. And if I may be allowed well before its time to twist a lyric from a song, the narrator seems to be asking Faret: "why would you want to stay down on the farm after you've seen 'Paree'"?

If for Saint-Amant, Paris is the city where all desire is apt to be fulfilled, as the empty cup is apt to be filled, for the poet, Damon, subject of Boileau's first satire, the precise opposite would seem to be the case. At one time the toast of court and city, eventually reduced to begging, he has abandoned Paris for some "antre ou roche" where creditors, collection agents, and detractors cannot get to him. Bidding *bon débarras* to the capital, Damon will end his stay in Paris not with a whimper but with a rhetorical bang, a scathing lament and accusation. In Boileau's words, Damon has "distilled his rage," an expression that serves to underscore the uncommonly concentrated conviction, if not power, of the tirade. What is more, the term *distill* is linked etymologically to the notion of dripping (*distillare*: to fall drop by drop). The verb can be seen, then, as suggesting something more than just the intensity and "rage" of the complaint. It tends also to evoke the erosive quality of life in Paris; and in so doing, to punctuate in a particularly telling, if implicit way, the idea that Damon has reached a kind of critical mass; that one too many drops of the moral poison defining Paris has fallen on him. These connotations of the term *distiller* would, incidentally, stand in dramatic contrast to one of the terms Saint-Amant uses to describe his Paris, namely, *abonder* ("Paris, enfin, ce petit monde, / Où tout contentement abonde"). This verb tends to underscore the enthusiasm and expansiveness of his argument by evoking the waves (ab/onde:*unda*) of pleasure and contentment characterizing a city awash in good cheer.

Damon attributes his own inability to find contentment in the city to a historical fact: times have changed. In this he tends to agree with Saint-Amant's narrator, who also saw a city in evolution. In Damon's eyes, however, the changes have been manifestly for the worse, especially with regard to the arts in general and poetry in particular: "Puisqu'en ce Lieu jadis aux Muses si commode, / Le mérite et l'esprit ne sont plus à la mode . . . ."[2]

The esthetic ("jadis au Muses si commode"), the moral ("le mérite"), and the intellectual ("l'esprit") are functionally and inextricably linked in the mind of the narrator, whose artistic misfortune would be the direct result of an unhappy evolution of the moral presuppositions defining Parisian society. Keenly—and proudly—aware of his difference, of that which would distinguish him from those types more at home in the new Paris, Damon will not hesitate to underscore the frankness and straight-forwardness that seem to be at the very foundation of his feelings of displacement: "Je ne puis rien nommer, si ce n'est par son nom. / J'appelle un chat un chat, et Rolet un fripon" (Boileau 24).

This irrepressible urge towards frankness, which Damon not only announces, but champions, can be taken as a will to moral and poetic power; and as such it must be considered near or at the very heart of the discomfort he experiences. The reader is invited to infer on the one hand that Damon's sense of himself as a poet is correlative to his sense of himself as a social critic, that poetry and commentary end up feeding each other in ways that lead inevitably to Damon's exclusion and eventual exile. Fueling the friction between Damon and the modern Paris is a basic conservatism, come, we are told, from his own rustic origins:

> Je ne sais point en lâche essuyer les outrages
> D'un faquin orgueilleux qui vous tient à ses gages,
> De mes sonnets flatteurs lasser tout l'univers,
> Et vendre au plus offrant mon encens et mes vers:
> Pour un si bas emploi ma muse est trop altière.
> Je suis rustique et fier, et j'ai l'âme grossière: . . .
> (Boileau 24)

Symptomatic of his rustic origins and mentality is a deeply felt pride that Damon tends to view in terms of personal heroism ("Je ne sais point en lâche essuyer les outrages"). Determined—indeed predetermined—to hold the moral and artistic line against the menace of the moderns, Damon has nonetheless come to recognize the futility of his own heroism. He has come to understand that his time may be past, precisely because the Paris he once knew has passed. In this light, it is interesting, at least for those who endorse more modern critical techniques, that at the very moment when he most assertively proclaims his pride and his difference, the terms he uses ("altière," "fier," "grossière") contain in them a homophonic allusion (*hier*), to those happier yesterdays when moral integrity and artistic accomplishment apparently issued in a natural way from this sense of self-worth. Such, however, can no longer be the case in the new Paris.

Faced with this moral inversion that he cannot tolerate and with the implied intolerance towards his out-dated poetry, Damon has come to realize that he is wholly dispirited. His soul, and with it, his enthusiasm and desire, have been as if ripped from his body: "Et je suis, à Paris, triste, pauvre et reclus, / Ainsi qu'un corps sans âme, ou devenu perclus" (Boileau 25).

Damon understands that to stay on in Paris is to run the risk of becoming a Parisian, which in the argument of the poem is to become what he most reviles. If, for the narrator in "Les Cabarets," Paris were the place to which any right thinking person would return, for Damon it is the place from which any right thinking person—including Saint-Amant oneself, who is named in the poem—would want to dissociate himself. Moreover, by passing judgment, casting aspersions, and cutting his losses, Damon would in fact be engaged in reclaiming his own soul. His effort is to reconstitute that part of himself which had too long been eroded by and sacrificed to immorality and soullessness.

The double loss—of identity and distinction—is attributable not only to the moral compromises Damon is fundamentally incapable of making, but also to the fact that he is obliged to rub elbows with a "foule effroiable de rimeurs affamés," a group he has to view with a certain ambiguity. On the one hand, his sympathy must extend to the general plight of poets in a society where poetry has been devalued and poets are reduced not only to the status of "rimeurs," but also to a state of indigence. On the other hand, however, he must also resent his own lack of distinction: he risks being absorbed into that same nameless group whose members do each other injustice by selling their souls and talents cheaply to the prevailing morality.

Given the moral decay of Paris and its ruinous impact on artists, the narrator can do nothing other than express an unmoving resolve to abandon the city:

> Quittons donc pour jamais une Ville importune
> Où l'Honneur est en guerre avecque la fortune
> Où le Vice orguelleusx s'érige en Souverain,
> Et va la mitre en teste et la crosse à la main:
> Où la Science triste, affreuse et délaissée,
> Est par tout des bons lieux comme infâme chassée?
> Où le seul art en vogue est l'art de bien voler:
> Où tout me choque: Enfin où . . . je n'ose parler.
> Et quel Homme si froid ne seroit plein de bile,
> A l'aspect odieux des moeurs de cette ville?
> (Boileau 36-37)

At this point in his ongoing—and redundant—complaint, Damon conjures up an exotic, almost ghoulish allegory. Honor, fortune, vice and knowledge vie with each other in what would be a titanic struggle for the soul of the city. In Damon's eyes, of course, the battle has already been lost—lost to the point that he himself is reduced to a dead end, to an inability, based certainly on a sense of the decorum he feels has been discounted in modern Paris, to express his final outrage ("Où tout me choque: enfin où . . . je n'ose parler"). Paris would have become a city of such negative moral temperament that a person of principle can only walk away without telling the whole story. Curmudgeon to the end, Damon does all the same find himself yet incapable of simply walking away. Rather, he hammers away once again at the place where moral decay and poetic expression intersect:

> Qui pourrait les souffrir? et qui, pour les blâmer,
> Malgré muse et Phébus n'apprendrait à rimer?
> Non, non, sur ce sujet, pour écrire avec grâce,
> Il ne faut point monter au sommet du Parnasse;
> Et, sans aller rêver dans le double vallon,
> La colère suffit et vaut un Apollon. (Boileau 37)

The reasoning here is telling in its ambiguity. On the one hand, it seems to want to posit that the proper place for publicizing and indicting what is wrong with Paris is poetry (Qui . . . n'apprendrait à rimer?") even though good poetry, that is, the kind of poetry associated with "mérite" and "esprit," has already gone out of fashion. And even if Damon does at the same time devalue this sort of expository poetry as unbefitting the higher aspirations of genuine poetic inspiration ("malgré muse et Phébus"), he ends up shifting his stance in a curious way: he seems to undermine the value of his own poetic inspiration by linking it to anger. Anger alone would be sufficient not only to inspire, but also to constitute, the material of his own remarks, themselves forming within Boileau's poem another "poem." And this other poem, put into question by the internal poet, Damon, would have to represent a less distinguished, less "meritorious" effort in order for those very readers who have forsaken the good poetry of the good old days to appreciate his salutary, if not exactly salvific, lesson.

Confronted with the double impasse of an inadmissible social order and the degraded status of his own poetic voice, Damon is forced to extrude the whole matter and to situate it on a theological plane:

> Pour moi, qu'en santé même un autre monde étonne,
> Qui crois l'âme immortelle, et que c'est Dieu qui tonne,
> Il vaut mieux pour jamais me bannir de ce lieu.
> Je me retire donc. Adieu, Paris, adieu. (Boileau 38)

The tone rings of the prophetic: God's thundering signals anger. Imprudent would be the one who opts to remain in a city which, it is implied, may someday hear more than mere thunder.

Whereas Boileau sends his hero off to self-imposed exile, La Bruyère gives a particularly incisive view of the lives led by those who stay. Marking his chapter, *De la ville*, is a semantic constellation that counts as its principal elements the correlated notions of imitation and theatricality. In this light, it should perhaps be recalled that at the moment La Bruyère is writing, Paris has already been forced into an imitative posture by an event of enduring socio-political importance, namely the definitive establishment of the court at Versailles. When Louis turned his back on the capital, taking his solar self and his entourage to Versailles, Paris lost a large measure of its allure. It is not therefore surprising that what grates and goads La Bruyère's Parisians is an urge for parity with the court: "Paris pour l'ordinaire le singe de la cour, ne sait pas toujours le contrefaire."[3] The difference is then between aping and imitating, between the most superficial representation and one that would claim to put Paris in meaningful apposition with the court. Now it is, of course, evident that both of these modes of representation that would regraft the court onto the Parisian psyche will come up short when compared to the original. Moreover, in the gap between the two terms—aping and imitating—Paris is not even able to get to the quick of its imitative gropings. The issue is complicated all the more by the fact that La Bruyère will characterize the court itself as a model of duplicity and falsehood. To imitate the court—and to imitate it badly at that—is to up the ante of artifice.

The particular example La Bruyère uses to argue his point is centered on the supposedly natural manners and mannerisms of a courtly woman when in the presence of a worthy man. His worth being as fundamental to him as her sensitivity is to her, an implicit contract of sympathy is drawn. He is at court; there is no need for further credentials. Such is not, however, the case of the *citadine* whose heart is set to thumping and whose wiles are put in motion not by the man himself or his merit, but by the sounds of his carriage and the visual *éclat* of his domestics' livery:

Une femme de ville entend-elle le bruissement d'un carrosse qui s'arrête à sa porte, elle pétille de goût et de complaisaince pour quiconque est dedans, sans le connaître; mais si elle a vu de sa fenêtre un bel attelage, beaucoup de livrées, et que plusieurs rangs de clous parfaitement dorés l'aient éblouie, quelle impatience n'a-t-elle pas de voir déjà dans sa chambre le cavalier ou le magistrat! (La Bruyère 216)

Her desire is piqued not by innate quality or worth, but by surface representations of status. For her sorry imitation of courtly ways, and because she is also guilty of affectation, La Bruyère ranks the city woman even lower than the person from the country she surely scorns. The shameless pursuit of superior public standing is not at all unlike play-acting. To affect is to pretend; it is to turn to false appearance. It is to disguise oneself to play a theatrical role, and the notion of theater is central to any understanding of La Bruyère's vision of Paris. Stylized *promenades*, for example, are taken not out of a desire for positive social exchange, but rather to honor certain conventions of manners and to "se rassurer sur le théâtre," the theater being at once the stage that is Paris, and its codes of behavior in deference to which the public persona always takes precedence over the private, supposedly authentic, person.

In this regard, La Bruyère reckons that "un homme de robe à la ville et le même à la cour ce sont deux hommes. Revenu chez soi, il reprend ses mœurs, sa taille et son visage, qu'il y avait laissés: il n'est plus si embarrassé, ni si honnête" (La Bruyère 209). The man at court and the man about town would be at parity: neither seems to dress himself in his true habits when in the public eye. The twist of La Bruyère's observation—the knife he twists into both actors—is that in reassuming their proper habits, stature and appearance at home, that is, in reestablishing a certain authenticity (*honnêteté*), they also lose something of that same authenticity. Now, it is, of course, true that the term *honnêteté* can be construed as meaning nothing more than politeness. If, however, the word is allowed to express its more fundamental semantic charge, the statement implies something very much akin to La Rochefoucauld's dark vision of the moral and social order; namely, that there is no escape from those psychic currents, which even though unperceived, nourish and determine behavior. In the special relief allowed by such a broader reading of the term— a reading that takes into account common notions of dignity, loyalty, and ethical propriety—faithfulness to self and to others would be more "genuine" in those situations where play-acting is the order of the day. In a view such as this, where the normal order of things is unflinchingly ironized, one is given naturally to sculpting an inauthentic self, which would in fact be an "authentic" self.

If this reading comes across as somewhat bold, it is all the same subtended by La Bruyère's insistence on a codified *amour-propre* and self-interest that in large part define middle and upper-class Paris. As we read in the opening fragment of the chapter,

L'on se donne à Paris, sans se parler, comme un rendez-vous public, mais fort exact, tous les soirs, au Cours ou aux Tuileries, pour se regarder au visage et se désapprouver les uns les autres. L'on ne peut se passer de ce même monde que l'on n'aime point, et dont on se moque. (La Bruyère 206)

With this slice of—and slicing into—Parisian life, the moralist focuses on the cynicism of the social machine. La Bruyère transmits loudly and clearly the silence with which the scene is set and reset, as well as the force of the unspoken invitation which is in fact a challenge. The Parisians, in the manner of dancers engaged in some stern and solemn choreography, look each other in the face to elicit and to proffer mutual disapproval—a disapproval predicated, of course, on the supposedly willing participation of the inferior being, the one being looked at and judged.

The term that perhaps best characterizes this phenomenon is *concours*, which in maintaining the complex etymological heritage of its latin origin (*concurrere*: to run together; to clash), can express simultaneously the notions of complicity and antagonism. In fact, La Bruyère will use this very term in writing of the *lieux d'un concours général*. On the one hand, he refers to the places of public frequentation, the Tuileries, the Cours-la-Reine and Vincennes, for example, and on the other, to the place of competition where

l'on s'attend au passage réciproquement dans une promenade publique; l'on y passe en revue l'un devant l'autre: carrosse, chevaux, livrées, armoires, rien n'échappe aux yeux, tout est curieusesment ou malignement observé et, selon le plus ou moins de l'équipage, ou l'on respecte les personnes, ou on les dédaigne.(La Bruyère 206)

It is in these places of competition that the *cliques* and *claques* assemble to pass judgment. Conversation takes on the character of stage dialogue and serves primarily to distinguish and dominate, to divide and segregate. The content of the discourse signifies less than its actual enunciation. In deference to the code, one talks for the sake of talking; or one talks for the benefit of the chance, but public, interlocutors who in turn raise the volume of their own discourse for the benefit of their own chance audience. This talk is punctuated by obvious gestures and the whole thing is solemnly repeated: "l'on passe et l'on repasse" (La Bruyère 207).

The ritual is at bottom an exclusionary one. Each *clique* cultivates its own garden; and in the manner of independent states within the city ("petites républiques"), these states establish borderlines across which the non-initiate is enjoined from stepping. Excluded from the discourse of the group, the unwitting interloper, especially one exhibiting superior, that is, threatening, qualities can do nothing right. La Bruyère writes, for example, of the woman who happens onto the scene, onto this stage, and does not strike the fancy of the *joyeuse bande*. She is doomed to reap scorn not only for the tone of her voice, but for her silence, for her shape, her face, her clothing, her entrances and her exits. Nor is this exclusionary feature trained uniquely on the outsider. It is already endemic to the "petite république" which, like some host organism, incubates the germs of disruption and division years before their public manifestation: "il y a toujours, dès la première année, des semences de division pour rompre dans celle qui doit suivre." What had started out as modest extravagance "degenerates" into "des pyramides de viandes et en banquets somptueux" (La Bruyère 208). These pyramids, the image of which already evokes death, will, however, retain no nuance of the monumental. Once it has received the *coup de grâce* (or is it the *coup de fourchette*?), the "republic" is no more spoken of than "les mouches de l'année passée." No more than last year's false beauty spots—or perhaps it is indeed last year's flies—flies that one cannot help but see devouring the forgotten, rotten discards from those pyramids of meat.

On a less spectacular, but no less pointed and effective level, the ethic of accretion and of conspicuous display prods members of families to pull together, to pool their resources (and their horses) to guarantee public approbation. This compliance with prevailing social pressures, while assuring the desired effect, namely, the "triumph" on the Cours-la-Reine or in the Vincennes forest, puts the family in question, the Crispins, on a par with a certain Jason who is in the process of bankrupting himself ("qui se ruine"). The same expression, *se ruiner*, appears in another fragment concerning those who, recently come into their inheritance, unwittingly put on a clown show for the city by putting on princely airs and ornament: "Par une dépense excessive et un faste ridicule [ils excitent] la raillerie de toute la ville qu'ils croient éblouir, et se ruinent ainsi à faire moquer de soi" (La Bruyère 211-12). And if some ruin themselves to the amusement of all Paris, others do it on the local stage only, i.e., in their own neighborhood, "le seul théâtre de leur vanité." In such cases, the *nouveau riche* bankrupts himself "obscurément" and for the benefit of "deux ou trois personnes qui ne l'estiment point" (La Bruyère 212). What is more, the happy few do not even hold their benefactor in high regard; and if he rides today in a fine carriage, in six months, La Bruyère observes, he will not even have the means to go on foot.

To go on foot: the notion is close to the heart of the moralist who at the end of this chapter on the city makes a critical comparison of the middle class Parisians of his day and their ancestors. The latter, he tells us, not only never learned the art of going without the necessities in order to permit themselves the superfluities, they never even saw the point of going for a carriage ride after a bad dinner. After all, "ils se persuadaient que l'homme avait des jambes pour marcher et ils marchaient." (La Bruyère 219). They walked, and their walking was in step with a lifestyle which, when viewed through the lense of nostalgia, would valorize the proportion, common sense, moderation and calm of the *anciens* while ridiculing the dissipation, exaggeration and frantic ineptitude of the *modernes*. And if from these and the other excesses La Bruyère spotlights in the 22 fragments on Paris could be precipitated a common feature, it might be something like dreariness. There is perhaps a certain liveliness in the activities of La Bruyère's Parisians, but there is no real life. The provocation of upward mobility and the jealousies fueling it, the demands of vanity, hardened by the competitiveness of the public stage make for a full, but ultimately vain and empty calendar.

Nowhere is this dour vision of things put more on display than in the portrait La Bruyère makes of the character he pointedly names Narcissus. The hero of this portrait is a modish social butterfly whose sole *raison d'être* is to be always in the right places at the right time and in the right togs. There is not the slightest wrinkle or blemish in his regime. And as La Bruyère puts it in a chillingly deadpan way: "Il fera demain ce qu'il fait aujourd'hui et ce qu'il fit hier; et il meurt ainsi après avoir vécu" (La Bruyère 213).

If I may be allowed, by way of extrapolation and synthesis, to draw something of a conclusion from these three disparate texts, we may see in them a narrative trajectory that takes us from the extremes of Saint-Amant and Boileau, to a kind of middle position in La Bruyère. Whereas Saint-Amant sees Paris as something of an earthly paradise where pleasure is defined and assured, Boileau will see the city as nothing short of hell on earth. It is the place where moral rectitude has been so beset and artistic orthodoxy so set on its ear that imprecation and flight become the only viable responses. For La Bruyère, unflinching observer maintaining a certain artistic distance from his subject, Paris would be that place where the pains and cares are not only ongoing, but, in their own especially cruel way, bearable.

Notes

1 Saint-Amant, *Œuvres poétiques*, ed. Léon Vérane (Paris: Garnier, 1930) 8-9.

2 Boileau-Despréaux, *Satires*, ed. Albert Cahen, Société des Textes Français Modernes (Paris: Droz, 1932) 22.

3 La Bruyère, *Les Caractères* (Paris: Garnier, 1962) 216.

Marie-Paule Laden

La Correspondance entre Belle de Zuylen et Constant d'Hermenches, ou comment être soi-même sans sortir de l'ordre

J'ecris par ce que je ne puis faire autre chose.

Depuis la publication de ses *Œuvres complètes*,[1] Isabelle de Charrière (1740-1805) est sortie de l'oubli. Cependant, si ses principaux romans, ainsi que sa correspondance avec Benjamin Constant sont l'objet d'études[2] et d'articles divers, les lettres qu'elle échange avec Constant d'Hermenches ne semblent pas avoir retenu les lecteurs. On peut s'étonner que ces lettres (maintenant facilement accessibles) soient négligées au moment où fleurissent les études consacrées à l'écriture épistolaire en général, et au roman féminin en particulier.

On peut en effet tirer de la correspondance clandestine entre Madame de Charrière, alors Belle de Zuylen, et Constant d'Hermenches, de multiples exemples illustrant les caractéristiques de l'écriture épistolaire dramatisées dans tous les romans de l'époque: Nécessité d'interrompre les lettres et d'écrire la nuit pour éviter d'être découverte, difficulté de faire parvenir ses lettres à d'Hermenches et de recevoir les siennes, demandes réitérées de brûler les lettres, exhortations à la prudence, etc... On peut dire sans exagération que les lettres qu'échangent Isabella van Serooskerken van Tuyll et David-Louis baron Constant de Rebecque, dit Constant D'Hermenches, de 17 ans son aîné, oncle du plus célèbre membre de la famille Constant et ami de Voltaire; on peut dire que cette correspondance qui s'étale sur une quinzaine d'années (Belle a vingt ans lorsqu'elle commence), se lit comme un roman de Richardson ou de Crébillon, dont l'établissement de l'héroïne constituerait l'intrigue. Le chassé-croisé de la douzaine de prétendants—les "épouseurs," comme les appelle Belle—et les diverses péripéties qui entourent son mariage, étant bien plus romanesques que tous ses romans réunis.

Rien ne manque au tableau: la personnalité D'Hermenches en premier lieu; Colonel d'un régiment suisse en Hollande, et dont la réputation n'est guère meilleure que celle d'un Valmont ou d'un Lovelace. Réputation que Belle n'ignore pas, et qui peut expliquer la réserve des premières lettres: "J'entends répéter que vous êtes le plus dangereux des hommes... J'écris pour vous faire plaisir et me justifier" (1: 127). On croirait entendre Mme de Tourvel. Tout comme Valmont et Lovelace, Hermenches perçoit bien que le fait de la correspondance prime son contenu; c'est pourquoi il déploie un savant mélange d'éloquence et de flatterie ("pour votre stile et la justesse de votre Esprit je vous mets de pair avec Voltaire, et Mme de Sévigné," 1: 157) pour engager Belle à poursuivre l'échange; avec succès, bien sûr: "Vous m'avez juré que je ne courois aucun risque, qu'il n'y avoit pas plus de danger a vous parler ou a vous écrire qu'a penser, eh bien je veux vous en croire quoique dans cette occasion votre parole ne paroisse pas un garant bien sur" (1: 120).

De façon caractéristique (c'est-à-dire, qui n'étonnera aucun lecteur de roman), Belle consacre ses premières lettres à dire qu'elle n'écrira pas ("Je ne cesse de donner les plus fortes raisons pour ne pas écrire et j'écris toujours," 1: 138); à demander qu'on brûle ses lettres ("a propos que faites vous de mes lettres? les brulez-vous?" 1: 365; "Brulez-les vite Monsieur et oubliez-les, mes craintes semblent leur donner plus de sens qu'elles n'en ont," 1: 119); à supplier qu'on ne lui réponde pas tout en indiquant plusieurs moyens de faire parvenir les réponses! ("Ce billet ne demande aucune reponse et je n'en attends point, si cependant il vous prenoit envie d'en faire une, adressez le couvert [c'est-à-dire, l'enveloppe] a Mme Geelvinck a la maison mortuaire de Mme de Delen . . . ," 1: 118-19).

La première partie de la correspondance entre Belle et Hermenches est d'ailleurs inscrite sous le signe de ce que Janet Altman a appelé "l'épistolarité,"[3] c'est-à-dire la conscience qu'ont les participants de l'échange épistolaire de lire et d'écrire. Belle se plaint même "d'une correspondance qui ne signifie rien, de lettres qui jusqu'ici ne parlent que des lettres mêmes" (1: 138). On dirait déjà l'amorce du cercle infernal que décrira Kafka à Grete Bloch en 1913: "et le pire, c'est qu'ensuite on échange des lettres qui ne traitent de rien d'autre que de la correspondance, des lettres vides, gaspilleuses de temps, dont tout le sens consiste à illustrer le tourment que représente une correspondance."[4] La relation épistolaire unissant Belle à Hermenches ne tourne cependant pas sur elle-même; nos protagonistes ont plutôt le sentiment de participer à une tradition épistolaire, sentiment perceptible à travers les multiples références à Voltaire, Mme de Sévigné, *La Nouvelle Héloïse* et autres romans de l'époque. Hermenches constitue, à cet égard, un bel exemple de ce que Roger Duchaîne[5] appelle un "écrivain épistolaire," c'est-à-dire celui dont les lettres, à travers un destinataire donné, s'adressent à un public plus large. Les exhortations de Belle pour qu'Hermenches brûle ses lettres ne relèvent donc pas uniquement de l'interdit moral qui pèse sur leur liaison, elle revendique aussi la position de "l'épistolier" pour qui les lettres doivent demeurer privées.

On pourrait multiplier les exemples; mon propos n'est cependant pas d'insister sur l'aspect exemplaire ou conventionnel de cette correspondance,[6] mais de dégager ce qui la fait sortir de la norme, ce qui appartient en propre à la future Mme de Charrière. Si l'on replace la phrase mise en exergue à cette étude dans son contexte, on s'aperçoit que loin de se plaindre du sort réservé à son sexe, Belle de Zuylen gourmande Constant d'Hermenches; elle lui écrit pour lui reprocher d'avoir manqué une des rares occasions qu'ils auraient eues de se voir en omettant de se rendre chez son oncle. (Signalons au passage que durant la quinzaine d'années que dure leur correspondance, Belle et Hermenches ne se voient que deux ou trois fois; ce n'est que dans ses lettres qu'Hermenches rencontrera véritablement Belle.)

"Me voici la plume à la main, elle ira cette plume au gré d'une tête folle; ne vous attendez pas a voir de la raison; ne croyez pas que j'écrive pour vous faire plaisir; j'ecris par ce que je ne puis faire autre chose. [Il est deux ou trois heures du matin et toute la maisonnée est endormie.] Non en verité je ne songe guere a vous faire plaisir, vous ne meritez pas de grandes attentions je suis mecontente" (1: 209). Cet extrait illustre bien le rapport qui finit par s'établir entre Belle et Hermenches: Belle mène la ronde; lorsqu'elle n'est pas le sujet de ses lettres, elle morigène Hermenches.

Malgré le pouvoir énorme que ses lettres confèrent à Hermenches, et en dépit de l'importance que Belle semble attacher à l'opinion ("Songez que ni mes parens ni le public ne me pardoneroient jamais cette etourderie [c'est-à-dire la correspondance] s'ils venoient a la savoir et soyez aussi discret que prudent je vous en conjure" [1: 119], implore-t-elle dès la première lettre à Hermenches), il apparaît bien vite que cette dépendance qu'elle professe à l'égard de l'autorité parentale et sociale, se double d'un autre discours qui vise à mettre en cause les valeurs sur lesquelles la société a son assise. Cette ambivalence s'exprime dès la deuxième lettre: "et pour ce qui s'apelle bienseance comme elle n'est fondée que sur l'opinion je ne vois pas grand mal a la violer lorsque cela n'alarme point la vertu, ni ne trouble le bon ordre" (1: 120). Il s'agit, bien sûr, pour Belle, de justifier cette correspondance illicite aux yeux de son correspondant aussi bien qu'aux siens propres; car il faudra quelques années (quatre ans) avant qu'Hermenches ne devienne le confident, le double devant qui elle pourra, comme elle le dit, "deployer son cœur" (1: 217). Mais de façon plus profonde, cette phrase annonce déjà un des thèmes sur lesquels reviendra avec une insistance presque obsessive, l'auteur des *Lettres de Lausanne*, des *Lettres neuchâteloises*, et de *Trois Femmes* (pour ne citer que les principaux romans). Comme certaines de ses héroïnes, mais de façon moins masquée, Belle exprime ici son refus de vivre dans l'opinion d'autrui tout en affirmant son allégeance à la règle sociale.

Au départ Hermenches est pour Belle à la fois L'Autre, la loi et celui qui lui permet de transgresser cette loi au moyen de chaque lettre. Il est donc à la fois l'obstacle et l'instrument de la révolte de Belle. C'est ce qu'elle exprime on ne peut plus clairement lorsqu'elle lui rappelle que c'est elle qui, violant toutes les règles de l'étiquette, l'a invité à danser lors de leur première rencontre: "Je veux que vous me sachiez gré d'avoir fait les premieres avances. Vous souvenez-vous chez le Duc? il y a quatre ans? Vous ne me remarquiez pas mais je vous vis; je vous parlai la premiere 'Monsieur vous ne dansez pas?' pour engager la conversation" (1: 222).

Quelle belle occasion de "violer la bienséance" sans "alarmer la vertu." On aurait tort d'assimiler la déclaration de Belle à la casuistique d'un Des Grieux; c'est le fondement de sa personnalité qui s'exprime ici, son rapport à la loi sociétale qui peut se résumer en une simple formule: révolte et respect de l'ordre, révolte et mesure. La correspondance avec Hermenches est le lieu idéal où peut s'exprimer cette ambiguïté vis-à-vis du système social. C'est dans ses lettres que se dévoile l'écart entre son refus de l'ordre fallacieux des préjugés et son désir de remplir des valeurs qui se définissent en creux. Il s'agit en effet d'être meilleur que la loi, de redonner un sens à des valeurs qui se sont érodées, telle la vertu: "Que la signification des mots décence, et pudeur, est arbitraire! que les idées touchant la vertu sont diferentes!" (1: 291). Or cette révision des valeurs ne peut, paradoxalement, passer que par une transgression de la loi symbolique. L'équivoque de sa correspondance avec Hermenches fournit à Belle l'occasion de l'effraction infinie, chaque lettre fonctionnant comme une répétition de la première rencontre. Elle insiste souvent sur le fait que ses lettres constituent une entorse au lien social, une transgression que chaque missive lui permet de réitérer: "L'air assuré de vertu que je prends en parlant de notre liaison et de notre correspondance est un air hipocrite; dans le fond elle n'est pas toujours si inocente" (1: 365). C'est d'ailleurs ce qu'on pourrait appeler sa conscience de l'effraction qui explique que la correspondance se poursuive pendant tant d'années alors qu'ils ne se voient pour ainsi dire jamais. On pourrait même dire qu'elle ne se poursuit que parce qu'il ne se voient pas; non pas parce que la lettre pallie à l'absence, comme pour la religieuse portugaise, mais parce qu'elle réitère une rupture avec l'ordre, rupture qui permettra à Belle de faire d'Hermenches le confident de ses désirs et de ses ambitions.

Hermenches est le confident idéal, en raison de sa réputation de libertin, sans doute, mais aussi parce qu'étant déjà marié, il ne pourra jamais prétendre au rang des "épouseurs." Il représente donc à la fois le risque et la sécurité. L'équivoque de sa position apparaît de façon éclatante lorsqu'il imagine de faire épouser à Belle son meilleur ami le marquis de Bellegarde, personnage superficiel et falot, incapable d'aligner deux phrases: "Je suis un peu fachée que mon ortographe soit plus correcte que celle du Marquis, mais cela vient de ce qu'il est si grand seigneur" (1: 220), remarque Belle avec humour; Hermenches le décrit cependant à Belle comme "un etre bien rare, par la verité de son caractere et la noblesse de ses sentiments, il est filosofe, il est gai, il â de l'esprit, il sait bien la musique" (1: 206).

Il suffit de remarquer que c'est son propre portrait que peint ici Hermenches pour comprendre que le mariage qu'il envisage pour Belle lui permettrait en fait de transformer leur échange épistolaire en mariage par procuration; car si Belle pouvait échapper à la tutelle de ses parents rien ne s'opposerait plus à ce qu'il la voie à son gré. C'est d'ailleurs ce qu'il exprime dans sa lettre du 12 août 1764: "Je vous verrai au moins a mon aise, je jouirai de votre amitié, de votre esprit, de vos consolations; si jamais je me suis fais une idée du bonheur sur cette terre, c'est en pensant que nous vivrons en societé, et que nous allons faire un trio de parfaite intimité tel qu'aucun poete n'a jamais osé l'imaginer encore" (1: 239-40)! Quelques années plus tard, après l'échec du projet de mariage avec son ami, Hermenches rêve encore au moyen d'épouser Belle par le truchement d'un autre: "Que mon fils n'a t il quatre ans de plus ma Chere Agnes et une compagnie aux gardes! je vous l'offrirois pour votre mari, ne pouvant vous epouser vous seriés au moins ma belle fille" (2: 71).

La position de Belle pendant l'épisode Bellegarde n'est guère moins ambiguë que celle d'Hermenches. Son rôle revient à celui d'un agent double: nous la voyons complotant activement avec Hermenches pour rendre le mariage possible tout en défendant passionnément le point de vue de ses parents dont la première réaction est, bien entendu, de s'opposer à cette union avec un Catholique. Comment expliquer l'engouement de Belle pour le marquis de Bellegarde, ou du moins, l'énergie extraordinaire qu'elle déploie pendant près de quatre ans pour persuader ses parents d'agréer à ce mariage? Ne va-t-elle pas jusqu'à rédiger elle-même la lettre de demande en mariage qu'enverra Hermenches à son père? C'est elle aussi qui s'informera auprès d'un évêque de la procédure à suivre pour obtenir une dispense du Pape. Toutes ces questions dépassent le marquis qui se bornera à insister sur les 100,000 Florins de la dot qu'il juge nécessaires pour redorer son blason. On s'expliquerait difficilement son enthousiasme pour un individu dont les lettres sont d'une platitude si affligeante (elle qui éconduira un prétendant parce qu'il n'a pas lu *Cinna*, et qui attache si peu d'importance aux quartiers de noblesse) si l'arrivée du marquis dans la ronde des "épouseurs" ne transformait complètement le rapport épistolaire entre Belle et Hermenches.

C'est à partir du moment où Hermenches se transforme en intermédiaire entre Belle et Bellegarde qu'elle se déprend de toute réserve à son égard, qu'elle lui "ouvre son cœur dans tous ses replis" (1: 217), et qu'elle se met à insister sur les exigences de sa sensualité: "Si j'aimois si j'etois libre il me seroit bien dificile d'être sage. Mes sens sont comme mon cœur et mon esprit, avides de plaisirs… Si je n'avois ni Pere ni Mere je serois Ninon peut-être, mais plus delicate et plus constante je n'aurois pas tant d'amants" (1: 217). Ou encore, un an plus tard: "Je ne puis plus suporter le celibat, c'est a dire le celibat dans sa rigueur car vivre sans mari et sans aucune gene n'est point un etat horrible" (1: 446). Il n'y a plus de sujets que Belle n'osera aborder dans ses lettres à Hermenches. C'est ainsi que dans une lettre qui a choqué Ph. Godet,[7] le premier biographe de Mme de Charrière, elle demande à Hermenches de la rassurer sur les implications pour sa descendance, du passé libertin du marquis: "Pouvez vous me rassurer sur les horribles suites que le libertinage peut avoir sur une femme et des enfans?" (1: 358). Dans la même lettre, elle s'inquiète même de savoir s'il reste assez d'énergie au marquis pour satisfaire une sexualité de 24 ans: "J'ai trouvé lorsqu'on a dit 47 ans que la diference d'age etait trop grande… Vous avez beau dire d'Hermanches j'ai des sens, mes desirs ne peuvent s'y tromper, dans dix ans j'en aurai peut-être encore. Je voudrai alors comme je voudrois aujourd'hui tout en prechant l'imortalité de l'ame caresser mon disciple, recevoir des caresses pour prix de mes sermons, et aprés avoir annoncé les pures joyes du ciel, eprouver les voluptés de la terre" (1: 358). C'est, nous le voyons, dans les lettres de cette période (1764-68) que Belle sort enfin de cet état de division et de sujétion dans lequel la maintenaient l'austérité des mœurs hollandaises et sa conscience filiale.

Il est important de s'arrêter un instant sur ce que représente exactement pour Belle le marquis de Bellegarde pour comprendre, non seulement la nature du rapport qui finit par se tisser entre Belle et Hermenches, mais aussi son rapport au monde. Bellegarde est en premier lieu celui qui alimente les lettres, celui qui attise le feu de la correspondance, comme elle le dit elle-même: "Si le marquis n'etoit pas au monde, aprés notre correspondance aprés ce feu qu'elle a pris depuis quelque tems, aprés tous ces aveux, je me croirois dans vos mains, et si je ne mettois des mers entre vous et moi il ne dependroit apparemment que de vous de me voir la plus foible des femmes" (1: 300). La présence du marquis (au nom prédestiné!) ne favorise donc l'intimité de l'échange que parce qu'il est aussi le pare-feu, l'écran qui permet à la correspondance de se poursuivre: "Mais sans le marquis jamais il n'y auroit eu ces lettres, ces aveux; car de m'en fier a la vertu… ce seroit avoir deja perdu la tête" (1: 300-01). On s'en est déjà aperçu, Belle ne fait pas grande confiance à la vertu, du moins à ce que l'on entend par ce mot lorsqu'on l'applique aux femmes.

On comprend donc mieux pourquoi Belle tient tant à Bellegarde malgré la platitude affligeante de ses lettres, et en dépit de son air de gentilhomme sur le retour. Il est celui qui lui permettra de voir Hermenches tout en la protégeant de lui: "Si je ne suis pas a votre ami si toujours je m'occupe de vous je serai un jour votre maitresse a moins que nous n'habitions les bouts opposés du monde" (1: 308). Mais il est surtout l'image, le reflet du contrat épistolaire, un signifiant disponible, un vide que l'on peut remplir à son gré, un peu comme les valeurs. Au fond Bellegarde fonctionne comme une lettre, il est pure médiation, à la fois terrain d'échange et écran. Ce que nous avons pu apercevoir de sa personnalité s'accorde d'ailleurs admirablement à ce "no man's land" qu'est l'épistolaire. En dépit des flots d'encre qu'il fait couler, le marquis n'est donc qu'un prétexte, une fiction, un personnage créé de toutes pièces par Belle; on pourrait même dire qu'il est une des créations romanesques les plus riches du futur écrivain.

Notes

[1] Isabelle de Charrière, *Œuvres complètes*, 10 vols. (Amsterdam: G.A. van Oorschot; Genève: Slatkine, 1979-84). Toutes les citations seront tirées de cette édition et les références seront signalées dans le texte. L'orthographe des épistoliers sera respectée.

[2] Voir l'ouvrage de C.P. Courtney, *A Preliminary Bibliography of Isabelle de Charrière* (Oxford: The Voltaire Foundation, 1980), auquel nous ajouterons quelques études plus récentes: "*Trois Femmes": le monde de Madame de Charrière* (Genève: Slatkine, 1981), d'Alix Deguise; "The Novels of Isabelle de Charrière, or, A Woman's Work is Never Done," *Studies in Eighteenth-Century Culture* 14 (1985)299-306, de Susan Jackson; " 'Quel aimable et cruel petit livre': Madame de Charrière's *Mistriss Henley*," *French Forum* 11 (1986) 289-99, de Marie-Paule Laden; *Madame de Charrière, les premiers romans* (Paris: Champion; Genève: Slatkine, 1987), de Sigyn Minier; et, plus récemment, un numéro spécial de *Eighteenth-Century Life*, 13 (1989), édité par Béatrice Fink et consacré exclusivement à Madame de Charrière.

[3] Janet Altman, *Epistolarity: Approaches to a Form* (Columbus: Ohio State UP, 1982).

[4] Cité par Vincent Kaufmann dans son beau livre sur *L'Equivoque épistolaire* (Paris: Minuit, 1990) 67.

[5] Roger Duchaîne, "Du destinataire au public: les métamorphoses d'une correspondance," *Revue d'Histoire Littéraire de la France* 76 (1976) 29-46.

[6] Sur l'aspect conventionnel de la lettre au dix-huitième siècle, voir en particulier Laurent Versini, *Le Roman épistolaire* (Paris: PUF, 1979) et Ruth Perry, *Women, Letters and The Novel* (New York: AMS, 1980).

[7] Voir *Madame de Charrière et ses amis, d'après de nombreux documents inédits*, 2 vols. (Genève: Jullien, 1906).

François Rigolot

Bridging Literary Generations: Sainte-Beuve's Romantic *Tableau* of the Renaissance

> Dans les critiques que nous faisons, nous jugeons moins les autres que nous ne nous jugeons nous-mêmes.
>
> Sainte-Beuve[1]

In August 1826, the French Academy offered a prize for an essay to be written on the progress of French language and literature from the beginning of the sixteenth century to 1610. Encouraged by his fellow Boulonnais, Pierre Daunou, Charles Augustin Sainte-Beuve, still a medical student, decided to compete for the award. But in February 1827, immersed in the discovery of the authors of the period, he was invited by Victor Hugo to the latter's reading of the *Préface de Cromwell* at the house of Emile Deschamps. One outcome was that he missed the deadline for the Academic competition (the award would be shared by Philarète Chasles and Saint-Marc Girardin). Another was that his Renaissance studies acquired a range that could not have been foreseen at the outset. The series of articles he composed for *Le Globe* was later published in the form of an ambitious book, the *Tableau historique et critique de la poésie française et du théâtre français au XVIe siècle* (principal editions: 1828, 1843 and 1876).[2]

Interestingly enough, Sainte-Beuve, who discovered Pierre de Ronsard at the same time he did Victor Hugo, chose Joachim du Bellay's position: his *Tableau* became the *Deffence et Illustration* of the Romantic *Cénacle*, the group of writers who rejected the neo-classical canon. Literary history took the form of a manifesto. Scholarly research and nostalgia for works of the past simply became a pretext for promotion of the modern school. At the beginning of the *Tableau*, Sainte-Beuve openly admitted that he had lost no opportunity of connecting his Renaissance studies to the literary questions stirring in his own time (1: 3).

In claiming sixteenth-century ancestry, Romanticism, instead of defining itself in the negative terms of rejecting the canon, restored a historical continuity that had been disrupted by the negativity of neo-classicism. The new periodization made *le grand siècle* appear as a simple episode, a sort of intermission, or a parenthesis opened within the French national tradition. According to Sainte-Beuve, "Cette fête monarchique de Louis XIV, célébrée à Versailles entre la Ligue et la révolution de 89, nous fait l'effet de ces courts et capricieux intermèdes qui ne se rattachent point à l'action du drame" (2: 38).[3]

Renaissance literature had been, by no means, completely forgotten during the seventeenth and eighteenth centuries, although much of its production had receded behind the great "masterpieces" of the neo-classical age as unfinished, unpolished and somehow immature literary sketches. Harsh judgments had been passed on Ronsard's style by Malherbe and Boileau; Rabelais's "vulgarity" had been held in contempt by La Bruyère and Voltaire; and Montaigne's self-centeredness had been condemned on moral grounds by Pascal. Although the eighteenth-century *philosophes* applauded the great Renaissance geniuses, they were unanimously troubled by their lack of clarity and "good taste."[4]

In the early 1800s the renewal of interest for the sixteenth century coincided with the revival of political history in official academic circles. Retrospectively, François Villemain's biography of Michel de l'Hôpital (1812) or Charles de Lacretelle's four-volume *History of France during the Religious Wars* (1814-1816) seem to have a foreshadowing effect on Alexandre Dumas's first "Romantic" drama (*Henri III et sa cour*, 1829) and Mérimée's first historical fiction (*Chronique du règne de Charles IX*, 1830). Even for Philarète Chasles, Sainte-Beuve's competitor for the Académie prize, Renaissance literary style is second to political considerations and therefore can only be understood in terms of the history of the period. In his diary, kept in English, he wrote: "I am preparing my *Essai on the sixteenth century History.* . . . My plan is to show how public manners, their variations, the deep passions of fanaticism, and zeal, and the changes of politics have altered the style of writing."[5]

Obviously the Renaissance appealed to the nineteenth-century imagination. It offered the Romantics a pseudo-historical framework in which to effect a "return to the origin" and justify their own esthetics. By means of the "old poets," the Romantic orphans were conducting a touching search for literary paternity. For them the "Pléiade" was a historical prefiguration of their own literary circle, the "Cénacle." As a locus of limitless possibilities, the sixteenth century had also to be the scene of every kind of failure. The theme of abortion underlies almost all writing on the subject. Ronsard's language is "prématuré," "né avant terme"; the Pléiade is "notre première poésie avortée." The sixteenth century as a whole is "un premier printemps trop tôt intercepté."[6] But this

Spring had its inspired hour. Its faults are ultimately redeemed by the extraordinary vitality of an immoderate, chaotic, in a word, *Hugolian*, period.

For Sainte-Beuve, the Renaissance—which he equated with the sixteenth century—was but the rough draft of another, polished and finished text, that of *le grand siècle*, an ordered mental universe where the "Classic," within the "Romantic" soul, had comfortably established residence.[7] This myth of the "grand siècle" presupposed a historical explanation, and it is not surprising that the literary "physiologist" should look for one in an eminently sensible location: the preceding century. In his *Cahier brun* Sainte-Beuve wrote: "Ce que je voudrais constituer, c'est l'histoire naturelle littéraire. . . . Ce que je fais, c'est de l'histoire naturelle littéraire. Etre en histoire littéraire, en critique, un disciple de Bacon, ce serait ma gloire."[8] The Renaissance thus became the immediate cause of classicism; it had seen the birth of printing and the disorderly diffusion of texts both ancient and modern; it explained and justified the masterpieces of the neo-classical age.

This postulate, which would prove a fruitful and enduring tenet of criticism, is clearly formulated in an 1827 article on La Fontaine: "La littérature du Siècle de Louis XIV repose sur la littérature française du seizième siècle."[9] Understanding Racine would be impossible without some familiarity with Jodelle and Garnier; so Molière is obscure without Rabelais; Boileau, if we forget Malherbe and, before Malherbe, Ronsard, Desportes and Regnier. This argument reappears in *Port-Royal*: La Fontaine is seen as forging the bond between the two centuries, a sixteenth-century poet in the seventeenth century:[10]

On a ce nom de La Fontaine sans cesse à la bouche quand on parle de nos vieux poètes, dont il fut, en quelque sorte, le dernier et le plus parfait. (*Tableau* 1: 130)

Quant au bon La Fontaine, lui qui se trouvait partout à l'aise, ne l'eût-il pas été plus qu'ailleurs en cette vieille France dont il garda les manières et le ton jusque sous Louis XIV? (*Tableau* 1: 186)

The same preoccupation is evident in his study of the theater: five periods are seen as reproducing the *ideal evolutionary schema* which leads, via the sixteenth and early seventeenth centuries, to those perfect—that is, French—masterpieces that are the plays of Molière and Racine. We recognize here a rationalist presupposition originating in the eighteenth century, that of "natural progress" and of "historical perfectibility" (*Tableau* 2: 360). Readers in the centuries to come will follow suit: lacking any real inherent value, the sixteenth century becomes only the *rough draft* of the *grand siècle*.

At times, however, the rough draft will indeed be judged as an inspired one: such is Rabelais. The Romantic in Sainte-Beuve is dazzled by this "œuvre inouïe," underlining through such a reaction the essential ambiguity of a work that "vous saisit et vous déconcerte, vous enivre et vous dégoûte" (*Tableau* 2: 6). Demolished is the legend of a bawdy Rabelais. The "Anacreon of Touraine" emerges from his arbor of vines (*Tableau* 2: 7); feasts of "style" are what actually interest the connoisseur of marrow. He writes, in 1850: "La débauche de Rabelais se passait surtout dans son imagination et dans son humeur; c'était une débauche de cabinet."[11] "Jamais la langue, jusque-là, ne s'était trouvée à pareille fête" (*Causeries* 3: 3). Sainte-Beuve finds in Rabelais's writing this "great feast," this "orgy" of the senses denied him in life. It is the orphan's "réveillon de Noël" (*Tableau* 2: 8-9).

Like Alcofrybas himself forbidding hypocrites to enter the Abbey of Thélème, Sainte-Beuve curses scholars who disturb the Pantagruelian banquet. Before Leo Spitzer, he leads the war against pedantic erudition: pedants are the kill-joys of style; their crime is to render its practice tiresome, failing in their obligation to "amener le lecteur à s'y plaire" (*Tableau* 2: 9). *Plaire* is indeed the rule of rules. This classic criterion does not in itself exclude erudition, but seeks to relegate it to the realm of the forgotten. Sainte-Beuve would prefer a Rabelais who is "simplement plaisant": Montaigne had been of the same mind.[12]

The myth of the style thus replaces the myth of the man. The "actual Rabelais," reconstituted by the physiologist, is of no interest to him. Gustave Lanson's reproach is foolish.[13] The Rabelais appreciated and prized by Sainte-Beuve is one who displays "le jet abondant et intarissable de [sa] parole."[14] It is an eloquence that, escaping all effort at recuperation, triumphs over every system and form of zealotry: "Je m'imagine que, quand on essaie de le tirer à soi, Rabelais se laisse faire et qu'il y va, mais pour en rire" (*Causeries* 3: 16). In short, Rabelais is not far from merging with the myth he created: that of the good giant, the "franc rieur" who, from his vantage point above the melee, as Pantagruel himself, covers the rank and file of his good readers with his tongue.

Hearty laugher he may be, but whom "good taste" would prefer less unmannerly. Always vigilant in Sainte-Beuve is a censor, formed at the Classical school, who permits only restrained instances of folly. However, the endless escapades of farcical lyricism offer a justification for obscene farce. "Saletés splendides."[15] The oxymoron stigmatizes the ambivalence of a judgment very close, in the end, to that of La Bruyère, a "monstrueux assemblage." Sainte-Beuve will apply this same judgment to the "Grand Siècle" in 1850: "Il y a deux Siècles de Louis XIV" (*Causeries* 1: 460). But the "charm of the rabble" is more acceptable in the sixteenth century than in the seventeenth century, because it is then attributed to good old Gallic naïveté.[16]

It is this "bonne vieille gaieté," at once tempered and brought into relief by a refinement characterized by better taste than found in the Middle ages, that accounts for Marot's charm (*Tableau* 1: 76). Marot, Rabelais, and Marguerite de Navarre, even while cultivating the Ancients, remained simple and natural (*Tableau* 1: 59). Sainte-Beuve admired this ingenuousness, and regretted not finding it in the Pléiade poets. In turning their back on the popular, Ronsard and his friends were at odds with the spirit of the age: "*Odi profanum vulgus* était leur devise, et elle contrastait d'une manière presque ridicule avec la prétention qu'ils affichaient de fonder une littérature nationale" (*Tableau* 1: 95).

According to Sainte-Beuve, whatever the force of the Pléiade poets' talent, we laugh *at* them each time we fail to laugh *with* them. So does Sainte-Beuve pass quickly over Joachim du Bellay's *Regrets* and *Antiquités de Rome*, preferring the satiric verve of the *Poète courtisan*. Again, it is because it is too "learned" that Ronsard's language is doomed to failure. Only his intimate poetry, that written in the "middle style," is really successful: it is Marot perfected, La Fontaine prefigured.[17]

It would not be too much of an exaggeration to say that Rabelais, insofar as he represents farce at its most naïve and vibrant, is the glass through which Sainte-Beuve appreciates the sixteenth century and judges its successes. His lexicon is quite revealing as one can judge from the following sample of quotations: about Clément Marot—"Il était trop *naïvement* de son siècle pour n'en être pas goûté" (*Tableau* 1: 59); about Ronsard and Du Bellay—they are "encore *naïfs* et déjà brillants" (*Tableau* 1: 132); about Jean-Antoine de Baïf—compared with La Fontaine, he had "l'avantange de la naïveté" (*Tableau* 1: 155); about Remy Belleau—he is not quite as successful as his friends for he lacks "simplicité" and "fraîcheur" (*Tableau* 1: 156); about Du Bartas and Desportes: they fail because of their "affectation" (*Tableau* 1: 173-81, 217); about d'Aubigné— his "rudesse grossière" is redeemed by his "sublime énergie" (*Tableau* 1: 242).

Indeed Sainte-Beuve's appreciation of sixteenth-century literature is betrayed by a redundant lexical pattern. The words "candeur," "naturel," and "vigueur" reappear constantly beneath the critic's pen. The Renaissance "bonhomie" is marked by the frequent use of the adjectives "bons" and "vieux" whose affective tonality is reinforced by the first-person possessive pronoun ("notre" and "nos"). Good kings, good bourgeois, and good monks people the stage of our old theater; and our old poets join together to sing, with an often coarse vigor, the song of King Henry.[18]

To Sainte-Beuve the sixteenth-century decor is that of the "painted paradise" envisioned by Villon. *Primus inter pares*, "le bon Louis XII y attrape sa chiquenaude comme les autres" and, behind the scenes, "le bon La Fontaine" takes lessons from the "bon Gaulois Rabelais" (*Tableau* 2: 339; 1: 91, 186). Laughing at human folly, the sixteenth century appears to the nineteenth century as a brotherhood of *Enfants sans souci* (*Tableau* 2: 296). For the satirical spirit, if it exists, is never far removed from a robust jollity. Audacity there is, but it proves a carefree audacity (*Tableau* 1: 234).

Here the sixteenth century diverges clearly from the eighteenth. If the two centuries share a certain taste for encyclopaedic knowledge and for ideas of reform, their "turn of mind" is radically different. Naïveté, in the case of the *philosophes*, can only be affected. The Bayles and Fontenelles make use of it as a strategem; and irony, absent in Rabelais, lurks in Voltaire behind a false ingenuousness.[19] The big-hearted souls of the sixteenth century roar with laughter while the wits of the eighteenth smirk and sneer. An ideal place, with all that this idealism can entail of the monstrous and imperfect, the sixteenth century remains unspoiled by zealotry and the worship of system. It has preserved a "pristine new spirit, *mens novella*."[20]

In Montaigne himself, it is the simply natural man who is the object of Sainte-Beuve's admiration. In writing *Port-Royal*, Sainte-Beuve had set himself to understand Pascal's genius; but instead he was swayed by Montaigne's "natural" greatness: "Montaigne, c'est tout simplement la nature: la nature pure, et civilisée pourtant . . . , la nature au complet sans la grâce" (*Port-Royal* 1: 836) [Bk 3]). Montaigne's skeptic indifference, his "mischievousness" and "slightly teasing trickery," clash with the overall tone of the sixteenth century. "Il y a déjà du Fontenelle chez Montaigne" (*Port-Royal* 2: 258 [Bk 3]).

The author of the *Essais* lacked that rough, "barbaric" force of the Renaissance which would have put him in tune with his century.[21] "La grande singularité de Montaigne, et ce qui fait de lui un *phénomène*, c'est d'avoir été la modération, le ménagement et le tempérament même en un tel siècle" (*Causeries* 4: 81). That vital and naïve force, constitutive of the myth, is missing in him. His withdrawal into himself is "maniaque"; his imitation, "singeresse."[22] Thus is his name virtually absent from the Hall of Fame ("*Tableau* d'Honneur") of the sixteenth century.[23]

The commerce between Sainte-Beuve and Montaigne would itself deserve a detailed study.[24] Certainly "il y a du Montaigne en chacun de nous," but especially in Sainte-Beuve, who no doubt recognizes too much of himself in Montaigne to adopt him as his model. Affinities between Sainte-Beuve and Montaigne are undeniable; they extend from the man to the writer. In the *Nouveaux Lundis*, Sainte-Beuve admits that the essayist and himself have never departed from each other for more than "la longueur d'un ongle" (*Nouveaux Lundis* 6: 25). They are both curious, prudent, repelled by dogmatic thought. What Sainte-Beuve writes about the style of his own C*ritiques et Portraits* could also be written about the style of the *Essais*: "Le véritable ordre est celui dans lequel je les ai écrits, selon mon émotion et mon caprice, et toujours dans la nuance particulière où j'étais moi-même dans le moment."[25] Both critical minds have the same conception of the evanescent course of things ("le passage"): "nous sommes tous mobiles et nous jugeons des êtres mobiles."[26] Yet Montaigne, the Pyrrhonist with "slightly thin nostrils" sends Sainte-Beuve an image of himself that he despises and whose existence he attempts to deny through the purifying admiration of a mythic sixteenth century (see *Port-Royal* 2: 259n1 [Bk 3]).

It is therefore no accident that the *Tableau* ends with a eulogy to La Fontaine and Molière: their works are seen as the epitome, the civilized—that is, redeemed by *good taste*—form of the inspired chaos of the Renaissance. Nothing was more alien, indeed, to the Renaissance mind than "l'équilibre intérieur" and "la possession de soi" which are, for Montaigne, "des valeurs suprêmes."[27]

But it is Rabelais and Montaigne, the century's only two "écrivains complets," who polarize Sainte-Beuve's thought (*Port-Royal* 1: 975). By the light in which he portrays them, they objectify in some fashion the ambivalence residing in the soul of Amaury, Sainte-Beuve's fictional hero in his novel, *Volupté*. The roars of the hearty laugher are met with the chuckle of the doubter (*Causeries* 3: 13; *Port-Royal* 1: 861). Yet we must note that the two writers are not frozen in an unequivocal attitude. Through his piquant language, Montaigne takes part in the tumultuous euphoria of the century's beginning; the Rabelais of 1850 evokes, in some respects, the Montaigne of *Port-Royal*: his laughter loses in heartiness what it gains in skepticism. The Romantic era is closed; for, after the Revolution of 1848, the sixteenth century can never be quite the same.

Notes

[1] Sainte-Beuve, *Pensées et Maximes*, ed. M. Chapelan (Paris: Grasset, 1954) 260.

[2] All references are to the Troubat edition of the *Tableau* (Paris: Lemerre, 1876). Volumes 1 and 2 will be indicated, with proper page numbers, in parentheses within the text.

[3] I have developed this point further in "The Invention of the Renaissance," in *A New History of French Literature*, ed. Denis Hollier et al. (Cambridge: Harvard UP, 1989) 638-44.

[4] See V.-L. Saulnier, "La Réputation de Ronsard au XVIIIème siècle," *Revue Universitaire* (March-April 1947) 20-40; Richard Switzer, "French Renaissance Poetry before Sainte-Beuve," *French Review* 26 (1953) 278-83.

[5] Quoted by Claude Pichois in his *Philarète Chasles et la vie littéraire au temps du romantisme* (Paris: Corti, 1965) 1: 267 ff. (ch. 4).

[6] *Tableau* 1: 125, and "Dédicace" of 1842 (2-3).

[7] See Pierre Moreau, *Le Classicisme des romantiques* (Paris: Plon, 1932), and Raphaël Molho, *L'Ordre et les Ténèbres, ou la Naissance d'un mythe du XVIIème siècle chez Sainte-Beuve* (Paris: Colin, 1972).

[8] These statements were made in 1847 and 1850. They are quoted by Roger Fayolle in his *Sainte-Beuve et le XVIIIème siècle, ou comment les révolutions arrivent* (Paris: Colin, 1972) 43. Hippolyte Taine will confirm this view: "Il [Sainte-Beuve] a importé dans l'histoire morale les procédés de l'histoire naturelle." *Journal des Débats* Oct. 17, 1869, quoted by Pierre Moreau in his *La Critique selon Sainte-Beuve* (Paris: Sedes, 1964) 68.

[9] *Œuvres de Sainte-Beuve*, ed. Maxime Leroy, Bibliothèque de la Pléiade (Paris: Gallimard, 1956) 1: 696.

[10] *Port-Royal*, ed. Maxime Leroy, Bibliothèque de la Pléiade (Paris: Gallimard, 1952) 1: 200 (Bk 1, ch. 6).

[11] "Rabelais's debauchery took place above all in his imagination and whimsy; it was a closet debauchery." *Causeries du Lundi,* in *Œuvres* 3: 3.

[12] *Port-Royal* 1: 835 (Bk 3). "Entre les livres simplement plaisans, je trouve . . . Rabelays . . . digne qu'on s'y amuse" (II, 10, 410). *Les Essais de Michel de Montaigne*, ed. Pierre Villey and V.-L. Saulnier (Paris: PUF, 1978).

[13] In his preface to *Hommes et Livres*, Gustave Lanson accuses Sainte-Beuve of using literary works to write biographies, thus eliminating their intrinsic "literary quality" (quoted by P. Moreau in his *La Critique selon Sainte-Beuve* 11). More recently Gérald Antoine has shown that, on the contrary, Sainte-Beuve could be seen as the father of stylistic criticism. *Sainte-Beuve et la critique contemporaine. Actes du Colloque de Liège (6-8 octobre 1969)* (Paris: Belles-Lettres, 1972).

[14] *Causeries du Lundi* (Paris: Garnier, 1857) 14.

[15] Article on Renan in *Nouveaux Lundis* (Paris: Calmann Lévy, 1879) 2: 401.

[16] Sainte-Beuve quotes Galiani and approves of his critical assessment: "Rabelais's obscenity was simply naïve" (*Tableau* 2: 22n1).

[17] According to Raymond Lebègue, Sainte-Beuve thought Ronsard was but "un Béranger supérieur." *Colloque Sainte-Beuve* (Paris: Armand Colin, 1970) 37.

[18] *Tableau* 2: 299, 310, 291, 374 and 402; 1: 106 and 187; 2: 114-15; *Œuvres* 1: 218; *Tableau* 1: 180. The reference to the song of King Henry is to Molière's *Le Misanthrope*, Act I, scene II.

[19] Bayle, for instance, is portrayed as constantly showing "un étonnement d'érudit qui joue la *naïveté* et couvre la malice" (*Tableau* 1: 315).

[20] This expression is used by Sainte-Beuve about Pierre Charron. See *Causeries du Lundi* 11: 216.

[21] Montaigne was brought up "comme un Emile du XVIème siècle" (*Port-Royal* 1: 836 [Bk 3]).

[22] *Port-Royal* 2: 258 (Bk 3). The word "singeresse" is used by Montaigne about himself in his chapter "Sur des vers de Virgile:" "Or j'ay une condition singeresse et imitatrice" (III, 5, 875).

[23] In his *Tableau* Sainte-Beuve speaks about Montaigne only in relation to other writers, for instance Mathurin Regnier (1: 234-35). The first article on Montaigne dates from 1851 (*Causeries du Lundi* 4); the second, from 1862 (*Nouvelles Causeries du Lundi* 2); the third, from 1863 (*Nouvelles Causeries du Lundi* 6).

[24] Some interesting work has already been done on the subject. See, in particular: Emile Faguet, "Montaigne annoté par Sainte-Beuve," *Revue Latine* 5 (1906) 449-76; and Donald M. Frame, *Montaigne in France: 1812-1852* (New York: Columbia UP 1940) 140-84.

[25] Lettre à Chaudes-Aigues, *Correspondance générale*, ed. J. Bonnerot (Paris: Stock, 1936) 2: 384.

[26] Epigraph to the contemporary *Portraits* of 1868. Both writers also share a particular love for the preposition "selon" as a mark of their relative point of view.

[27] *Nouveaux Lundis* 6: 251. Sainte-Beuve also declares: "J'appelle Montaigne le Français le plus sage qui ait jamais existé" (ibid. 2: 177).

Suzanne Nash

In the Wake of Victor Hugo: The Poetry and Politics of Indebtedness

Two years after Hugo's funeral, in 1887, Emile Zola predicted that France's national poet would have no progeny: "Victor Hugo, qui a traîné derrière lui des cortèges de fidèles, ne laissera pas un disciple pour reprendre et fonder la religion du maître. Tout ce vaste bruit . . . s'éteindra peu à peu autour de l'écrivain mort."[1] Fifty years later Paul Valéry began his radio address commemorating Hugo's death by insisting on his relevance for contemporary debate on poetry:

On prétend que Victor Hugo est mort, et qu'il l'est depuis cinquante ans. . . . Mais un observateur impartial en douterait. Hier encore, on s'attaquait à lui comme à un simple vivant. On essayait de l'exterminer. C'est là une grande preuve d'existence. . . . Quand un écrivain, après un demi-siècle qu'il a disparu, excite encore des discussions passionnées, on peut se reposer du souci de son avenir. . . .[2]

As Valéry suggests, strong writing provokes strong judgments because it requires strong redefinitions; the longer these judgments continue to be made, the more fundamental the redefinitions would seem to be. When a writer's critical energy extends beyond distinct cultural boundaries and time periods, his writing becomes not only an agent for significant change, but a means for understanding the direction of that change itself. One hundred years after his death it is becoming apparent that Victor Hugo's work can no longer be contained within a single cultural moment, as Zola and other important contemporary writers, who were challenging the values which appeared to lie behind high Romantic art, needed to believe. By looking at shifts in the reception of Hugo's poetry since the 1860s—on its assimilation and transmission by Parnassian and Symbolist schools as well as by such major poets and founders of modernism as Baudelaire, Mallarmé, and Valéry, for example—one can better understand certain key issues underlying the creative activity which has accompanied serious cultural redefinitions in our century.

My title, "The Poetry and Politics of Indebtedness," means, on the one hand, to underscore the important difference for contemporary writers between public and private testimonies when the poet in question is a revered national

figure of the colossal proportions of Hugo. On the other hand, it means to
suggest that differences in reception can also reflect shifts in critical bids for a
kind of philosophical authority, that is, in the way the definition of authority is
being implicitly posited. Put another way, the history of Hugo's reception is
also a history of changes in esthetic ideology, in our understanding of the nature
of literary language, how it works, and to what ends.

From the 1840s until his death in 1885, Hugo's every move was news. To
be invited to his table was to be recognized, or, as one poet put it, to receive an
envelope post-marked "Guernsey" meant literary baptism.[3] Nothing seemed to
touch or threaten Hugo's position as poet laureate of France, based as it was on
the adulation of both public and the literary worlds. He was seen by everyone,
even his detractors, as having single-handedly brought the almost dead genre
of lyric poetry back to life; and the breadth, range, and sheer quality of his
production was such that every poet living during his lifetime and in the
generation immediately following felt him there as a kind of hovering presence—setting standards, challenging, defying, intimidating, even absorbing
and redirecting his heirs' achievements for new creations of his own. Somehow, this older poet and mentor always seemed to remain in the avant-garde,
and this, to the annoyance of many serious writers, despite official approval.
His poetry became a kind of source book for what was possible for all poetic
practice. Hugo, of course, saw it that way too. As he wrote in "A un poète," one
of the several *artes poeticae* of *Les Rayons et les ombres* (1839): "Sois petit
comme source et sois grand comme fleuve" (*OC* 6: 74).

It is around this conception of Hugo's work as source and origin of the
modern lyric that I have organized my study of his reception, since the
acknowledgment of a writer as source requires the poet writing in the wake of
that source to redefine or justify his own enterprise. The threat Hugo posed was
that, if he did restore the French lyric to the preeminence it had enjoyed during
the sixteenth century, he may also have brought that tradition to a culmination
once and for all, and this before he was even dead. As Emile Verhaeren said in
1891, "Hugo mort, il a paru que la poésie fut morte."[4] The way individual
poets reacted to or sought to resolve the dilemma posed by Hugo's claim to
both cultural ("fleuve") and divine ("source") authority is more than anecdotal; it tells us the story of fundamental redefinitions taking place in French
cultural history during the post-Romantic and early modernist period.

The debate concerning textual authority which opposed the reproduction
of an original and sacred model to an individual writer's originality came into
being quite inevitably with the development of an historical awareness.[5] By the
nineteenth century and following the Revolution of 1789, this awareness
seemed to permeate all aspects of cultural production in France, even to the
point of determining the genres and distribution of literary representation. One
may speculate that the paradoxical need to see the marginalized, solitary

individual as representative of both historical and sacred truth is related to the fact that the political events following the Revolution of 1789 repeatedly belied the liberal and progressivist ideology underlying eighteenth-century revolutionary thought. In any case, politics and poetics became subtly intertwined both in the symbolic figuration of the artist as Prometheus or Miltonic Satan[6] and in the more seamy jostling for personal recognition which took place in the *cénacles* and literary press of the times. Divine Presence was a memory of what once was and what could be, but its voice could only be heard through a post-lapsarian figure, emerging from the oceanic chaos of history. This figure's heretical gesture of self-divinization conflated, for a brief cultural moment, the opposing notions of Origin and originality and permitted all sorts of worldly aspirations to coexist with messianic function.

Victor Hugo or "Olympio" was the self-appointed prophet for his century, undisputed *chef d'école* and respected statesman right up until the disaster of 1848. In the 1830s lyric poetry, all but dead since the Renaissance, would be the medium for his oracular and educative purpose:

> Peuples! écoutez le poète!
> Ecoutez le rêveur sacré!
> Dans votre nuit, sans lui complète,
> Lui seul a le front éclairé!
> Des temps futurs perçant les ombres,
> Lui seul distingue en leurs flancs sombres
> Le germe qui n'est pas éclos.
> Homme, il est doux comme une femme.
> Dieu parle à voix basse à son âme
> Comme aux forêts et comme aux flots!
> ("Fonction du poète," *Les Rayons et les ombres*)

When he went into exile for twenty years during the reign of Louis Napoleon, he became the disembodied symbol of a lost utopian dream. His authority was thus strengthened by his absence, because he became a living ideal who might return and disprove the apparent failure of the Revolution. During his absence and after the profound disillusionment of the 1848 Revolution, challenges to Hugo's role as spokesman for his time began, nevertheless, to present themselves, but they had Hugo's own, increasingly experimental and increasingly visionary poetry to contend with. If they could ridicule Hugo's claim to Divine authority, they could not deny the extraordinary nature of the texts which flowed steadily across the channel of his exile to lay claim to that authority.

The violence of Hugo's younger contemporaries' reactions may be seen to stem from the fact that, as Maurice Souriau points out, the great poet survived and continued to write well beyond the cultural moment of which he was the spokesman. By the 1850s Romanticism was on the decline, and the utopian and messianic aspects of its production were being challenged on all fronts. But if the temple of Romanticism was losing its stones, there Hugo stood, *pierre de touche* for everyone, insistent figure of authority, "Bête comme l'Himalaya," as Leconte de Lisle was reported to have quipped,[7] commanding attention and admiration with each new work commemorating that outdated vision in a language which never ceased to stupify. One hundred years after his birth, in response to the poll taken in 1902 asking who was the greatest French poet living or dead, it would provoke Gide's exasperated and admiring reply, "Hugo,—hélas!"[8]

At the root of the differences in the reception of Hugo are changes in the understanding of the nature of the creative subject and its relationship to language. For some, Hugo is conceived of as a divinely inspired source, a body of essential truth; for others he is seen as a great forger or master craftsman who, through the lucid manipulation of tools, dismantled the fixedness of French prosody, producing possibilities for new structures within which culturally distinct voices could be heard. In short, for some he was an origin which must be imitated or disproved; for others, his importance lay in his recognition of the historical nature of art, its provisional rootedness in contemporary culture. Hugo himself contributed to both essentialist and historicist versions of himself, since in "Réponse à un acte d'accusation" and many other polemical poems he claims to be the true "originator" of the language appropriate for his century.

Leconte de Lisle, who, ironically, inherited Hugo's seat at the French Academy in 1887, presents an interesting paradox in regard to this question of how other poets conceived of Hugo's authority. He was the first outspoken challenger to Hugo's position as *chef d'école* when he published his inflammatory preface to the *Poèmes antiques* in 1852,[9] declaring war on Romanticism. Flaubert would call that preface a "belle engueulade aux artistes modernes" (cited by Souriau 228). In his effort to dethrone Hugo, Leconte de Lisle felt determined to refute the popular view that Hugo's poetry was the legitimate source of the modern lyric. He wages his *coup d'état* around the central issue of origin and originality in this preface. Never mentioning Hugo's name, he asks his contemporary poets, "Qui vous a conféré le caractère et le langage de l'autorité? . . . Quel dogme sanctionne votre apostolat?" and then asserts that whatever this authority may have appeared to be, it is now meaningless at best and corrupting at worst. Leconte de Lisle sentences it to death. "Allez! vous vous épuisez dans le vide et votre heure est venue. Vous n'êtes plus écoutés" (218).

His own claim to authority is based on his refusal to allow personal feeling or contemporary events to color his language. He writes, not to persuade, but to purify language through its learned evocation of ancient Greek models. Until this purification process takes place, however, poetry cannot be used to educate the public, as Hugo had said that it should: "La Poésie . . . n'enfantera plus d'actions héroïques; elle n'inspirera plus de vertus sociales; parce que la langue sacrée ... réduite ... à ne plus exprimer que de mesquines impressions personnelles, envahie par les néologismes arbitraires, morcelées et profanées, esclave des caprices et des goûts individus, n'est plus apte à enseigner l'homme" (Leconte de Lisle 216-17). Thus, Leconte de Lisle's battle for authority is waged entirely through a revalorization of the concept of the sacred Original and against the contemporary cult of individualized expression: "Il n'est rien de plus inintelligent et de plus triste que cette excitation vaine de l'originalité propre aux mauvaises époques de l'art" (219-20). One must leave the field of political action and personal confession (this the year after the publication of Hugo's *Napoléon le Petit*) to enter the ivory tower of purification through the study of the poets of antiquity—Homer. Aeschylus, Sophocles, "qui représentent la Poésie dans sa vitalité, dans sa plénitude et dans son unité harmonique" (218).[10]

Only the ancient Greek poets can serve as models—the Latin poets and the entire Christian cycle, including Dante, Shakespeare, and Milton, are all corruptions of the great originals. Modern poetry has become a troubled source, a second hand, and morally dangerous art: "La source n'en est pas seulement troublée et souillée, elle est tarie jusqu'au fond. Il faut puiser ailleurs. . . . Rien de moins vivant et de moins original . . . une autolâtrie d'emprunt" (220). In one fell swoop, Leconte de Lisle negates most of French literary history since the Renaissance and presents himself as the forger of a new, clean language.

In so arguing, Leconte de Lisle substitutes one *poet vates* for another, Homer for Hugo, but the idea of the poet as unique and authoritative subject is very much in place in this struggle by one authority to replace another for the official control of language. He takes a position which refuses cultural autonomy to his century at the same time that he redefines genius as the ability of each individual to recreate, through learned processes a perfect imitation of the ancient source. Even more than the Romantics, whom he attacks for their emphasis on personal suffering, this self-styled "impersonal" poet places value in the constitutive genius of the creating subjectivity to carry out his project. Just as the concept of impersonality may disguise a powerfully authoritarian subject, the imperative of detachment from history used to refute Hugo's claim of "artiste civilisateur" disguises a profoundly historical project. The subject of Leconte de Lisle's work, as he himself is proud to point out, is the historic reconstruction of antiquity—its great battles, its myths, its legends. In the Preface to the *Poèmes et Poésies* of 1855, he announces an epic soon to be finished on the heroic and sacred period during which mysterious tribes came from the Orient to inhabit Europe. Here he seems to be engaged in the very *history* which brings the concept of divine origin into a cultural context, alluding, as he apparently is, to the aryan myth of the pure origins of Germany which contemporary philologists were in the process of theorizing.

One should not underestimate today the importance of the Parnassian movement in the development of the French lyric and in the formation of most of the poets whom we consider as founders of modernism. However disingenuous, Rimbaud's letter to Banville in 1870 is a case in point, "Que si je vous envoie quelques-uns de ces vers, c'est que j'aime tous les poètes, tous les bons Parnassiens puisque le poète est un Parnassien."[11] We will see to what extent poets such as Mallarmé, Valéry or Baudelaire adopt and reinterpret Leconte de Lisle's terms in their own efforts to evaluate Hugo's importance; and yet there is not a single account of Leconte de Lisle by a major poet which does not stress his limitations and even characterize him as a somewhat ridiculous figure of authority. This may be because the very ambiguities underlying his claim to authority made him both adaptable and expendable as those claims underwent more rigorous redefinitions. One thing is clear. He mistook the means for the end in his experimentation with poetic language, not knowing how to go beyond his own normative criterion. His genuine concern for the materials of his craft—rhyme, rhythm, diction—did more to restrict than to empower his avant-garde followers. This is particularly obvious in his reaction to the *vers libristes* who came on the scene in the 90s and who referred to him as the Abbé Delille of their century. To hear Leconte de Lisle rave about what they were doing is to understand why:

Ce sont des vandales! Ce sont des démolisseurs incapables de réédifier ce qu'ils voudraient mettre en ruines. Ils appellent convention ce qui est la loi fondamentale de L'Art. . . . J'affirme qu'en poésie cette loi est lyrique, primordiale, éclatante à l'esprit comme le soleil lui-même; et la preuve, c'est que si le rythme du vers et l'écho de la rime n'avaient pas existé avant moi, je sens que je les aurais inventés, car étant tout enfant, j'ai bercé mes idées en strophes, avant d'avoir rien lu. (Cited by Souriau 424)

Clearly "le Chef de l'Ecole Parnassienne" conceives of himself as the source for all possible lyric poetry, as lyric poetry incarnate, and Parnassianism as a temple or monument whose laws, once learned, are never to be disputed. After him, as one poet put it on the occasion of his death, "Les portes du temple élevé en l'honneur des vers à rime et à mesure fixe sont fermées."[12] Although his disciple, Heredia, did not introduce changes into those rules, even he occasionally permitted himself irregularities to make a point, as in this case of hiatus from a line reminiscent of Hugo's image of poetry as *tas de pierres*: "Le temple est en ruine en haut d'un promontoire" (cited by Souriau 441).

Within the temple of Parnassus, there was, however, already a much greater rift than the occasional breaking of a rule of prosody. That rift was in the person of Théodore de Banville, all the more dangerous, perhaps, because he ostensibly carried out the dictates of the high priest more ably than any other of his followers, and in so doing undermined the concept of a poetry of revealed truth most completely. In a sense, Banville was to Leconte de Lisle what the court jester was to the king; in fact, well before Picasso or Apollinaire, he chose the clown as an analogue for the poet: "Le clown! le poète! . . . c'est une seule et même personne. . . . Il y a dans tout habile arrangeur de mots un acrobate . . . s'élancer avec agilité et avec certitude à travers l'espace, au-dessus du vide, d'un point à un autre, telle est la suprême science du clown, et j'imagine que c'est aussi la seule science du poète."[13] Banville was adopted by those great poets in the margins of the schools and most willing to experiment with new forms—Hugo himself, whose *Chansons des rues et des bois* show the influence of Banville's *Odes funambulesques*; Verlaine, who called him the paradigm of the lyric poet; Rimbaud, whose early reworkings of old genres were inspired by Banville's practices; and especially Mallarmé, for whom he represented the ideal of a new poet, detached from his empirical self, drawing his inspiration from the complex possibilities of the structures and history of the French language in an elocutionary suspension of being: "Théodore de Banville . . . n'est pas quelqu'un, mais le son même de la lyre. Avec lui je sens la poésie m'enivrer . . . et bois à la fontaine du lyrisme."[14]

The article Mallarmé wrote in 1892 at the time a commemorative monument was being erected for Banville in the Luxembourg reveals a fundamental difference between his and Leconte de Lisle's concepts of authority. Whereas Leconte de Lisle would close poetry and her acolytes within the confines of the sacred temple of Parnassus, Mallarmé refuses all such controlling gestures for a new concept of language and creativity. He finds it fitting that Banville should reside now, "Tel qu'en Lui-même," in the open decor of the Luxembourg rather than locked away in the emptiness of the Panthéon, like poor Hugo, who according to Mallarmé, deserved to be liberated from such a fate as well. Banville's poetry is, like nature, part of a rhythmic and sonorous decor, not fixed in the soil as stones of reference: "Une ligne, quelque vibration, sommaires et tout s'indique. Contrairement à l'art lyrique comme il fut, élocutoire, en raison du besoin, strict, de signification" (Mallarmé 522). He should be represented by a new kind of monument—one which gives up its fixity and thus becomes, paradoxically, "Le Verbe . . . plus massivement lié à la nature" (522). For Mallarmé, Banville accomplished *La divine transposition, pour l'accomplissement de quoi existe l'homme, va du fait à l'idéal. . . ."* His work as "un théâtre prestigieux" and himself as "être de joie et de pierreries, qui brille, domine, effleure" (522-23) suggest that authority resides in creative possiblities rather than any substantive definition of being. It is as verbal acrobat, "être de pierreries," that Mallarmé places him on Mt. Olympus as one of the select, "Harmonieux comme un poème et charmant comme un décor" (521). Twice in his eulogy, Mallarmé connects Banville with Hugo—perhaps out of respect for Banville's own life-long admiration for Hugo, but also because Mallarmé himself understood Hugo as having renewed the process of liberation of the French lyric which had ended for almost two centuries. In *Crise de vers* he dates the renewal of the lyric with Hugo's loosening of the alexandrin, which instead of "vers monument" became in his hands "instrument héréditaire," released from its predictable rhythms and from the grip of authority to be picked up and passed through the curious and experimental hands of future generations—first by Henri de Régnier and Jules LaForgue, who added or substracted a foot here and there from the sacred twelve, and then by the truly revolutionary *vers libristes*, "une mutinerie exprès, en la vacance du vieux moule fatigué . . . infractions volontaires . . . dissolution du nombre officiel . . . à l'infini." Once the initiative was yielded to words, a liberated chain of subjects could be born and with that a true merging of originality with origin in the self-reverberating text:

Selon moi jaillit tard . . . la possibilité . . . de se moduler à son gré. Que tout individu apporte une prosodie, neuve, participant de son souffle . . . le dire retrouve chez le Poète . . . sa virtualité . . . le vers . . . vous cause cette surprise de n'avoir ouï jamais tel fragment ordinaire d'élocution. (Mallarmé 361-68)

Banville's own life-long admiration for Hugo seems to reflect this change from an authoritarian concept of poetic authority represented by Leconte de Lisle to Mallarmé's depersonalized notion of poetic writer. In a sense, he stood as an intermediary between Victor Hugo and the generations which followed, linking Romanticism to Parnassianism on the one hand, and Parnassianism and Symbolism on the other.[15] From the beginning of his career in 1842 until his death, Banville wrote scores of poems celebrating Hugo's genius. One of his most famous is "Semper adora," written in 1887, two years after Hugo's funeral, in which he castigates his contemporaries who, only now that the Master is dead, dare attack him and claim his place. Calling these poets "les nains joyeux," and echoing the "Bons appétits, messieurs" speech from *Ruy Blas*, Banville writes, "Ils crièrent, montrant leurs appétits flagrants: / A présent qu'il n'est plus, nous pouvons être grands."[16] In fact, Banville quotes from Hugo throughout "Semper adora," thus making the poem a tribute to Hugo in Hugo's own style. He does so both through his use of allusion ("Maître, je suis un flot parmi les flots sans nombre"), recalling such poems as "Oceano nox," for example, and through his use of prosodic technique, where the integrity of the alexandrin is frequently broken by a change of voice. His final pledge of fidelity evokes Hugo's own pledge in "Ultima verba," from *Les Châtiments*, to be the guarantor of his century's freedom, even if he is the last person left to defend that right:

Tant que je vivrai sous les grands cieux qui se dorent
O Père, je serai parmi ceux qui t'adorent,
Fidèles, et *s'il n'en reste qu'un, je serai*
Celui-là plein d'amour et le cœur ulcéré![17]

Banville's italics repeat word for word, but with the added emphasis of enjambement, Hugo's famous challenge to the pygmy usurper, Louis Napoleon.

Most of the poems of the 1880s, "La Statue de Victor Hugo" or "A Victor Hugo," for example, both written in '81 in celebration of the poet's 80th birthday, are constructed from clear echoings of Hugo's work: "O! parle! ravis-nous, poète! Chante encore / . . . / Les chefs d'œuvres futurs qui germent sous ton front" (*Fournaise* 164). Rather than to look for new words to demonstrate his originality as author, Banville combines Hugo's words to produce new effects as if author and language were one and the same. Humor and surprise are key agents in this process which depends upon the reader's recognition of the *dramatis personae* of Hugo's vast work. This use of citation or pastiche, depending upon one's critical perspective, is what identifies the shift in the conception of creativity which I have said characterizes Banville's relationship to his acknowledged master. In the early poems to Hugo, during the 1840s Hugo is represented in Romantic terms, as an isolated genius who, like Homer, Aeschylus, or Shakespeare, was divinely chosen to sing the Harmony of the Spheres. The younger poet conceives of his own project as a kind of reverent blasphemy, Prometheus stealing the fire of the gods to sit on Mt. Olympus as one of the select ("A Olympio," *Les Stalactites*).[18] The fact that Banville conceives of his vocation as stealing the fire to reach Mt. Olympus, however, already would suggest the shift from a Romantic concept of poet-seer as unique and privileged center of activity to a concept of poet as forger or craftsman more typical of the mature Banville who would write in "Le Forgeron" of 1887, "ce vulcain farouche . . . qui semble plutôt un ouvrier qu'un Dieu." With this change in the concept of the poet's function comes a concomitant shift in focus from the content of the divine message to its representation in language.

> Avec tous les outils, esclaves de mon zèle,
> Je repousse l'airain, je lime, je cisèle,
> Je grave, curieux, ardent, inassouvi,
> Seul avec mon cerveau plein d'images, servi
> Par des figures d'or que j'ai faites moi-même.
> Le métal fulgurant change comme un poème:
> Il est devenu lyre où dort un chant divin,
> Armure, coupe offerte à la gloire du vin,
> Sceptre, épée aux brillants éclairs, de sang avide,
> etc. (*Stalactites* "Le Forgeron," 265)

Verse can be or sing anything secular or divine so long as it is properly formed.

In his *Petit Traité de versification française*, published in 1877, Banville says that every aspiring young poet should find a great model—a Homer, Shakespeare, or Hugo—and study that model as one would a Bible to learn all of the techniques of the Master, because it is only by learning the rules of art that one can *go beyond those rules.* (In 1864 Banville wrote Hugo: "Lisant chaque jour *Les Contemplations* et *La Légende des siècles*, comme les anglais lisent la Bible ... ayant, je crois, pénétré presque tous les secrets de la construction matérielle de ces vers immortels, je les admire mille fois plus qu'auparavant.")[19] He characterizes Hugo as a model who liberates, saying that 9/10 of the words exiled from poetry were "délivrés" by his verse. In his maturity, Banville was using citation to make this point. If he adopted the words and techniques of the Master, as we have seen him do in "Semper adora," he did so both to recognize his source and to demonstrate his ability to use that source for new effects. The sheer variety of voices quoted from within Hugo's work—Ruy Blas, the Queen, Olympio, Hugo in exile—subverts the integrity of a unique, authoritative voice, and suggests that no poetic subject, however grand, can be a simple origin.

For Banville, as for Mallarmé and the early Valéry, poetry is ideally a pure form—a sonorous verbal structure free of discursive elements, governed by its own system of relationships. Rhyme would be his starting point for the creation of this overall unity, the best rhymes being those where the sound and the meaning of the rhyme words are farthest apart. The subject matter of a poem should be as small, insignificant, unpretentious as possible and should never distract from its setting (or as Mallarmé might say, its "décor"). The lyric, then, is defined by its style. But if sound is privileged in Banville's theorizing, it is less as an expression of an individuated presence than as an abstract linguistic category. His *Petit Traité* presents not an opposition between sound and grammar, but a grammar of rhymes. Voice and writing are not antithetical categories as in much Romantic thought, but aspects of the same thing, and therein lies his modernism. Some of Banville's most significant tributes to Hugo can be found in what establishment critics of his time saw as one of his most insignificant collections, the *Odes funambulesques*, published in 1857, one year after *Les Contemplations* and the same year as *Les Fleurs du mal*. It is a collection which offers extensive use of parody. Alvin Harms has pointed out, for example, that the subtitle "Autres Guitares" is a borrowing from Hugo's "Autre Guitare" of *Les Rayons et les ombres*, and compares Banville's "V . . . le baigneur" with Hugo's "Sara la baigneuse," from *Les Orientales*.[20] Banville's derision can be read as a playful commentary on the muddying of sources:

Hugo
Sara, belle d'indolence, / Se balance / Dans un hamac, au-dessus / Du bassin d'une fontaine / toute pleine / D'eau puisée à l'Illyssus;
Banville
V . . . , tout plein d'insolence / Se balance, / Aussi ventru qu'un tonneau / Au-dessus d'un bain de siège, / O Barège / Plein jusqu'au bord de ton eau!

Although Banville never gave up the idea that the ability to combine sounds springs from a kind of system of divine correspondences, his practice of authority is very different from Leconte de Lisle's. It is not surprising, for example, that most of the *Odes funambulesques* were first published anonymously in journals of the time and that his preface to the first edition would state that they did not deserve to be signed since they were only experiments in form with no claim to represent an individual's thought. The Hugo to whom Banville was undyingly loyal was not the *poet vates*, but the master of structures and forms—ode, ballad, epic, drama—of rhythm, diction, grammar, and rhyme—the poet of whom Mallarmé would say "Hugo c'est le Verbe," of whom the uneasy Baudelaire would write that he semmed to have *eaten* the dictionary of the French language, and whom Valéry would call "Créateur par la forme."

Banville and Mallarmé may have begun the redefinition of Hugo's importance as source, but it was really not until Valéry's radio talk in 1935 on the occasion of the 50th anniversary of Hugo's death quoted at the beginning of this article that the contemporary reversal in Hugo's reception began to take place. In this talk Valéry uncompromisingly rejects the concept of Hugo as vatic source, insisting on the individual and historical nature of his genius as rational interpreting critic and creator of forms. It is clear from comments in Valéry's *Cahiers*, especially between the years 1915 and 1922 when he was writing his own greatest poetry, that Hugo was no demi-god to be worshipped uncritically:[21]

Musical quality of his verse
1918—Hugo ne sait pas moduler. . . . Le changement de ton lui est inconnu. . . . C'est un grandissime poète dont la voix m'est désagréable. (2: 1091-92)

Vocabulary
Hugo a un vocabulaire riche—mais pauvre ou du moins médiocre. La richesse vraie est le nombre des mots X le nombre moyen des emplois significatifs qu'on sait leur donner . . . Un trop puissant rhéteur prend le mot qui vient—et le jette à toute force, comme un hercule prend pour arme toute chose qui lui tombe sous la main. . . . Hugo prenait des mots énormes . . . et il les maniait . . . si aisément . . . qu'il donne l'impression qu'ils sont vides . . . "Farouche" -"Infini"-"Immensité"— (2: 1092)

Composition
1920-21—C'est un grand faiseur de vers et de morceaux. . . . Sa composition est nulle. . . . Quand elle existe, elle n'est que celle d'un récit . . . . (2: 1096)

Yet as time went on, Valéry was struck more and more by the beauty of these fragments, especially when, in 1931, he came upon the unedited notes for *Tas de pierres*, written in Hugo's huge handwriting on blue paper. With this discovery Valéry begins formulating a concept of lyric poetry not as "poésie pure," so much as work in process constructing and deconstructing itself in a kind of never ending excess of creativity—the concept which a poet such as Francis Ponge, for example, will articulate more fully in his essays in *L'Atelier contemporain.* "Un poème complet," Valéry will say of one of these pieces found among Hugo's papers, "serait le poème de ce poème à partir de l'embryon fécond" (2: 1118). Shortly before his death, the new poet laureate of France would write:

1942—Insomnie adoucie—J'ai couché avec le plus beau vers *possible.* C'est le Hugo: "L'ombre est noire toujours même tombant des cygnes." Il n'y a aucun moyen ni espoir de faire mieux. (Celui-ci et "le dur faucheur avec sa large lame avance / Pensif et pas à pas, vers le reste du blé" ["A Théophile Gautier"] domine toute la fabrication française.) La bizarrerie d'idée du premier lui permet le contraste simultanément phonique et sémantique des mots extrêmes *ombre-cygnes.* C'est un vers immense—4.8.13 muettes—et le contraste oire—ou—our—dans le cadre des *m,n.* (2: 1135)

In 1935 Valéry ends his eulogy by saying that Hugo was the most powerful, long-lasting, and constantly evolving form-making consciousness ever known. Each time he picks up a volume of Hugo's poetry he finds confirmation of that fact.

One name has been conspicuously absent from this sketch of Hugo's influence, and that name is, of course Baudelaire. So much has been written on the complex relationship of these two writers that any attempt to capsulize it would be inadequate. I would like to end, however, by referring to Baudelaire's much commented "Le Cygne," written in 1860 and dedicated to Victor Hugo for inclusion in the 1861 edition of *Les Fleurs du mal,*[22] because in it I believe Baudelaire addresses the issue around which this essay has been organized— that is, the status of poetic authority. He does so by allegorizing the shift away from the concept of origin as ultimate guarantee to the concept of origin as the discovery of one's fundamentally temporal condition within a creative process which is by no means progressive and linear, but always and at the same time caught in a dialogue between past and present.[23]

Many have noticed the ambiguity of a tribute in which Hugo is unmistakably represented as one of the "exilés, ridicule et sublime . . . oubliés dans une île," who like the benighted swan of Ovid or Virgil's Andromaque or "bien d'autres encore," stare into an empty source which they mistake for a fullness, "Un ruisseau sans eau" or un "Simoïs menteur," and dream of returning through its mediation to the plenitude of a former existence. These are the deluded figures who inspire a poetry of nostalgic remembering by a lyric voice which knows itself to be once and for all caught in the history of change: "Le vieux Paris n'est plus! La forme d'une ville / Change plus vite, hélas! que le cœur d'un mortel." Yet one cannot help noting that as the lyric voice insists upon its exiled condition within a fragmented world, through broken forms such as parenthesis, powerful enjambement, and the use of the tri-meter, it does so at the moment in the line when the word most reminiscent of Hugo ("hélas") is introduced. Thus tribute is paid to the historical Hugo ("créateur par la forme") at the same time that the concept of Hugo as prophet is being undermined, implying perhaps that Hugo as poet understood something that Hugo as thinker did not. Even more telling are the citations of Hugo's "Tristesse d'Olympio" in "Le Cygne," because it is in that poem that Hugo had expressed most eloquently his own exile within a temporal condition and separation from the source of his inspiration. Hugo's poem, written in the past tense, is about the poet's return to a lake, which he calls "divin miroir," in search of the experience of fullness which he had known there with a loved one the year before (vol. 6). Like Andromaque, whose tomb to Hector is a reproduction of the river around Troy, "Pauvre et triste miroir où jadis resplendit / L'immense majesté de vos douleurs de veuve," the poet looks into the lake and instead of finding there his original experience of fullness, interiorizes the lake as tomb: "Hélas, Il se sentit le cœur triste comme une tombe." The following stanzas articulate the discovery of the permanence of change—the discovery which Ovid's swan does not want to know in Baudelaire's poem, but which the modern lyric voice recognizes with "Le vieux Paris n'est plus . . ." Echoing this line, Hugo's stanza begins: "Que peu de temps suffit pour changer toutes choses / . . . / Et comme vous brisez dans vos métamorphoses / Les fils mystérieux où nos cœurs sont liés." As in "Le Cygne," what was once nature—the old menagerie of the Caroussel—is being turned into stone: "On a pavé la route âpre et mal aplanie," and the traces of the lovers' experience have almost disappeared:

> De tout ce qui fut nous presque rien n'est vivant.
> Et comme un tas de cendre éteinte et refroidie
> L'amas des souvenirs se disperse à tout vent.
> D'autres vont maintenant passer
> Où nous passâmes.

Instead of the permanence of the natural lake, the source will become the poet's tears of loss: "Vers quelque source en pleurs qui sanglote tout bas." Yet the poetry of memory, in which perception is never immediate, but always already representation surpassing any possible account of its origin, will constitute a new kind of imaginative permanence for both poets. As Baudelaire puts it in Part II of "Le Cygne," "Paris change! mais rien dans ma mélancolie / N'a bougé . . . / Et mes chers souvenirs sont plus lourds que des rocs." Hugo ends his poem: "C'est toi qui dors dans l'ombre, o sacré souvenir."

In his essay "On the Question of the 'Structural Unity' of Older and Modern Lyric Poetry," Hans Robert Jauss has, I think correctly, identified what is "modernist" about Baudelaire's treatment of the swan theme in "Le Cygne," and in so doing, made clear an important difference between Hugo's and Baudelaire's understanding of poetry as imaginative substitution for experience.[24] Baudelaire desacralizes the originary experience behind the poem in a way Hugo does not. The menagerie swan, which inspires the analogy with Virgil's Andromaque, is less dignified than his literary substitute. His recreation "presupposes a destruction and estrangement of the familiar objective world at the beginning of the creative act" in a way Hugo's text does not. Like Baudelaire's classical references, Andromaque and the swan, Hugo allows the earlier experience of his visit with his loved one to the lake to "shine through" in a way which suggests the primacy of that experience over its recreation through memory. Baudelaire, as Jauss points out, does just the opposite. He strips the real world of its familiar aspect by introducing a mythical reference based on a personal recollection of an entirely enigmatic and private sort. The reader cannot guess the significance of the Andromaque reference until the end of Baudelaire's new construct. The poem thus establishes, according to Jauss, its own origin and originality within the chaos of other poetic voices.

Baudelaire echoes Hugo's word of remembering, "o sacré souvenir," in his own final stanza of a poem which refuses to end, thus placing Hugo's voice within a chorus of texts from which history has lost its progressivist shape and there is no privileged ground to control the flux of experience: Virgil, Racine, Vigny, an anonymous medieval bard, "et bien d'autres encore." His source, then, is a shared language of change, hope, and disillusionment:

> Ainsi dans la forêt où mon esprit s'exile
> Un vieux Souvenir sonne à plein souffle du cor!
> Je pense aux matelots oubliés dans une île,
> Aux captifs, aux vaincus! . . . à bien d'autres encore!

In light of Baudelaire's subversive rewriting of Hugo's tribute to himself as Olympio, or the egotistical sublime, it may be fitting to end this study of Hugo's influence on the French lyric tradition with a metaphor which Valéry gives in his notebook of 1916 for the influence of all great poets on tradition:

On peut considérer les types de notre poésie, Racine, Hugo, Baudelaire, etc. comme des instruments chacun plus approprié à tels effets et plus adopté par sa langue choisie, ses rhythmes, ses images à telles ou telles nécessités. Il n'est pas impossible de conjuger ces violons, ces "cuivres" et ces "bois" pour posséder un orchestre. . . . Il suffit de rappeler que chacun de ces poètes est dans le langage, que leurs effets sont distincts, incomparables, non contradictoires dans la suite. Il faut, naturellement, savoir orchestrer. (2: 1080)

Notes

[1] Pierre Albouy, "La Vie posthume de Victor Hugo," in Victor Hugo, *Œuvres complètes*, ed. Jean Massin, 18 vols. (Paris: Le Club Français du Livre, 1968) 13: ix. All references to Hugo are from this edition, indicated in the text as *OC*.

[2] Paul Valéry, *Œuvres*, ed. Jean Hytier, 2 vols. (Paris: Gallimard, Bibliothèque de la Pléiade, 1957) 1: 583.

[3] Maurice Souriau, *Histoire du Parnasse* (Paris: Spès, 1929) xli.

[4] Emile Verhaeren. *Impressions* (Paris: Mercure de France, 1928) 3: 176-77, cited by Souriau 443.

[5] In his study of the source topos, *Origin and Originality in Renaissance Literature* (New Haven: Yale UP, 1983), David Quint demonstrates through close textual analysis how these differing concepts of authority coexist in an unresolved and contradictory way in many highly self-conscious Renaissance works. He articulates the issue with admirable clarity: "The source topos emerged at a moment when, under the impact of a new historical consciousness, the Renaissance literary text was seeking to re-examine—and represent—the source of its fictions' authority. That consciousness allowed the text to be read as the exclusive creation of its historical human author and could thus question the claims to a nonhistorical transcendent truth which had been advanced for the text by traditional modes of allegorical reading and writing. . . . Ultimately at issue was the question of which of those fictions were dependent upon systems of revealed truth or belonged instead to an autonomous secular domain" (ix-x).

[6] Quint 211. Quint's final chapter presents Milton as a transitional writer whose powerful representation of "the interference which Satan's secondary, counterfeit imitation succeeds in placing around an originary divine significance describes the general problem of meaning in the world after the Fall" (213). Although other Renaissance scholars have criticized Quint's interpretation of Milton for being too modern, it certainly elucidates the choice of Milton's Satan as Romantic prototype by nineteenth-century poets.

[7] Xavier de Ricard in *Revue des Revues* (February 1902) 305.

[8] *L'Ermitage* (February 1902), Survey on "Les Poètes et leur poète." I think Albouy is quite right in interpreting this "Hélas" as a rather back-handed compliment: "Ainsi, le mot célèbre de Gide est surprenant, en ce sens que, de la part d'un jeune symboliste comme lui . . . on aurait attendu la réponse donnée par plusieurs autres: Baudelaire, ou Verlaine, ou même Mallarmé. Or, Gide reste fidèle à Hugo. Que signifie alors le hélas? Qu'il est fâcheux qu'on ne puisse vraiment pas porter un autre jugement? Ou que Gide s'en veut à lui-même d'une telle préférence, persistant au bout du compte?" (xiii)

[9] All quotations are from the following edition: *Œuvres de Leconte de Lisle: derniers poèmes*, ed. Charles Marie René (Paris: Alphonse Lemerre, 1899).

[10] Leconte de Lisle would translate Homer's *Iliad* in 1866 and *The Odyssey* in 1867.

[11] Arthur Rimbaud, *Œuvres*, eds. Suzanne Bernard et André Guyaux (Paris: Garniers, 1981) 341.

[12] Emile Verhaeren, *Impressions* 98-101, cited by Souriau 429.

[13] Théodore de Banville, *Critiques*, ed. Victor Barrucand (Paris: Fasquelle, 1917) 422, cited by Souriau 77. It seems clear that Mallarmé wrote his "Pitre châtié" in reaction to Banville's poem.

[14] All quotations are from the following edition: Mallarmé, *Œuvres complètes*, eds. H. Mondor and G. Jean-Aubry, "Théodore de Banville" (Paris: Gallimard, 1965) 520.

[15] See Aaron Schaffer, *The Genres of Parnassian Poetry* (Baltimore: Johns Hopkins UP, 1944) 235. Schaffer quotes F. Charpentier, one of Banville's critics in this regard: "D'une de ses ailes il relie le Romantisme au Parnasse et de l'autre le Parnasse au Symbolisme."

[16] All quotations are from the following edition: Banville, *Dans la fournaise* (Paris: Charpentier, 1892) 41-43.

[17] The last stanza of Hugo's "Ultima verba": "Si l'on n'est plus que mille, eh bien, j'en suis! si même / Ils ne sont plus que cent, je brave encore Sylla; / S'il en demeure dix, je serai le dixième; / *Et s'il n'en reste qu'un, je serai celui-là!*"

[18] All quotations are from the following edition: Banville, *Œuvres, Les Stalactites* (Paris: Alphonse Lemerre, 1889) 92-94.

[19] *Revue de France* (1 April 1923) 317, cited by Souriau 62.

[20] Alvin Harms, *Théodore de Banville* (Boston: Twayne, 1983) 47-48.

[21] All quotations are from Judith Robinson's edition of the *Cahiers*, 2 vols. (Paris, Gallimard, 1973).

[22] All quotations from "Le Cygne" are from the following edition: Baudelaire, *Œuvres complètes* (Paris: Gallimard, Bibliothèque de la Pléiade, 1975) 1: 85-87.

[23] See Paul de Man's reading of this poem in "The Rhetoric of Temporality," *The Rhetoric of Romanticism* (New York: Columbia UP, 1984).

[24] In *Aesthetic Experience and Literary Hermeneutics*, trans. M. Shaw, Theory and History of Literature 3 (Minneapolis: U of Minnesota P, 1982) 228-34.

Alain Toumayan

Barbey d'Aurevilly and Flaubert: Engendering a *Diabolique*

In his presentation of *Les Diaboliques*, Jacques Petit identifies two critical elements in the common inspiration of the six stories: "Les deux éléments essentiels de la 'genèse' des *Diaboliques* me paraissent être: l'influence de Balzac et la réaction de Barbey contre son époque."[1] Petit's precision with regard to what one might call "influence" sources and his vagueness with respect to polemical inspirations have oriented many critical readings of Barbey towards studies of intertextual connections with those writers that Barbey admired such as Balzac, Stendhal, and Walter Scott. Less attention has been paid to the polemical dimension of Barbey's works and specifically to the relations which his fiction describes with such writers as Flaubert, Hugo, and Zola. Thus, Barbey's indebtedness to Balzac in both the formal and thematic inspiration of his fictional works is well-known and well-attested.[2] Flaubert's works, however, are rarely, if ever, cited as possible sources—even polemical or ironical ones—of some of Barbey's literary works. Furthermore, while the creative possibilities of Barbey's critical works have been lucidly assessed,[3] the critical possibilities of his fictional works (in other words, the possibility of reading intertextual connections as something more significant than simply sources) have rarely been discussed,[4] which is perplexing given Barbey's acknowledgment of the coherence of his critical and creative endeavors.[5]

In this essay, I propose to analyze the system of references linking Barbey's short story, "Le Bonheur dans le crime" and Flaubert's *Madame Bovary*. I argue that this connection not only accounts for certain features of Barbey's story but guides a reading of it as a polemical answer, in both moral and esthetic terms, to Flaubert. I shall first establish the link of Barbey's story with Flaubert's novel, then seek to understand its ramifications.

The plot of "Le Bonheur dans le crime" is a simple one. The story is recounted by one doctor Torty to a narrator who retells it addressing himself on one occasion to another character who bears only the name, "Madame." Hauteclaire Stassin was the only child of a fencing instructor who had established himself in the "aristocratic" city of V(alognes). Upon her father's

death, the young woman, an accomplished fencer herself, continued the lessons
and fell in love with a local aristocrat, the count Serlon de Savigny who was
taking fencing instruction from her and, at the time, was betrothed to another
member of the local aristocracy, Delphine de Cantor. Shortly after the latter's
wedding, Hauteclaire disappeared without a trace. Doctor Torty, called to the
count's castle by the illness of the countess, recognized Hauteclaire who was
now employed as the countess's chambermaid. Shortly thereafter the countess
died, apparently victim of a terrible mistake: Hauteclaire had given her some
concentrated ink in place of her medication. After an official period of
mourning, the count married Hauteclaire and, despite moral indignation and
ostracism by the residents of the town, Serlon and Hauteclaire lived happily
ever after. Only the doctor, the countess's personal physician, knew the truth:
that Serlon had hidden his mistress under his wife's nose and that Hauteclaire
had murdered the countess. In fact it is revealed that the countess herself knew
of both the adultery and of the murder but refused treatment and demanded that
the doctor confirm the accidental version of the events in order to save her name
and the aristocracy of the town from the scandal and the dishonor of a
poisoning.

It is through the three figures of the countess of Savigny, Hauteclaire, and
Dr. Torty that reference, both direct and—as I shall suggest—indirect, is made
to *Madame Bovary*. The most explicit reference to Flaubert is made through the
character of the countess of Savigny, specifically in the episode of her
poisoning. The fact that the countess is poisoned by ink, not coincidentally the
substance for writing, is unusual enough that Serlon de Savigny feigns surprise:
"Mais, docteur, ce n'est pas possible! est-ce que l'encre double serait un
poison?" (ORC 117). Barbey's repeated mention of the poisonous ink and the
countess's mention of "le goût horrible de cette encre avec laquelle ils m'ont
empoisonnée" (ORC 118) evoke Emma's poisoning, one of the first symptoms
of which is "cet affreux goût d'encre."[6] The obvious nature of this symbolic
link underscores, however, great differences in character between Emma and
the countess, a contrast which I will describe more fully below.

Like the character of the countess, the character of Hauteclaire would
appear to constitute a marked qualitative contrast to Emma. All of her attributes
are excessive and exceptional: her physical and emotional strength, her
strength of character and, in particular, her imperviousness to sentimentality,
guilt, and social ostracism. Indeed, in his essay on *Madame Bovary*, Barbey's
analysis of the character of Emma describes quite precisely the opposite of the
qualities with which he has endowed Hauteclaire: Emma is described as "une
âme faible,"[7] "la femme médiocre" (OH 208), "cette espèce d'être faible sans
grandes passions, sans l'étoffe des grandes vertus ou des grands vices, inclinant
de hasard au bien comme au mal" (ibid.); or, finally, Emma is "cette nature si
peu exceptionnelle" (ibid). But if Barbey reads Emma as a weak, failed, or

mediocre soul, Baudelaire in his essay on *Madame Bovary*, reads Emma very differently.[8] And Baudelaire's reading of Emma describes very precisely many of the atttributes that Barbey will give to Hauteclaire in "Le Bonheur dans le crime." In a less focused but no less brilliant article than Barbey's, Baudelaire stresses the virile nature of Emma, her fundamentally masculine characterization. Flaubert, Baudelaire writes, "n'a pas pu ne pas infuser un sang viril dans les veines de sa créature, et . . . madame Bovary, pour ce qu'il y a en elle de plus énergique et de plus ambitieux, et aussi de plus rêveur, madame Bovary est restée un homme. Comme la Pallas armée, sortie du cerveau de Zeus, ce bizarre androgyne a gardé toutes les séductions d'une âme virile dans un charmant corps féminin" (OC 81). Emma is, according to Baudelaire, "une petite Lady Macbeth" (OC 82) or, more simply, "voilà l'homme d'action!" (OC 83). Barbey uses, among others, the figures of both Pallas (ORC 95) and Lady Macbeth (ORC 88) to characterize Hauteclaire but, more importantly, in the character of Hauteclaire, he develops precisely that androgynous, virile femininity which so fascinates Baudelaire a propos of Emma. Comparing Serlon and Hauteclaire, the narrator writes, "c'était la femme qui avait les muscles, et l'homme qui avait les nerfs" (ORC 85); or, in another characterization of her, "Hauteclaire, que je croyais l'homme des deux dans leurs rapports d'amants" (ORC 122), a situation which, of course, recalls Emma's relations with Léon who, Flaubert writes, was more Emma's mistress than she was his: "il devenait sa maîtresse plutôt qu'elle n'était la sienne" (MB 361). (While not lost on Barbey, who notes that in her relations with Léon "elle est l'homme de cette nouvelle intimité" [OH 211], this side of Emma's character does not alter his initial assessment of her.) The fact that Hauteclaire's profession is that of weapons instructor contributes of course to this fascination; she is "cette St. Georges femelle, dont la beauté . . . égalait le talent d'escrime" (ORC 93). And the narrator notes, in a passage which develops Baudelaire's analysis of Emma's seductive appeal: "Les hommes sont tous les mêmes. L'étrangeté leur déplaît, d'homme à homme, et les blesse; mais si l'étrangeté porte des jupes, ils en raffolent. Une femme qui fait ce que fait un homme, le ferait-elle beaucoup moins bien, aura toujours sur l'homme, en France, un avantage marqué" (ORC 96-97). While her profession of fencing instructor accounts, in part, for Hauteclaire's seductiveness, the fencing becomes a rather crude metaphor of Torty's for the sexual relations between Serlon and Hauteclaire following his voyeuristic observation of their nocturnal fencing practice, "voilà donc toujours leur manière de faire l'amour" (ORC 112), an association which is crudely reinforced when, reacting to Serlon's feigned impatience with the countess's prolonged illness, Torty muses to himself: "mais si je guérissais ta femme, . . . tu ne ferais pas des armes et l'amour toute la nuit avec ta maîtresse" (ORC 115). While the fencing, in its literal meaning, is the basis of Serlon's and Hauteclaire's relationship (since they first meet when Serlon takes instruction from her) one will recall that one of Emma's first disillusions in her marriage is the fact that Charles does not know how to "faire des armes" (MB 70).

A similar intertextual configuration, mediated by Barbey's and Baudelaire's critical essays on *Madame Bovary*, is present in the case of the character of Torty. Torty is first characterized by Barbey's narrator as an astute, penetrating, and cynical observer of human nature: "il était devenu un de ces impitoyables observateurs qui ne peuvent pas ne point être des misanthropes" (ORC 83). And it is as observer—and voyeur—that Torty repeatedly characterizes himself in his relations with Serlon, Hauteclaire, and the countess.[9] The association of the quality of acuity of observation with the medical profession is made in Barbey's characterization of Flaubert himself as author/narrator (Barbey does not distinguish) of *Madame Bovary*. According to Barbey, Flaubert lays bare Emma's soul with "une main de chirurgien" (OH 206), he seizes nuances "comme un chirurgien pince les veines" (OH 209). Flaubert is, writes Barbey, "de la véritable race des romanciers; c'est un observateur . . ." (OH 208). Elsewhere, Barbey writes that Flaubert is "un véritable nosographe de la corruption" (OH 211), he praises his language for its "précision presque scientifique" (OH 212), and he reproaches "an observateur de l'acuité de M. Flaubert" (ibid.) for the spareness of his portrayal of provincial mores.

If the characterization of Torty reproduces the traits which Barbey has attributed to the author of *Madame Bovary*, there is another characteristic of the figure of Torty which is evocative of Flaubert's novel in Barbey's story. It is specifically Torty's claim that in contemporary society, doctors have replaced priests as confessors: "—Le médecin est le confesseur des temps modernes, — fit le docteur avec un ton solenellement goguenard. —Il a remplacé le prêtre, Monsieur, et il est obligé au secret de la confession comme le prêtre" (ORC 89). This is a remark that was of considerable interest to Barbey: he reproduced it in the following form in his *Pensées détachées*: "Dans une société qui devient de plus en plus matérialiste, le confesseur, c'est le médecin" (ORC 1628) and, according to Petit, it serves as a pretext for the entire story of "Le Bonheur dans le crime" (ORC 1288). In any case, Torty makes this claim to the narrator early in the story and the claim to secrecy serves to signal ironically the start of Torty's secondary narrative in which, of course, he reveals the secret; Torty goes on "Et il va le tenir . . . comme le prêtre! . . . Venez par ici. Nous allons causer" (ORC 89). The narrative will confirm Torty's claim since, as she was dying, the countess confided the truth of the crime to Torty with the stipulation that he not reveal it. Now one will recall the episode in *Madame Bovary* in which Emma consults the abbé Bournisien in their classic "dialogue de sourds." While in his essay on *Madame Bovary*, Barbey glosses this episode quite quickly, reading it solely as an attack on the Church, Baudelaire, in his essay on *Madame Bovary*, does not. Baudelaire finds it one of the most remarkable, powerful, and modern scenes in Madame Bovary. (Baudelaire has italicized the word "moderne.") Baudelaire summarizes the episode in the following manner: "Le bon curé Bournisien, uniquement préoccupé des polissons du catéchisme qui font de la gymnastique à travers les stalles et les chaises de l'église, répond avec candeur: 'Puisque vous êtes malade, madame, et puisque M. Bovary est médecin, *pourquoi n'allez-vous pas trouver votre mari?*'" (OC 85, Baudelaire's italics). In fact, all Bournisien says to Emma when she mentions to him that she is not well is "Mais, M. Bovary, qu'est-ce qu'il en pense?" (MB 158). Baudelaire's misquote of Flaubert is instructive since what Baudelaire does is to interpret a question which Flaubert, initially at least, leaves ambiguous, specifically the fact that Bournisien refers Emma to Charles as a doctor and not as her husband, assuming therefore a physical rather than spiritual etiology of her affliction. (It is only in his following question that Bournisien makes this distinction: "il ne vous ordonne pas quelque chose?" ibid.) In other words, Baudelaire interprets the scene in the very terms that Barbey then develops in "Le Bonheur dans le crime" in the case of Torty: the doctor being called upon to replace the priest as confessor. Furthermore, as is clear in the previous quotes, this substitution[10] is variously attributed by Barbey to modernity (Torty says "le médecin est le confesseur des temps *modernes*," my emphasis) or to materialist ideology, itself synonymous with the modern for Barbey ("une société qui devient de plus en plus *matérialiste*," my emphasis). I have noted Baudelaire's emphasis on the word "moderne" in connection with this episode in *Madame Bovary* while the charge of materialism is leveled at Flaubert by Barbey in his essay on the novel, "M. Flaubert n'a point de spiritualité. Il doit être un matérialiste de doctrine comme il l'est de style . . ." (OH 212).

While many of the elements in the network of references to *Madame Bovary* are rather common and even formulaic narrative ingredients in nine-teenth-century fiction—elements such as the doctor-observer and the virile, androgynous woman—a pattern of direct and indirect, explicit and veiled references to *Madame Bovary* is quite palpable in Barbey's "Le Bonheur dans le crime" and these references describe two areas in which Barbey's story is answering Flaubert: in his moralism and in his estheticism.[11]

The moral horizon of Barbey's story is made extremely clear in its title, which, of course, evokes Sade's *Les Infortunes de la vertu*, and requires no extensive commentary here. Indeed, not only do Barbey's protagonists get away with murder, suggesting that crime sometimes does pay (one thinks of Vautrin tempting Rastignac with such a proposition in *Le Père Goriot*), they live happily ever after. So Barbey's story, in a very general sense, ostentatiously rejects the notion that crime, or transgression, if not punished by a social, legal, or moral apparatus, would inevitably be punished by the onerous psychological burden of guilt.[12] But in a more specific way, both of Barbey's female protagonists (which one is the "diabolique" is subject to discussion) describe a scenario of success in those areas in which Emma presents a portrait of failure. Hauteclaire succeeds as an adulteress—she challenges the implied moralism that holds that Emma, as an adulteress, must be punished. And the countess of Savigny succeeds, so to speak, as a victim. As noted, it is through the image of their poisonings that Emma and the countess are associated. In marked contrast to Emma, whose Romantic and sentimental illusions about death ("Ah! c'est bien peu de chose, la mort! . . . je vais m'endormir, et tout sera fini!" MB 406) are so cruelly destroyed, the countess never loses her composure nor her aristocratic demeanor. Even as she is dying, the countess is able to calculate strategically the social consequences of her death and to affirm certain principles (as archaic and reactionary as they might be), thus demonstrating, again in contrast to Emma, her total control of herself and her complete mastery even of the situation of her own death. It is through the example of this remarkable force of will that the countess then counters Emma's "âme faible." In this way, both women answer the commonality of Emma, they are extreme and exceptional characters driven by uncompromising and powerful passions and both of them thus openly and explicitly answer the formulaic sentimental-ism of repentant or tormented criminals and punished adulteresses.

Related to the question of the sentimentalist moralism of *Madame Bovary* is the question of the estheticism inherent in the artistic depiction of the banality of bourgeois mores. This point virtually erupts in Barbey's scathing attack on *L'Education sentimentale* in which the incidence of the words "vulgaire," "vulgarité," "médiocre," and "médiocrité" to describe both the book and its characters is extraordinary.[13] It is thus clear that Barbey's creative esthetic is diametrically opposed to that of Flaubert.[14] The operative principles in Barbey's esthetic are excess and transgression; for Barbey, literature is the privileged province of the exceptional, the monstrous, the transgressive, and the *expérience limite*.[15] *Les Diaboliques*, in general, and "Le Bonheur dans le crime," in particular, bear this out: like Torty who would like to write his memoirs which would be "un traité de tératologie" (ORC 125) and whose interest in Serlon and Hauteclaire derives from their monstrous qualities (ibid.), Barbey himself notes in the preface of *Les Diaboliques* that the protagonists of his stories are monsters.

In his study of Laclos's *Liaisons dangereuses*, André Malraux offers the following assessment of Flaubert's protagonists: "les personnages principaux de Flaubert sont bien souvent des personnages de Balzac conçus dans l'échec au lieu de l'être dans la réussite."[16] Barbey, apparently, would concur and "Le Bonheur dans le crime" can be considered an attempt to reverse the situation described by Malraux, that is, to conceive a Flaubertian protagonist "dans la réussite." Finding an inspiration for this in Baudelaire's analysis of *Madame Bovary*, Barbey creates a critical story, an elaborate motley of references and allusions, reactions, judgments, and criticisms many of which are directed at

Flaubert and answer both the moralism and the estheticism that Barbey perceives in his works. Thus can "Le Bonheur dans le crime" provide an example of a polemical and ironic literary inspiration of Barbey's works and suggest that when Barbey formulates moral and esthetic questions in his fiction, he tends to do so in relation to, and occasionally by means of, other authors. In synthesizing Barbey's own and Baudelaire's critical reflections on Flaubert and specifically on *Madame Bovary*, "Le Bonheur dans le crime" demonstrates that while Barbey's fictional writings are distinct from his extensive critical corpus, they are consistent with it, they complement it, and indeed are informed by it.

Notes

[1] "Notice" in Barbey d'Aurevilly, *Œuvres romanesques complètes*, ed. Jacques Petit (Paris: Gallimard, Bibliothèque de la Pléiade, 1966)2: 1274. Hereafter ORC will refer to this edition and to this volume of Barbey's works.

[2] Largely due to the excellent work of Jacques Petit in his Pléiade edition of Barbey's novels, in his *Barbey d'Aurevilly Critique* (Paris: Les Belles Lettres, 1963) and in his *Essais de lecture des "Diaboliques" de Barbey d'Aurevilly*, Lettres Modernes (Paris: Minard, 1974). In the latter work Petit does broach the subject of the polemical dimension of some of Barbey's works. See *Essais de lecture* 70-71.

[3] I am thinking of Nichola Anne Haxell's essay, "Barbey d'Aurevilly, 'Creative Critic' of Baudelaire," *Symposium* 41.3 (1987) 174-87. Haxell's essay is in part inspired by Rosemary Lloyd's study, "Baudelaire's Creative Criticism," *French Studies* 36 (1982) 37-44.

[4] A notable exception would be Allan Pasco, "A Study of Allusion: Barbey's Stendhal in 'Le Rideau cramoisi,'" *PMLA* 88 (1973) 461-71.

[5] See, for example, Philippe Berthier, *L'Ensorcelée, Les Diaboliques de Barbey d'Aurevilly: une écriture du désir* (Paris: Champion, 1987) 8.

[6] Gustave Flaubert, *Madame Bovary*, Folio (Paris: Gallimard, 1972) 406. Hereafter MB will refer to this edition of the work.

[7] Barbey d'Aurevilly, "Madame Bovary," in *Le XIXᵉ Siècle: des œuvres et des hommes* (Paris: Mercure de France, 1964) 1: 206. Hereafter OH will refer to this edition and to this volume of the work.

[8] Charles Baudelaire, "Madame Bovary," in *Œuvres complètes*, ed. Claude Pichois (Paris: Gallimard, Bibliothèque de la Pléiade, 1976)2: 76-86. Hereafter OC will refer to this edition and to this volume of Baudelaire's complete works. Barbey's essay appeared in the October 6, 1857 edition of *Le Pays*, Baudelaire's essay in the October 18, 1857 edition of *L'Artiste*. There is no doubt that Barbey was aware of Baudelaire's essay given their relations and given the fact that in his essay on *Madame Bovary*, Baudelaire approvingly evokes Barbey and two of his works, *L'Ensorcelée* and *Une Vieille Maîtresse*. One should recall that during the summer of 1857, Barbey had written but not published an essay on *Les Fleurs du mal* which Baudelaire would consider a significant piece of evidence in his legal defense. On the relations between Baudelaire and Barbey, see Claude Pichois's comments in Baudelaire's *Correspondance* (Paris: Gallimard, Bibliothèque de la Pléiade, 1973) 1: 873. See also Pichois's and Ziegler's *Baudelaire* (Paris: Julliard, 1987) 346, 349, 370, 371. In addition, see Petit, *Barbey d'Aurevilly Critique* 179-85 and Petit's essay "Baudelaire et Barbey d'Aurevilly," *Revue d'Histoire Littéraire de la France* 67 (1967) 286-95. Finally, see Gisèle Corbière-Gille, *Barbey d'Aurevilly critique littéraire* (Paris: Minard, 1962) 168-73.

[9] On the subjects of voyeurism and exhibitionism in *Les Diaboliques*, see Petit, *Essais de lecture des Diaboliques* 136-47. See also Eileen Boyd Sivert, "Narration and Exhibitionism in *Le Rideau Cramoisi*," *Romanic Review* 70 (1979) 146-58 and Marcelle Marini, "Ricochets de lecture: le fantasmatique des 'Diaboliques,'" *Littérature* 10 (1973) 4, 5. Finally, see Nabih Kanbar, "Evolution de la figure du témoin dans *Les Diaboliques*," in *Barbey d'Aurevilly cent ans après 1889-1989*, ed. Philippe Berthier (Geneva: Droz, 1990) 255-94, and in the same collection one can usefully consult articles by Max Milner and Jean Bellemin-Noël on this problem.

[10] The dialogue or the tension between medicine, or, more generally, science, and religion is a persistent preoccupation in Barbey's thought and art. I have proposed an analysis of *L'Ensorcelée* in terms of this question in my *La Littérature et la hantise du mal*, French Forum Monographs 69 (Lexington, KY: French Forum, 1987). On the question of Torty's role as doctor and confessor, see Raymonde Debray-Genette, "Le Récit autologique: 'Le Bonheur dans le crime,'" *Romanic Review* 64 (1973) 44.

[11] While Petit argues for a different thematic inspiration for "Le Bonheur dans le crime," it is noteworthy that it is also a polemical and intertextual one, and it is also mediated by Baudelaire. Petit cites the following judgment on Hugo's *Les Misérables* which is attributed to Baudelaire and which, according to Petit, Barbey could have heard: "Ah! . . . qu'est-ce que c'est que ces criminels sentimentals, qui ont des remords pour des pièces de cent sous, qui discutent avec leur conscience pendant des heures, et fondent des prix de vertu? Est-ce que ces gens-là raisonnent comme les autres hommes? J'en ferai, moi, un roman où je mettrai en scène un scélérat, mais un vrai scélérat, assassin, voleur, incendiaire et corsaire, et qui finira par cette phrase: 'Et sous ces ombrages que j'ai plantés, entouré d'une famille qui me vénère, d'enfants qui me chérissent et d'une femme qui m'aime, —*je jouis en paix* du fruit de tous mes crimes.'" Cited by Petit in ORC 1279, also in *Barbey d'Aurevilly Critique* 180-181n70. Also cited (with some slight variants) by Pichois in Baudelaire, OC 1182. And in his *Essais de lectures des Diaboliques*, Petit argues that "*Les Misérables* jouent un rôle de repoussoir dans la conception du 'Bonheur dans le crime'" (71). I see my argument with respect to "Le Bonheur dans le crime" and *Madame Bovary* complementing not contradicting Petit's. As noted, the character of the intertextual reference is similar to the one I am claiming here. Moreover, I find it entirely plausible that Barbey's story is responding to both Hugo and Flaubert: two of his most persistent enemies whose works Barbey never ceased to attack in his critical essays. While I agree with Petit that Barbey might have heard, and would certainly have been interested in Baudelaire's opinions on *Les Misérables* (the reverse is certainly true, as Baudelaire's disavowal of his own essay on *Les Misérables* makes clear; see Baudelaire's letter to Madame Aupick in *Correspondance* 2: 254 [Pichois ed.]), there is no doubt that Barbey would have read Baudelaire's essay on *Madame Bovary* since, as noted above, in it Baudelaire discusses Barbey's works. In a similar thematic vein, one can recall Altamira's words to Julien in *Le Rouge et le Noir*: "Si malgré les bons offices du prince d'Araceli, je ne suis pas pendu, et que je jouisse jamais de ma fortune à Paris, je veux vous faire dîner avec huit on dix assassins honorés et sans remords" (2: 9).

[12] I think that Petit discounts too categorically the possibility of *Thérèse Raquin* being one of the polemical sources of "Le Bonheur dans le crime" (See ORC 1311.). It is clear that Barbey's story openly challenges the sentimentalism in the notion that criminals who successfully evade the law might be tormented by guilt. After the murder of the countess, Serlon and Hauteclaire are a bona fide example of conjugal happiness, as the story's title makes so clear. Furthermore, Zola, like Flaubert and Hugo, is a persistent target of Barbey's critical articles.

[13] Barbey d'Aurevilly, "L'Education sentimentale," in *Le XIXᵉ Siècle: des œuvres et des hommes* (Paris: Mercure de France, 1966) 2: 156-63. On Barbey and Flaubert, see Petit, *Barbey d'Aurevilly Critique* 528-31; see also Gisèle Corbière-Gille 204-08. While the charge of vulgarity (in its literal meaning no doubt) is not an unusual one in Barbey's critical idiom, it is a criticism that Barbey also levels at Hugo in Barbey's first essay on *Les Misérables*.

[14] Baudelaire had seen this very clearly in his essay on *Madame Bovary*. Indeed, Baudelaire places Barbey and Flaubert at opposite ends of the creative spectrum. While Barbey's literature is concerned with "les miracles de l'exception" (OC 78), Flaubert's originality, according to

Baudelaire, is to craft a work of art that is "vulgaire dans le choix du sujet," whose style is deployed on "un canevas banal," and which is concerned with "l'aventure la plus triviale" (OC 80).

[15] Pierre Colla also notes this feature of Barbey's esthetic. See *L'Univers tragique de Barbey d'Aurevilly* (Brussels: La Renaissance du Livre, 1965) 53, 54.

[16] *Le Triangle noir* (Paris: Gallimard, 1970) 33.

Mary Donaldson-Evans

The Morbidity of *milieu*: *L'Assommoir* and the Discourse of Hygiene

Through the years, Zola's *L'Assommoir* has been the object of numerous critical articles and monographs. Like the novel itself, many of these have focused on the heroine, Gervaise Macquart, whose metamorphosis from an appetizing young woman to a repulsive *clocharde* is traced by the narrative. While it is clear even to the casual reader that this transformation owes something to both heredity and environment, the precise reason for her decline and the moment at which it begins are a subject of some debate. Most critics see in Coupeau's fall from the roof a turning point, and Gervaise's alcoholic heredity is assigned an important role. Kathryn Slott believes Gervaise to be a victim of gender oppression: "The true focus of *L'Assommoir* is less how Gervaise's weakness ruins her life than how alcohol brutalizes men who in turn abuse women."[1] Joy Newton, while avowing multiple factors in her decline, first lays the responsibility at her own door ("Son ambition de s'établir est . . . la cause du drame et de la tragédie qui s'ensuivent"),[2] then, in a subsequent article, exonerates her, attributing her degradation to "a combination of three...factors for which she is in no way responsible: accident, crippling fatigue, and loneliness."[3] Marcel Girard accuses Gervaise of *faiblesse* and *gourmandise*,[4] and Jacques Dubois, without denying the influence of environment, asserts that "[t]out au long, l'héroïne est le principal agent de sa perte."[5]

All of these interpretations are defensible, and I do not wish to take issue with them. However, in proceeding along the path laid by Jacques Dubois, whose socio-critical reading pays special heed to the traces of diverse ideologies to be found in the novel, I would like to examine Gervaise's demise through the microscope of nineteenth-century medical discourse, particularly on subjects relating to hygiene and the working class. Such an approach suggests itself naturally when one is dealing with a novel as preoccupied with cleanliness and dirt as is *L'Assommoir*. I should like to argue for a restricted reading of the concept of *milieu*, one which pays special attention to the work environment of the *blanchisserie*. In short, it is my conviction that Zola intended to expose through his novel the corrupting influence of the laundry, an influence so pernicious that it can transform a woman whose every attribute identifies her with thrift, industry and purity into the incarnation of waste, sloth and filth. Seen from this perspective, Coupeau's fall, the ultimate occupational hazard of the roofer, has a counterpart in the less dramatic but no less destructive perils of Gervaise's chosen occupation.

At the beginning of the novel, Gervaise is coded as the incarnation of freshness and health. A recent arrival from Plassans, she has a glowing complexion, blond hair, white teeth. She is further identified with whiteness by her moral qualities (she is "douce comme un mouton, bonne comme du pain")[6] and by her profession. Drawn to those who, like her, are the incarnation of cleanliness (the blond-bearded Goujet lives with his mother in an immaculate apartment), Gervaise makes a virtue of both physical and moral *propreté*. She has been chastened by her youthful adventures with Lantier which resulted in a premature maternity, and she tells Coupeau in no uncertain terms that sexual relations no longer interest her. Yet by novel's end she has attempted to prostitute herself, she is described as "un tas de quelque chose pas propre" (731) and, as John Frey so succinctly puts it, "only her odour recalls her to the story" on the last page of the novel.[7] Indeed, she has assumed a shape that assimilates her to *entassement, saleté* and *odeur*, nouns used repeatedly in hygienist discourse to describe the conditions in working class neighborhoods.

I should like to suggest that Gervaise Macquart is poisoned by the fetid air of the laundry just as surely as Coupeau is killed by the "poison" of alcohol. Simply stated, the task of laundering clothing is identified not only by its feminine specificity but also by its risks. Zola had represented a different aspect of this danger in *La Fortune des Rougon* where the death of Gervaise's mother had been associated with laundering duties resulting from "une fluxion de poitrine qu'elle a prise en allant laver le linge de la famille . . . et en le rapportant mouillé sur son dos."[8] In *L'Assommoir*, on the other hand, the danger appears to be "in the air." If machines breathe freely in the universe of this novel (the still at Colombe's; the steam machine in the wash-house), the characters cough and splutter with various respiratory ailments (Maman Coupeau has asthma; Clémence suffers from a head cold, Coupeau has a persistent cough, etc.) and the verbs *suffoquer* and *étouffer* are noticeable by their frequency. The fear of asphyxia, a danger to which the medical community constantly alerted the populace in the latter half of the nineteenth century, is evoked twice in the novel. In fact, there is throughout the work a whole network of allusions to the quality of the air (including innumerable evocations of various odors), constituting a subtext which orientates our reading of the novel.

It has often been pointed out that Gervaise's universe is inscribed within a space limited by two constructions which in the nineteenth century evoked death, the slaughterhouse and the hospital. However, since the hospital is also associated with the possibility of healing, the more important common denominator shared by these two geographic perimeters is their association with foul and unhealthy odors. In one of the earliest scenes in the novel, Gervaise looks with disgust towards the walls of the old slaughterhouse, "noirs de leur massacre et de leur puanteur" (380). Discussions regarding the generally insalubrious nature of the *abattoir* were common currency in the contemporary medical press, and physicians were relentless in their struggle to dislocate these *tueries* to the periphery of the city. If by novel's end the slaughterhouse is being demolished, the Lariboisière Hospital, that other limit to Gervaise's horizon which had been under construction in the opening pages, now has its full complement of indigent sick, and its halls reek of a nauseating "odeur de fièvre à suffoquer" (696). In addition, the more general stench of poverty that hangs heavily in the air of les Batignolles and assumes various forms contributes to what one might term *la morbidité du milieu*. Zola singles out for special mention the "air chargé d'alcool" of the cabaret (410), the odor of "soupe à l'oignon" (422) emanating from workers' kitchens, and the repulsive smells that permeate the corridors of the huge apartment buildings on the rue Neuve de la Goutte d'Or, including "l'odeur fade des logis pauvres . . . poussière ancienne, saleté rance" (416) and the stench and "humidité fétide" (422) of the plumbing. However, there can be no doubt that the most memorable description of odors in this novel, equal in importance to that of the celebrated "symphonie des fromages" in *Le Ventre de Paris*, is the one which takes as its subject the *odor sui generis* which fills the small laundry during a ritual sorting of the linen:

Le triage dura une grosse demi-heure. . . . Dans l'air chaud, une puanteur fade montait de tout ce linge sale remué. . . . [Gervaise] n'avait aucun dégoût, habitué à l'ordure; elle enfonçait ses bras nus et roses au milieu des chemises jaunes de crasse, des torchons raidis par la graisse des eaux de vaisselle, des chaussettes mangées et pourries de sueur. Pourtant, dans l'odeur forte qui battait son visage penché au-dessus des tas, une nonchalance la prenait . . . elle se grisait de cette puanteur humaine, vaguement souriante, les yeux noyés. Et il semblait que ses premières paresses vinssent de là, de l'asphyxie des vieux linges empoisonnant l'air autour d'elle. (505-06)

Zola's use of the verb *se griser* to describe the effect of the laundry's stench upon Gervaise suggests a parallel with alcoholism, and the arrival of a drunk Coupeau in the midst of the sorting process has clearly symbolic value. In a similar manner to Gervaise, his inebriation is characterized by indolence and a state of sexual arousal. After resisting his somewhat comical displays of affection, Gervaise finally allows him to kiss her:

Elle s'abandonnait, étourdie par le léger vertige qui lui venait du tas de linge, sans dégoût pour l'haleine vineuse de Coupeau. Et le gros baiser qu'ils échangèrent à pleine bouche, au milieu des saletés du métier, était comme une première chute, dans le lent avachissement de leur vie. (509)

"Premières paresses . . . première chute": Zola could hardly be more explicit. As *blanchisseuse*, his heroine has made a business of managing filth. She is aptly named: Gervaise *gère la vase*, so to speak. But in allowing all of the soiled and malodorous linen in the neighborhood to invade her private and public space (for the laundry serves as her home) she is putting herself at risk of infection, metaphorically speaking. It is common knowledge that Zola sub-scribed to Taine's theory on the influence of the occupational environment, believing, with the philosopher, that "le métier crée des variétés dans l'homme comme le climat crée des variétés dans l'animal."[9] However there is more at stake here than the power of an occupation to transform its practitioners. Dubois comes close to the mark when he says "nous reconnaissons . . . la marque du positivisme inspiré de Taine. Elle se concrétise dans la fameuse influence du milieu, poussée ici à l'extrême et, dans le cas de Gervaise Macquart, jusqu'à l'imprégnation, l'osmose et les formes typiques de la réduplication" (122).

Indeed, Gervaise is literally impregnated by filth until, in the end, she becomes indistinguishable from it. Hence the episode near novel's end when she eats something disgusting on a dare, in order to earn money, represents the final alignment of her personal life with her professional practice. Filth is quite literally her business: it is by taking in *la saleté* that she earns a living. And her laundry is penetrated, not only by the literal filth of the soiled linen, but by such incarnations of moral slime as Virginie Poisson and Lantier. The dream of a refuge against the world's ills is illusory: the boutique may keep out the cold but it is not impervious to dirt. What Dubois does not appear to notice, or in any case does not elaborate, despite the detailed attention he accords to ideology and bourgeois discourses on the poor, is the mechanism by which this "osmosis" is effected. Jacques Allard hints at a causal relationship between Gervaise's profession and her decline: "L'entreprise de blanchissage du quartier était fondée justement sur l'accumulation de linge sale dans la boutique. D'où la paresse (suite à l'action asphyxiante du linge) et, conséquemment, la misère."[10] I would like to take this observation a step farther by proposing that in order to understand Gervaise's demise, we must see her as a victim of "contamination" by her *milieu*. Gervaise has somehow contracted a moral illness more deadly than the most virulent physical disease, an illness charac-terized first by indolence which is experienced as a *jouissance*, then by an erotic fascination with filth: "la saleté était un nid chaud où elle jouissait de s'accroupir. Laisser les choses à la débandade, attendre que la poussière bouchât les trous . . . cela était une vraie volupté dont elle se grisait" (644). In order to comprehend the means by which this "contamination" occurs, it is useful to have some knowledge of nineteenth-century medical discourse on disease transmission.

For the greater part of the nineteenth century, the means by which diseases were communicated was improperly understood. Until the 1880s, some years after Pasteur made his groundbreaking discoveries which eventually resulted in the triumph of germ theory, the prevalent belief, inherited from the eighteenth century, held that disease was the product of noxious odors resulting from decaying matter, effluvia of various sorts, and bodily excretions, especially (but not exclusively) of the sick. As the century wore on, miasma theory (as it was known) came increasingly under attack by contagionists (those who believed that disease was communicated from person to person or indirectly by objects carrying a morbific agent). By the 1870s, the non-contagionists had conceded with regret that unhealthy air was not always malodorous ('il est bien regrettable qu'à chaque miasme ne soit pas surajoutée une odeur désagréable, avertissant de sa présence");[11] however it was an article of faith that the overcrowding of populous sections of the city always produced unhealthy air: "l'accumulation d'organismes, sains par ailleurs, dans un espace relativement restreint, vicie l'air d'une façon particulière en y répandant . . . ce que l'on appelle habituellement le miasme de l'encombrement . . ." (432).

In a period wracked by epidemics, such a conviction had enormous implications. The example of cholera alone will suffice to illustrate the fears that haunted the nineteenth-century bourgeois imagination. Asiatic cholera (*cholera morbus*) came ashore in Europe for the first time in 1829 and was to return several times before the century's end, making its last appearance in France in the summer of 1885, in Toulon. The disease, which killed approximately half of those who contracted it, was characterized by uncontrollable vomiting and diarrhea. Although its etiology and means of transmission were unclear, researchers had, by mid-century, identified what they believed to be predisposing conditions for the spread of cholera, including crowded and filthy living conditions, humidity, and lack of sunlight. There was a proliferation of hygiene manuals intended for the general public, and in text after text, bourgeois readers were lulled into complacency by the same comforting refrain: "La suette, le choléra, le typhus, la fièvre typhoïde, etc. n'ont pas d'instincts aristocratiques, et l'on sait à merveille que ces fléaux aiment volontiers loger dans les quartiers pauvres" (Fossangrives 138). Observation had borne out the accuracy of this formulation: in the case of cholera in particular, the urban poor were most severely affected. The only problem was that one could not assign limits to *l'air vicié* that was believed to circulate in working class neighborhoods. *La classe laborieuse* was indeed *dangereuse*, not in a criminal sense but as a source of illness.

How could the health of the general population be protected? There were two approaches. With *l'haussmannisation de Paris*, Napoléon III had attempted to widen the distance between the affluent and the destitute, the healthy and the unhealthy,[12] thus effecting a symbolic quarantine of the workers in shrinking *faubourgs* of the city. Social reformers and members of the medical profession did their part by pleading for improved hygiene among the proletariat. Attention shifted from the public to the private spheres: concern for the salubrity of the streets had been growing since the dawn of the century, as Parent-Duchâtelet's work on sewers had demonstrated as early as 1836. Now, however, a link was established between body, home, and street: if the reigning powers had to assume responsibility for rendering the streets more healthful, personal cleanliness and the tidiness of one's home were within the province of the workers themselves. The moralizing discourse of hygiene, directed at all classes but with special urgency at the *peuple*, promoted *propreté* as a virtue second to none. Julia Csergo's monograph on nineteenth-century hygiene, *Liberté, Egalité, Propreté*,[13] demonstrates the degree to which cleanliness was valorized as an emblem of worth and moral probity. Her play on the famous revolutionary slogan is deeply significant. One was not expected to fraternize with the worker but rather to inculcate in him values which would make him less repugnant, less threatening to bourgeois health. Where would these values be taught? Above all in the home, by wives and mothers. Medical discourse was most insistent on this point: women, who were viewed as the representatives of the medical profession within the home, were to carry the hygienist message to their families. As Alain Corbin puts it, in *Histoire de la vie privée*, "ce sont elles qui, au sein de la famille, gèrent les choses de la santé."[14]

In addition to its nefarious role as a cause of cholera, an unhealthy home environment was held to be responsible for the "contagion" of alcoholism. The argument went as follows: after long hours of work in dirty factories, men deserved to return home to a clean house. Those who were saddled with negligent wives would delay their return, stopping instead for a drink at the local cabaret. This habit would soon lead to chronic inebriation, a condition that became known only in 1852 as alcoholism.[15] Like cholera, then, the specter of alcoholism intensified fears of the class that was known as "the great unwashed." However, unlike cholera, alcoholism's danger was not that it might be transmitted to the upper classes ("la contagion de l'exemple" was felt to be operative only among the poor), but rather that under its influence, workers would become restless, revolutions would be fomented. In the seventies and eighties, the Commune was cited as an example of mass madness brought on by excessive drinking, and statistics on the number of ex-Communards to be hospitalized for alcohol addiction was tabulated as proof of the phenomenon.[16] To solidify the connection between what were indentified as the twin scourges of the proletariat, cholera and alcoholism, it was asserted that alcoholics were particularly susceptible to the cholera infection, to which they succumbed more rapidly than those who abstained from drink. Once again the responsibility was placed squarely on the shoulders of womankind. Keep your home clean, Madame, and you will live in health and happiness, if not in prosperity: this was the moralizing message of hygienist discourse. To disobey this bourgeois imperative was to condemn one's familly to a demoralizing slide into poverty, filth and disease.

Contemporary literature on hygiene, particularly when it treated the connection between lack of cleanliness and cholera and alcoholism, confirms the hypothesis I have already introduced concerning Gervaise's decline and enables us to read *L'Assommoir* from a new perspective. It is true that Zola made no secret of his direct sources for the novel, such as Denis Poulot's *Le Sublime*, Jules Simon's *L'Ouvrière*, Delvau's *La Langue verte*, and Dr. Magnan's *De l'alcoolisme*. However, scholars who consult only the "official" sources, without taking into consideration the more general context of contemporary medical discourse, are afflicted with a form of intellectual tunnel vision which can seriously handicap their understanding of the novel.

Although Zola began thinking about *L'Assommoir* as early as 1868, most of the actual writing was done in a twelve-month period between 1875 and 1876. Studies of the *fiches préparatoires* show that the idea of making his working-class family victims of the curse of alcoholism came late to Zola, and that his original intention was merely to tell the tale of a working-class woman. From the beginning, he had settled upon her occupation: she was to be a laundress. From this he never waivered, and the reader is left to ponder the reasons which lay behind this choice. What did the laundress represent for the Frenchman living in the second half of the nineteenth century?

Firstly, the laundress was intimately associated with the hygienist project. Unlike the *ménagère*, whose duty in this domain did not extend beyond the familial sphere, the laundress was responsible for the cleaning and maintenance of the clothing of the entire neighborhood. Alain Corbin has observed that in the lower classes, personal hygiene was for a long time interpreted to mean wearing clean clothes rather than bathing, whence the central role played by the *blanchisseuse*. The entry for *blanchissage* in the nineteenth-century Larousse dictionary confirms this view of the laundress: "L'industrie du blanchissage est intimement liée à l'hygiène publique, et occupe une classe nombreuse de travailleurs qu'il est urgent de protéger contre les inconvénients et les dangers de leur profession."[17] In fact, sending one's laundry out to be washed, rather than taking it to the *lavoir* oneself, was a relatively recent phenomenon, especially in the lower classes, and was not without serious disadvantages, since disease was believed to be spread through the wash water. The laundress herself was most at risk, and nineteenth-century medical discourse ranked this profession among the most dangerous for women. Philippe Patissier, in his 1822 *Traité des maladies des artisans*, observes that

les chemises et le linge imprégnés de mille saletés . . . exhalent des odeurs fétides. Considéré sous ce dernier point, le métier de blanchisseuse est sans contredit l'un des plus dangereux; ces ouvrières peuvent en effet contracter les maladies contagieuses par le linge qu'elles manient, et qui récèle les émanations du corps des malades.[18]

Even towards the end of the century, when miasma theory no longer held sway, the fundamental belief in this occupational hazard remained firm: "When washing the clothes of the sick, they [laundresses] are exposed to contagion."[19] Like alcoholics, laundresses were believed to be particularly vulnerable to epidemic diseases, not only because infection was somehow transmitted through clothing, but also because the very conditions in which they were obliged to work were insalubrious.[20] City laundries, generally on the ground floor of multi-storied buildings, had little direct sunlight; the atmosphere within was warm and moist, conditions believed to augment the activity of miasma as well as to cause a sense of extreme fatigue.[21] Furthermore, the noxious smells emitted by the laundry, combined with the vapors produced by cleaning agents and the coke-burning stove on which irons were heated, poisoned the atmosphere and caused asphyxia. In short, the air in the typical laundry was polluted to the point of being *irrespirable*. Laundresses were subject to a host of other ailments as well, resulting from constant exposure to heat and steam, inadequate perspiration because of the moist air, prolonged periods of standing, often on a wet floor, immersion of the hands and arms in hot, alkaline water, and hard physical labor.

Such was the bleak picture of life in the laundries, as painted by a reform-minded medical profession eager to improve workers' conditions. Superficially, at least, it has little in common with the apparently idyllic tableau sketched by Zola. Although the shop is humid and dark ("les murs pissaient l'humidité et on ne voyait plus clair dès trois heures de l'après-midi," 497), Gervaise perspires abundantly, contracts no contagious diseases, suffers no rhumatism or other occupation-related illness, and indeed appears to thrive in the hothouse atmosphere of her shop which is likened on several occasions to an *alcôve* and resembles a boudoir more than a sweatshop. The image of Gervaise and her employees sipping coffee and luxuriating in the cocoon-like warmth as they watch passersby bundled in overcoats on a bitterly cold winter's day, or of the scantily clad employees bleaching and ironing until late into the night as a titillated Goujet looks on discreetly from his assigned place in a corner of the room, hardly seems to conform to the picture of professional misery drawn by the physicians. To be sure, Gervaise's situation is not typical. As *patronne*, she employs a washerwoman, Madame Bijard, who completes the first steps in the long washing process in the *lavoir*. Moreover, as a "blanchisseuse de fin," she limits her practice to certain items of clothing (collars, sleeve guards, men's shirts, ladies bonnets, scarves, etc.), leaving the heavier work of laundering sheets, towels, etc. to others. Finally, as proprietress of her own shop which doubles as her home, she does not violate her "feminine domesticity" and is thus spared the wrath of physicians who, echoing Michelet's diatribe against women driven to work by the Industrial Revolution ("Ouvrière, mot impie . . . !")[22] decry the gainful employment of wives and mothers who are of necessity neglecting their domestic duties. Theoretically, at least, Gervaise "has it all."

In practice, of course, this is hardly the case, and despite the positive valorisation of the little laundry, which appears to stand in symbolic counter-point to Colombe's destructive *assommoir*, the domain of men as the laundry is that of women, this textual space is only apparently utopian. It does offer, like the cabaret, an escape from the misery of working class life, but this escape is fleeting indeed, and like that of alcohol, can be seen merely as "un paradis artificiel" which is ultimately destructive. On one level, the novel can be read as a struggle for dominance between the laundry and the cabaret, two spaces to which the narrative gives significant religious connotations, suggesting that they have become the modern substitute for religion, that once effective "opiate" of the people. At the beginning of the novel, Gervaise worships at the altar of Hygeia, the goddess of cleanliness. She reigns over her laundry while a devoted Goujet admires her "pareillement à une sainte vierge," a role she relishes. Her own hygienic standards are irreprochable: she is "propre comme un sou" (442) and she takes loving care of her meager possessions, "[ayant] une religion pour [ses] meubles" (465). Gervaise's example illustrates the growing influence of the medical profession and the hygienist movement which it spawned. In this age of scientism, the doctor has replaced the priest as director of public conscience, and cleanliness has become a cardinal virtue. This shift in emphasis from the moral to the physical is accompanied by a blurring of the distinction between the two: the good are by definition clean, and cleanliness is a signifier of goodness. This is not simply an example of the old cliché according to which cleanliness is next to godliness: in hygienist discourse, cleanliness replaces godliness.

By novel's end, however, Gervaise has joined the cult of Bacchus, and it is Colombe's cabaret, "illuminé comme une cathédrale pour la grande Messe" (769), that has emerged victorious in the battle for the souls of the poor. How can we explain the triumph of alcohol which flies in the face of the medical community's repeated warnings of the horrors of alcoholism and its tireless proselytizing on behalf of the "religion" of hygiene? Interestingly enough, an examination of the popular discourse as reproduced by Zola testifies to the fact that the hygienist message *did* get through, for there is a persistent confusion between the moral and the physical which is especially prevalent in the sexual domain. Moral and physical "filth" go hand in hand, and words evoking uncleanliness are repeatedly pressed into service to describe "sins" of a sexual nature. To give but one example, the word *saleté* is used as an epithet for sexual intercourse ("Vous ne songez qu'à la saleté" [407], says Gervaise to Coupeau in the early days of their courtship), illicit sexual activity (the relationship between Boche and Mme Gaudron is characterized as a "saleté," 499), and vulgar jokes ("la saleté de Sophie," 719; "[Clémence] lâcha un mot cru, une saleté," 507). This contamination of the physical and the moral is operative on another level as well, for the most unkempt of this novel's characters, those whose laundry smells the most foul are the sexually promiscuous. Early in the novel, Virginie is characterized as "une saleté" (397). The wanton Madame Gaudron brings in a packet of laundry that is so rank Gervaise vows never to accept her business again, whereas the spinster Mlle Remanjou deposits clothing that is never soiled, "ce qui prouvait qu'à cet âge-là on est quasiment comme un morceau de bois, dont on serait bien en peine de tirer une larme de quelque chose" (508).

The result of this coincidence of moral and physical impurity is that the clothing brought in to be laundered tells an often sordid tale of debauchery. In an era when clothing had a marked social value among the bourgeoisie as camouflage for corporeal imperfections and enhancement of (especially femi- nine) beauty,[23] a scene which features clothing in a treasonous role cannot fail to suggest an implicit contrast between la bourgeoisie and le peuple. This brings me back to my analogy with religion. Semantically inscribed as a meeting point between filth and cleanliness, Gervaise's blanchisserie may be likened to a confessional where the sins of the quartier are revealed and symbolically cleansed. The triage is the moment of truth, and Gervaise delights in this operation during which "on déshabillait . . . tout le quartier" (508). The prurient curiosity of Zola's laundresses is in conformity with the image promoted by the medical press which, not content to outline the physical risks of various occupations, insisted on providing a "moral profile" of the women who engaged in them. The laundress, according to official wisdom, is particu- larly fond of "la danse, les spectacles, les cafés et les plaisirs de l'amour."[24] Zola emphasizes this weakness for the "pleasures of love" in his fiction. It is not by chance that the promiscuous Mouquette in Germinal is a laundress, or that the voluptuous Clémence takes special interest in ironing men's shirts. Also in keeping with current stereotypes, Zola's laundresses are characterized by their vulgar language and crude jokes. Before Gervaise acquires her boutique, Goujet avoids the company of such women, and lowers his head when he must pass by their shops: "il n'aimait pas leurs gros mots, trouvait ça dégoûtant que des femmes eussent sans cesse des saletés à la bouche" (474). Later in the novel, Lantier will take pleasure in the company of these same women, "des filles pas bégueules" (608).

The vulgarity of the blanchisseuse, her preoccupation with sensuality, appear as a natural consequence not only of the knowledge gained through the laundering of personal garmets, but also of the sexual disponibilité and indolence engendered by inhaling the body odors emitted by the soiled clothing. The role of corporeal odors in the evolution of sexuality has been discussed in detail in Alain Corbin's remarkable treatise on the history of olfaction, Le Miasme et la jonquille.[25] Zola establishes an unmistakably causal relationship between the professional duties of the laundress and her immorality; in so doing, he betrays the influence of the discourse of hygiene which displayed an almost obsessive preoccupation with "la puanteur du pauvre" and a growing repugnance for strong animal smells. Unlike the bourgeois, whose olfactory pleasures had proceeded to more delicate perfumes that masked body odors, the poor, with their allegedly primitive sexuality, were believed to be stimulated by the violent smells of bodily excretions.[26]

Gervaise is thus "infected" with a languid sensuality that overcomes her energy, her industry, and her moral indignation, and this ultimately devastating influence of the environment upon her suggests an analogy with miasma theory. Although the word *miasme*, found so frequently in the works of a Flaubert or a Balzac, does not appear in *L'Assommoir*, the fact that Zola subscribed to this theory is not in doubt (Corbin 241). Moreover, the text is shot through with allusions to the stench of poverty, as concentrated in the laundry and in the huge apartment building, the spaces that Gervaise is condemned to inhabit and in which the tale of her degradation unfolds. Gervaise herself, reflecting upon her first entry into the maison de la rue Neuve de la Goutte d'Or, pinpoints that moment as decisive in the turn her life has taken: "Depuis le jour où elle y avait fichu les pieds, elle s'était mise à dégringoler. Oui, ça devait porter malheur d'être ainsi les uns sur les autres, dans ces grandes gueuses de maisons ouvrières; on y attrapait le choléra de la misère" (778). The promiscuity of crowded living. A grinding poverty of epidemic proportions. One easily recognizes the clichés of medical discourse. Gervaise has indeed become infected with "le choléra de la misère," an infection which was borne in the acrid air of the little laundry.

A distinction must however be made between the fears articulated by hygienist discourse and Zola's literary transposition thereof. Gervaise does not fear cholera; she fears "le choléra de la misère." She does not contract a physical malady, but a moral one which takes her from *la paresse* to *l'alcoolisme*. And if alcoholism is presented as contagious (indeed, Poulot's preface to *Le Sublime* exploits the medical metaphor in laying bare the epidemic nature of this pathological condition),[27] it is disassociated from political activism in *L'Assommoir* where the most outspoken proponents of labor reform are Goujet and Lantier, both of whom are characterized by their sobriety. Finally, the cabaret and the *lavoir*, which at the time had the reputation of being centers of seditionist activity, here set the scene for disputes and discussions of a distinctly apolitical nature. In short, the conditions of working class life deplored by hygienist discourse and faithfully reproduced by Zola are presented not as potentially destructive to society at large but as self-destructive, threatening above all to the proletariat.

The walls of the *abattoir*, "noirs de leur massacre et de leur puanteur," had established a connection between *death* and *stench*. Death, particularly when provoked by the violent and repeated slaughter of animals, smells bad. Gervaise, who at first finds the odor repugnant, will eventually be seduced by the animal odors of her customers, then by the odor of death as represented by Bazouge, the *croque-mort* (another example of the "osmosis" which makes one resemble one's occupation). In the novel's final passage, it is death itself which causes the odor that poisons the air. Gervaise *is* that odor. By infecting the air with the stench of her decaying corpse, Gervaise is achieving a posthumous revenge against those who poisoned her with the rancid odor of their vice.

The *Petit Robert* gives, as the first definition of the verb *infecter*, "imprégner d'émanations dangereuses et malsaines." What better phrase to describe the pathogenic force of the working-class community on Gervaise Macquart? In an operation analogous to the spontaneous combustion of old Macquart's alcohol-soaked body, described so vividly in *Le Docteur Pascal*, Gervaise's body self-destructs after being permeated, infected by the filth of others. Viewed in this light, she takes her place naturally among the surrogate victims enumerated by Naomi Schor, and *L'Assommoir* fits into the general pattern of what Schor terms the "founding myth . . . the ritual slaying or expulsion of the scapegoat, or pharmakos."[28]

In his original project for *L'Assommoir*, Zola wrote to the editor Lacroix that he had a social agenda, that of demanding "de l'air, de la lumière et de l'instruction pour les basses classes" (Girard 14). Later, defending in his 1877 preface his controversial portrayal of the working class, he claimed to have written "le premier roman du peuple qui ne mente pas qui ait *l'odeur* du peuple" (373-74, emphasis added). Zola's use of *odeur* to signify *authenticité* and his insistence on the need to provide a healthier environment for the working classes offer extra-textual support for my thesis regarding the importance of atmosphere, conceived in a *physical* sense, on the heroine's destiny. Through a process which owes much to miasma theory, Gervaise Macquart has been metaphorically infected by the environment in which she lives and works. We must wait for Nana to redress that wrong.

Notes

[1] "Narrative Tension in the Representation of Women in Zola's *L'Assommoir* and *Nana*," *L'Esprit Créateur* 25.4 (1985) 99.

[2] With Claude Schumacher, "La Grande Bouffe dans *L'Assommoir* et dans le cycle Gervaise," *L'Esprit Créateur* 25.4 (1985) 20.

[3] "The Decline and Fall of Gervaise Macquart," *Essays in French Literature* 16 (1979) 62.

[4] "Notice," *L'Assommoir* (extraits) (Paris: Larousse, 1972) 24.

[5] *L'Assommoir de Zola: société, discours, idéologie* (Paris: Larousse, 1973) 39-40.

[6] Emile Zola, *L'Assommoir*, in *Les Rougon-Macquart*, Bibliothèque de la Pléiade Edition (Paris: Gallimard, 1961) 2: 502. Subsequent references to the novel and its preface, given in the text of the essay, will be to this edition.

[7] *Aesthetics of the Rougon-Macquart* (Washington, DC: Studia Humanitas, 1978) 135.

[8] Pléiade edition (Paris: Gallimard, 1960) 1: 148.

[9] Quoted by Henri Massis, *Comment Emile Zola composait ses romans* (Paris: Charpentier, 1906) 153.

[10] *Zola: le chiffre du texte* (Grenoble: PU de Grenoble, 1978) 88.

[11] J.B. Fossangrives, *Hygiène et assainissement des villes* (Paris: Baillières, 1874) 398.

[12] In his *Encyclopedia of Medical History* (London: MacMillan, 1985) 62. Robert McGrew asserts that cholera was the impetus behind urban renewal.

[13] *Liberté, Egalité, Propreté* (Paris: Albin Michel, 1988).

[14] "Cris et chuchotements," in *Histoire de la vie privée*, 4 (Paris: Seuil, 1987) 595.

[15] Dr. Ernest Monin, *L'Alcoolisme: étude médico-sociale* (Paris: Octave Doin, 1917) 54.

[16] Susanna Barrows, "After the Commune: Alcoholism, Temperance, and Literature in the Early Third Republic," in *Consciousness and Class Experience in Nineteenth-Century Europe*, ed. John M. Merriman (New York: Holmes and Meier, 1979).

[17] Pierre Larousse, *Grand Dictionnaire universel du XIXe siècle* (Paris: Larousse et Boyer, 1866-90); "Blanchissage," 2: 800.

[18] *Traité des maladies des artisans* (Paris: Baillière, 1822) 254. Ambroise Tardieu, in his *Dictionnaire d'hygiène publique et de sobriété* (Paris: Baillière, 1852), is more cautious: "Nous ne pensons pas que les blanchisseuses soient exposées à contracter des maladies contagieuses pendant les opérations qui constituent le blanchissage lui-même; mais il ne serait pas impossible qu'en recevant et en triant le linge à blanchir, elles ne vinssent à contracter le germe d'affections transmissibles" (1: 157).

[19] J.T. Arlidge, *The Hygiene, Diseases and Mortality of Occupations* (London: Percival & Co., 1982) 118.

[20] See Léon Poincaré, *Triaté d'hygiène industrielle à l'usage des médecins et des membres des conseils d'hygiène* (Paris: Masson, 1886).

[21] See *Dictionnaire des sciences médicales* (Paris: Panckoucke, 1821) and Sir Thomas Oliver, *Occupations from the Social, Hygienic and Medical Points of View* (Cambridge: Cambridge UP, 1916).

[22] *La Femme*, 2nd. ed. (Paris: Hachette, 1860) 22.

[23] Philippe Perrot speaks in *Le Travail des apparences* (Paris: Seuil, 1984) of "la production vestimentaire du mirage anatomique" (169).

[24] M. Cadet-Gassincourt, quoted by Patissier 256.

[25] *Le Miasme et la jonquille* (Paris: Aubier Montaigne, 1982).

[26] Lantier, for example, likes the smell of musk (cf. 601), a perfume that was said to emphasize, rather than camouflage, bodily odors.

[27] "Nous avons fouillé, ouvert à plein couteau toutes les plaies, les pustules de ce corps qui se décompose, nous l'avons présenté tel qu'il est, rien de plus. Vous ne le croycz pas assez avancé, vous pensiez qu'il était moins atteint. Quand vous le regardez il vous fait peur. Ah! tant mieux s'il vous épouvante. Oh! prenez garde, c'est épidémique et très-contagieux, le sublimisme. . . ." Denis Poulot, *Le Sublime ou Le Travailleur comme il est en 1870 et ce qu'il peut être*, 2nd ed (Paris: Lacroix, 1872) 6.

[28] *Zola's Crowds* (Baltimore: Johns Hopkins UP, 1978) 4.

Vicki Douillet Toumayan

A Generation of Ballerinas: Degas's and Halévy's Dancers

The second half of the nineteenth century in France, and in particular in Paris, was perhaps one of the moments when the rapport between painters and writers was at its most intimate. Both portrayed their era, working in different mediums, but choosing the same themes, the same motifs. Their common interest in art drew them together as professionals, occasioning not only many discussions at favorite cafés but also visits at home. Degas, not an anomaly of his time, was connected with Zola, Paul Alexis, Paul Arène, Villiers de l'Isle-Adam, Duranty, Mendès, Albert Mérat, and Ernest d'Hervilly, with whom he frequented the Café Gerbois, the Goncourt brothers, Ludovic Halévy, and later on Stéphane Mallarmé and Paul Valéry.[1]

Ludovic Halévy was one of those who entered the circle of Degas's close friends as is witnessed by the latter's correspondence. It was the ballet and the Opera which linked the two men both professionally, as artists, and socially, as friends. Halévy grew up in a family of theater people and eventually took an active part writing plays and collaborating on operas. He was Offenbach's librettist. Thus he had first-hand knowledge of the world both on and backstage. He was a "flâneur" within the Opera, roaming its many corridors and absorbing all that took place. He would record his conversations with the wealthy who attended the performances, with the ballerinas and their mothers whom he knew well and with whom he chatted freely, and with the maids who were veritable encyclopedias of information on the intrigues of Opera life, and he attended rehearsals as well as the actual productions themselves. His writings, both fiction and non-fiction reflect this knowledge. The vignettes of the Opera, appearing sporadically in his *Notes et Souvenirs*, a journal for the years 1871-1872, his short stories concerning the ballet: "The Most Beautiful Woman in Paris," 1894, "Mariette," 1883, and "A l'Opéra," 1883, and finally his novel, *La Famille Cardinal* published in 1880 (parts of it were published earlier in other collections, 1872), all are based on his actual experiences. In particular, the latter, as he reveals in his *Carnets,* is based on a real interview with the mother of a ballet dancer.

Degas, although not as intimately connected with the Opera by profession, managed to infiltrate its private world, partly through the influence of Halévy, who, for example, could arrange for his friend to attend an "examen."[2] Thus during the period 1870-1885, before Degas shut himself off from the world, when he frequented the theaters and race-tracks, and dined out, the familiarity with the ballet which he acquired as an avid Opera-goer (he had a season's subscription) (LD 66) was given a second dimension by his visits back-stage, his attendance at rehearsals, and his presence at ballet classes (Son 9). His method was similar to Halévy's in that the notes he took of what he heard and saw furnished the raw material for his works. He came to know the dancers well, at least well enough for one to ask his intercession in getting her a raise in salary (LD 73-74). Degas also seems to share Halévy's predilection for what takes place at the Opera away from the public eye: more of his works on the theme of the ballet and the opera are devoted to scenes of the corridors behind stage and in the classrooms of the Opera than to actual views of the production, just as Halévy devotes most of his text to stories of the dancers' personal and off-stage lives rather than to their profession and affords only a rare, fleeting glimpse of the actual performances.

It was perhaps due to this mutual interest as well as to their friendship that Halévy requested Degas to illustrate his novel, *La Famille Cardinal,* for the 1880 publication (Degas accordingly started making studies as early as 1877). But, while Halévy's novel ostensibly generated Degas's monotypes, it was evidently their very different perceptions of the ballet world, arising from radically opposing perceptions of their society, that resulted in Halévy's discontentment with the monotypes which Degas produced as illustrations and in Halévy's ultimate rejection of them. Indeed, if we examine the works of Halévy and of Degas which were generated by this third art form, ballet, we see two markedly different portrayals of the ballerinas as a small subclass of women in the nineteenth century.

The dancers, whom both Degas and Halévy chose to portray, were always female although there were male dancers at that time. Even the harlequins whom Degas shows are actually female.[3] Furthermore, they are usually the "coryphées," those who appear in groups and not lone stars. However, Halévy was not sensitive to the dichotomy of the ballet dancer's life as was Degas. The latter was aware of the artificiality and hypocrisy of the opera world which created such a contrast between the dancer on and off-stage. This is revealed in his sonnets: "Partez, sans le secours inutile du beau, / Mignonnes, avec ce populacier museau / Sautez effrontément, prêtresses de la grâce! / En vous la danse a mis quelque chose d'à part, / Héroïque et lointain. On sait de votre place. / Que les reines se font de distance et de fard" (Son 33-34). Degas contrasted the beautiful, ethereal, and rhythmic vision which appeared on stage with the hard-working, perhaps vulgar, and ugly girl that the dancer was when seen close-up. Halévy, however, depicts the ballerina on and off-stage as a charming, vivacious, beautiful creature. Consequently, there seems to be very little correspondence between the character, Virginie, "joliment débourrée"[4] in *La Famille Cardinal* and Degas's pictorial translation of her into the rather homely, awkward dancer of the monotype, "Au foyer."[i] Degas's vision of the dancers, often heavy, coarse-featured, and even perhaps slightly deformed at the joints due to their occupation (pl. 62), does not coincide with that of Halévy whose dancers are seen even behind the stage as "jolies filles" (FC 62), "vêtu(es) de soie et de satin" (FC 38), moving "lestement" (FC 38), "charmant(es) à voir" (FC 64). Furthermore, Degas's dancers often reveal their vulgarity in their poses and gestures when caught out of the spectator's vision. We see them scratching, yawning wide, and even sitting in provocative positions which recall those of the prostitutes in his brothel scenes (pl. 21, 28, 114, 133, 203). Halévy's ballerinas, on the contrary, never lose their charm and even when seen in private moments remain coquettishly attractive: they "frétillaient gentiment devant la grande glace . . . se détirant pour rompre leurs maillots, faisant bouffer leurs jupes de gaze" (FC 64). While Halévy may superficially recognize the discrepancy between the woman and her persona, this observation is relegated in his novel to a brief, incidental allusion to the false hair of some of the dancers.[5] Degas, on the other hand, emphasizes this discrepancy; he repeatedly thematizes it, making it the focus of such works as the monotype of a dancer putting on her make-up.[ii]

   The ballerinas working out in class are also depicted differently by the artist and the writer. The elements are the same; Halévy's description in "A l'Opéra" could easily be applied to many of Degas's paintings—the room: "une grande salle carrée, le plancher légèrement incliné, un poêle de faïence, des banquettes pour les mères . . . voilà le décor. Des barres d'appui courent le long des murs . . ." (PtC 245-46), the girls: "en costume de danse. . . . Décolletées, bras nus, robes de mousseline blanche, ceinture de soie bleue, rouge, rose . . ." (PtC 246). But there the similarity ends. The atmosphere evoked is completely different. For, although the author sees the dancers as "presques toutes maigres, grêles, efflanquées," exhibiting "un air de hardiesse, de courage, et de bonne humeur" (PtC 246), and while he recognizes the rigor of a dancer's training, it is all dismissed lightly with the remark that "elles aiment leur état, elles aiment l'Opéra, elles aiment la danse. Leur métier est rude, mais elles l'adorent" (PtC 246). Hence, the mood is animated and gay, the girls are "riant, criant, gambadant" (PtC 246), and they are often talking to and confiding in one another. In Degas's classroom scenes, the emotional tone is quite different. The rapport between the dancers is not seen as one of great comradery. Rather, when not performing together they often choose to be alone, either to practice or to rest. This lack of interaction and disregard for each other's presence is reflected in their gaze and their body language: they look in different directions and turn away from one another (pl. 17, 116, 187). Even when they are pictured as communicating, they remain fairly expressionless (pl. 201). No warmth of friendship is suggested. And, Degas's dancers do get tired. In several scenes of dancers resting, Degas conveys the sense of exhaustion, emphasizing it by his choice of point of view. Seen from above, bending over, in a space cut by a very low horizon line, the ballerinas seem crushed with fatigue (see for example pl. 99).

While Halévy and Degas both describe the dancers as composites of different pieces all of which must be in order for the perfect running of the machine, Halévy attenuates the inhumanity; Degas emphasizes it. Thus Halévy describes an examination where seven dancers go through an exercise together, detailing the action of each part of the body: "les sept petites mains gauches des sept petites danseuses viennent se plaquer, toutes en même temps sur leurs sept petits cœurs, et les sept petites mains droites viennent ensuite se plaquer sur les sept petites mains gauches. . . . Les sept petites têtes s'abîment comme par un mouvement mécanique . . ." (PtC 235). Here the affectionate term "petits" and the amusing tone set by the repetition obviate any criticism which the mechanical aspect might elicit. Degas is not so kind. His dancers in "Trois danseuses exécutant 'Développe à la seconde'" (pl. 35) have all the aspects of robots. The fact that their faces are often not completely visible and that they are also frequently not well differentiated (for example in some works [such as pl. 240], dancers seem to be mirror images of each other and in other works we seem to have the same dancer seen in several different poses) contributes to the impression of their being anonymous dolls, mass-produced for public entertainment. Also, the dancers sometimes seem to dissolve into the backdrop (pl. 232), thus being rendered no more important than the non-human props of the production. (Huysmans sensed this in Degas's dancers also: "dans des tableaux de danseuses . . . [il] avait déjà si implacablement rendu la déchéance de la mercenaire abêtie par de mécaniques ébats et de monotones sauts. . . .")[6] Degas also truncates his dancers abruptly, isolating parts of the body, thus again suggesting the piecemeal composite (pl. 45, 112).

There is, in particular, an emphasis on the legs, introducing an element of eroticism which is lost on today's public. But, for Degas's and Halévy's generation, the tutu which revealed the legs was still fairly new as a costume for ballerinas (Browse 47), and considered to be quite "risqué" at the time. McCabe, an Englishman, then traveling in France, noted that "the dress of the dancers [is] as slight as the law, which is by no means prudish, will permit."[7] Thus the display of the legs calls attention to the sexuality of these women. And Degas and Halévy chose to portray their dancers, almost without exception, in that costume, even in classroom scenes (although Degas sometimes adds a shawl or shows bloomers underneath the skirt to remind us that the ballerina is also a working-girl). Degas further evokes the sensuality of the ballerinas in

such paintings as "Les danseuses aux cheveux longs" where he devotes his
attention to the dancers' seductively long hair (pl. 160, 162, 163), and in others
where his rendering of the skin tone by several colors which melt into one
another creates a vivid, palpitating effect.[8]

This erotic aspect suggests another dimension of Degas's and Halévy's
ballerinas: their work was not restricted to the realm of public entertaining; they
were employed, as well, in entertainment of a much more private nature. The
dancers of this generation were often the mistresses of wealthy men, the top-
hatted "habitués" of the Opera. In fact, the ballet was somewhat of an exclusive
brothel for members of the Jockey Club.[9] Both Halévy and Degas intimate what
this relationship was like through comparison of the dancers and race-horses—
again Degas is the harsher critic. In one of his sonnets he describes a horse as
"tout nerveusement nu dans sa robe de soie" (Son 26). Halévy assimilates the
two as well; he says of the ballerinas: "Elles attendaient là le signal du défilé
et faisaient ainsi en l'air l'effet d'un peloton de jolis petits chevaux, encensant,
piaffant, se cambrant, se cabrant et se préparant à charger" (FC 64). Degas
translates the literary simile into a pictorial one. He was preoccupied with the
motifs of the race-track and those of the ballet during the same period and his
scenes of groups of dancers, milling around, waiting to go on stage, remind one
of his paintings of race-horses. For example, compare "Les danseuses roses
avant le ballet" (pl. 181) and "En attendant l'entrée" (pl. 139), with some of his
"Horses"[iii] done around 1883-85. There are compositional parallels in the
diagonal lines and similar points of view of horses and dancers, seen from
different angles, which link the two motifs. This assimilation has a deeper
significance. Both the horse and dancer depend on their legs for their careers,
and the horse is often an erotic female symbol. What was demanded of both
horses and dancers was the same: performance on command. Often Jockey
Club members would watch their dancers work out, just as they watched their
horses, and Degas shows both in his pictures (compare "At the race-track:
Spectator and Horses" [pl. 30 and Minervino pl. 434] with "Répétition d'un
ballet sur la scène" [Minervino pl. 772]).

The mothers of the ballet dancers were instrumental in setting their
daughters up with the Jockey Club members and other men of wealth. The
figure of the mother appears repeatedly in Degas's works and in Halévy's
fiction; she is often more important than the dancers themselves. Again
however, Halévy differs from Degas in his amused, affectionate attitude toward
these matriarchal figures which contrasts with the painter's more realistic and
perhaps harsh attitude. Degas does seem to have been influenced by Halévy
here since in several of his works[iv] (pl. 34, 102) even apart from his illustrations
for the book, the mother resembles Madame Cardinal whom Halévy describes
as "Une grosse dame, d'une mise négligée, un vieux tartan à carreau sur les
épaules" (FC 5).

For both artists, the mother was a dual figure in relationship to her daughter—both parent and business-woman whose saleable commodities were her daughters. The former relation is developed in Halévy's *La Famille Cardinal* where Madame Cardinal, despite her daughter's break with her wealthy lover, is more concerned with her child's health than with the bad turn of events (FC 13). The strange dichotomy of the two seemingly unreconcilable facets of the mother is evoked with a good deal of humor both in a scene where Madame Cardinal insists on attending to her sick daughter although her lover insists that he can do it and in the scene where the living arrangements are decided upon for, although Virginie is to become a mistress of a Marquis, she is not to leave her family. Degas occasionally, though rarely, depicts affection displayed between mother and daughter, thus giving little emphasis to the mother in her role as a parent. In the "Classe de danse de M. Perrot" (pl. 22), there is a mother perhaps embracing her daughter at the far end of the room. In "Préparation pour la classe" (pl. 39) we see a dancer affectionately encircling her mother with her arms.

This pastel also seems to emphasize the dual role of the mother. We see two mother-daughter couples which resemble each other enough to be the same one, just portrayed in different positions and in different attitudes, thus reflecting two very different aspects of the same relationship. The couple closest to the window conveys a sense of the matter-of-fact, business-like quality of the relationship in marked contrast to the affection exhibited by the couple to the right. This dichotomy is also evoked in "La Famille Mante" (pl. 72, 73) by use of a similar technique to depict another duality—that of ballerina as dancer and as child. But here Degas is more cynical. We see two sisters, one in a dancer's costume and one in street clothes. They look so much alike that they may be thought of as two aspects of the same person. The mother is devoting all her attention to the dancer, ignoring the "little girl." This is emphasized by the fact that while the heads of the mother and girl in costume are pointing along the same axis, the girl in street clothes is looking in a different direction. Furthermore, the background is divided into light and dark, separating the sisters and setting each girl in one of the resulting two segments of space; the mother is basically in the same space as the dancer. In "L'attente" (pl. 7) we again see a woman and child, mother and daughter since they are seated together at one end of a long bench. But the physical proximity of the two belies any true intimacy between them as there is no communication or interaction; the woman sits rather determinedly and indifferent, ignoring the girl who is massaging her ankle, perhaps in pain.

The mothers of the ballet dancers were, as far as can be deduced from Halévy's works, essentially business-women in a large sense. The mother of Mariette, the eponymous heroine of one short story was a "fruitière," others were "couturières ou blanchisseuses" (PtC 230). Thus they were used to coldly calculating profits. Their daughters, then, became just another source of income. We see Madame Cardinal evaluating objectively the beauty of her daughter; she sees her as "pas la plus belle. Faut pas d'aveuglement maternel. Marie Fernot est mieux que Virginie" (FC 7). She can ignore any maternal prejudice which could interfere with her business. Similarly as regards Pauline, the younger of her two daughters, she (Madame Cardinal) is on guard that she not take on a lover right away as her value will increase when she is older: "à quoi bon se presser, je vous le demande? La petite sera encore plus jolie l'année prochaine que maintenant" (FC 8). That this was the usual rather than the exceptional attitude of the ballerina's mother is suggested by Halévy in "Mariette" where the heroine's recounting of her own mother's attitude ("Je n'ai jamais trouver ça bien, ces mères qui passent leur vie à tâcher de se faire donner des choses par leurs filles. Il faut aimer ses enfants pour eux-mêmes et pas pour le plus ou moins de profits qu'on en retire")[10] is met with astonishment by the other dancers in the Opera.

As a business-woman, the dancer's mother has usurped the role of the father as provider for the family, and in her need to maximize profits she takes on traditional male character traits, suppressing her sentimental, "womanly" side. In *La Famille Cardinal* we see that all is controlled by the mother; Monsieur Cardinal is inept and the family would get along as well, or in fact better, without him. In the short stories concerning the ballet, the father is totally absent. It is then significant that Degas entitles his work "*La Famille* Mante" although no father is present. Furthermore, that the mother has moved into the "male realm" is suggested by the fact that in Degas's works she is usually shown in dark dress (as are the male figures: orchestra members and Opera "habitués") which contrasts with the light ballet costumes. Also, during the classes, the mothers may sometimes act as extensions of the professor (always male). Halévy describes a classroom scene where the dance-instructor, helpless in bringing his class to order abandons his role as director of proceedings, allowing maternal authority to discipline the unruly group of girls as he passively waits (PtC 250). In Degas's "La classe de danse. 'Adage'" (pl. 34), the connection between instructor and mother is literal: the figure of the mother touches that of the professor and in "La répétition dans la salle d'un 'Pas de trois'" (pl. 98), the mother is linked pictorially with the professor by her proximity, by the fact that only those two (of those on the right side of the prominent line down the floor) are facing toward the left, and by her occupancy of the straw-seated chair which in Halévy's "A l'Opéra" is the seat of the instructor (the mothers usually sit on benches along the walls). This mother is reading "Le Petit Journal," the newspaper always read by Halévy's mothers too. The dance instructor can also be seen as surrogate father in that he represents discipline, is older, and forms a couple with the mother in these scenes.

The mother's morality seems to be one of expediency. One must simply be practical: she and her daughters need money so there is nothing wrong with their way of obtaining it. This outlook is reflected in Madame Cardinal's remark in reaction to contempt shown by a priest: "Est-ce que c'était ma faute à moi si j'étais née dans la médiocrité et si ma fille était dans la danse au lieu d'être dans l'aristocratie?" (FC 119). Feeling thus justified she becomes unabashed in seeking her ends and tyrannical in directing her daughters' lives. She keeps them under strict surveillance, even watching them back-stage where, in principle, she is forbidden to go. We see Madame Cardinal reprimanding Pauline with a slap for accepting a kiss from an admirer back-stage and her daughter subsequently is fined for her mother's trespassing. In Degas's monotypes for the novel, this mother is also seen behind the sets and in the corridors but rather than the comical madame of Halévy's novel, she is more of an ominous figure. In some works, for example (Janis pl. 195, 196), the silhouettes of the stage back-drops echo that of Madame Cardinal thus assimilating her and insinuating that her presence is an integral part of the performance and that she is always in the background. The manner in which the silhouettes jut into the picture space of the dancers, sometimes even eclipsing one, suggests the domineering mother who is always "butting in," managing even the private lives of her daughters. Madame Cardinal arranges her daughters' lives without consulting them. Thus she is against Virginie's affair with an actor and sets things up with the marquis alone. As she says in commenting on Virginie's indifference, "c'était sans importance, on n'avait pas besoin d'elle" (FC 22).

As a woman who enters the male world of business transactions, the mother is seen also as somewhat of an equal of the "habitué" of the Opera who wishes to "purchase" her daughter. This is suggested in Halévy's works by her brashness with even the highest of nobility. In Degas's works this is reflected in "La loge de la danseuse" (pl. 60, 61) where the "entreteneur" and mother are at the same level and both provide dark contrasts to the radiant ballerina. They are also both in relatively the same position in relation to the ballerina and this physical parallelism in the picture suggests that their positions in life in regard to the dancer were parallel: they both profited from her.

This top-hatted "habitué" of the Opera is a figure which recurs with the frequency of a leitmotif in Degas's ballet pictures. In addition to his presence in the "loge" of the dancers, he appears conversing with ballerinas in the corridors of the Opera, as in the monotypes to illustrate *La Famille Cardinal*, or half-concealed, watching the dancers from the edge of the stage or behind a backdrop (pl. 51, 55, 172a, 175, 180, 208). In the latter representations, he appears as a dark, sinister, lurking figure, a shadow always behind the ballerinas. The top-hatted man is almost always the lover of one of the dancers, her "entreteneur." Dancers' salaries, graduated to correspond to the hierarchy of their roles, were low for all but the real stars. McCabe noted that "the average salaries are low. The majority are so small that their recipients can scarcely live upon them" (McCabe 674). According to Halévy, "Pour les petites, vingt sous quand elles figurent le soir à l'Opéra. . . . Puis devenues grandes, elles entrent dans le second quadrille et gagnent de sept à neuf cents francs par an. Après quoi, elles avancent lentement. . . . Du second quadrille, on passe dans le premier, de mille à onze cents francs; du premier quadrille dans les secondes coryphées, de treize à quatorze cents francs; des secondes coryphées dans les premières, quinze cents francs. Enfin après des années . . . on devient petit sujet! . . . de seize cents francs à deux mille francs. C'est la fortune! C'est la gloire" (PtC 247). But it seems that the official salary was only a token, that the real income for these girls came from their roles as mistresses, and that in fact they entered the profession with this aim (or more accurately, their mothers engaged them in dancing with this goal). McCabe alludes to this practice in speaking of the Parisian gossip: "You will see heroines (among them ballerinas) of the stories that are told you, living in a style utterly beyond the salaries which they receive for their professional services, and you will not be slow in forming your conclusions as to the manner in which the difference is made up" (McCabe 675). For Halévy's dancers, this is a universal principle, a condition taken for granted. Thus Virginie selects the marquis, as she says, "puisqu'il faut que je prenne quelqu'un" (FC 18). That there was nothing out of the ordinary in this relationship is also revealed by the remarks of Mariette's mother. She explains the career of her ballerina-daughter saying: "Regardez-moi cette enfant-là . . . elle est trop jolie pour être fruitière. . . . Elle tournerait mal dans les Batignolles. Eh bien! du moment qu'une enfant doit mal tourner, autant la voir mal tourner dans le grand monde" (MA 72). And she accepts the relationship of Mariette and her suitor, for "Savez-vous ce qu'elle gagne . . . à l'Opéra? Quinze cents francs, dont il faut bien retirer mille francs d'amendes [for missed rehearsals and misbehavior backstage]. Et savez-vous ce qu'elle dépense? Pas loin de cent mille francs par an; la pauvre chérie. . . . Eh bien voilà le monsieur qu'elle a choisi pour payer tout ça" (MA 81). Besides the actual presence of the suitors in Degas's pictures, the jewelry of the dancers testifies to their liaisons, for the bracelets and earrings which they almost invariably wear during performances are probably gifts, as is mentioned in Halévy's works.

Who were these top-hatted "habitués"? Usually, they were "d'un certain âge," men well into middle-age as is revealed by those of Degas's pictures where they are seen closely enough for one to be able to discern their age, for example, in "La loge de la danseuse" (pl. 60, 61) and in "Le ballet de 'Robert le Diable'" (pl. 8, 9). Identification of these men in the audience can be deduced from the fact that they are in the same seats as those in Halévy's story: "à l'orchestre à droite dans un coin peuplé de vieux habitués" (FC 62). For the mothers of the dancers, respectable seniority was important, as one says, "Il fallait avoir des poils gris sous le menton. . . . des hommes sérieux . . . (pour) nos enfants" (PtC 242). In fact, to assure the quality of admirers for her daughter she wished to implement a policy whereby she would "flanquer à la porte des coulisses de l'Opéra, par mesure générale, tout ce qui n'a pas quarante-cinq ans. . . . Quand un homme a passé la quarantaine, c'est déjà une garantie pour une mère" (PtC 243). Thus the "entreteneurs" were old enough to be the fathers of these sixteen and seventeen-year-old dancers. As with the instructor, then, a male figure becomes a surrogate of the father. This is more explicit in Halévy's "A l'Opéra" where a mother describes one as "un véritable père pour les danseuses" (PtC 242) and in *La Famille Cardinal* where Madame Cardinal lauds Monsieur de Glayeul for his fatherly good advice to her daughter (FC 54). In "La loge de la danseuse" Degas evokes the paternal aspect of the "habitué" by showing the latter and the mother in similarly solicitous postures vis-à-vis the ballerina, thus rendering him the male counterpart of the mother.

Obviously, these top-hatted frequenters of the ballerinas backstage were men of money. They were also from the highest echelon of society. As McCabe noted, "The women [i.e., dancers] are the objects of the most determined gallantry on the part of the wealthy and titled gentry of Paris . . . the loftiness of some of the names [is surprising] . . . Counts, Dukes, Princes" (McCabe 675). This is also evident in Halévy's stories where the admirers mentioned are, for example, the marquis, "un roi," Monsieur *de* Glayeul, "un sénateur," and "le premier secrétaire d'une grande ambassade étrangère" (FC 68). The importance to the ballet of this upper class and of the social structure which is its context is emphasized in *La Famille Cardinal* where Madame Cardinal states "Pauline n'est pas casée, et j'aurai probablement du mal à la caser sous la République, tandis que sous l'Empire, il faut être juste, ça allait tout seul. . . . Je sais bien qu'il en faut des hommes comme il faut, parce que, sans ça nos pauvres petites, . . . qu'est-ce qu'elles deviendraient?" (FC 45). The same sentiment is reiterated, more explicitly by a ballerina's mother in *Notes et Souvenirs*; she tells Halévy: "Si l'on faisait voter les mères de danseuses sur la question de la forme de gouvernement, . . . elles se prononceraient à l'unanimité pour la monarchie."[11]

In the ballet world which Halévy depicts, there is "entre les deux sociétés [the lower class of the dancers and the upper class of their lovers] une sorte de fusion . . . fusion de manières et de langage" (MA 77). An air of familiarity between the top-hatted men, the dancers, and their mothers pervades. Also, the social fusion is realized more concretely in *La Famille Cardinal* where Virginie becomes the legitimate wife of the marquis.

For Degas, however, the two social worlds rarely came together. On the contrary, they are sharply differentiated. In one monotype (Janis pl. 49) of a back-stage scene the figures of two top-hatted men are placed so as to extend the corridor and cut off Madame Cardinal, suggesting quite the opposite of the amicable rapport described by Halévy. Degas also uses his palette to contrast the realm of the "habitué" and that of his dancer. The stark, black figure of the top-hatted man, who appears behind the scenes, or in the audience (pl. 8, 9), does not blend into the fluid, pastel world of the ballerina.

We must note, nevertheless, that the melding of the two classes is occasionally suggested in Degas's work. In "Danseuse au bouquet derrière une femme à l'éventail" (pl. 106) and "Au ballet, la femme à l'éventail" (pl. 109) the shape of the dancer's skirt echoes that of the fan held by a well-to-do (judging by her first row box seat) lady in the audience. The fan motif similarly links the ballerina and the woman spectator in many other pictures where the ballerinas hold fans (pl. 22, 116, 117, 199, 208, 210, 212, 213).

The class distinction between ballerina and "habitué," then, seems to be based more on gender than on social rank. This is further substantiated by the fact that the black dress of the orchestra members (all male but not upper class) sets them apart from the colorful ballerinas just as much as the "habitué's" formal dress does him. And, as we have seen, the mother, who also usually appears in dark clothes, fits more into the male role. The two classes, then, are not upper and lower but male and female: the male ("habitué," dance instructor, orchestra member, mother) directs, manipulates, and exploits; the female obeys, performs, produces.

This male/female relationship has obvious implications in regard to Halévy's and Degas's rapport with the dancers. They are themselves, to a certain extent, the male manipulators and exploiters. Like the top-hatted suitor, Halévy directs the private lives of the dancers in his stories and profits from real life dancers in so much as they furnish material for these stories. Degas too profits from them in using them as a source for his subject matter. Furthermore, just as the dance instructor arranges and manipulates the bodies to create an image for public consumption, so also does Degas in his paintings. And like the "habitués" he often has a commercial relationship with the dancers: he uses them as models in his studio; he too pays them to perform. Indeed, in some of his works, Degas assimilates himself with the dance instructor and elsewhere with the "habitué" by adopting their point of view. For example, in "La leçon de danse" (pl. 17) and "Trois danseuses exécutant 'Développe à la seconde'" (pl. 35) he seems to have viewed the scene from the position of the dance master, while in "Le ballet de 'Robert le Diable'" (pl. 8, 9) and "Au théâtre, Le ballet vu d'une loge" (pl. 110) he seems to have observed all from the "habitué's" viewpoint.

But for the most part, in his works, Degas remains detached from the dancers, as well as from the top-hatted men and the mothers. He does not participate in their world as does Halévy who becomes a fourth protagonist in his stories. While Halévy writes in the first person, Degas paints in the third person (perhaps depicting himself once, but then only as an illustration for *La*

Famille Cardinal—in one monotype [Janis pl. 49], one of the men is an artist according to the Halévy story). Unlike Halévy, Degas depicts only what he observes as the objective "flâneur" at the Opera, without going into the homelife and events related to the dancers as persons distinct from their profession. This is underlined by his selection of scenes to illustrate for Halévy's book. Thus in one sense, as opposed to Halévy, he denies them a full personality; they remain simply ballerinas and not full-dimensional women.

Yet in a more important sense, it is in Degas's work that we find the more complex portrayal of the women whom his dancers represent. In his objectivity, Degas records the harsh reality of their lives as well as the beauty of their art, whereas Halévy subjectively edits his episodes so that his ballerinas, whether in public or in private, remain simply pleasant fictions. Degas's distance from the ballerinas brings the viewer closer to the real woman than does Halévy's apparent intimacy with them. The author's dancers never do more than entertain a complacent reader; the artist's disturb the viewer and provoke a social awareness. Hence, while Halévy paints a more flattering portrait of the ballerinas of his generation (and while Degas has been accused of misogyny for his unflattering depictions of women in general—and certainly many of his ballerinas are *not* pretty), it is ultimately Degas who paradoxically proves to be the more sympathetic to them.

Notes

[1] Edgar Degas, *Huit Sonnets* (New York: La Jeune Parque, Wittenborn and Co., 1946) 8. Henceforth, references to this work will be designated by "Son" with page numbers in parentheses.

[2] Edgar Degas, *Lettres de Degas* (Paris: B. Grasset, c. 1931) 63. Henceforth, references to this work will be designated by "LD" with page numbers in parentheses.

[3] Lillian Browse, *Degas, Dancers* (London: Faber and Faber, 1949) 52.

[4] Ludovic Halévy, *La Famille Cardinal* (Paris: Calmann-Lévy) 7. Henceforth, references to this work will be designated by "FC" with page numbers in parentheses.

[5] Ludovic Halévy, *Les Petites Cardinal* (Paris: Calmann-Lévy) 237. Henceforth, references to this work will be designated by "PtC" with page references in parentheses.

[6] J.-K. Huysmans, *Certains* (Paris: Tresse and Stock, 1889) 23.

[7] James D. McCabe, Jr., *Paris by Sunlight and Gaslight* (Boston, 1870) 673.

[8] Camille Mauclair, *Degas* (Paris: Hyperion Press, 1937) 163.

[9] Ellen Moers, *The Dandy* (New York: Viking Press, 1960) 273.

[10] Ludovic Halévy, *Un Mariage d'amour* (Paris: Calmann-Lévy, 1883) 73. Henceforth, references to this work will be designated by "MA" with page references in parentheses.

[11] Ludovic Halévy, *Notes et Souvenirs* (Paris: Calmann-Lévy, 1889) 155.

List of Plates

[i] Lillian Browse, *Degas, Dancers* (London: Faber and Faber, 1949) pl. 179a. Henceforth, all references to plates will be from this work and designated by number in parentheses unless otherwise indicated.

[ii] E. P. Janis, *Degas' Monotypes* (Greenwich, Ct.: New York Graphic Society, 1968) pl. 186.

[iii] F. Minervino, *L'Opera Completa di Degas* (Milan: Rizzoli Editore, 1970) pl. 702, 703, 704.

[iv] Camille Mauclair, *Degas* (Paris: Hyperion Press, 1937) pl. 119, 126.

Albert Sonnenfeld

Mallarmé and His Music

Ed Sullivan was named Chairman of Romance Languages and Literatures at Princeton precisely at the moment I defended my Ph.D. thesis there and became Instructor! As my new boss his first words to me were: "I want you to be in charge of your own course." That sounded encouraging, but the course Ed had in mind was "lower intermediate French," a slow track for underachievers with an extra evening session for under-underachievers, who existed, albeit in limited supply, even at Princeton. From the subsoil of such unpromising beginnings flowered a collegial association and friendship which now spans more than thirty-two years! Ed was my loyal and encouraging supporter as my career developed at Princeton, and I have tried over the years to reciprocate that loyalty. Ed's energetic sense of entrepreneurship in 1960 helped establish the Princeton Series at the Presses Universitaires de France, and with his editorial guidance I prepared my revised thesis to inaugurate the Series. We wrote a book together, *Témoins de l'homme* (Scribner's, 1965), an ambitious anthology of short fiction the proceeds of which, Ed maintained, would pay my children's college tuition. Alas, we overestimated the potential quality of language instruction and learning, and the royalties barely paid a year's laundry costs! But more importantly, the collaboration cemented our friendship. Ed was by far the best organized and fairest-minded Chairman the Romance Languages and Literatures Department had known; he became an outstanding Dean of the College and presided over major curricular reforms. At whatever level of eminence he had attained, Ed Sullivan remained accessible to, and concerned with, "his" departmental colleagues, and I turned to him frequently when it became my turn to chair "his" department.

Of course, Ed Sullivan did a lot for Princeton University, but it is his selfless support of generations of colleagues and students that I must gratefully evoke as the most appropriate collective motivation for this *Festschrift* to which I am honored to contribute.

J'abomine les écoles . . . , et tout ce qui est professorial
appliqué à la littérature qui, elle, au contraire, est tout à fait
individuelle.[1]

In the light of my epigraph, one need hardly speculate as to what the
Master's reaction to such a normative and professorial title as "Qu'est-ce que
le Symbolisme" would have been. Yet as always with the proponent of "énigme
en poésie," there is the enigma of the poet himself: the imperfect Wagnerite
obsessed with Wagner, the mocker of journalistic typography ("le réel parce
que vil") who kept up a massive social correspondence and produced innumerable *vers de circonstance*, the apostle of silence who kept writing, the denigra-
tor of the professorial who professed weekly in the rue de Rome, and, above all,
in his extensive magisterial pronouncements on poetry, its mission and technique. For Mallarmé, his many encomia to Music project an ideal luminosity
to which his poetry was only an imperfect and shadowy accompaniment.

The uncial letters must be Valéry's, pernicious though their influence may
have been on the always elusive topic of music and Poetry: "Ce qui fut baptisé
le Symbolisme, se résume très simplement dans l'intention commune à
plusieurs familles de poètes (d'ailleurs ennemies entre elles) de 'reprendre à la
Musique leur bien.' Le secret de ce mouvement n'est pas autre."[2] Pernicious,
because, in a Mallarméan perspective, the result is the cult of prettification à la
Verlaine, or the excess of lexicographical rigor from René Ghil to André Spire,
as we apply to Poetry an essentially alien vocabulary: melody, timbre, harmony,
etc. In Valéry's definition, the key words ("reprendre à la Musique leur bien")
are in quotation marks, for they derive from Mallarmé's *rejection* of Music in
Crise de vers, written with "un indéracinable sans doute préjugé d'écrivain,"
proclaiming his mission to be

un art d'achever la transposition, au Livre, de la symphonie ou uniment de reprendre notre bien:
car ce n'est pas de sonorités élémentaires par les cuivres, les cordes, les bois, indéniablement mais
de l'intellectuelle parole à son apogée que doit avec plénitude et évidence, résulter, en tant que
l'ensemble des rapports existant dans tout, la Musique. (OC 367-368)

And, in a letter to René Ghil (1885), "Cet acte de juste restitution qui doit être
le nôtre, de tout reprendre à la musique."[3] The ultimate enigma, not to say
paradox, is that what Mallarmé sought to recapture from Music was not its
sonorous expressivity, but its silence, the "sound of silence," if you will; and
to this impossible ideal he remained surprisingly faithful. Tragically, or perhaps
ironically, the embodiment of the problematic of Music for Mallarmé was
Wagner, the inventor of the continuous melody, to whom silence was anathema:

La grandeur du poète se mesure surtout par ce qu'il s'abstient de dire, afin de nous laisser dire à nous-mêmes, en silence, ce qui est inexprimable; mais c'est le musicien qui fait entendre clairement ce qui n'est pas dit, et la forme infaillible de son silence retentissant est la *mélodie infinie*. (Bernard 19) (Wagner's Letter to Villot)

It is because of Wagner's "Trompettes tout haut d'or pâmé sur les vélins" (OC 71) that Mallarmé must apostrophize the "Génie" of Bayreuth, reluctantly: ". . . ô Wagner, je souffre et me reproche, aux minutes marquées par la lassitude, de ne pas faire nombre avec ceux qui, ennuyés de tout afin de trouver le salut définitif, vont droit à l'édifice de ton Art, pour eux le terme du chemin" (OC 546). Mallarmé's own "Salut" (originally entitled *Toast*, in 1893) contains the expression of his esthetic of the music of silence: "Rien, cette écume, vierge vers / A ne désigner que la coupe/ . . . Le blanc souci de notre toile" (OC 27). The greeting "Salut" becomes salvation; the cup becomes the "coupe" of verse; the white sail becomes the blank canvas. The public recital of the sonnet "Toast" at the banquet of *La Plume* is transformed into the vast silence of fourteen octosyllabic lines on a printed page, a virtually blank canvas.

In his early "Hérésie(s) artistique(s)" in *L'Art pour tous* (1862) Mallarmé articulates his musical credo. The sacred implies mystery, and, like religion whose arcana are unveiled only to the predestined elite, Art has its sheltered secrets:

La musique nous offre un exemple. Ouvrons à la légère Mozart, Beethoven ou Wagner, jetons sur la première page de leur œuvre un œil indifférent, nous sommes pris d'un religieux étonnement à la vue de ces processions macabres de signes sévères, chastes, inconnus. Et nous refermons le missel vierge d'aucune pensée profanatrice. (OC 257)

The mystery is twofold: the unsanctified reader of scores sees only the procession of undecipherable signs on a page minimally darkening the whites between the bar-lines, minute traces of ink. The "seul prédestiné," it is implied though not stated, knows how to read these signs and to transpose them into a silent concert taking place within the sphere of ideality, the *mind's ear*, as it were; and this "reading" gesture is both horizontal and vertical, as he will seek to realize in *UN COUP DE DÉS*. "Un solitaire tacite concert se donne, par la lecture, à l'esprit qui regagne, sur une sonorité moindre, la signification: aucun moyen mental exaltant la symphonie ne manquera, raréfié et c'est tout—du fait de la pensée" (OC 380). This from *Le Livre, instrument spirituel*. The book is the "instrument of the mind or spirit," but the mind is the performing instrument of the score embodied in the book. Far from being merely an *odi profanum vulgus*, seen retrospectively these lines tell us that seeing the incomprehensible procession of musical signs is the very act of perceiving the mystery of the unstated, while deciphering them is the charge of the ideal creator and reader "magiquement produit par certaines dispositions de la parole; où celle-ci ne reste qu'à l'état de moyen de communication matérielle avec le lecteur comme les touches du piano" (Bernard 75) [Letter to Edmund Gosse]. We have here what is an esthetic of reading, of interpretation and of creation. Little wonder, then, that Mallarmé's ideal page resembles that mysterious score: "je préfère selon mon goût, sur page blanche, un dessin espacé de virgules ou de points et leurs combinaisons secondaires, imitant, nue, la mélodie—au texte, suggéré avantageusement si, même sublime, il n'était pas ponctué" ("Solitude," OC 407). The use or rejection of these signs is what distinguishes verse from prose, "nommément tout notre art," and the abundant, disconcerting and perplexing use of these "signes convenus" represents the poet's attempt to make his prose obscure, mysterious, syntactical; in short, Mallarmé's mature prose attains the density and "musicality" of "poetry," whether labeled "Poèmes en prose" or "Crayonné au théâtre."

Despite Mallarmé's ballet of commas in his prose, he fails to achieve his purported ideal of expressive punctuation to the same extent as the self-consciously simplistic Maeterlinck. In *Pelléas*, the 4th Act Love Scene contains 15 ellipses in eight lines of dialogue (or if one prefers at 3 dots per ellipsis, 45 dots); it is in these interstices that the true vagueness of the symbolic Idea purports to dwell, "le théâtre du silence." Mallarmé, far more genuinely philosophical and in many ways as much esthetician as poet (despite his avowed disdain for the "professorial"), writes about the ineffable without achieving it in radical form before *UN COUP DE DÉS* and the fragmentary "Le Livre." He will use minimalization ("Une ligne d'azur mince et pâle serait / Un lac . . . Non loin de trois grands cils d'émeraude, roseaux") [*Las de l'amer repos*], much the way he speaks of music:

Si je recours, en vue d'un éclaircissement ou de généraliser, aux fonctions de l'Orchestre, devant lequel resta candidement, savamment fermé notre musicien de mots, observez que les instruments détachent, selon un sortilège aisé à surprendre, la cime pour ainsi voir, de naturels paysages; les évapore et les renoue, flottants, dans un état supérieur. Voici qu'à exprimer la forêt . . . suffit tel accord dénué presque d'une réminiscence de chasse . . . Une ligne, quelque vibration, sommaire et tout s'indique. ("Théodore de Banville," OC 522)

The brush stroke of the Chinese painter on the printed page is minimal darkening of the pure Ideal of the white page ("le vide papier que la blancheur défend") by the short poem, the sonnet, the *Chansons bas*, the *Petit air*: "Ce sont les blancs qui me donnent le plus de mal! Ils ont la valeur des *silences* en musique. Ce sont eux qui créent le rêve, l'ineffable" (Bernard 41). Or: "Vraiment entre les lignes et au-dessus du regard cela se passe en toute pureté, sans l'entremise des cordes à boyaux et des pistons comme à l'orchestre, qui est déjà industriel; mais c'est la même chose que l'orchestre, sauf que littérairement ou silencieusement" (Bernard 75, Letter to E. Gosse).

The paradoxes of Mallarmé never cease to amaze: *L'Après-midi d'un faune*, a loquacious poem of more than 100 verses, narrates the move toward the silent inner concert of the mind. Repeated attempts to recount the vision of the two nymphs in musical narrative by the musician-faune ("qui cherche le *la*") *fade* and fail until they are minimalized into: "Une sonore, vaine et monotone ligne." But even this is too much sound of music; the vision retreats into silence, vision, dream, the ultimate music. As the poet states in *Le Livre, instrument spirituel*:

Plus le va-et-vient successif incessant du regard, une ligne finie, à la suivante, pour recommencer: pareille pratique ne représente le délice, ayant immortellement, rompu, une heure, avec tout, de traduire sa chimère. Autrement ou sauf exécution, comme de morceaux sur un clavier, active mesurée par les feuillets—que ne ferme-t-on les yeux à rêver? (OC 380)

The next line begins: "Un tacite concert se donne, par la lecture, à l'esprit. . . ." Or, from the essay on Banville: "Une ligne, quelque vibration, sommaires et tout s'indique" (OC 522); and from *La Musique et les lettres*: "moins le tumulte des sonorités, transfusibles, encore, en du songe" (OC 648).

In a book-length study, one should turn clearly now, *in extenso*, to the whiteness of the pages of *UN COUP DE DÉS*, barely darkened by the sparseness of Mallarmé's text, and to his necessarily fragmentary "Le Livre," as the closest approximation of the ideal of the silent musical score described in his 1865 *L'Art pour tous*. That aspect of Mallarmé as musician of silence has been admirably studied by Suzanne Bernard, by Robert G. Cohn,[4] and Jacques Schérer.[5] But I would like to conclude with a short, further rumination on Mallarmé and his Music. It was only around 1885, his daughter Geneviève wrote, that Mallarmé began attending concerts! He had forbidden her to take piano lessons. It was ironic that the musician who inspired his reflexions, his admiration, fear, and disdain was Richard Wagner, a look at whose scores would convince one that he is the antithesis of Mallarmé's "concert tacite." That is the fault of the incontrovertible coincidences of History. In the hope of leading the reader from the printed page to the printed score, and thence to listening on record or through the inner ear of the professional decipherer of musical mysteries in awe of whom Mallarmé stood in *L'Art pour tous*, I would like to take the chance of evoking here, as quintessentially Mallarméen in esthetic, conception and execution, a composer of whom Pierre Boulez said: "[Il] représente le seuil de la musique nouvelle: l'homme indélébile." Here are descriptions of that music:

Webern's FIVE PIECES FOR ORCHESTRA represent his attempt to undermine the tyranny of Wagnerism. In barely five minutes, he argues for an economical esthetic of sighs and whispers rather than the screams and breast-beating popular with his peers.[6]

The brevity of Webern's musical utterance bewildered audiences that were used to the expansive, explicit, exuberant, and repetitious style of the late Romantic period, as seen in the works of Wagner, Strauss, etc. But what really shocked them was the terrific degree of concentration in Webern's music, which seemed to reduce musical matter to a few drops of precious essence. For the first time in its history, music became so lean and transparent that its single elements seemed to float in isolation between air-pockets of total silence. Not only each tone, but also its inflection, its manner of vanishing into nothingness, took on unheard-of, almost frightful significance.[7]

Autant la brièveté de ces pièces parle en faveur de celles-ci, autant il est nécessaire aussi de parler en faveur de cette brièveté. Que l'on considère quelle sobriété exige une expression aussi concise. Chaque regard peut développer en un poème, chaque soupir en un roman. Mais pour enfermer tout un roman en un simple geste, tout un bonheur dans un seul souffle, il faut une concentration banissant tout épanchement sentimental. Ces pièces ne seront comprises que par ceux qui croient qu'on ne peut exprimer avec des sons que ce qui ne peut être exprimé qu'avec des sons.[8]

If, in Sartre's words, Giacometti had taken the fat off space to reach the skeleton, Webern and Mallarmé reached the same sublime ascesis in their own art. "Seuls seront touchés ceux qui auront la foi. Puisse ce silence se faire entendre d'eux!" said Schoenberg of Webern. "Je réclame la restitution au silence, impartial," wrote Stéphane Mallarmé.

Notes

[1] *Œuvres complètes* (Paris: Gallimard, Bibliothèque de la Pléiade, 1951) 969. Hereafter OC will refer to this edition of Mallarmé's works.

[2] Suzanne Bernard, *Mallarmé et la musique* (Paris: Librairie des Lettres, 1951) 11.

[3] Stéphane Mallarmé, *Correspondance,* vol. II 1871-1885, eds. Henri Mondor and Lloyd James Austin (Paris: Gallimard, 1965) 286.

[4] Robert Greer Cohn, *Toward the Poems of Mallamé* (Berkeley: U of California P, 1980) and *L'Œuvre de Mallarmé: Un Coup de Dés* (Paris: Librairie des Lettres, 1951).

[5] Jacques Schérer, *Le "Livre" de Mallarmé*, nouvelle édition (Paris: Gallimard, 1977).

[6] Robert Craft, "Program Notes" for *The Complete Works of Anton Webern* (LC No. R-56-1077, 1956) 6.

[7] Ernst Krenek, "Anton von Webern: A Profile," in *Anton von Webern: Perspectives* (Seattle: U of Washington P, 1966) 4.

[8] Arnold Schoenberg, cited by Claude Rostand, *Anton Webern*, Musiciens de Tous les Temps (Paris: Seghers, 1969) 104.

Armand Hoog

1900 au pluriel

Cette soi-disant "Belle Epoque," cette vaniteuse, cette piaffante, cette esbrouffante "Belle Epoque," à peine y songe-t-on que s'alignent aussitôt les vieux clichés, les poncifs rebattus, aussi arbitraires que les figurants exotiques—mandarins chinois à nattes, bayadères en saris multicolores—qui défilaient sur les trottoirs roulants de l'Exposition Universelle de 1900. "Belle Epoque!" Sous ce titre, cinquante ouvrages, dont un petit volume à couverture rose tendre de Paul Morand, enjolivé d'ornements style nouille, célèbrent nostalgiquement les jupes évasées de Paquin et Worth, *L'Aiglon* d'Edmond Rostand (le nouveau Corneille), Mistinguett, Emilienne d'Alençon, le *Quo Vadis* de Sienkiewicz (grand succès de librairie de l'année), les peintures "parisiennes" de Jean Béraud (dîneurs en frac, femmes du monde décolletées, officiers en uniforme déambulant sur les boulevards), le théâtre de Sardou (on va représenter *Patrie*, remarquable navet), les commencements scabreux de Colette (premiers *Claudine* signés Willy), le cher maître Anatole France, Robert de Montesquiou, l'esthète des *Chauves-Souris* et des *Hortensias bleus*, et le Chat Noir, et le Club des Hydropathes et les Jemenfoutistes et les Hirsutes,[1] et les *Salons* des Champs-Elysées, où triomphent Bouguereau, les sous-Bouguereau, les moins que sous-Bouguereau. La "Belle Epoque," enfin.

Ce bric-à-brac amusant qui se restreint à peu près au Paris des théâtres, des cabarets (Maxim's, fondé en 1893), de Montmartre, et du huitième arrondissement, n'est, bien sûr, qu'un décor artificiel et pittoresque, dont s'enchante la "petite Histoire." Une génération littéraire, au sens propre du terme, lui correspond-elle? Historien de la Troisième République, Jacques Chastenet a proposé de circonscrire la "Belle Epoque" entre les années 1899 et 1911. Significatif, ce *terminus a quo* de 1899. Parce qu'à cette date est à peu près liquidée la génération littéraire dont on trouve le catalogue guignolesque, ou le faire-part anticipé de décès, dans *Le Déséspéré* de Léon Bloy.[2] Patronymes, plus ou moins révélateurs, de personnages fictifs. Ils ne réussissent pas à déguiser (ils n'avaient pas cette intention) les écrivains de la génération née entre 1840 et 1860, les grands noms d'*avant* la fin du siècle. Qui est Gaston Chaudesaigues, "troubadour homme d'affaires," "un des plus bas mercantis des lettres," "plagiaire à la longue chevelure," "juif auvergnat né dans le Midi?"

C'est Alphonse Daudet. Daudet disparaît en 1897. Qui est Andoche Sylvain, "à la barbe épaisse et sale, au teint de viande crue et bleuâtre, à l'œil injecté et idiot?" C'est Armand Silvestre, qui va mourir en 1901. Mérovée Beauclerc, "pion sérénissime, inaltérable, absolu," "moniteur et répétiteur de la conquérante médiocrité," c'est Francisque Sarcey, mort en 1899. Auquel se peut comparer "l'heureux bouddha du Collège de France," "le Dieu des esprits lâches," c'est-à-dire Renan, mort en 1892. Gilles de Vaudoré, "romancier ithyphallique," "bellâtre de garnison qui affole les caboulotières," c'est Maupassant, mort en 1893. Léonidas Rieupeyroux, "hypocrite véhément," "fleur de crasse," c'est Léon Cladel, mort en 1892. Raoul Denisme, "raté félibre et gluant chroniqueur," c'est Paul Arène, mort en 1896.

Quelques autres, également placés dans cette galerie de sagouins, sont encore présents vers 1900 au bataillon de la vieille littérature mais ils ne comptent plus, tels que Abraham Prosper Beauvivier, "cabot sacrilège," "salisseur d'âmes," qui est Catulle Mendès (il mourra en 1909). Seuls de ce jeu de massacre vont survivre Bourget (mort en 1935), Richepin (mort en 1926), Elémir Bourges (mort en 1925). Echappés à la férocité de Bloy: Mallarmé (mort en 1898), Zola (mort en 1902), Edmond de Goncourt (mort en 1896), Loti (mort en 1923). Albert Samain disparaît en cette année 1900.

1899-1900, un seuil donc pour la littérature autant que pour le calendrier. Le passage d'un siècle à l'autre apporte (selon les tempéraments) soit un frisson eschatologique, soit un sentiment de renouveau. Fin du dix-neuvième siècle ou aube du vingtième? Décadence ou renaissance? On interrogera les uns et les autres. "Littérature," en ce tournant du siècle, ne signifie pas seulement esthétisme, beau style, "prose d'art," ce qu'on trouve dans la poésie, le théâtre, le roman. Autour de 1900 les idées politiques, philosophiques, religieuses ont au moins autant d'importance. Et les lecteurs (de livres, de revues, de journaux) auront bien aussi quelque chose à dire. A travers eux se forment et s'organisent les représentations collectives. 1900, ce n'est pas seulement les jeux et gaîtés de la "Belle Epoque." 1900 se lit au pluriel.

Fin de Siècle

D'abord, chez beaucoup, cette sensation de décadence, de deuil. Le bout du rouleau. L'épuisement du dix-neuvième siècle. Tout ce qu'il a laissé derrière lui. Ces ruines. Les dieux morts: Hugo, Taine, Renan. Le vieillissement irrémédiable d'une époque. Ses derniers feux érotiques. Veillée funèbre avec odeur de décomposition.

Bien révélateur, ce "journal littéraire illustré" qui s'appelle en 1900 *Le Fin de siècle*. M. Robert Burac l'a feuilleté. Catulle Mendès sexagénaire y publie *Sous la chemise*. Titres des feuilletons: *Enfilons des perles* ou *Chairs épanouies*, *beautés ardentes*.[3] Alliance de la tristesse fin de siècle (le duc de Guermantes a de ces mélancolies nostalgiques quand il se rappelle les musiques passées) et de l'"érotisme à corset et bottines à boutons," comme dit Armand Lanoux.[4] Bien le maître de ce genre, Mendès. Maître de la "perversité subtile," avec une certaine chaleur lyrique et l'aptitude à fabriquer des livrets d'opéra (*La Reine Fiammette*, 1898). Il correspondrait assez bien, littérairement parlant, à un d'Annunzio ventripotent, les cheveux gras dans le cou. Il mourra en 1908, écrasé par un train sous le tunnel de Saint-Germain.

Dès 1893, un médecin hongrois installé à Paris, Max Südfeld dit Nordau a établi le procès de cette fin de siècle. Selon lui, la fin d'une civilisation. *Dégénérescence* aura un retentissement considérable en France, bien que l'auteur s'y attaque surtout à Wagner, Ibsen et Tolstoï, témoins de l'"hystérie universelle." Nordau applique à la littérature et à la société le diagnostic que l'aliéniste et le psychiatre italien Lombroso applique à la criminalité (*L'Homme délinquant*, 1897). Approche médico-sociologique qui est, au même moment, celle des professeurs Adrien Proust et Ballet, dans leur *Hygiène du neurasthénique* (1897). La "neurasthénie" ambiante, le docteur Proust y voit, comme Nordau, un phénomène de civilisation. Les classes privilégiées en sont avant tout les victimes.[5] Préoccupations d'ordre moral, soucis professionnels, "vexations de l'amour-propre," crainte des examens, "course aux plaisirs," en somme l'existence de la bourgeoisie, des intellectuels, de l'aristocratie parisienne. Il ne se doute guère, derrière ses gros bouquins, l'éminent professeur, membre de l'Académie de médecine, que la célébrité de son patronyme ne sera pas due à ses savants ouvrages mais à la carrière mondaine de son salonnard de fils. (Ainsi, vers le même temps, Charles Gide, professeur au Collège de France, fondateur de l'"école de Nîmes," qui publie en 1900 son fameux catéchisme, *La Coopération*, se douterait-il que son neveu André, auteur en 1897 d'un petit livre confidentiel intitulé *Les Nourritures terrestres*, maintiendra seul la gloire du nom?) Lorsque, la même année 1897, le professeur Proust diagnostique dans les hautes classes de la société une "émotion excessive," Marcel a vingt-six ans. En fait d'émotivité, quel beau sujet d'observation il peut offrir à son père! Le professeur mourra en 1903 sans avoir rien lu de son fils qu'un maigre volume, *Les Plaisirs et les Jours*, édité à compte d'auteur. En 1899 un écrivain belge, Hippolyte Fierens-Gevaert, a publié à son tour un ouvrage sur *La Tristesse contemporaine*, qui retient l'attention de la critique.[6] Fierens-Gevaert parle de Leopardi, Schopenhauer, Wagner, Tolstoï, passe en revue l'individualisme artistique, le nihilisme philosophique, l'"internationalisme," le "néo-christianisme," la littérature "alcoolique," dénonce les "écrivains malades," déplore (encore un) l'influence de Baudelaire, mentionne au passage *l'Union pour l'action morale* de Paul Desjardins—drôle de salade. Examinant le livre de Fierens-Gevaert, le critique Joseph Ageorges estime, lui aussi, que "les classes supérieures sont certainement atteintes de la maladie. . . . La désespérance, la fatigue, la mélancolie deviennent parfois des états ordinaires, des habitudes morales, jusqu'à des attitudes mondaines" (196). Attention. Cet Ageorges appartient à une famille spirituelle minoritaire en 1899 mais dont l'influence va grandir: les catholiques démocrates—ceux qui prennent parti, en ce moment même, pour Dreyfus (les Viollet, les Leroy-Beaulieu, les abbés Pichot et Frémont). Pas beaucoup de complaisance chez eux pour les "classes supérieures" de la "Belle Epoque." La France aurait-elle perdu, demande Ageorges, son "fluide vital?"

"Décomposition du siècle": la formule se trouve, un an avant 1900, dans un ouvrage qui va faire du bruit, *Le Soleil des morts.*[7] Mi-roman, mi-essai, autobiographie d'une génération, "la génération de l'année terrible." L'auteur: Camille Faust, dit Camille Mauclair, fort connu en son temps (il mourra en 1945). Né en 1872, au lendemain de la guerre franco-prussienne et de la Commune. Ce familier de Mallarmé met en scène dans son récit des poètes et des "intellectuels" bien représentatifs du moment. Qu'est-ce que l'art? Une maladie. "On a l'art comme on a la phtisie." Tristes, ces jeunes gens. "Nous ne sommes pas gais: nous sommes nés au sein même de la mort. . . . Ce pays a une névrose au cœur." Derrière ses porte-voix, Sylvaine Armel, Manuel Hélicourt, André de Neuze, c'est l'auteur lui-même que j'entends, qui arrive à la maturité dans l'avant-dernière année du siècle. Malheureuse génération! "Rongée intérieurement par l'idée de l'inutilité de l'effort. . . . Elle se sentait déjà gardienne d'un tombeau. . . . Les grandes énergies étaient dépensées, il n'y restait que les sensations raffinées, l'efflorescence fragile des délicatesses. . . . Comme les Byzantins occupés de controverses minutieuses et savantes, dans un empire illusoire et exténué. . . . L'odeur de décadence . . . une odeur exquisement fanée et captivante. . . . La modernité du sang pauvre. . . ."

Verlaine avait déjà chanté, au temps des *Poèmes Saturniens*, "Je suis l'Empire à la fin de la décadence," mais le propos n'était pas attaché à une date précise. Voici maintenant 1899, qui n'est sans doute que la quatre-vingt-dix-neuvième année du siècle mais l'ultime chiffre des 1800. Le pathétique de ce 99, sa charge eschatologique, inspirent des images de ruine, de déliquescence. Un vacillement, une dégringolade. Sur le siècle qui a vu passer Napoléon, Victor Hugo et Taine, un rideau tombe. Et songez que le scandale de Panama, c'était hier. Que le président Carnot a été assassiné par un anarchiste en 1894. Que nous sommes en pleine affaire Dreyfus. Que le président Félix Faure vient de mourir à l'Elysée au cours d'un exercice amoureux (février 1899). Que l'on s'apprête à persécuter de nouveau les catholiques. Que le socialisme monte. Que l'on attend la guerre sociale. Enfin que la France se dépeuple (39 millions d'habitants) en face d'une Allemagne menaçante (67 millions). Oui, c'est bien la décadence. Mauclair répond à Verlaine en évoquant "tout le tralala des fins d'Empire." En cette même année 1899 Milosz, le poète lithuanien d'expression française, futur spécialiste des apocalypses, publie son *Poème des décadences.*

Je note, en septembre, un article d'Emile Bauny, *Au pays des intellectuels*:[8]
"Sommes-nous descendus véritablement au dernier degré du byzantinisme?"
Cette fin de siècle contient en effet une foule de germes de dégénerescence.
"Etes-vous bien sûrs, ô sombres prédiseurs de notre décadence, de n'avoir pas
contribué, pour une large part, à cette dissolution sociale. . . ."

Fin de siècle... L'obsession de l'anéantissement, Loti la trimballe
voluptueusement depuis toujours, jointe à une parfaite nullité de pensée. Le
livre qu'il donne en 1899 s'intitule *Reflets sur la sombre route*. On ne saurait
mieux dire. "L'idiot" dira cruellement André Breton à la mort de Loti en 1923.
Mais au tournant du siècle on l'adore, ce Loti, on le voit aussi grand que
Chateaubriand. En 1902 ce sera *Les Derniers Jours de Pékin*. La hantise du
couchant, des feux suprêmes. Loti aurait mieux fait de mourir à ce moment-là.

"Déliquescente psychologie littéraire de cette fin de siècle," avait dit Léon
Bloy dans *Le Déséspéré*. La psychologie religieuse, elle aussi, peut avoir sa
déliquescence. Anatole France publie, en 1899, *L'Anneau d'améthyste*. On y
voit opérer un abbé Guitrel, qui enseigne l'éloquence sacrée au grand séminaire
de Tours. Touché par ce néo-christianisme, et cet individualisme artistique, ce
"modernisme" que stigmatisent les Nordau et les Fierens-Gevaert. A
l'indignation de son ennemi, l'abbé Lantaigne, supérieur du séminaire, il
dissèque les états d'âme et les crises psychologiques de Notre-Seigneur devant
des séminaristes admiratifs, qui voient en lui "un prêtre fin de siècle."[9]

Aube de siècle

En tête du troisième cahier de la deuxième série de ses *Cahiers de la
Quinzaine*, Charles Péguy annonçait, le 20 décembre 1900:

> A nos anciens et à nos nouveaux abonnés
> nous ne donnons
> ni un réveille-matin . . .
> ni un roman de Sienkiewicz
> ni une cave à liqueur . . .
> ni la vérité toute faite . . .
> ni des vers d'Edmond Rostand . . .
> ni le résultat complet des courses
> ni un pardessus pour dix francs . . .

Qu'est-ce qu'il va leur donner alors, Péguy, à ses abonnés (quelquefois
récalcitrants)? Le contraire de ce que donnaient les émotifs, les décadents, les
byzantins. Moins de frissons et de désespérances, moins de symbolisme, de
crépuscules, de lys au bord des étangs. Les premières séries des *Cahiers de la
Quinzaine* offrent des textes de Romain Rolland, Georges Sorel, Tolstoï,

Bernard-Lazare, des frères Tharaud, d'Anatole France, Daniel Halévy, François Porché, Louis Gillet, Robert Dreyfus, Paul Desjardins. Laissons les *Cahiers*. Un peu partout dans la nouvelle génération, un sentiment de renouveau et de responsabilité. Recevant André Theuriet sous la Coupole en 1898, Paul Bourget s'était demandé quel serait le legs du "siècle finissant" au "siècle commençant." Bourget posait la question sans donner la réponse. Il nous est plus facile, aujourd'hui, de regarder en arrière. Si je m'en tiens à l'année 1900, dernière du siècle finissant mais première à changer de millésime, la production littéraire montre bien le passage de l'*avant* à l'*après*. Encore d'hier *La Ténébreuse* de Georges Ohnet, le romancier populaire des "Batailles de la vie," que la critique ne cesse de brocarder, que le public ne cesse de consommer. Encore d'hier *Les Vierges folles* de Marcel Prévost, *Les Médailles d'Argile* d'Henri de Régnier, *Au milieu du chemin* d'Edouard Rod. Peut-être voudra-t-on joindre à cette liste le livret que Gustave Charpentier a écrit pour son opéra *Louise*, en même temps qu'il en composait la partition. Ou *Le Journal d'une femme de chambre* d'Octave Mirbeau. Ici une mention particulière. Mirbeau est une étoile du siècle finissant comme du siècle commençant. Une étoile naine mais une étoile tout de même. Après avoir été monarchiste et catholique il a écrit *Le Jardin des supplices*, maintenant il récidive dans la porno. L'embarras de la gauche est visible. Elle est volontiers puritaine, la gauche. Or Mirbeau est un militant dreyfusiste. On l'a vu à Rennes l'an dernier pour le deuxième conseil de guerre où Dreyfus a été pour la deuxième fois condamné avec "circonstances atténuantes." Si *L'Aurore*, le journal de Clémenceau, se bat les flancs pour louer "la portée sociale du courageux livre," Péguy et ses amis réagissent moins complaisamment: "Ni un chef d'œuvre ni une œuvre. M. Octave Mirbeau a surtout collaboré à *L'Aurore* en lui fournissant un nombre assez considérable de points de suspension." Et: "Quelle saleté!" Et: "Dégoûtant, rien que dégoûtant" (*Cahier* du 16 novembre 1900). Et puis encore deux noms d'hier. 1900 voit paraître *Ubu enchaîné* d'Alfred Jarry (qui mourra en 1907) et *Ne nous frappons pas* d'Alphonse Allais (qui mourra en 1905). Pour Barrès, c'est un peu différent. *L'Appel au soldat* de Barrès, troisième volet du "roman de l'énergie nationale," paraît aussi en 1900. Fin d'un chapitre politique. Mais Barrès a encore toute une œuvre devant lui.

De vrai nouveau? Deux petits livres d'auteurs inconnus et sans succès, *Connaissance de l'Est*, d'un certain Paul Claudel (dont les aventures sentimentales à Fou-Tchéou ont eu un certain retentissement dans les seuls milieux diplomatiques) et l'*Album de vers anciens* de Paul Valéry. Il faudra attendre longtemps pour que la gloire vienne à ces deux-là. Mais la gloire vient tout de suite à la comtesse Anna de Noailles, dont *Le Cœur innombrable* est sur le point de paraître. Dans vingt ans, c'est Valéry qui détrônera Anna de Noailles.

Le choc du changement de siècle, avec sa résonance épiphanique, on va l'entendre ailleurs. Voici un essai de J. Angot des Rotours, *Aube de siècle* (Paris:

Perrin, 1898). *Le XXème Siècle*, c'est une "revue d'études sociales." Du poète catholique Edward Montier, un *Salut au Vingtième Siècle*.[10]

> Un siècle est né; salut! Salut! Un siècle est né.
> Nous vous louons, ô Dieu, qui nous l'avez donné!
> . . . Nous vous offrons ce siècle à son premier matin.
> Car vous seul en savez ici-bas le destin. . . .

Dans sa barbe le socialiste Jules Guesde avait déjà proclamé, en 1897, que "le commencement du siècle prochain sera le commencement d'une ère nouvelle." Et Jean Jaurès, l'autre socialiste, rival acharné de Guesde, va saluer à la fois le nouveau siècle et l'avènement d'un nouvel ordre social: "Il dépend de nous, dans la période vraiment grande où nous allons entrer, d'achever dans l'ordre intellectuel l'œuvre de la République française. . . ."[11] Ce n'est pas au socialisme guesdite ou jaurésien que pensait le graveur Albert Robida quand il publiait en 1883 son *Vingtième Siècle*. Dessins d'anticipation montrant des embouteillages d'hélicoptères à mi-hauteur des rues parisiennes. A chacun son vingtième siècle. Politiques ou dessinateurs, ils seront bien étonnés.

"Génération de rhéteurs," dira François Mauriac de cette génération de 1900 dans une préface à la réédition de *Cinq Années de ma vie*, d'Alfred Dreyfus.[12] Mauriac oppose à l'"homme le plus étranger à toute rhétorique," ce capitaine d'artillerie victime d'une erreur absurde, bizarrement incapable d'exprimer pour sa défense la moindre émotion, les écrivains de talent comme les médiocres phraseurs (de droite et de gauche) qui ont déversé sur la France, pendant ces cinq années, les torrents de leur éloquence.

A cause de l'Affaire, la littérature se politise, la politique devient littéraire. "Tous hommes de lettres," écrit Daniel Halévy, "telle fut l'affaire Dreyfus. Ainsi avons-nous, d'une part, Lucien Herr, doctrinaire hégélien, et Péguy, poète, d'autre part, Maurice Barrès, romancier hégélien (?) et Déroulède, poète."[13] Jean-Denis Bredin note à son tour "la multitude des articles dans lesquels Rochefort, Drumont, Barrès, Clémenceau, Jaurès, Lemaître, Brunetière, Lucien Herr, Zola firent appel à l'opinion, car les journalistes de l'Affaire furent le plus souvent des écrivains."[14]

Cette magnificence rhétorique a trouvé pour s'exprimer des journaux aux titres moins magnifiques. A l'aube d'un siècle enclin à se croire triomphant, la presse conserve sa désolante propension à utiliser un adjectif diminutif où se manifeste le goût du médiocre bien caractéristique de la Troisième République. Les articles les plus éloquents de Jaurès ont paru dans *La Petite République*. Le socialisme français possède un autre journal, organe de l'"Unité socialiste révolutionnaire" (guesdiste), *Le Petit Sou* (qui fait parler de lui en août 1901 quand il offre en prime à ses lecteurs, à un prix exceptionnel, des fusils Gras réglementaires transformés en fusils de chasse. René Viviani, avocat et député socialiste, rédacteur en chef de *La Petite République*, plaidant pour son confrère, évitera au *Petit Sou* de gros sous d'amende). Dans le camp anti-dreyfusard, l'organe fondé à la fin du Second Empire par Moïse Milhaud ("Ayons le courage d'être bête!"), devenu en 1900 un mastodonte de presse, passant le million d'exemplaires quotidiens, se nomme *Le Petit Journal*. *Le Petit Parisien*, fondé en 1876, approche seulement du million. La province fournit *Le Petit Marseillais, La Petite Gironde, Le Petit Méridional*. On ajoutera à ces enseignes pitoyables *Le Petit Soleil, Le Petit Illustré, Le Petit Français illustré, Le Petit Journal illustré, Le Petit Journal des Enfants, Le Petit Corbillard* et, *last but not least, Le Petit Echo de la Mode*, qui déguise sous l'humilité de son titre un puissant tirage et restera longtemps un géant de la presse hebdomadaire.

Plus tard dans le siècle Edouard Herriot, homme politique radical-socialiste et académicien, déplorera la manie française du "petit" (ma petite maison, ma petite femme, mes petites économies, signes de l'acceptation d'un destin chétif). Mais qui en fut responsable plus que cette presse de la Troisième?

Le progrès et la raison

Par contraste avec cette symbolique misérabiliste, le grand évènement intellectuel (je dis bien intellectuel) de l'année, c'est l'"Exposition universelle internationale." Pas seulement cette foire qui aligne sur les deux rives de la Seine palais en toc, belvédères, minarets, pavillons rococo où les visiteurs étrangers, mélangés aux provinciaux applaudissent les danses du ventre. Pas seulement le trottoir roulant qui relie les Invalides au Champs de Mars et inspirera à Courteline son amusant *Article 330*, que représente en décembre le Théâtre-Antoine.

L'Exposition est sérieuse. L'Exposition est d'abord une manifestation philosophique, une profession de foi, l'affirmation de valeurs intellectuelles et morales. Selon le décret constituant du 13 juillet 1892, elle avait été conçue comme "la synthèse et . . . la philosophie du XIXème siècle." Quelle philosophie? Celle d'Auguste Comte, sur laquelle Lucien Lévy-Bruhl vient de faire paraître un livre.[15] Comte, écrit à ce propos Emile Faguet—non sans quelque déplaisir— n'est "ni plus ni moins que le roi de la pensée du XIXème siècle." Le sociologue Mentré renchérit: "Non, l'Exposition n'est pas une monstrueuse Babel. . . . C'est une œuvre immense, il est vrai, mais pénétrée de méthode et de clarté. . . . Pour le dire d'un mot, l'Exposition est le triomphe du positivisme." Mais l'ambition des organisateurs va plus loin. C'est au vingtième siècle qu'ils pensent, à la "philosophie" du nouvel âge. Cette philosophie, elle se résume en quelques mots: perfectibilité humaine, développement inévitable et automatique de la civilisation. L'Exposition "se fait l'apôtre de l'idée de *progrès* . . . elle se propose ouvertement de célébrer l'*humanité*." Citations de Renan et de Jules Simon, et Mentré d'affirmer superbement: "L'idée d'organiser scientifiquement l'humanité n'est pas une utopie."

Echantillon de cette foi en l'amélioration de l'esprit; "Rien de plus instructif à cet égard que la revue des essais qui ont abouti à la bicyclette moderne, du véloci*fère* au véloci*pède*, en passant par la draisienne. . . . Il faut remercier M. Picard d'avoir donnée cette 'leçon de choses' aux pessimistes et aux néo-rousseauistes." Adversaires du progrès, tenez-vous bien!

Qui est ce Picard qui donne, à grand renfort de vélocipèdes, des leçons aux rousseauistes attardés? Il s'agit d'un homme qui, pour être aujourd'hui oublié, n'en a pas moins été un des maîtres de 1900. Alfred Picard, commissaire général de l'Exposition, est déjà l'auteur du *Rapport général* sur la précédente Exposition, celle de 1889, celle de la Tour Eiffel et du Centenaire de la Révolution française. Dans ce monumental *Rapport* (neuf volumes) M. Picard cite longuement, à l'appui de sa propre philosophie, l'*Esquisse d'un tableau historique des progrès de l'esprit humain* de Condorcet. Qui rédigeait imperturbablement son livre en 1793 et 1794 avant de s'empoisonner pour échapper à la guillotine des progressistes jacobins: "Si le perfectionnement indéfini de notre espèce est, comme je le crois, une loi générale de la nature . . . ."

A l'aube de ce siècle qui va commencer par les massacres d'Arménie, les massacres de Crète, les pogroms de Russie, se poursuivre par la première guerre mondiale, les guerres civiles en Allemagne et en Russie, la seconde guerre mondiale, le goulag soviétique, les camps de concentration nazi, les atrocités japonaises, l'extermination des opposants politiques, des Polonais, des Juifs, des Tziganes, et connaître enfin les explosions de Hiroshima et Nagasaki, on rêve un instant devant les déclarations de ce Picard: "Certes, vouloir qu'aucun grain de sable ne soit broyé dans le mouvement qui emporte la terre, c'est folie; mais les crises s'espacent, les souffrances deviennent moins longues, et la masse est plus heureuse. . . ." Attendez seulement quelques années, monsieur Picard...

Julien Benda se précipite à son tour au secours du progrès, ou plutôt décharge sa bile (déjà! il a trente-trois ans en 1900) contre "les ennemis de l'Exposition."[16] Benda inaugure la longue carrière d'inquisiteur qui le mènera, de *La Trahison des clercs* à *La France byzantine*, à dénoncer tout ce qui est intuition, art, poésie, bergsonisme, religion, jusqu'à ce qu'il ne reste plus, après ce jeu de massacre, que les pâles figures que Barrès nommait plaisamment en 1897 "les grands hommes à l'usage du baccalauréat."[17] Il appartient, ce Julien Benda, à la cohorte des fils de Renan et de Marcelin Berthelot, avec les historiens Charles Seignobos et Alphonse Aulard, le sociologue François Simiand (*alias* François Daveillans dans *La Revue Blanche*), le philosophe Lucien Herr, le philosophe député Jean Jaurès, en somme les "intellectuels" (le mot date de l'Affaire Dreyfus). "Progrès" signifie vision paradisiaque de l'histoire, un hégélianisme rose, dépourvu de tragique, la religion de la science ("Nous croyons," avait dit Renan dans *l'Avenir de la science*, "à l'humanité, à ses divines destinées, à son impérissable avenir"). Ce progrès-là, Jean Jaurès le chante: "Car le rêve d'universelle félicité et de croissante perfection humaine qui exaltait ma jeunesse d'écolier, je sens que j'y suis resté fidèle dans ce qu'on appelle la politique, et je sais gré au socialisme d'avoir donné pour moi un corps à mon beau songe."[18] Le mot "rêve" et le mot "songe" dans la même phrase. Jaurès, un génie onirique.

Mais ils ne sont pas tous d'accord. Romain Rolland a vingt-sept ans lorsque Jaurès conjugue le rêve et le songe avec la *croissante perfection de l'espèce humaine*. Rolland, élève de l'Ecole normale, où Jaurès l'avait précédé de quelques promotions, avait noté la "discussion irritée" qu'il eût, aux alentours de sa vingt-deuxième année, avec un certain D... "Lorsqu'il m'oppose cet argument: 'En quoi servent-ils [les écrivains français de la fin du siècle] au développement de l'humanité?' je lui réponds en souriant: 'Pardon! Dîtes-moi seulement: vous croyez au Progrès?'—'Comment? si j'y crois?'—'Très bien, cela suffit'—'Comment si j'y crois? Mais tout le monde y croit! Qui donc n'y croit pas?'—'Moi par exemple.'"[19] Ne voilà-t-il pas, en ces années-charnière, un dialogue révélateur de deux familles d'esprits, l'une et l'autre issues du dix-neuvième siècle, celle qui a le sens et comme l'aperception du tragique de l'histoire, celle que bercera jusqu'au bout une utopie indéfectible?

Avec le "Progrès," la "Raison." Mot gigogne, ambigu, qui couvre plus d'une signification. Mot qui s'accompagne paradoxalement, autour de 1900, d'une effervescence de passions. Prenez *La Raison, journal international hebdomadaire de philosophie, de sociologie, de littérature*. Vous attendez quelque chose de comparable à la *Revue de Métaphysique et de Morale*, que publie alors la librairie Alcan, et qui s'efforce, gravement, sagement (quelquefois pesamment) à la sérénité philosophique. Or *La Raison*, où écrivent les poètes Laurent Tailhade et Gustave Kahn, les politiques Henry Bérenger et Gustave Téry, est tout simplement un brûlot partisan, où déferle la violence anticléricale. Le chansonnier Montéhus y donnera une *Marche anticléricale* dont je recopie le premier couplet:[20]

> Contre les vendeurs de bêtises,
> Contre ceux qui faussent le cerveau,
> Contre les tenanciers de l'Eglise
> De la raison levons le drapeau . . .

La Raison va défendre l'action du ministère Combes contre les congrégations, contre ce que M. Combes lui-même appelle "les vieilles croyances, plus ou moins absurdes."[21] Un personnage considérable de l'intelligentsia parisienne, Alphonse Aulard, historien de la Révolution française, admire par-dessus tout, dans cette Sorbonne où il enseigne, la fresque de la grande cour sur laquelle on lit "Raison, rien que Raison." Refus par conséquent de toute croyance religieuse, de toute philosophie spiritualiste. Selon son disciple Georges Belloni, la "raison" était "le dieu spirituel" d'Aulard. Favoriser "ce qui unit les Français, à savoir la raison, et non ce qui les divise, à savoir la religion."[22] Pas surprenant qu'en avril 1902 le socialiste Péguy (qui commence à s'énerver devant la dérive anticléricale et politicarde des dreyfusards) accuse Aulard de "surdité mentale" (926, 5 avril 1902). Cette surdité semble affecter beaucoup d'oreilles. Significative, l'affaire Brunetière. Ferdinand Brunetière, professeur, écrivain, directeur de la *Revue des Deux Mondes*, une quinzaine d'ouvrages de critique littéraire, élu à l'Académie française en 1893. Brunetière a publié récemment un *Manuel de l'histoire de la littérature française*. Il s'y affirme admirateur de Bossuet. En même temps, il a osé parler de la "faillite de la science." *La Petite République* s'enflamme: "Ce qui me paraît monstrueux, c'est qu'un professeur laïque dont le premier devoir est d'apprendre à ses élèves la valeur et le bon usage de la raison, s'applique insolemment à convaincre la raison d'erreur, d'imposture et d'imbécillité. . . . Crime de haute trahison, s'il en fût!"[23] L'auteur (anonyme) de cette diatribe est sans doute Gustave Téry, philosophe devenu journaliste. Un écrivain mineur. Mais Jaurès, également philosophe et journaliste, n'est pas, lui, un personnage mineur. Et pour Jaurès, à un étage intellectuel supérieur à celui de Téry, la raison, c'est d'abord le refus de tout mystère, de l'obscur, des profondeurs. Dans sa thèse de 1891, *De la réalité du monde sensible*, il définissait l'inconnaissable, "une maison fermée sur une ruelle sombre et un mystère de mélodrame." Le 21 novembre 1898, dans un discours à la Chambre des députés, il affirmait "que la seule raison suffisait à tous les hommes pour la conduite de la vie." Selon Alexandre Zevaès, qui fut son collègue au Parlement, "la théorie bergsonienne de l'originalité inexprimable de la vie individuelle a le don de l'exaspérer."[24] Est-ce parce que Jaurès se fait de la "raison" cette idée aggressive qu'il s'est décidé à soutenir dans sa persécution anticléricale Emile Combes, petit bourgeois étriqué et vindicatif (ancien professeur de séminaire passé à l'ennemi), aussi éloigné que possible d'un socialisme lyrique et généreux? Etrange combinaison, chez ce Jaurès, de rêve visionnaire et d'une théorie réaliste des objets de la connaissance. Au moins trouve-t-il, à défendre son rationalisme, une éclatante imagerie. Ce n'est pas le cas d'un de ses collègues, Charles Dumont, qui vient d'être élu en 1898 député du Jura. Charles Dumont a été croyant, il ne croit plus qu'en la "raison." Devenu ministre des travaux publics, il expliquera un jour sa philosophie rationaliste à la fin d'un banquet officiel en des termes trop remarquables pour qu'on ne les cite pas: "Je respecte la foi que je n'ai plus mais en la respectant je me crois obligé de défendre dans nos écoles la cause de la libre pensée. Pourquoi la raison qui suffit à l'homme fait ne suffirait-elle pas à l'enfant et comment un jeune esprit ne reconnaîtrait-il pas comme le nôtre que ce n'est pas la Bible qui a découvert toutes ces merveilles modernes qui s'appellent le télégraphe, le téléphone, l'aéroplane? Notre vie, aujourd'hui, doit être un cri de confiance dans la raison. . . ."[25]

N'y aura-t-il personne pour dénoncer l'ambiguïté du mot *raison*, pour en proposer une interprétation plus riche, moins sectaire? On va retrouver ici l'incorruptible Péguy, le plus pur des dreyfusards, qui ne fut animé par aucun calcul politique, rien que par le souci de la justice, et voulut que cette justice fut appliquée à tous, pas seulement à un parti. Le quatrième de la troisième série des *Cahiers de la Quinzaine* (5 décembre 1901) réunit sous le titre *Etudes socialistes* les articles que Jaurès vient de publier au cours des derniers mois dans *La Petite République*, avec une longue lettre amicale de Jaurès à Péguy. Pour ouvrir le cahier, un avertissement de Péguy, *De la raison* (835 sqq.):

La raison ne procède pas de l'autorité gouvernementale. . . . C'est manquer à la raison que de vouloir établir un gouvernement de la raison. . . . La raison ne procède pas de l'autorité religieuse. Il fallait une insanité inouïe pour oser instituer le culte de la déesse Raison. . . . La froide répétition politique de cette insanité, la commémoration concertée de cette insanité constitue l'indice le plus grave d'incohérence ou de démence, de déraison. . . . Nous n'avons pas dénoncé les religions d'hier pour annoncer la religion de demain, pour prêcher quelque religion nouvelle. . . . La raison ne procède pas de l'autorité parlementaire. . . . La raison ne procède pas de l'autorité démagogique. . . . C'est fausser la raison que d'imaginer, comme l'a rêvé Renan, un gouvernement spirituel de la terre habitée, un gouvernement des intellectuels omnipotent. Une république de cuistres ne serait pas moins inhabitable qu'une république de moines. . . . Un catéchisme est insupportable. Mais un catéchisme de la raison tiendrait en ses pages la plus effroyable tyrannie. . . .

Et encore ainsi pendant des pages. Vers la fin de son "avertissement" Péguy livre le fond de sa pensée:

Nous savons que la raison n'épuise pas la vie et même le meilleur de la vie; nous savons que les instincts et les inconscients sont d'un être plus profondément existant sans doute. . . . Nous ne défendons pas la raison contre les autres manifestations de la vie. . . . Nous la défendons contre les manifestations qui, étant autres, veulent se donner pour elle et dégénèrent ainsi en déraisons. . . .

Très bien, Péguy. On se demande seulement ce qu'a pu penser Jaurès en lisant ces pages où s'ébauchent des perspectives bien éloignées de son rationalisme, la découverte de l'inconscient, l'ouverture aux profondeurs, le bergsonisme. Mais nous ne sommes qu'en 1901. Chacun des deux hommes a son chemin à lui à parcourir jusqu'en 1914. Et en 1914 ils disparaîtront tous deux.

Qu'il commence donc maintenant, ce vingtième siècle, ce siècle terrible, qui va rendre dérisoires les rêveries de croissante perfection humaine et nécessaire une plus profonde conception de la raison. La génération littéraire qui se lève va dépasser les problèmes de "fin de siècle" et d'"aube de siècle." D'autres confrontations l'attendent. Le nietzschéisme, l'anarchisme, le marxisme. De cette génération nouvelle bon nombre vont être tués au cours de la grande guerre. J'ai connu deux survivants, l'un et l'autre nés en 1885. Chaque fois que j'ai rencontré François Mauriac, il m'a parlé (avec nostalgie, un peu de gêne, quelque remords) de la période 1906-1910 où il connut mon père aux côtés de Marc Sangnier. Chacun, Mauriac et mon père, ont écrit sur ces années un roman dont je parlerai ailleurs.[26] *L'Enfant chargé de chaînes* se termine vers 1910, *Rédemption* en 1914. La "Belle" Epoque est bien morte. Une autre commence.

Notes

[1] *L'Esprit fumiste et les rires fin de siècle*, anthologie (Paris: Corti, 1990); Séverine Jouve, *Les Décadents, bréviaire fin de siècle* (Paris: Plon, 1989).

[2] *Le Désespéré*, 1886 (Paris: Club des Libraires de France, 1955) 283, 287, 299, 300, 301, 306, 324, 325.

[3] Charles Péguy, *Œuvres en prose complètes*, éd. Robert Burac (Paris: Gallimard, 1987) 1: 1637.

[4] "La mystérieuse affaire Steinheil," in Gilbert Guilleminault, *La Belle Epoque* (Paris: Denoël, 1958) 363.

[5] Voir l'analyse que fait Théodore Zeldin du livre du Dr. Proust dans son *Histoire des passions françaises* (Paris: Seuil, 1979) 5: 91 sqq.

[6] Le livre de Fierens-Gevaert paraît en janvier 1899 dans la Bibliothèque de Philosophie Contemporaine. Joseph Ageorges en rend compte dans *Le Sillon* (25 août 1899) 192-200.

[7] Camille Mauclair, *Le Soleil des morts* (Paris: Ollendorf, 1898).

[8] *Le Sillon* (septembre 1899) 259 sqq.

[9] *L'Anneau d'améthyste* (Paris: Calmann-Lévy, 1899).

[10] *Le Sillon* (10 janvier 1901) 32.

[11] Article de *La Petite République* (3 août 1902).

[12] Le livre de Dreyfus, racontant, de 1894 à 1899, son arrestation, sa condamnation, son séjour à l'île du Diable, sa seconde condamnation, puis sa grâce, a paru pour la première fois chez Fasquelle en 1901. Il est réédité en 1962 avec la préface de Mauriac.

[13] Daniel Halévy, *Péguy*, réédition (Paris: Grasset, 1943) 76. Halévy a vécu l'Affaire dans le camp dreyfusard.

[14] Jean-Denis Bredin, *L'Affaire* (Paris: Julliard, 1983) 655.

[15] Lucien Lévy-Bruhl, *La Philosophie d'Auguste Comte* (Paris: Alcan, 1900). L'article de Mentré, "L'Exposition et les divers courants sociaux," auquel je vais emprunter, a paru dans *Le Sillon* (25 octobre 1900) 241-57.

[16] *La Revue Blanche* (15 juin 1900).

[17] Maurice Barrès, *Les Déracinés*, 1897, édition définitive (Paris: Plon, 19??) 35-36.

[18] *La Petite République* (28 juillet 1893). Cf. Barrès, *Enquête aux Pays du Levant* (en 1914) (Paris: Plon, 1923) 2: 178, sur Jaurès orateur: "Et soudain, la figure congestionnée, le cou et la poitrine tendus à se rompre, les bras courts, le voici qui s'élance hors du plan rationnel, loin des réalités, dans ce monde indéterminé de la musique et des espérances. C'est alors qu'il était lui-même! C'est alors qu'il me plaisait supérieurement! Il délirait. . . . Il m'attirait un peu de la même manière que les bacchantes du Liban et les derviches tourneurs de Konia. . . ."

[19] Romain Rolland, *Le Cloître de la rue d'Ulm* (Paris: Albin Michel, 1952) 253.

[20] Cité par René Rémond, *L'Anticléricalisme en France*, éd. Complexe, (Bruxelles, 1985) 209.

[21] Discours de Combes, présidant à Beauvais la pose de la première pierre d'un futur lycée, mars 1896. "Dans un temps où les vieilles croyances, plus ou moins absurdes, tendaient à disparaître, les principes de la morale se réfugiaient dans les loges" (de la Franc-Maçonnerie).

[22] Georges Belloni, *Aulard, historien de la Révolution française* (Paris: PUF, 1949) 35, 71, 130.

[23] *La Petite République* (9 janvier 1901).

[24] Alexandre Zevaès, *Jean Jaurès* (Paris 1951) 48.

[25] Discours prononcé à la Roche sur Yon en 1911. Cité par Marc Sangnier, *Discours*, III (Paris: Bloud et cie, 1913) 96-97.

[26] François Mauriac, *L'Enfant chargé de chaînes*, a paru dans le Mercure de France en juin et juillet 1912 et en volume, chez Grasset, 1913; Georges Hoog, *Rédemption* (Paris: Bloud et Gay, 1916).

Carol Rigolot

Ancestors, Mentors, and "grands Aînés": Saint-John Perse's *Chronique*

In a volume honoring the long career of a distinguished man of letters, it seemed fitting to offer as my contribution the study of a poem composed by an eminent poet as he looked back on his own career. Saint-John Perse wrote *Chronique* in 1959, at the age of 72, just a year before receiving the Nobel Prize in Literature. (He went on to write—and sail and travel—for many more years.)

Throughout all of Perse's poetry, one can hear the echoes of literary ancestors whose voices and visions colored his own. Claudel, Hugo, and Dante loom large in his literary genealogy, preceded by Virgil, Homer, and the biblical psalmists. But in *Chronique* these voices have a particular resonance, for it is very much a poem about literary generation and the debts we owe to mentors and models, and about the "grands Aînés,"[1] who shaped Saint-John Perse's development as a poet.

To enter the world of *Chronique* is to hear, in the first instance, the personal voice of a narrator, and perhaps even the autobiographical voice of a poet, confronting old age and beyond. Saint-John Perse bestows on his narrator an urgency and a poignancy that communicate the sentiments of a man looking back on a long life. The personal echoes are frequent and moving. Yet, at the same time, *Chronique* belongs to a long lineage of works that reflect on time, aging and immortality. Cicero's *De Senectute* is a classic in a genre that includes writings by Seneca, Plutarch, Montaigne, Hugo and innumerable others. In addressing the "Grand âge" of *Chronique*, Saint-John Perse is at the same time engaged in a conversation with his predecessors, the "grands Aînés" of his literary tradition.

From the beginning, we realize that Saint-John Perse's debate with his mentors will be very different from the dialogues I and my colleagues have had across the years with Edward Sullivan. For Perse's conversation with his mentors is a problematic one:

Nous en avions assez du doigt de craie sous l'équation sans maître . . . Et vous, nos grands Aînés, dans vos robes rigides, qui descendez les rampes immortelles avec vos grands livres de pierre, nous n'avons vu remuer vos lèvres dans la clarté du soir: vous n'avez dit le mot qui lève ni nous suive. (392)

In these lines Perse's discourse evokes great voices of the past, not as voices but as silent stone giants descending the immortal staircase of history. What is this word they have not been able to say, the "mot qui lève ni nous suive," this "word that would live and be with us" (as Robert Fitzgerald translates it)?[2] And what is the poem's brief with the Elders and their books of stone?

One of the narrator's principal disputes is with the portrayal of aging that the Elders have bequeathed to us. Saint-John Perse, in the eighth decade of his life, seems resolutely unwilling to accept the idea that time inevitably brings diminution, and this is clearly a fundamental preoccuption of the poem. Its title is meant to be interpreted in the etymological sense of the Greek word *Kronos*, as Perse explained in a famous letter to Dag Hammarskjöld: "Sous son titre, *Chronique*, à prendre au sens étymologique, c'est un poème à la terre, et à l'homme, et au temps, confondus tous trois pour moi dans la même notion intemporelle d'éternité" (1133). All of these elements —earth, man and time— are present. But I would like to focus here on time, and to see how Perse's view of time informs his dialogue with his ancestors and illuminates his poetics.

When we travel to the origins of our western literary tradition, we come, by most reckonings, to the ancestor whom legend portrays as the blind and aged Homer. In one of our founding texts, the *Iliad,* Priam laments to his son Hector the misfortunes which are augmented by old age (XXII: 39-66): "Have compassion also on me, the helpless one, who can still feel, ill-fated; whom the father, Kronos's son, will bring to nought by a grievous doom in the path of old age, having seen full many evils."[3] Here, Kronos and old age are already contiguous as they are again in *Chronique.* But Perse will re-write Homer—and the subsequent tradition—to contradict how these classical authors depict aging.

Plato played an important role in fixing the topoi of old age. His *Republic* begins with the old man Cephalus telling Socrates what it is like to be old: "The majority of us bemoan their age: they miss the pleasures which were theirs in youth; they recall the pleasures of sex, drink, and feasts, and some other things that go with them, and they are angry as if they were deprived of important things."[4] But Cephalus himself has a more sanguine view: if one's life is "moderate and contented, then old age too is but moderately burdensome" (4). The essence, he concludes, is to lead a just life. This opening conversation, which appears above all to be a way to set the scene, actually had a great influence on later writers, for it was one of the first formulations of the standard complaints of old age and of the exhortation that our fate in old age owes more to character than to birthdays. Aristotle, Cicero, Seneca and Plutarch all write about aging, but, ultimately, the portrait of old age in classical antiquity is a rather gloomy one, painting it as a time of reason, virtue and peace (at best), but also of diminution, resignation and waiting.

At the end of the Renaissance, Montaigne adds his voice to this ongoing meditation about old age. Steeped in classical authors, he tends to thematize aging in their manner. In the essay "De l'aage" (I, 57), he remarks how Hannibal and Scipio and almost all the great people of ancient times had accomplished their deeds by the age of 30. "Quant à moy, je tien pour certain que, depuis cet aage, et mon esprit et mon corps ont plus diminué qu'augmenté, et plus reculé que avancé."[5] What happens with age—after 30!—according to Montaigne, is that "la vivacité, la promptitude, la fermeté, et autres parties bien plus nostres, plus importantes et essentielles, se fanissent et s'alanguissent" (ibid.). Montaigne accords the very last words of his writings to old age. The final essay of Book III ends with a quotation (in Latin) from Horace's prayer to Apollo:

> Grant me but health, Latona's son,
> And to enjoy the wealth I've won,
> And honored age, with mind entire
> And not unsolaced by the lyre.
>   Horace[6]

This poetic lyre of Horace and Montaigne belongs, of course, to all poets. But when Saint-John Perse takes it up in *Chronique,* it is to protest the image, inherited from Montaigne and from antiquity, of old age as a time of decline. At the age of 72, Saint-John Perse proclaims another vision of age, different from the ancestral wisdom. And it may be that his protest is most vehement against a most recent ancestor: Victor Hugo.

Hugo is indeed a formidable forefather, before whom any twentieth-century poet might understandably feel a Harold Bloomian anxiety of influence. On earlier occasions, Hugo has been present, explicitly or implicitly, in Perse's prose and poetry, as I have suggested in other studies.[7] And I would argue that Hugo can be felt once again in *Chronique.*

The presence of a literary ancestor may not be totally surprising in a poem that is placed under the sign of the mythological Kronos, who was defeated by his son Zeus and relegated to the darkness of Tartarus. Kronos's presence in the poem sets the stage for another father-son drama, this one between a writer and at least one of his "grands Aînés" (392). I would contend that, as Zeus attacked his father Kronos, Perse, in a certain sense, takes on the ancestral figure of Hugo to rebut his vision of old age.[8] It is as if in *Chronique,* the literary descendent tried to get the last word over his Elder. And I would argue that *Chronique* can be read, at least in part, as a reply to a specific poem—*Tristesse d'Olympio*—one of Hugo's best known and most widely anthologized works, one that a French schoolboy would have been likely to study, and one whose very title proclaims the importance of the mythological lyre in Hugo's poetic vocation. Although *Tristesse d'Olympio* is a lyric poem, significantly different from the more epic *souffle* of *Chronique*, it contains specific textual and thematic elements to which I believe Perse is replying in his work.

Hugo was in his thirties when he composed *Tristesse d'Olympio*,[9] but in the poem he imagines the desolation of old age as he relates the story of a man revisiting sites of a past love. (Literary historians assimilate this pilgrimage to Hugo's own travel in October 1837 to the village of Les Metz, where he had previously spent some idyllic time with Juliette Drouet.) The tone of *Tristesse* is doleful, for the presence of both narrator and his beloved seems to have vanished from the surroundings:

> De tout ce qui fut nous presque rien n'est vivant;
> Et, comme un tas de cendre éteinte et refroidie,
> L'amas des souvenirs se disperse à tout vent! (st. 15)

In his Romantic desolation, the narrator feels old and decrepit, describing his mental state as old age, although there is no indication of his actual age. Like any authentic Romantic sufferer, he is old before his time, and he conveys throughout the poem bleak visions of old age. It is a time without vigor or force:

> Toutes les passions s'éloignent avec l'âge,
> L'une emportant son masque et l'autre son couteau,
> Comme un essaim chantant d'histrions en voyage
> Dont le groupe décroit derrière le coteau. (st. 33)

Indeed, the portrait of age drawn by Hugo in the final stanzas of *Tristesse d'Olympio* is terrifying:

> . . . ces jours où la tête au poids des ans s'incline,
> Où l'homme, sans projets, sans but, sans visions,
> Sent qu'il n'est déjà plus qu'une tombe en ruine
> Où gisent ses vertus et ses illusions; (st. 35)

This tomb-like man is compared to someone advancing step by step along a darkened ramp toward an abyss. And the poem ends in a place as dark as Kronos's Tartarus—devoid even of starlight: "dans cette nuit qu'aucun rayon n'étoile" (st. 38).

If old age in Hugo's poem is a time and place of darkness, this is decidedly not true for the narrator of *Chronique* who refutes, virtually point by point, the characterizations of old age that were formulated by a Victor Hugo who was only 35 years old. It is as if Perse reversed the chronology, becoming the Elder who, at age 72, could teach the young Hugo what old age is really like. For Hugo, old age was a Romantic stance, the Romantic hero being, almost by definition, a man "vieux avant l'âge," whereas Perse could describe old age as a real situation.

The protagonist of *Tristesse* wanders all day, then at nightfall begins a thirty-stanza lament. *Chronique* also takes place at nightfall: "Fraîcheur du soir sur les hauteurs" (389). But it is far from a lament, for the call is to action: "Lève la tête, homme du soir" (389).

The protagonist of *Tristesse* is described as a "paria" (st. 8) contemplating the scenery as an outsider. By contrast, the observer in *Chronique*, looking out on a vast geography reddened by the sunset, dominates the scene. "La face ardente et l'âme haute" (391), he is king of the site and the moment: "Notre royaume est d'avant-soir, ce grand éclat d'un siècle vers sa cime" (392).

Hugo's poem is filled with images of light and dark, where old age represents darkness and death. What remains of our existence is "un tas de cendre éteinte et refroidie" (v. 15). But *Chronique* denies these ashes: "l'embrasement d'un soir" (390); "Fièvre là-haut et lit de braise" (390); "Grand âge, vous mentiez: route de braise et non de cendres" (391); or, finally , "Ceux qui furent aux choses n'en disent point l'usure ni la cendre, mais ce haut vivre en marche sur la terre des morts" (399). Perse's insistence on *braise*—glowing embers—in place of Hugo's *cendre*—cold ashes—signals the radical difference between his vision and that of his predecessor.

In *Tristesse d'Olympio* we learn that nature has been instructed to erase us from the places we have lived: "[Dieu] dit à la vallée, où s'imprima notre âme, / D'effacer notre trace et d'oublier nos noms" (st. 30). The narrator is banished from the setting; he can remember the past, but he has no role in the present. No traces remain of his life with the woman he loves. Even their names are forgotten. In *Chronique* Perse takes up this same dialectics of naming and anonymity, but in a way that underscores his disagreement with Hugo. When Perse's narrator observes that "Notre race est antique, notre face est sans nom" (393), his assertion is not meant to be plaintive:

Errants, ô Terre, nous rêvions . . .

Nous n'avons point tenure de fief ni terre de bien-fonds. Nous n'avons point connu le legs, ni ne saurions léguer. Qui sut jamais notre âge et sut notre nom d'homme? Et qui disputerait un jour de nos lieux de naissance? Eponyme, l'ancêtre, et sa gloire, sans trace. (395)

By contrast with the lament in *Tristesse* over losing one's name, the narrator of *Chronique* seems to valorize his anonymity, linking it to dreams, and declaring in subsequent stanzas that his identity does not reside in names, but in other realities, like the "pierre du vieux fusil de noir" (395) or the "pâte de corail blanc sciée pour les terrasses" (396). Nor does the ancestor ever have a name in this poem. He is "Eponyme"—someone who gives his name to a place—but he is never himself named, as if the narrator were conveniently erasing all genealogy. He does precisely what Hugo's narrator most fears: "D'effacer notre trace et d'oublier nos noms." The ancestor remains nameless in *Chronique*, as do the "grands Aînés" earlier in the poem. Even worse, the ancestor leaves behind no vestige of his accomplishments: "sa gloire, sans trace." It is intriguing that Perse and Hugo use the same word "trace." Moreover, Hugo's expression "effacer notre trace" is echoed homophonically in Perse's verse "Notre race est antique, notre face est sans nom." If indeed *Chronique* pursues a debate with Victor Hugo, it is a double comeuppance for this literary predecessor to be rendered anonymous, leaving behind no sign of his glory.

Hugo's poem focuses on an individual narrator who laments his past and finds his only consolation in memory: "ô sacré souvenir" (st. 38). When he says *nous*, he is referring to the couple he formed with the woman he loves, and his *nous* often feels like a disguised "*je*." In *Chronique* the narrator also says *nous*, but his song is collective as well as singular. He is a series of individuals whose voices ultimately speak for humanity and for the multiplicity of human experience: "Grand âge, nous venons de toutes rives de la terre. Notre race est antique, notre face est sans nom" (393); "Et le temps en sait long sur tous les hommes que nous fûmes" (393). In *Tristesse* the narrator laments to his beloved that all signs of their passage are gone: "De tout ce qui fut nous presque rien n'est vivant" (v. 15). By contrast, in *Chronique* "tous les hommes que nous fûmes" live on in some mysterious way that lies at the heart of the poem. For Perse takes the drama of old age and elevates it to a universal scale, with time extending both backward and forward. He assimilates one lifetime into the geological time frame of a "nuit dévonienne" (401), stretching back, beyond the early devonian period of earth formation to a mythological past, where he finds Cybèle, the wife and sister of Kronos: "Et la grenade de Cybèle teint encore de son sang la bouche de nos femmes" (391). Cybèle's presence spans time from the beginning to the present. In the other direction, *Chronique* seeks to extend limitlessly forward, "car notre route tend plus loin" (391). Perse takes the journey of an individual, as related in *Tristesse d'Olympio*, and extends it past old age to something beyond: "Pour nous chante déjà plus hautaine aventure" (403).

Ultimately, the debate between Perse and Hugo goes beyond a disagreement about old age to embrace vaster questions of life and poetics. *Chronique* seeks, in all ways, to go beyond the limits that dominate in *Tristesse d'Olympio*: beyond the metrical limits of measured verses and quatrains; beyond the narrative limits of one protagonist; and beyond the chronological limits of one lifetime. This effort to go beyond limits takes Perse out of the lyric into the epic; out of autobiography to a story of humanity; and out of time to a striving for eternity: "Le temps que l'an mesure n'est point mesure de nos jours . . . Et ceci reste à dire: nous vivons d'outre-mort, et de mort même vivrons-nous" (391).

This enigmatic affirmation of life in and beyond death assumes its fullest meaning when placed in the larger context of Perse's complete work, where the role of death evolves progressively. In *Pour fêter une enfance*, life and death were envisaged as components of a total universe where death seemed a natural part of an integrated world: "Et l'ombre et la lumière alors étaient plus près d'être une même chose" (25). In the second period of Perse's poetry, from *La Gloire des Rois* through *Vents*, life and death divided off as antithetical elements in a dualistic world. In A*mers*, the first poem of synthesis, references to death are more frequent than in any other of Perse's poems, not only because it is such a long work but, more importantly, because in *Amers* two protagonists, lover and poet, confront the fact of mortality. One discovers in love and the other in art a force stronger than death.

Chronique fits into Perse's œuvre as a sequel to these discoveries. In this poem we circle back to the insular paradise of *Eloges* and the "bois moucheté des Iles" (395), but with a narrator who is enriched by the quests of a lifetime. "Et nous rentrons chargés de nuit, sachant de naissance et de mort plus que n'enseigne le songe d'homme" (397). The life-death dichotomy seems to have found at least a temporary resolution in *Chronique*: "Notre grief n'est plus de mort . . . La mort est au hublot, mais notre route n'est point là" (399). This realization allows the protagonist to affirm that "de mort même vivrons-nous" (391). Where Hugo lamented old age, Perse celebrates the rituals of ever-renewing life: "toute cette immensité de l'être et ce foisonnement de l'être, toute cette passion d'être et tout ce pouvoir d'être, ah!" (397). And he focuses on what comes afterward: "il est d'autres naissances à quoi porter vos lampes" (392). *Chronique* closes with a liturgical gesture of divestment in which the protagonist prepares for death, for the alliance with "cette heure de grand sens" (397). The narrator-priest strips away his past in order to appear at the threshold, with free hands: "Nous élevons à bout de bras, sur le plat de nos mains, comme couvée d'ailes naissantes, ce cœur enténébré de l'homme où fut l'avide, et fut l'ardent, et tant d'amour irrévélé . . ." (404).

If in *Tristesse d'Olympio*, shadow and darkness bring terror, Perse in *Chronique* revalorizes darkness, making it an exalted quality: "cette part en nous divine qui fut notre part de ténèbres" (394). In response to Hugo's protagonist who asks "N'existons-nous donc plus? Avons-nous eu notre heure?" (st. 16), Perse's narrator declares a new vocation: "notre lit n'est point tiré dans l'étendue ni la durée" (391); "Nous sommes pâtres du futur" (401).

But *Chronique* ends with many questions, for the narrator declares us shepherds of the future without knowing of what it consists; he stands ready to offer up his life, without knowing to whom: "L'offrande, ô nuit, où la porter?" (404). This question stands at the crossroads where Perse's ontology and poetics come together. And it seems clear that the answer lies, at least in part, in art itself.

In one particularly colorful scene, Indians engage in their eagle dance:

Jadis les hommes de haut site, la face peinte d'ocre rouge sur leurs mesas d'argile, nous ont dansé sans gestes danse immobile de l'aigle. Ici, de soir, et face à l'Ouest, mimant la verge ou le fléau, il n'est que d'étendre les bras en croix pour auner à son aune l'espace d'un tel an: danse immobile de l'âge sur l'envergure de son aile. (399)

In this "danse immobile" they live the seeming contradiction of intense action and apparent motionlessness (a contradiction that is not unlike the stone statues of the elders, processing down a ramp even though they are immobilized in stone.) For the privileged time of the eagle dance, Indians stand with arms extended, resembling a cross or a scale, in a posture of intense immobility, as if somehow making time stand still. And the poet seems to suggest that in a work of art one can capture the intensity of life and the permanence of eternity. Both creation and creator transcend chronology by entering into this privileged space-time of the work of art: "Nos œuvres vivent loin de nous dans leurs vergers d'éclairs. Et nous n'avons de rang parmi les hommes de l'instant" (395).

If *Chronique* takes as its point of departure a disagreement with the "grands Aînés" of the literary past, with the long lineage of voices lamenting old age, it ultimately extends far beyond this debate to proclaim its own vision of time and art. Saint-John Perse gives a cosmic dimension to the lament of old age and incorporates it into a larger meditation about poetics and life. Certainly, the stakes were larger for him than for the 35-year-old Hugo, for Perse is also, through *Chronique*, challenging his own mortality. If the stone effigies of the "grands Aînés," processing down the staircase of history, did not possess answers to the questions of existence, if they did not offer the "word that would live and be with us," Perse takes up the lyre in *Chronique* to find this word. In response to the Elders and to the "équation sans maître" (392), he attempts a "chant du Maître" (404). This means transforming the *Tristesse d'Olympio* into a truly Olympian song, translating its lyrical voice into an epic work, "comme chant d'honneur et de grand âge" (404).

Saint-John Perse's debate with Victor Hugo and with his other literary ancestors is a complex one, and clearly as formative in its own way as the much happier conversations that I have been privileged to share with the mentor whom we honor in this volume. The protagonist of *Chronique* may not ultimately have found all the words that are needed: "la chose est dite et n'est point dite" (397). But in his effort to turn Hugo's cinders into embers: "route de braise et non de cendres" (391), he has nevertheless succeeded in having the last word—at least in time—over one youthful ancestor among the "grands Aînés" of his cultural tradition.

Notes

[1] Saint-John Perse, *Œuvres complètes*, Bibliothèque de la Pléiade (Paris: Gallimard, 1972) 392. All subsequent references to Perse's works will be indicated in parentheses in the text.

[2] St.-John Perse, *Collected Poems*, Bollingen Series 87 (Princeton: Princeton UP, 1983) 583.

[3] Homerus, *The Iliad*, trans. Lang, Leaf, Myers (New York: The Modern Library, n.d.) 402.

[4] Plato, *Republic*, trans. G.M. A. Grube (Indianapolis, IN: Hackett Publishing Co., 1974) 3.

[5] Michel de Montaigne, "De l'aage," in *Œuvres complètes*, eds. Albert Thibaudet and Maurice Rat, Bibliothèque de la Pléiade (Paris: Gallimard, 1962) 313.

[6] Montaigne, "De l'expérience," III, 13, 1097.

[7] For example, in "Victor Hugo et Saint-John Perse: *Pour Dante*," *French Review* 57 (1984) 794-801.

[8] Zeus's own son, we recall, is Perseus, or Persée. Whether or not Saint-John Perse's *nom de plume* echoes a kinship to this mythological Perseus-Persée (and I have suggested elsewhere that it does), it is clear that mythology is a factor in *Chronique*.

[9] "Tristesse d'Olympio" was composed in 1837 and included in the collection *Les Rayons et les ombres* (1840). References to the poem are drawn from Hugo, *Poésies*, "Lettres Françaises," Vol. 2 (Paris: Imprimerie Nationale, 1984) 287-93. Quotations from the poem specify the stanza number in parentheses.

Kirk Anderson

Chronicles, Maxims, and "la Petite Histoire": Some Célinian Precursors

A well-traveled paradox would have it that Louis-Ferdinand Céline's writing represents the unlikely marriage of a revolutionary style and reactionary ideas. This suggests that in philosophical or ideological terms, Céline is a traditionalist whereas on the level of form, he would be the consummate modern, the innovator, the stylist who, looking back, finds nothing worthy of imitation. The case of his relationship to Gobineau would confirm as much: the author of the *Essai sur l'inégalité des races humaines* provides Céline with "non seulement une doctrine mais un climat et des mécanismes mentaux," as Philippe Alméras maintains, while in their use of language, the two could hardly resemble one another less.[1] The first wrote in the sort of academic French which the second blamed on Amyot and disdainfully called *style du bachot*.

The dichotomy, though, is somewhat too neat. A perceptive and even voracious reader, Céline professes admiration for a series of writers reaching back into the late Middle Ages, writers noteworthy not so much for their ideas (who needs ideas? he told his interviewers over and over, the encyclopedias are full of them) as for their expression. Taking a cue from remarks made by the author himself, I would like to emphasize that Céline's writing has formal and not just ideological precedents, and moreover that he recognized this.

With few exceptions, the texts Céline claims to respect or emulate would not fit under the heading "prose fiction." One advantage to considering his final trilogy, *D'un château l'autre*, *Nord*, and *Rigodon*, as chronicle or *témoignage* rather than as novels is that it makes his place in a literary tradition more apparent. That tradition belongs largely to writers who transcribe experiences rather than imagine them. But Froissart, Tallemant des Réaux, Chamfort, and Lenotre have more than this in common. Much of Céline's interest in these four, and consequently my own, lies in the way they select and present the *petit fait vrai*. In the *Chroniques*, in *Historiettes*, in *Produits de la civilisation perfectionnée*, and in *Paris révolutionnaire*, the anecdote or veridical detail enjoys a privileged status, often at the expense of narrative continuity and philosophical transcendence.[2] An evaluation of the so-called "German" trilogy should take some account of these precedents.

Froissart (1333-c. 1400)

Céline often referred to his final trilogy as a "chronique," and his mention of Joinville, Villehardouin, Commynes, and Froissart in interviews of the period, as well as in the trilogy itself, suffices to eliminate any doubts as to just what sort of chronicle he meant. I single out Froissart because, more than the other three, he illustrates what is typical of the genre: chronological organization, gratuitous detail, little explanation, and a predilection for color at the expense of plot. Gaston Boissier sums up an 1874 study with the remark, "On peut dire que ses *Chroniques*, si pleines d'erreurs dans les détails, sont merveilleusement exactes pour l'ensemble et qu'elles nous donnent l'idée la plus vraie de son temps."[3] This judgment of Froissart's chronicle prefigures, almost to the letter, a widely-held view on Céline's.

The declarations of absolute fidelity to fact which regularly interrupt Céline's narrative cannot be wholly dissociated from his adoption of the label "chronique," but neither can they explain a specific preference for Froissart over, for example, Ranke, whose name has become synonymous with the telling of things "as they really were." His remarks on the subject encourage us to consider other criteria: "Je ne sais pas si Froissart . . . , Joinville ou Commines ont fait exprès d'être mêlés aux événements qu'ils décrivent... Ils se sont trouvés là par la faute des circonstances historiques. Moi aussi je me suis trouvé dans une histoire... ... Comme eux j'ai été mêlé à de drôles de salades."[4] One feature distinguishing medieval historiography from its modern descendant is the dual status of the writer who is also a witness or even participant. For present-day readers, who tend to associate truth with objectivity, a true account supposes some distance between the narrator and the events described. However, like his medieval forebears, Céline considers immediacy as synonymous with veracity: "j'ai lu bien des reportages, ci!... là!... sur Siegmaringen... tout illusoires ou tendancieux... travioles, similis, faux-fuyard, foireux... que diantre!... ils y étaient pas, aucun!... au moment qu'il aurait fallu!..."[5] And by techniques such as the extensive use of the present of narration, he seeks constantly to convey that immediacy.

Mixed up in the confusion of Germany's destruction and collapse, the narrator of *Rigodon* compares himself to an ant in a pile of iron filings (731). The ant's perspective prevents it from understanding the outside forces that may have given shape to the pile, and so it wanders back and forth, noting the position of each particle but not presuming to explain the configuration. Chronicles like Froissart's also ignore the kind of perspective that makes history intelligible by reference to chains of causality. Although he may sum up an anecdote about a greedy doctor with the remark "De telles verges sont battus tous médecins" (935), Froissart usually limits himself to the role of a recorder, one who simply puts events to paper so that they will not be lost to posterity. His characteristic "je vous recorde" (734) expresses this intention as clearly as Céline's "je dois tout vous noter! je vous note!"[6] Their principal duty, both quotations suggest, is to establish a record, giving to the "si brutal net événement" its first linguistic incarnation (*Rigodon* 823).

Both chroniclers not only "record" or "note" events, but explicitly say that they are doing so, and for the benefit of whom. Despite more recent notions of "objectivity," the shifters "I" and "you" in no way hinder the documentary endeavor; in fact, they highlight it in a way not possible if the subject and indirect object of "je vous note" were excluded in favor of a strictly third-person discourse. Critical objection to Céline's use of the term "chronique" is often based on his failure to efface himself from his narration: Frédéric Vitoux, for example, calls the true chronicler an "image type de l'écrivain 'classique' . . . qui s'efface devant l'histoire," and in whose text "le discours . . . est insigni-fiant."[7] This characterization might well apply to Ranke or Thierry, but hardly describes Froissart's *Chroniques*, in which references to the writer's "je" and the reader's "vous" appear again and again.

F ormulaic allusions to the past and future of the narration, as well as to its present, count among the topoi which Céline resuscitates for his own chronicle. These statements too refer not to what happened, but to the relation of what happened. His repeated "je vous raconterai" echoes Froissart's "Or conterons de"; reminders like "je vous ai déjà dit" recall the medieval "vous avez ouï comment," as if the writer felt a need to assure us that the organization of the text has not been left to chance. Moreover, in the absence of narrative suspense and a well-knit plot, promises of what will follow serve to maintain the reader's interest. *Rigodon*'s narrator claims that by imitating the ant in the filings, he will resist the temptation to philosophize, and Froissart rarely even feels the urge, yet neither exhibits much concern for what Fustel de Coulanges, historiography's Flaubert, called "la chasteté de l'histoire." These texts betray an acute aware-ness of the reader and deliberately call attention to the narrative act which produced them.

Like the practitioners of the *nouveau roman* (*La Jalousie* and *D'un château l'autre* are published the same year), Céline dispenses with conven-tions of plot, character, and thematic unity. His *Féerie pour une autre fois* had failed critically and commercially for no other reason. But one need not see in this gesture a categorical break with the past; passing mention of Froissart, Joinville, and Villehardouin reminds us of a literary code which in fact predates the "classical" one. Hayden White's distinction between chronicle and history aptly characterizes the difference between Célinian chronicle and the classic novel. For White, chronicles and histories differ not as genres but as "level[s] of conceptualization."[8] Explanation is inherent to the histories of Marx or Toqueville because they operate at more abstract levels of conceptualization, while chroniclers, considerably less concerned with plot, interpretation, and overall structure, may have more closely approached the ideal of bare reporting. In short, a Froissart narrates without narrativizing. Criticisms of early historical practice, notes White, rest upon an essentially moral foundation:

[T]his value attached to narrativity in the representation of real events arises out of a desire to have real events display the coherence, integrity, fullness, and closure of an image of life that is and can only be imaginary. . . . If it were only a matter of realism in representation, one could make a pretty good case for both the annals and chronicle forms as paradigms of the ways that reality offers itself to perception.[9]

The realism evoked here is the only kind Céline seeks. What modern readers of Froissart might call incoherence is one of the more significant justifications for Céline's preference of the term "chronicle" to designate his trilogy. He suggests as much in the opening pages of *Nord*: "imaginez une tapisserie, haut, bas, travers, tous les sujets à la fois et toutes les couleurs... tous les motifs!... tout sens dessus dessous!... *prétendre vous les présenter à plat, debout, ou couchés, serait mentir...*" (318, my emphasis). Hence he defends the apparent disorder of his narrative by insisting on its mimetic truthfulness, forgoing a cohesive plot in favor of an imitative chaos.

A nostalgia for the Middle Ages comes to light as early as the aborted "Légende du roi Krogold," passages of which figure in *Mort à crédit*. In general, the fascination is with linguistic rather than political circumstances: the history of the language since the Renaissance, writes Céline in a short piece on *Gargantua* and *Pantagruel*, is the story of the triumph and subsequent tyranny of Amyot's French over that of Rabelais, who, as the title informs us, "a raté son coup."[10] Amyot's academic style would unfortunately impose itself on Voltaire, Bourget, and in the end an entire "littérature de bachot et de brevet élémentaire" (*Herne* 45). Because they were lucky enough to have preceded all this, medieval writers had no obligation toward a sort of truthfulness which emasculates the language: "Je pourrais inventer, transposer... ce qu'ils ont fait, tous... cela passait en vieux français... Joinville, Villehardouin l'avaient belle, ils se sont pas fait faute, mais notre français là, rabougri, si strict mièvre, académisé presque à mort . . ." (*Rigodon* 841). An interview from this period betrays the same regret: "Même les chroniqueurs, Froissart, Joinville, tous ils ont laissé une place très large à l'affabulation, à la force des mots, à leur musique."[11] Céline has as little regard for pure fiction as he does for factual writing which, shunning style, deprives the language of its musicality. It seems natural, then, that he should evoke a writer who records lived experience through a conscience that is unashamedly literary.

Tallemant des Réaux (1619-1690)

The author of *Historiettes* receives a single mention in the trilogy: "les romanciers écrivent toujours les mêmes romans. . . . à tout bien voir, garniture lianes de fortes pensées... Tallemant suffit, compact, vous met tout, pognon, les crimes, l'amour... en pas trois pages..." (*Nord* 499). Published correspondence and interviews, though, contain more than a half-dozen such references, all of which express approval on Céline's part, if not a literary affinity. A witness close to him during the years of the trilogy recalls that "De Tallemant des Réaux à Georges Lenotre, il se passionnait pour la 'petite histoire,' genre auquel il attachait son œuvre."[12] The anecdotes related in Tallemant des Réaux's *Historiettes*, whose very title evokes "la petite histoire" that would make Lenotre's fortune over two hundred years later, defile the most illustrious figures of sixteenth- and seventeenth-century France so irreverently that upon first publication (1834) mandarins like Victor Cousin considered the text a forgery. Like Céline, Tallemant adopts a casual, even conversational tone ("Il faut que je conte une chose de lui qui est plaisante"; "Parlons un peu de ses amours") and, perhaps certain that his work will not reach the public during his lifetime, he does not flinch before some of the same *gros mots* that brought *Mort à crédit* so much censure (129, 161). Particulars concerning the private lives of the nobility often satisfy a desire for realism by humanizing them. His penchant for anecdotes involving various bodily functions could be called either an apex of bad taste or an earnest project to remind readers that the great and powerful did not escape the laws of biology. In either case, the parallel with Céline on this level needs little amplification.

The *Historiettes* make even less claim to continuity or overall unity than Froissart's *Chroniques*; each section begins with a literary portrait and relates anecdotes intended to fill out and authenticate the characterization. "[C]e ne sont que petits Mémoires," warns the preface, "qui n'ont aucune liaison les uns avec les autres" (11). As the quotation from *Nord* indicates, Céline admires these vignettes for their concision and their cynicism. The trilogy contains some comparable sketches, mainly in the first volume: Pétain, prisoner of the Reich, lives like a king with sixteen meal cards per day, while Pierre Laval hoards Lucky Strikes and refuses audience to anyone who might ask him for one. Other dignitaries of the Collaboration—Bridoux, Abetz, Chateaubriant—receive similar treatment, and consequently certain members of the far right cried treason when *D' un château l' autre* was published a decade after the post-Occupation purges.

Such portraits-cum-*historiettes* are fewer in *Nord* and *Rigodon*, and yet by his reduction of history to personal foibles and vices, by his subversion of the

Plutarchian tradition of Great Men history, Tallemant des Réaux becomes a noteworthy predecessor. Whereas battlefields, courtrooms and amphitheaters provide the settings for typical historians, Tallemant prefers the bedroom, the boudoir, and the water closet. He cultivates his difference in an age whose official historiography usually smacks of panegyric: "je prétends dire le bien et le mal sans dissimuler la vérité, et sans me servir de ce qu'on trouve dans les Histoires et les Mémoires imprimés" (11). Behind the voyeuristic appeal, though, lurks a contention that the public personality reveals itself best in private life, and thus that these anecdotes are perhaps as relevant as they are amusing. Tallemant, like Saint-Simon after him, recognized that banal incidents can reveal character traits with implications too wide to ignore. Private vices and personal quarrels were his stock-in-trade, and their influence on History (with a capital H) is implied throughout. His nineteenth-century detractors considered him "un esprit malin et pervers, heureux de se vautrer dans l'ordure, et qui noircissait à plaisir les personnages les plus vénérables"; Céline, more than familiar with such condemnations, saw in him a literary ancestor and kindred spirit.[13] Had he not admitted to his typist, reading the proofs of Voyage au bout de la nuit, "Il faut noircir, et se noircir" (Herne 211)?

Chamfort (1740-1794)

The Produits de la civilisation perfectionnée belong on the one hand to the tradition of Tallemant and Lenotre, and on the other to that of La Rochefoucauld, Pascal, and La Bruyère; Chamfort had divided them into "Caractères," "Anecdotes," and "Maximes et Pensées." One's initial contact with the text highlights the intentional irony of its title, since the "Caractères" and "Anecdotes" in particular unmask the eighteenth-century aristocracy much as the Historiettes had done to an earlier one, in a context where this gesture has political implications which Tallemant could not have imagined. Both the anecdotal and the moraliste dimensions of the work are germane to my discussion, and both doubtless interested Céline. "Je vous recommande Chamfort parmi les humoristes français," he writes to Milton Hindus, "la quintessence de l'esprit de finesse—Schopenhauer lui doit tout—sans l'avoir jamais avoué" (Herne 128). The remark evinces an enthusiasm which seems constant; in other comments made immediately after the war, Chamfort supposedly prefigures Céline himself, each of them belonging to a long series of French writers who became victims of revolutionary purges (CC7 258, 303). But the choice of predecessor transcends biographical matters, and Chamfort's misanthropy has a resonance strangely familiar to readers of Céline. "[L]e public me paraît avoir le comble du mauvais goût et la rage du dénigrement," he responds to those who wonder why he has not published anything recently, "s'il y a un homme sur la terre qui ait le droit de vivre pour lui, c'est moi, après les méchancetés qu'on m'a faites à chaque succès que j'ai obtenu" (17-18). It is significant that despite the considerable achievements of Enlightenment historiographers, this writer can still imply that portraits and anecdotes are worthy of more than idle curiosity, as if narrative histories might not provide a complete picture of the past. In any case, Céline recognizes and admires Chamfort's contribution to literary forms he often integrated into his own work.

The recommendation to Hindus could apply to any part of the *Produits de la civilisation perfectionnée*, but given that the preceding and following sections of this essay both deal with a champion of "la petite histoire," the emphasis here will fall on the *moraliste*. Albert Camus preferred Chamfort to La Rochefoucauld not only for obvious ideological reasons, but also because the former depicts rather than legislates, rarely generalizes, and avoids the contrived symmetry of La Rochefoucauld's antitheses. In fact Chamfort's first "maxime générale" warns against the abuse of maxims. "Le paresseux et l'homme médiocre," he writes, "donnent à la maxime une généralité que l'auteur . . . n'a pas prétendu lui donner" (21). Elsewhere, Chamfort marks his distance from La Rochefoucauld by accusing him of having judged an entire palace (i.e., human nature) on the basis of the latrines (25). But as his (ironic) title suggests, he will insist more on the depravity of civilization than on the goodness of uncorrupted human nature. Indeed many of the "Maximes et Pensées" read like the work of a resigned but more cynical Jean-Jacques. Still others, in tone, in phrasing, and in thought, could have come directly from *Voyage au bout de la nuit*: "Vivre est une maladie dont le sommeil nous soulage toutes les seize heures. C'est un palliatif. La mort est le remède" (49); "L'Ecriture a dit que le commencement de la sagesse était la crainte de Dieu; moi, je crois que c'est la crainte des hommes" (49). What is most curious is not that Chamfort died while recovering from a gruesome suicide attempt, but that he had once mustered the faith to write pamphlets for the republican cause.

Maxims like La Rochefoucauld's—cynical, categorical, and reductive—find a natural place in Céline's writing as early as the dissertation on Semmelweis: "L'Homicide est une fonction quotidienne des peuples. . . . Il ne convient pas plus d'irriter les foules ardentes que les lions affamés."[14] *Voyage au bout de la nuit*, which some have read as a compendium of highly quotable proverbs, would in any event suffer greatly by their omission. Recent French quotation dictionaries devote as much space to Céline as literary manuals, a sure sign that discrete well-turned phrases were not the least of his writerly achievements. However the one-sentence paragraphs so prominent in *Voyage au bout de la nuit* rarely reappear afterward. Maxims in the later works, like Chamfort's, tend to be less lapidary, less categorical, less aphoristic:

Le confort fait bien déconner (*Château* 228)

dans les circonstances tragiques y a toujours deux clans, ceux qui vont voir couper les têtes, ceux qui vont pêcher à la ligne (*Nord* 324)

vous savez n'est-ce pas aux débâcles tout le monde fauche les papiers de tout le monde... (*Nord* 396)

les êtres humains restent pas comme ça sur une émotion... faut qu'ils fassent une maladie... (*Nord* 592)

tous les grands redressements nationaux commencent par des vols de literie... (*Nord* 616)

quand y a la guerre on tombe tout le temps sur des bancalots, fatal!... (*Rigodon* 818)

The recourse to aphorisms, regardless of the message they express individually, implies that events can be explained by reference to human nature, and that the human condition through the ages never really changes. The medieval histori-ographer also worked on the premise that no epoch differed fundamentally from his own. Nevertheless, the chronicler and the *moraliste* are at cross-purposes in Céline's late work, the absence of explanation being the salient feature of chronicle, as the narrator himself has defined it in his passage on the ant and the filings. He cannot choose between a text that shows without explaining (like Froissart's) and one that explains without showing (like the "Maximes et Pensées"). If one wanted to refute the chronicler pose, the frequent intrusion of these "considérations" or "philosophies" would be a strong argument against it (*Château* 164; *Nord* 445).

G. Lenotre (1857-1935)

In a brief exposition of his literary preferences, the narrator of *Bagatelles pour un massacre* declares, with neither preamble nor explanation, "je me ferais mourir pour Lenôtre."[15] As is so often the case in the pamphlets, the hyperbole conceals some measure of sincerity. In *D'un château l'autre*, written some twenty years later, the name comes up once more: "Ça sera un jour bien amusant qu'un autre Lenôtre des temps à venir retourne les tombes et les statues, les auréoles et les 'Actions'..." (41). A similar remark in a letter to Paraz concerns the assassination of Céline's first publisher, Robert Denoël: "Je vois qu'on ramone beaucoup l'affaire du mystère Denoël. C'est pas fini–Ah les Lenotre 2000 ils auront du pain!"[16] Lenotre is the pen name of a historian best remembered for his anecdotal version of the Revolution and First Empire, most of which was published just about the time of Céline's birth under the title *Vieux papiers, vieilles maisons*. This treatment, which he called "la petite histoire," seeks neither narrative continuity nor third-person objectivity, and this at a time when positivists like Langlois and Seignobos set the parameters for historical writing. More important, Lenotre favors the sort of details which conventional histories had passed over. Describing himself as a "lecteur gâté par les reportages minutieux si fort en vogue à notre époque," he sought to depict the Revolutionary era the same way periodicals documented his own (xii). His notorious curiosity and the meticulous research which it inspired emphasized particulars of diet, dress, fashion, and speech as well as the Parisian topography and architecture which set the stage for the momentous events to which most histories limit themselves. "Combien de fois," he exclaims in a foreword, "en parcourant les pages qu'ont inspirées à Michelet et à Lamartine les sombres journées de la Terreur, j'essayai de reconstituer en esprit, à l'aide de leurs narrations, la salle où siégeait la Convention, les prisons, les comités. Comme j'aurais préféré à ces grandes compositions qu'ils ont laissées le moindre croquis pris d'après nature!" (xii). Few accounts but his would teach us the name of Danton's charwoman. Or he devotes entire chapters to forgotten bit players of the historical drama. Some of these lesser-known figures influenced events in a way that, in Lenotre's treatment, appears decisive in retrospect; others simply contribute to our impressions of what might be titled "everyday life during the French Revolution." Amusing trivia? Such was Lenotre's own opinion when he began his research, but once finished, he concluded that "rien n'est inutile en histoire," and that his fastidiousness had permitted him to "rectifier sur bien des points, et non des moins importants, les récits des grands historiens de la Révolution" (xiv).

Céline always preferred to cite writers that his interlocutor had not likely read—Tallemant, Chamfort, and Lenotre, among others—thus satisfying a penchant for "la petite histoire" in the literary domain. Beyond this, however, Lenotre's project appeals to him because it confirms his view that history's most visible phenomena are superficial if not deceptive, and that its true motors (individual greed and aggressivity, in Céline's adaptation) lie well hidden. The indiscrete researcher thus becomes an instrument of history's revenge. The remarks in *D'un château l'autre* and in the letter to Paraz reveal a confidence that facts about the Occupation unearthed by disciples of Lenotre will ruin many undeserved reputations and clear the way for historical revision. Surprisingly, though, the trilogy contains very little partisan muckraking in comparison to the correspondence. Color and immediacy override political usefulness in the selection of facts and details. Those eager to elicit sympathy for the plight of the German civilians or for the undeserving victims of the *épuration* in France might find the "chronique" a worthwhile source, but so might their opponents.[17]

At the height of the war, Céline's passion for the historically neglected found expression in a preface to a volume entitled *Bezons à travers les âges*, where he wrote, "Beau poète celui qui s'enchante de Bretagne! de Corse! . . . Chanter Bezons, voici l'épreuve!" (*Herne* 33). This taste for local history resurfaces in *Nord*, where we learn that Neuruppin is not only the birthplace of the writer Fontane, but also that Frederick II exercised his troops there, on occasion whipping soldiers to death (566, 386). A description of the Sigmaringen castle provides an opportunity to remark upon the misdeeds of the Hohenzollern princes, their "cent mille rapts, rapines, assassinats, divorces, Diètes, Conciles..." (*Château* 184). Indeed, the castle becomes a metaphor for history itself: above, "les hauts, le visible, formidable toc, trompe-l'œil, tourelles, beffrois, cloches... pour le vent! miroir aux alouettes!...": below, deep in the bowels, "l'or de la famille!... et les squelettes des kidnappés . . . quatorze siècles d'oubliettes!..." (*Château* 107). The trilogy abounds in anecdotes which betray the same taste for what Lenotre called "les petits côtés des grands événements" or what Céline calls history's "petits à-côtés marrants," from bishop Agobart's denunciation of Dagobert's court, to Louis XIV's reluctance to change doctors, to Richelieu's sexual prowess (*Château* 250, 225, 56; *Rigodon* 850). That Berliners neatly arranged and numbered the bricks of their bombed-out houses so as to facilitate reconstruction, that Pétain was entitled to sixteen food cards, that the last Vichy consul to Dresden owed his life to a packet of coffee: this information too belongs to "la petite histoire," and here Céline is not merely relaying what he has found in other texts (*Nord* 333; *Château* 123, 210). That such material might be significant as well as entertaining is explicit in one of *D'un château l'autre*'s more picturesque asides; at a juncture where anything less than complete confidence in the eventual triumph of the Reich is considered treason, post offices across Germany are full of collectors queueing up for stamps bearing Hitler's portrait:

moi je serais Nasser, moi par exemple, ou Franco ou Salazar, je voudrais voir si mes pommes sont cuites, je voudrais vraiment être renseigné, ce qu'on pense de moi... je demanderais pas à mes polices!... non!... j'irais voir moi-même à la Poste, les queues aux guichets pours mes timbres... votre peuple collectionne?... c'est que c'est joué!... ce qu'il doit y avoir de collections 'd'Adolf Hitler' en Allemagne! ils s'y sont mis, on peut le dire, des années d'avance! (248)

Provident philatelists in the Vichy enclave at Sigmaringen are especially lucky—they can collect stamps of Pétain as well.

Froissart provides a narrative that is self-consciously literary and at the same time ideologically unassuming, if not naïve. His fortune lay in having exercised the craft long before literature and fact separated into opposing camps, and before the imitation of a classical rhetoric choked all the verve and vulgarity from the language of Rabelais. Tallemant des Réaux's *Historiettes* serve as an antidote to neo-classical grandeur both in form and in theme. In a work based on interruption and digression, Tallemant reduces everyone to a biological common denominator. The pretentions of his subjects make them ideal targets for such an attack. Tallemant reminds one of a character from a much earlier and better-known Céline novel: "Elle visait bas, elle visait juste." Chamfort represents the best of two worlds: as a moralist, he preaches a social cynicism which, for the author of *Voyage au bout de la nuit*, equals lucidity; as an anecdotist, he provides both models of and justifications for his misanthropy, taken from the courts and salons of the late *ancien régime*. Chamfort's version of "la petite histoire" is the most openly tendentious of those considered here, while Lenotre, who coined the expression, exemplifies modest, meticulous, and disinterested research. Furthermore, Lenotre's claim that "nothing is unimportant in history" implies that Céline's chronicle merits our attention no less than De Gaulle's memoirs. Finally, the promotion of local color gives the author of *D'un château l'autre* a precedent for his "tourisme et pleine Histoire!" (111).

I ventured at the start that these four writers dignify Céline's affection for the *petit fait vrai*. Chamfort, the only one to philosophize in earnest, is at pains to limit the scope of his observations (Céline lauds his finesse), and redeems himself as it were with a text that is the most fragmentary of the group. The other three remain indifferent to what Céline disparagingly called "idéas" and "messâges," and none of them adopts the measured rhetoric of Amyot or Gobineau. Given his low tolerance for anything that hints at grandiloquence (in language) or abstraction (in thought), perhaps literary "modesty" would be a fair term to explain their appeal. Modesty seems to be the only lesson Céline acknowledges after his ideological blunders: the closest he comes to contrition for his anti-Semitic campaign is to admit, "Là j'ai péché par orgueil, je l'avoue, par vanité, par bêtise."[18] However, present-day Lenotres have already turned up enough evidence to challenge the claim that such was the extent of his "sin."

Notes

[1] Philippe Alméras, *Les Idées de Céline* (Paris: Bibliothèque de Littérature Française Contemporaine, 1987) 83.

[2] I will quote from the following editions: Froissart, *Chroniques* (selections), in *Historiens et chroniqueurs du Moyen Age*, eds. Albert Pauphilet and Edmond Pognon (Paris: Gallimard, 1952); Tallemant de Réaux, *Les Historiettes* (Paris: Balland, 1986); Chamfort, *Maximes et Pensées, Caractères et anecdotes* (Paris: Gallimard, 1970); G. Lenotre, *Paris révolutionnaire, ouvrage illustré de 60 dessins et plans inédits d'après les documents originaux* (Paris: Firmin-Didot, 1895).

[3] Gaston Boissier, "Froissart restitué d'après les manuscrits dans une édition nouvelle," *La Revue des Deux Mondes* (1 February 1875) 694.

[4] *Cahiers Céline 2: Céline et l'actualité littéraire, II, 1957-1961* (Paris: Gallimard, 1976) 25, 38. In subsequent references, this volume will be identified between parentheses as *CC2*.

[5] *D'un château l'autre*, in *Romans II* (Paris: Gallimard, 1974) 136. All subsequent quotations from *D'un château l'autre*, *Nord*, and *Rigodon* are also taken from this Pléiade edition.

[6] *Féerie pour une autre fois II, Normance* (Paris: Gallimard, 1954) 31.

[7] Frédéric Vitoux, *Louis-Ferdinand Céline: misère et parole* (Paris: Gallimard, 1973) 112.

[8] Hayden White, *Metahistory* (Baltimore: Johns Hopkins UP, 1973) 5.

[9] Hayden White, *The Content of the Form* (Baltimore: Johns Hopkins UP, 1987) 24-25.

[10] "Rabelais, il a raté son coup," rpt. in *L'Herne: L.-F. Céline* (Paris: L'Herne, 1972) 44-45. Amyot was Plutarch's translator. This collection of texts will be referred to as *Herne* in subsequent quotations.

[11] *Cahiers Céline 7: Céline et l'actualité, 1933-1961* (Paris: Gallimard, 1986) 455. In subsequent references, this volume will be identified as *CC7*.

[12] Pierre Monnier, *Ferdinand furieux* (Lausanne: Age d'Homme, 1979) 200.

[13] The quotation comes from Antoine Adam's introduction to the Pléiade edition of the *Historiettes* (Paris: Gallimard, 1960) xvi.

[14] *Cahiers Céline 3: Semmelweis et autres écrits médicaux* (Paris: Gallimard, 1977) 20.

[15] *Bagatelles pour un massacre* (Paris: Denoël, 1937) 216. The record does not show that Céline and Lenotre ever met, although the latter was less than two years dead when the former wrote this line. ("Lenôtre" is a common misspelling.)

[16] *Cahiers Céline 6: lettres à Albert Paraz, 1947-1957* (Paris: Gallimard, 1980) 237.

[17] P.-A. Cousteau, successor to Brasillach as editor of *Je suis partout* in 1943, violently attacked Céline in the press as soon as *D'un château l'autre* had reached the shelves. The unsympathetic portrayal of Vichy "martyrs," as I noted above, provoked indignation on the far right.

[18] Interview with Albert Zbinden, rpt. in *Romans II* 939.

Virginia A. La Charité

The Poetics of Neo-Formalism

French poetry of the 1970s and 1980s is marked by renewed interest in the crisis of form which dominates twentieth-century literature. The position of the "iconic" poets in the 1960s may be said to signal the end of surrealism, which flourished into the 1950s with the emergence of the "metapoetry" of Bonnefoy, Jaccottet, Dupin, Bouchet, even Jean Laude. On the other hand, it was the decade of the 1960s which brought to the literary scene a veritable renaissance of letters. At the very historical time in which it became fashionable to avoid the term *poetry* and embrace a skeptical attitude towards the logic of language, major French publishing houses began to release new editions of previously published poets, making available in affordable editions those works of poetry which shaped the genre in the twentieth century. Apollinaire's awareness at the end of "La Jolie Rousse" that the new must in turn become old and give way to a newer new—"Esprit nouveau"—serves as the threshold of a historical perspective, which is presently engendering attention to the poetic past. Recognition of how the twentieth century is becoming history is found first in the rediscovery of the freshness, originality, and poetic intensity of Reverdy, Eluard, Queneau, Artaud, Péret, Tzara, Aragon, Desnos, and Soupault. Identification of poetry as an evolutionary, not revolutionary, mode of expression has also refocused the reading of the poetry of Char, Michaux, Ponge, Jouve, Guillevic, and Leiris, as their works also began to reappear in bookstores. Curiously, most of the rediscovered and reread poets are former surrealists, and all of them acknowledge their indebtedness to Baudelaire, Rimbaud, Lautréamont, and Mallarmé, whose work has also undergone a rebirth in terms of republication and critical study. Rimbaud, for example, was the subject of more scholarly attention in the 1960s and 1970s than any other poet, a phenomenon perhaps initiated by René Char's edition of Rimbaud in 1957. On the other hand, Mallarmé dominated poetry studies in the 1980s.

The increase in attention to the poetic legacy of the twentieth century has been reinforced by the involvement of the poets themselves in editorial work, critical studies, and translation. In particular, the translation of the avant-garde poets of other countries, especially the non-francophonic poets of Germany, Italy, Russia, and the United States has further revitalized interest in poetic expression in general. Emphasis on what Roland Barthes has phrased as "le plaisir du texte" or focus on the poem as a social communication and not as a linguistic or literary exercise emerges in the 1970s and 1980s as a dominant pattern in poetic practice. From this perspective, the meta-iconic debate in the 1960s and early 1970s and the appearance of so many literary magazines and reviews in support of that debate contributed greatly to renew the genre of poetry: its distinguished past, its contradictory present, and its promising future. The number of disparate views on the what, how, and why of the poem may have seemed at one point to threaten the actual continued existence of poetry; in some instances, the debate resulted in such quarrels that the practice of poetry was nearly replaced by a concentration on theory, even theory redoing theory. While, at one time, poetry appeared to be on a self-destructive course, captured by *Le Mécrit* of Roche and the historic revolution of 1968, the debate actually served as a stimulus to reflection on the fundamental problem of writing poetry. New questions on the reading process, the nature of prose, and the definition of a line of verse began to be asked. Hence, the climate of the decades of the 1970s and 1980s may be seen as one of regeneration, a refocusing of interest in the exploration of form.

To be sure, regeneration of poetry in the last two decades includes experimentation, especially with regard to the mechanical and scientific aspects of the publication process brought about by the computer age and rapid changes in technology. In André Frenaud's *La Sorcière de Rome*, 1973, for example, the changes of persona are based on the changes in typeface. Nevertheless, underlying the multiple modes of poetic practice is a defense of poetry in both its formulation and its articulation. Reversion, inversion, subversion, and perversion have given way to version, just as reforming, deforming, and unforming (restructuring, destructuring, unstructuring) are variations on the act of formation. Recognition that both the naming function of the metapoets and the nominalization process of the iconics alter the condition and generate differentiation has brought about acceptance of the poem as an enactment of relationships even when that act brings about loss: loss of contact, loss of identity, loss of the authority of referents. Acceptance of the loss of the model is, then, the established framework for the writing and reading experience. No longer fascinated by newness ("la nouvelle vague"), nor attracted to revolutionary ideologies, much less concerned by a heightened consciousness of contradictions, twentieth-century French poets are presently engaged in elucidating the process of transformation which sets the poem apart from other modes of written expression and yet aligns it with modes of plastic communication. Concerned with neither creation nor derivation, poetry is undergoing a return to basics which is characterized first and foremost by a renewed interest in the beginnings of the crisis of form which so dominates this century: Mallarmé's "notion pure" of "le texte véridique," outlined primarily in his "Crise de vers."

The contradictions of Rimbaud's structure of departure ("partir pour partir"), especially in his *Saison en enfer*, lead to the appropriation of all identity, his famous "JE est un autre," and recalls Baudelaire's unresolved binaries at the end of *Les Fleurs du mal*. The language-reality tensions of the nineteenth century lead to silence, the end of a poetics of representation in form and language. But it is this very mark of silence which Mallarmé authenticates, affirming the poem as that act which converts a thing seen into a thing expressed. The act of writing so generates its own accomplishment in the act of reading that the poem is its own guarantee of being "véridique." As the poet who ushers in the twentieth century, especially the years of "modernism," Mallarmé is the same poet who towers over the final decades of the century, "post-modernism."[1] Where the first 60 to 70 years may be said to be marked by the persuasive presence of the Mallarmé "hybrid" poem, the last years are overshadowed by his preoccupation with how to write a line of verse. Even those poets who at present concentrate on the more scientific aspects of the writing-reading process share in the Mallarmé legacy, for he was the first to incorporate the technicalities of the medium of print into the esthetics and practice of poetry.

Mallarmé so towers over the poetics and poetry of the last decades of this century that Mallarmé studies are undergoing considerable revision and renewed vigor. It may well be that post-modernist writing is so attracted to Mallarmé's work that the poetry of the 1980s is generating rereadings of Mallarmé. Certainly, scholarly interest has notably shifted from Rimbaud to Mallarmé. While a given surrealist spirit and sense of poetic activity remain in evidence, there is at the same time the adoption of an optic which views the writing of a poem through the investigative techniques posited by Mallarmé. For Roubaud, it is a matter of "le vers très exactement que nomme Mallarmé." The emerging poetic theories offer a modernized, contemporary application of Mallarmé's inquiry into the technical features which identify a poem and create poetry. Where the century began in a crisis of form—a rejection of nineteenth-century constraints and conventions and an admiration of Mallarmé's poetic practice, the century is ending in a crisis of form—a rejection of the twentieth-century practice of non-form and an adoption of Mallarmé's theories of poetic restraints: his "Crise de vers."

For Mallarmé, poetry is unlimited in agreements and disagreements, manifested in its interactive components rather than by its generic relationships. His "hybrid" poem is adapted by Reverdy and readapted by Ponge in his "prôeme." Mallarmé is an acknowledged precursor of the surrealists, especially in their emphasis on creative activity, as well as a forerunner of Roche's proclamation that poetry does not exist. For Mallarmé, there is no distinction between poetry and all other forms of spoken or written expression; poetry is not a separate genre, for all traces of expression are poetic. In this way, he initiates the contemporary view that poetry is neither a subject nor an object because the text is its own subject and object, not the preservation of a given form, function, message. The poem is a communication which affirms exist- ence because the poet speaks: "Je dis: une fleur!" Transformation, then, occurs through the sharing of the act of speech, an inquiry into the form of the response: limited signification or unlimited possibilities of meaning, no matter how illogical those possibilities may be. Mallarmé's well-known expression of wonder that "la Pénultième est morte" finds its twentieth-century counterpart in concern over the what and the how of the poetic venture—the problem of form and procedure in a conjunction of contradictions. Intersection confers poetic value, effectively counterbalancing social, economic, political, and historic circumstances. As the century lives out its final decade, the poetic act embraces change as testimony to human grandeur; the poem is formal evidence of confidence in change as the sign of exchange.

un ordre risque de s'établir / dans la claustration
A.-M. Albiach

The ongoing search for fundamental structures of the poetic act in the late 1970s and throughout the 1980s leads to recognition of the writing code as a system of formal constraints, which forge chains of reading directions. Acting as triggers to reader consciousness, the rules of poetic construction emerge as the sign of the poem. Even visual deceits of paginal design obey certain principles of assembly and disassembly. While words may no longer enjoy privileged meaning and language may be reduced to the level of a gesture, generation of written expression remains embedded in the space of a page. The formalities of verse and prose—what Mallarmé calls "l'unique vocable du poëte"—persist and provide a unity despite all efforts to eliminate these formalities as barriers to a purity of the writing-reading experience, purity in the sense that it is beyond attitudes, not tied to moral, historical, or social events.

Barriers which in the past brought about reader distance from the text have been recognized and identified and cease to be a concern. In fact, it is now commonly accepted that erudite references and details tend to alienate rather than integrate. Apollinaire's "La Chanson du mal-aimé," for example, charms in its lyrical enthusiasm for the conversion of experience into art, but its vocabulary of elitism demands such pedantic decoding that the text nearly negates its own imagistic projection. What rescues "La Chanson du mal-aimé" is, first, its troubadorial consciousness that art is stable, and second, Apollinaire's celebration of the traditional *dire-lire* harmony so perfected later by Eluard in his rhythm or "murmure." Eluard and the surrealist generation profited from Apollinaire's self-appraisal in "La Jolie Rousse," the "Raison ardente," which advocates a fiction which invents experience and creates the possibility of new associations. While the break with the nineteenth-century and Apollinarian legacy of perceiving relationships and textures may seem to have been finalized by the iconic and parapoetic shift from writer responsibility or textual coding to full reader responsibility and authority for textual decoding in an effort to unite poetry and criticism through the investigation of writing as process, post-modern poets remain interested, nonetheless, in the nature of creation. Even the extreme iconic poets whose work seems to defy the very existence of a reader pay strict attention to order and arrangement, for deliberate destruction of order is based on the identification and understanding of order. What may appear as intentional violations of the tenets of "good" writing, the ABCs of composition, especially as practiced by parapoets and extreme iconics, are the very tenets or restraints which compose the communication. Hence, those restraints emerge as the points of inquiry by those poets who are termed the "new formalists."

Turning to an investigation into the actual components of composition, poets in the 1980s agree that a poem is not determined by fixed divisions (stanzas or paragraphs) or by the rigid adoption of given metric and rhyme schemas. Rather, the poem is determined by its *vers*, which is the constituent element of poetry. *Vers*, in French, is a noun form, a line of verse; in fact, the expression *faire des vers* means to write poetry. *Vers* is also a preposition of place, denoting a direction, toward or towards. The *vers* is, then, both the what and the how of poetry, according to both literary tradition and use and as ordained by the dictionary. *Vers* is the undeniable age-old and contemporary mark of the poem. Because *vers* is the one semantic, linguistic, and syntactical law which identifies, affirms, and indicates poetic passage, it is the governing principle of writing poetry. *Vers* is the substance and the procedure; it is what distinguishes poetry from everything else. Therefore, the nature of the poetic act cannot be separated from attention to the rigors of the line of verse, which orders the relations of the phenomena of written vocables.

The new formalists are less interested in the disposition and arrangement of the poem than in the configuration of the text: the adjustment of the lines or parts. The adjustment of the formal components into a code of communication guides the reader to make physical connections among the printed signs and confer upon those signs a psychological value. Hence, there is an effect on the reader from his textual experience, but the immediate cause of that effect may remain undetermined, there being only the chain of the lines of verses. The effect is the connection made by the reader, whether that connection comes about through the exercise of imagination and intuition or through an inference of the facts of the verses on the page. Neither inductively derived, that is, concretely demonstrable, nor self-evident, that is monophoric and monovalent, each line of verse performs as a corridor in the white space, a guide to an implied and indicated destination (*vers*) which is poetry. As a corridor or aisle, each line of verse connects with each other and from each other to another, providing passage to the poetic experience. Physically real and visible, the line itself is a phenomenon which appears in varying sizes, shapes, positions, even styles. Each line is a necessary unit in the construction of the whole, and each in turn poses the problem of its own importance, for each has a bearing on the effect of the passage. The language and the syntax of each verse may be distorted and the context may remain suggested rather than specified, but a construction is undeniably present, solid in its very mobility, and, consequently, architecturally logical, even if not philosophically rational.

The formalism of the line of verse is Mallarmé's "fil conducteur" of and to meaning. It is the poetic statement, determined by its own restraints, shaped by its very existence on the page. The convention of placing a word in paginal space is instructive as a reader sign; it is recognition of authorial ordering. Each verse is a positive attenuator which involves the reader in a rhythm of poetic passage. The written is fixed in print, organized by the assembly of each line, no matter how brief or expanded that line may be. Each line is a form, which contributes first to the shape of the page, modifying in turn each preceding line, and second to the configuration of the poem. In this sense, neo-formalist poetry is generative and reformist.

There is no neo-formalist group. Poets who are identified as new formalists include those who are also committed to experimental poetry, for the examination of the constraints of a line of verse is in many respects experimental. Neo-formalists are not in control of the text in the same way that a formalist exercises total authority over the form and therefore the message of his work. On the contrary, they consider the line of poetry as the syntactical element of unity, asserting what is allowable in the reading. It is not a discipline in the sense of objective study to master a field of knowledge or gain an expertise in a chosen craft, but a discipline which acknowledges the authority of the line of verse to direct the reader to a meaning. The new formalists grant complete power of textual arbitration to the reader, who follows the rules set out by the directional signs, the lines of verse.

Nearly all poets who may be described as neo-formalists, such as Jacques Roubaud, Lionel Ray, Anne-Marie Albiach, Henri Deluy, Alain Veinstein, Claude Royet-Journaud, are also translators and fully involved in editorial work. They admire the metapoets who dominated the scene in the 1950s and the iconics of the 1960s, as well as the surrealists whose works were republished in the 1960s and 1970s. Their interest in the evolution of twentieth-century poetry is evidenced not only in the number of poetry anthologies which have appeared in the past 15 years, but also in a new enthusiasm for the works of Reverdy, Queneau, Char, Michaux, Guillevic, Leiris, Ponge, Jouve, and Jabès. Their awareness of the pattern of change which characterizes the poetry of the century brings about awareness of the one unchanged contour of the poem: the verse. Even in self-destructive and auto-critical nihilism, the power of the vocable remains; Aragon's dada poem, "Suicide," which consists of the 26 letters of the alphabet, a variation of Tzara's single-letter poem, "Z," rejoins Roche's *Le Mécrit* in a testimony to the force of the poetic vocable as verse. It is the verse which creates the tension in Baudelaire's post-Romantic binaries, Rimbaud's use of prose, surrealist texts, iconic deformation and dissolution. For Jacques Roubaud in *Dire la poésie*, 1981, it is a marriage between "des articles / du vocabulaire" and memory, actually "la diction mémorisée," which causes the poetic to come forth through the faculty of speech. The voice of poetry is then the reader's voice, which enunciates order, and that order of the text becomes his possession: "Dans l'île lente de la voix la connaissance poésie . . . la possession par ma voix n'est plus qu'un ordre / instantané." While the poem resists explanation, it remains irresistible: "La mémoire dans la voix de poésie demeure / explication intérieure et non l'intérieur sortant de / soi." Where traditional poetry relied on meter to create poetic memory, poetry in the 1980s relies on a line of poetry which intervenes in white paginal space, as in the spacings of Roubaud's lines, to create its poetic code of rhythm in the voice, which "reads" the line and the space simultaneously, ordering the text through spoken or vocalized effects, literally formalizing the text into poetry. For Michel Deguy, this genre of writing brings full circle poetic figuration: "la technique littéraire traditionnelle se renversant en littérature de la technique qui s'achève."

In the work of Pierre Oster, it is reliance upon poetic formalities—rules of limitation—which give a poem solidity, an identifiable corpus: "Des dieux, rocheux, ligneux, rugueux, / Affermissent notre alliance. Ils gardaient, inspectaient des îles mobiles. / Ils m'enjoignent d'être fidèle." His "religion du relief" throughout *Vingt-neuvième Poème*, 1985, is based on the reversal of the obstructionism of materiality (the physicality of a word, its fixity in the medium of print, and its arrangement on the page). The form is its own function and the text is a two-dimensional bas-relief, jutting out from the frame of the page. Lexical, semantic, and syntactical restraints are incorporated into the conventions of the printing process, as the contours of language and reality emerge in a corridor of order and coherence.

Reforming the barriers of resistance—textual restraints—into pathways of circulation exerts the power of the verse. For Anne-Marie Albiach, "*la page accentue la distance*," requiring performative lines of verse, a theater in which the lines are horizontal demarcations of vertical "ouvertures" or possibilities:

"trajectoire de l'objet / où la trajectoire / retrouverait le sujet." The white space is literally the stage, while the verses are the actors and the stage props, as well as indicators of scene changes and set design. However, Albiach does not advocate a theater of poetry. On the contrary, the theatrical design serves as a concrete demonstration of how reality appears in human terms: language. While words themselves are things, non-human material objects, their arrangement and direction arc a human act of projection and a summons to order.

The text is a corporeal trajectory with the physical properties of a project which is both visible and invisible. The poem does not "mean," does not reflect an idea or contain a specific message; rather, the text "is" its performance. The reading process consists of choices: which lines of words lead to which others? The text is an intermediary, organized first by the writer, then verbalized by the reader's performance, the discovery and affirmation of an ordering. Anti-symbolist and anti-metaphysical, the poem of the new formalists rejects the notion of a reality beyond reality. The subject is the self, neither objectively nor subjectively, but a living personality which experiences a sense of life and of meaning through reading. Reading is experience, rather than living as experience, and it is a conscious act of creation. The poet's style, attention to the verbal rearrangement of perspectives on the page, communicates the opportunity to experience being, to create an art of life.

Apollinaire's "lyrisme plastique . . . concret, direct" merges with Mallarmé's view of "une écriture corporelle" in the rigorously concentrated verbal tension between the act of experience and the state or condition of existence. Relations are verbal in the plastic property of the printed poem. A doubling between the physical appearance of the word, its visible form, and the verbalization of that word, its invisible form, presents language as a formal drama, in which the traditional arts of pleasing and doing (*art de plaire* and *art de faire*) are so intertwined that the language of the text becomes the measure of the authenticity of experience. Authority for the meaning of the poem emerges from reader familiarity with the choices on the page. Interaction among and between the lines of verse is a social act of participation. The text is both subject and object, and its verbal units are both tools to the point and the point itself in a balance between reassembly and disassembly, structure and procedure, the imagination and real, even commitment and disengagement. Fundamentally lucid, neo-formalist poetry has no moral perspective, no political position, no nostalgia for a pre-modern Eden, no sense of despair over the historical circumstances of the present, no apprehension about the uncertainties of the future. Non-ideological, except perhaps for the adoption of a surrealist attitude towards poetry as a form of fact or truth, the neo-formalists equate expression and experience. Textual appeal lies not in emotion, but in the operation of the intelligence, consciousness of the experience of expression, captured in the lines of verse.

The formalities of the text demand analysis and synthesis at the same time. Drawing upon textual limitations and conventions (orthography, syntax, dictates of print in the permissible range of typographical and topographical variations, including preordained restrictions on white space), the elements of formal closure become the directional signs of an open invitation to the unlimited. Verbal invention is a problem of consciousness; awareness of the constraints engenders curiosity about the possibilities of overcoming those limitations. Experimental poetry, including Oulipo writing, is based on verbal inventiveness as a form of lucidity, a characteristic which aligns neo-formalists with even certain parapoetic practitioners. Hence, some poets, such as Jacques Roubaud, Claude Royet-Journaud, Alain Veinstein, and Michel Deguy may be described as proponents of both experimental poetry and neo-formalism. The major difference in the two "categories" lies in the approach to verbal invention. Where the experimentalists rely on scientific procedures, especially mathematics, neo-formalists concentrate on the problem of writing poetry, *faire des vers*. Where experimentalists tend to alienate the reader through technical gamesmanship and the mechanics of translation, which in some instances negates language, neo-formalists reject the notion of game-playing in their advocacy of the intelligible word and reader. Jacques Roubaud's *Trente et un au cube*, 1973, is an example of experimental poetry in its nature as a stylistic exercise in linguistic conversions to a mathematical language and Japanese culture, but it is also a neo-formalist work in its reliance on an astute and intuitive reader to forge chains of meaning in the performance of a dialogue of communication. The very title testifies to experimental re-creation or systematic and systemic translation as well as neo-formalism, the act of creation within the formalized conventions and restraints of literature. Verbal invention connects the two approaches; the difference lies in the direction of passage—the act of reading. On the one hand, *Trente et un au cube* demonstrates textual closure, in particular the post-facto diagrams which order the relationships; on the other hand, it projects unlimitedness because the diagrams are neither self-evident nor susceptible to alteration, serving as the only viable demonstrable solution. Perhaps too much emphasis has been placed on Roubaud's mathematical formation and interests, bringing out the scientific nature of his writing, but ignoring the fact that the science of mathematics is a formalism which applies principles to a process; algebra, for example, is a symbolism of numbers and the solution to certain problems is a matter of esthetic choice, "le plus élégant." In this respect, Roubaud recalls the algebraic formulae used by Benjamin Péret in his very surreal work, *Le Grand Jeu*, 1928, and Mallarmé's use of a cube in *Un Coup de dés*.

In fact, it is Mallarmé's distribution of the parts of his *Coup de dés* which appeals greatly to the neo-formalists, particularly to Roubaud. The Mallarmé structure is tightly-knit, literally immoveable in its arrangement of different type sizes on the white page. At the same time that it is severely restrained by the dictates of print on white space and the technical limitations imposed by the printing industry, *Un Coup de dés* is multivalent in its possible readings, interpretations, interrelationships—intertextuality. The formal presentation of a figure in space (the di or cube, constellation, storm at sea, sinking sea vessel) is a constraint of coherence, which prevents intermediaries: the poem is virtually "un coup de dés" and its principle of operation or "fil conducteur" is its system of presentation. Immobility is then the poetic circumstance of mobility, textual plurality.

Accordingly, Roubaud pays homage to Mallarmé for being the first to recognize that free verse threatens the existence of the genre of poetry and is not a viable substitute for meter: "le vers est partout dans la langue." While Roubaud admires Valéry's insistence that form should precede content and poetic form should be crafted by the severe restraints of versification, he also appreciates Aragon's conversion to the formal lyrical tradition of poetry in his post-war texts and use of memory as a structure, not a theme. However, it is especially Mallarmé's "forme vers," which Roubaud rewrites as a single term, "forme-vers," that generates interest in the conjunctive structure of form and identifies neo-formalist poetry of the 1980s. In this sense, Roubaud's 1978 *La Vieillesse d'Alexandre* may be seen as the credo, if not the manifesto for a new formalism.

Drawing on cultural history, what identifies French verse from that of other cultures and languages is the alexandrine 12-syllable line, perfected by Victor Hugo. According to Roubaud's title, Mallarmé's aged shipwrecked captain is Hugo, and his ship is the alexandrine line, and they both go down in the debris of free verse. The rage of the old master at the break-up of his ship is Mallarmé's recognition that free verse is destroying "forme vers" as the organizing principle of the basic operation of Poetry: rhythm.[2] The neo-formalist concern is not to return to the strict rules of versification, but to analyze, discover, identify, and grasp what culturally makes a poem poetic. For them, the word *text* is unpoetic and anti-poetic; only the word *poem* is acceptable and authentic. Consequently, it is not a matter of meter and end rhyme, but a question of rhythm which is at the basis of French verse or "forme-vers." In turn, examination of rhythm leads to an investigation into the peculiarities of the French language, and one of its most salient characteristics is the mute "e," which is pronounced or unpronounced depending on its position in a word or thought group. Mallarmé was the first to be acutely aware of the inconsistencies of the mute "e." Oulipo fascination with phonetic games continues Mallarmé's interest in lexical and linguistic oddities and reflects an affinity with neo-formalist interest in discovering the written form which cannot be reduced beyond itself, cannot be transposed to another system, cannot be translated, transmuted, or transformed. The very form of a word or poem has a dramatic impact, as the effects of the poet's chosen verse form emerge as affects for the reader.

Mallarmé's equation of versification with style and his continual experimentation with the formalities of prose and verse, always preferring to work within and upon the technical restraints of versification, becomes the basis of twentieth-century neo-formalism. The deliberate, calculated, and finely calibrated layout of his *Coup de dés* even serves as a basic pattern for the design of neo-formalist poetry. And, like Mallarmé's ultimate poem, it denies a systematic linear procedure in its utilization of a maximum amount of space, on which the black type appears to take on a mathematical, if not geometrical, form. Each page is an architectural framework of space, which isolates combinations of letters and words, organizes groupings into discernible units, and permits the identification of contrast between parts, as well as the recognition of relationships and unity between groupings. Language is not a Racinian hidden structure, but the structure itself, and that language is a social and cultural act of French poetry, captured in Roubaud's title, *Quelque Chose noir*, 1986: "L'encre et l'image se retrouvent solidaires et alliées / Comme l'oubli et la trace."

The three basic principles of neo-formalism may, then, be summarized as visual representation, oral performance, and the structuration of memory. The first tenet is the layout of the poetic plan, the arrangement of the printed units of the poem, using white paginal space as the organizing element. Finding a poetic model in Mallarmé's *Un Coup de dés*, the layout is usually stylized, often mixing type selections: weight (bold, medium, light), point size (gradations from large to small, upper and lower cases), and choice of face itself (roman or italic). The typographical and topographical design of the poem on the page correlates the medium of communication with the message. Word placement is deliberate; the choices are scientifically determined, usually based on the authority of the dictionary. The technical constraints of the printing process (shape and size of the page, signature form, margins) combine utilitarian concern with artistic election in paginal presentation. The page takes on form, becomes itself a verse form in its array of patterns which divide and subdivide the white space into identifiable blocks of printed matter, grouping and regrouping words into phrases and phrases into paragraphs or stanzas: form.

The physical presentation in across and down patterns, vertical and horizontal grids which resemble word games, challenges the reader as spectator to determine visually the correlations between the words, phrases, groupings, blocks. The text may be read in the normal reading grid of a Western language, left to right, top to bottom, or it may be read in juxtaposed positions, even in reversals of the grid. A factor which determines the adoption of the reading grid as well as the recognition of several possible grids is the oral performance of the text, which goes beyond and often nullifies the semantic, linguistic, and syntactical codes which the visual arrangement displays. The act of speaking, of reading the text aloud, forces a reevaluation of the visual impression of the codes in operation in the poem. Only when a speaker enunciates the verse form do rules of pronunciation and choices surface for reading decisions. Pronouncing or not pronouncing a mute "e" becomes important only when the written line is translated into human speech. Rules of linking also come into consideration, for in conversation there is a tendency to overlook linkings which are mandatory in formal discourse and formal reading. Hence, the verb *dire* dominates neo-formalist poetry, as in the title of Roubaud's volume, *Dire la poésie*. Verbalization of the poem, what the reader says (*dire*), is further complicated by borrowings from other cultures, languages, and disciplines, and by punctuation, its use and its omission. In the punctuated text, the reader-speaker must determine the length of the pause for a comma, semi-colon, colon, period; in the unpunctuated text, the reader-speaker faces the problem of the spaces between words and phrases set out in a single line: how to read one space or three spaces, how to punctuate the work at hand. Similarly, capitalization may be present for the purposes of emphasis, which only an oral performance dramatizes. Reliance upon punctuation—its presence or its absence—affects both visual and oral coordinates. In *Quelque Chose noir*, for example, Roubaud interjects slashes to present a linguistic absurd as poetic logic: "Je pense: 'Et l'affreuse crème / Près des bois flottants /.'" Traditionally, the use of the slash mark indicates a line division in a stanza or verse; giving the reader the poetically visual sign of the slash signals a need to change the oral performance of the line so that it is poeticized, making acceptable what would have otherwise been a nonsensical line.

The faculty of speech, *dire*, is essential in neo-formalist creation. The common act of direct discourse, speaking, frees the poem from external compulsion. Neither descriptive nor prescriptive, speech initiates an intimate dialogue between the reader and the poet, objectivizing thought, desire, and emotion. Denying progression in time and space, the basic dimensions of reality, the dialogue is limited to the actual moment of enunciation. The poem is because the poet speaks and the reader replies in speech. The intellectual nature of the visual layout is modified by the intuitive nature of oral performance: feeling what one speaks. The reader's act of reading aloud animates the immobility of the static lines of type, forging new angles of conjunction between effect and affect. To see is to speak, and to speak is to see.[3] Generative without a translative intermediary, the rhythm of direct discourse uncovers verse in the language. Language is the force of life, the force of poetry.

The third characteristic of neo-formalist work is memory, primarily reader memory. The visual and oral pivots of conjunction generate reader aspiration to integrate the angles detected by the eye and voice. The framework of white space makes possible a bringing together of psychological and sensorial memory as well as intellectual recall, generating an artistic reality which gains meaning from the reading grids and vocal decisions adopted. The reader crosses and crisscrosses the paginal space of the poem, drawing upon the lexical, semantic, and syntactical clusters which intellectually indicate a poem from among the verse forms. The reader's memory makes tactile and oral associations, emotionally detecting poetic form in the spaces between and around the imposing black print: ink and the image are interdependent and allied. While representation (the act of writing) precedes interpretation (the act of reading, first in terms of formal discourse and second in terms of the direct discourse of enunciation), memory re-presents the devices of the original system or plan of presentation. While that original system may not be subject to translation by the reader into another system, it is identifiable as a poetic form because of its cultural constraints and rigorous distribution in verse form. Form is poem, authenticated in human acts and terms. Language itself is not human: it is the voice which animates language which is human and it is through the voice, the enunciation of what the eye sees and what the curious mind identifies, that language gains its sense of life, its poetry. Direct discourse is an act of memory in the response to perform the poem, read it aloud and therefore actualize it. Reader memory draws upon study of the formal structuring, the layout, and recognition of rhetorical devices (their preservation or violation) in effecting verbalization of the predetermined visual appearance of the poem. Interaction between seeing, speaking, and remembering communicates the experience of being, "meaning" in human terms, and poetic truth.

More structuralist than semiotic in orientation, neo-formalism assumes the presence of a reader in the act of interpretation and restructuration. The poem is a plurality: white space and black ink, image and layout, poet and reader, effects and their affects, representation and interpretation, act and art, art and life. The neo-formalist poem is also—perhaps even more importantly so—a plurality of the predominating poetic patterns in twentieth-century French poetry: Apollinaire's plastic sense of language in his "calligrammes,"[4] Reverdy's mastery of topography and theory of conjunction through "le mot juste," the surrealist attitude towards language as a living element and the marvelousness of the everyday world, Michaux's combination of graphic art and written expression, Char's pulverized crispation, Ponge's phenomenological "prôemes" or hybrid creations, even existential equation of acting and being. The metapoetic view that language is an ordering—reader response confers value—and the poem is a plastic and social invitation conjoins iconic disjunction, linguistic freedom from logic, and interest in technical contradictions. Synthesis and analysis correspond, as process and procedure co-respond in the rigors of the neo-formalist verse-form.

Notes

[1] For Mallarmé scholars, there is frequently a disparity between his practice and his theories. Nowhere does the disparity emerge more clearly than in the poetry of this century. Yet, as Marcelin Pleynet has so astutely pointed out, even the most literal adherents of Mallarmé's cerebral technical approach are latter-day surrealists.

[2] Curiously, Mallarmé was ambivalent towards Hugo's poetry, at times praising his work and at times expressing dissatisfaction with it. Basically, Mallarmé criticizes Hugo for his symmetrical use of space and obvious delineated demarcations in the arrangement of the lines of verse. While Mallarmé may not have advocated free verse poetry, he did not condemn it; for example, *Un Coup de dés* may be read as a free verse poem and his "Toast à Emile Verhaeren," found among his papers after his death, is composed in free verse.

[3] Mallarmé favored the oral performance of poetry. His well-known statement, "Je dis: une fleur!" summarizes the ultimate poetic act of creation. The flower *is* because the poet speaks and the reader vocally responds; communication occurs in the form of a voiced dialogue, and the flower is evidence of the exchange.

[4] A *calligramme* refers to a figure which is formed by the topographical layout of the letters, while an *ideogram* is generally restricted to a work which is diagrammatic in nature. Apollinaire's adoption of the term *calligramme* aims at "une idéalisation de la poésie vers-libriste et une précision typographique" (letter to André Billy, 1918). Basically, Apollinaire sought a marriage between plastic art (the sketch) and the written free verse line.

Léon-François Hoffmann

Haitian Créole Literature: An Overview

Even though barely 10% of the citizens of Haiti are able to use their official language, and despite the country's enormous rate of illiteracy, elite Haitians have always put a great premium on writing elegant French, free from regional variations. They have used it to produce a venerable and distinguished literature in which all genres are represented. There are two main explanations for this characteristic of elite culture.

The first is that, from 1804 on, elite Haitians have considered themselves as spokesmen for all Black peoples. They have postulated that the first black independent republic's duty was to serve as an inspiration and an example to all Blacks—whether in the African motherland or in New World exile—in their own fight for independence and human dignity. Further, they felt it their duty to give the lie to the notion, generally accepted in the Western world, that Blacks were intellectually inferior and unfit for self-government. From this perspective, it was important to show that Haitians were quite capable of handling that most perfect creation of modern civilization, the French language. Every Haitian ambassador who delivered a speech in flawless French, every writer who composed a play or a novel favorably reviewed in the Parisian press felt he was performing a patriotic duty and striking a blow for the cause of Black dignity.

The second explanation is that the literate Mulattos and Black generals who took over power after expelling the French made sure that education was reserved for their class. To keep the masses powerless, it was important to keep them illiterate. Education was conducted only in French, which effectively made it inaccessible to the overwhelming majority of the population. The illiteracy rate in Haiti today is still estimated at between 85 and 93%, although it is impossible to know how many lower-class Haitians have lately become literate in Créole due to the efforts of religious and lay volunteers. To a considerable degree, class status in Haiti was, and still is, linked to fluency in the official language. Even more than flawless oratory, publication confers great prestige; to have authored a novel or a collection of poems generally ensures a place at the top of the social ladder. As a result, until the middle of the twentieth century, a larger number of titles were published by Haitians in proportion to the whole population than by citizens of any other New World country except the United States.

Not only did the Haitian elite adopt a fetichistic attitude towards *le français de France*, they also disparaged Créole, asserting that it was a debased, corrupted form of French, fit for communication with social inferiors (créolophone peasants, manual laborers, house servants etc.), but quite unsuitable for any form of serious written expression. To be sure, all Haitians without exception are fluent in Créole and have never hesitated to use it when addressing close relatives and friends in informal conversation. But French is called for in front of one's school-age children or in any formal situation. It may still, in fact, be considered impolite to address even a lower-class person for the first time without using a few words of French. So that, in asking directions from a peasant, one might say: "Bonjour, Madame, pourriez-vous me dire *ki bò lakay chèf sèksion an ye?*" However, even in more or less formal situations, Haitians seldom hesitate to use a particularly pungent Créole expression. Whence the humorous saying: "Il est difficile de commencer une phrase en français s*ank ou pa finil an kreyol.*"

While the emergence and development of literature in Haitian Créole is a recent and still tentative phenomenon, authors—ever since Haitian literature began and with increasing frequency—have included some Créole in their writings. They did so very timidly at first: one might find occasional Créole words for which there is no metropolitan French equivalent, words belonging to the vocabulary of *vodùn*, for instance, or for local plants or dishes. In works published outside of Haiti, in France especially, these words are usually footnoted. Since authors can hope to reach more than the small local readership only by publishing abroad, they take good care that foreign readers not be puzzled by what—to them—might be strange expressions. With time, the number of Créole expressions increases. Proverbs come to be included. A given character may even utter a whole sentence in Créole. In 1949, Clément Magloire St. Aude published a fine novel, *Parias*, in which expository passages are in elegant French and the dialogues in Créole without footnoted French translations. The book was published in Port-au-Prince, and Magloire St. Aude aimed it exclusively at a Haitian audience. Anecdotes and short stories written in a mixture of French and Créole frequently appear in nineteenth and twentieth-century newspapers. Haitian playwrights, such as the famous Languichatte, use Créole for comic effects, just as Molière used French patois.

Very few eighteenth-century texts written entirely in Créole (poems such as "Lisette quitté la plaine," written by a French *colon*, for example, or Sonthonax's proclamation of the abolition of slavery) have come down to us. Indeed, such texts are extremely rare until about 1950. Aside from occasional religious pamphlets, a few collections of Créole proverbs, with their French equivalent or translation, might be mentioned. In 1901, Georges Sylvain

adapted the fables of La Fontaine in Créole under the title *Cric? Crac!*
Significantly enough, an anonymous Haitian reviewer confessed that: "Most of
the time, I had to consult the French translation that the author had the foresight
to include at the bottom of the page." The fact is that while all Haitians were
fluent in Créole they were quite unused to seeing it transcribed. Even today,
many Haitian readers claim to have great difficulty in reading Créole; coupled
with the snobbish disdain towards Créole, still considered as an inferior means
of expression, this narrows even more the number of potential readers of Créole
texts. What our anonymous reviewer stated in 1901 still holds true for many
literate Haitians: "We do not know how to read Créole, and we do not want to
learn how to read it."

Beside the proverb collectors and the adapters of La Fontaine, a few poets,
Oswald Durand (1840-1906) being the most famous, composed occasional
poems in Créole. These are generally either humorous or archly sentimental:
everyone agrees that Créole is a very witty, picturesque language or, as most
Haitians would say "dialect" or "patois," and that it is well suited for amorous
badinage.

Since the middle of the twentieth century, a certain number of Haitian
intellectuals have been arguing for the recognition of Créole as a full-fledged
language, well suited for intellectual discourse, and especially for the literary
expression of authentic Haitianity. More and more poets are composing in
Créole, although the greatest part of the recent Haitian poetic production is still
in French. As might have been expected, the real breakthrough came with the
emergence of Créole theater. Félix Morisseau-Leroy's 1953 adaptation of the
Antigone legend *Antigone en créole* created a sensation. In 1973, Nono Numa's
Jénéral Rodrig, an adaptation of Corneille's *Le Cid* was performed.
Franketienne's 1978 *Pélin tèt* was a great success. Haitian Créole theater is a
vital, fascinating genre, and is well received by the overwhelming majority of
Haitians, both in Haiti and in the diaspora. This is because of its intrinsic
qualities, to be sure, but also because a play can be attended and does not
necessarily have to be read, thus bypassing the real or pretended difficulty
Haitians claim to have in deciphering Créole. And besides, theater is after all
dialogue, and all Haitians agree that Créole is particularly suited to oral
expression.

As for novels in Créole, the list is still quite short. The first was Franketienne's
remarkable *Dézafi*, published in 1975. Unfortunately, many Haitians did not
make the sustained effort to read 300 pages of admittedly difficult Créole, and
preferred to read the French adaptation of this fine novel, published in France
four years later. Émile Célestin-Mégie's *Lanmou pa gin baryè* (1975), Carrié
Paultre's *Tonton Libin* (1978?) and Morisseau-Leroy's *Ravinodyab*, published
in Paris in 1982 with an appended French translation, seem to me less
successful.

To conclude this rapid survey, one should mention the publication of the first Haitian history book in Créole, Rolph Trouillot's 1977 *Ti difé boulé sou histoua Ayiti* and the recent translation into Créole and publication in Switzerland of Ulrich Fleischmann's excellent monograph *Ideologie und Wirklichkeit in der Literatur Haitis.*

Cautiously optimistic predictions can be made about the future of Haitian Créole literature. Especially since the fall of the Duvalier regime in 1986, Créole is rapidly gaining acceptance as a full-fledged language: article 5 of the 1987 constitution even states "Le créole et le français sont les langues officielles de la République;" in other words: "Kreyòl ak Franse se lang ofisyèl Repiblik Hayiti." It is being used by more and more Haitians in an ever-increasing number of social contexts. Most radio and TV stations now include frequent Créole language programs in their broadcasting schedules. The use of Créole in primary schools is finally beginning to be allowed, if not encouraged. Catholic and Protestant congregations conduct most of their services in the vernacular. Créole periodicals are being published in Haiti and abroad. The growing influence of English has lessened the fetichistic attitude towards French. Slowly, perhaps, reluctantly, at times, more and more educated Haitians are becoming proficient in reading Créole. There is no doubt that the virtual readership for Créole texts is increasing. But of course, now as before, this virtual readership will be exclusively Haitian, and only by using French can authors hope to reach a wider audience.

Readers of literature, as opposed to readers of religious texts, newspapers, self-help pamphlets, etc. are a small, conservative, smug minority. To date, this minority still prefers to read French or, for that matter, English for relaxation. Consequently, the increasing social acceptance of Créole is not reflected by a corresponding increase in the number of Créole titles being published. Créole literature still awaits the emergence of a readership willing and able to support it. It still consists mostly of slim, inexpensive collections of poems. An informal survey of people I know in Haiti reveals that not one of them owns a copy of Lyonel Desmaratte's remarkable *Mouché Défas*, a Créole adaptation of Molière's *Tartuffe*, published in 1983. After those of Franketienne, Célestin-Mégie and Morisseau-Leroy, no novel in Créole has—to my knowledge—been published.

Still, more and more Haitian high-school and university students are becoming interested in Créole literature and wish to see it thrive. When they enter the job market and can afford works of literature, they will no doubt be more willing than their elders to invest in them. The trickle-down effect should eventually affect the production of literature, and the increase in the potential readership cannot fail to be reflected in an increase in production.

Since its emergence as a literary language is so recent, Créole, while complex and pungent, is only beginning to develop what we might call literary styles. Most Créole literary texts imitate oral, basically colloquial expression.

The fifth poem in Milo Rigaud's twelve short poems published in 1933 under the title *tassos* may serve as an example:

-si ou vlé bilié chagrins,	If you want to forget your troubles
si ou vlé bilié malhès,	If you want to forget your pain
pouqui ou pas bouè clarin?	Why don't you drink some clairin
-main, canmarade-là pas ouè	But my friend doesn't understand
cé en France m'yé;	That I am in France;
m'mète chèché,	I can look,
m'mète la-priè,	I can pray,
m'mète rélé,	I can cry,
m'mète piaffé	I can stamp my feet,
si m'vlé blié chagrins,	When I want to forget my troubles,
si m'vlé blié malhès,	When I want to forget my pain
m'pape joinne gn'crasse clairin.	I can't find a drop of clairin.
coument ou 'ta vlé	How can I help
m'pas songé pays-à?	Thinking of home?

This may be an extreme example, but the fact remains that Davertige, Morisseau, Phelps, Depestre and most other Haitian poets who write sophisticated, linguistically elaborate poetry do so in French. There are probably two reasons for this. The first is that most Haitian poets writing in Créole adhere to a populist ideology, and wish to serve as spokesmen for their forgotten, unsophisticated countrymen. The second is that in Haiti, speculative, analytical, in other words "formal" writing has always been done in French. With the increase in philosophical theorizing, sociological analysis, psychological research, and scientific exposition in Créole, not only will adequate Créole words and expressions be coined, but a "written" language, as different from the colloquial as "written" French or English or German are from their respective "spoken" varieties will emerge. And this "written" Créole is in fact being elaborated day by day, in the Créole review *Sèl*, in *Ti difé boulé sou istoua Ayiti* and elsewhere. This is not to disparage in any way literature that uses the direct, essentially oral brand of Créole, but to suggest that we can expect a gradual development of the kind of literary language exemplified in Frankétienne's *Dézafi*. We can expect Créole to develop many different stylistic registers and this evolution is to be welcomed.

Finally, one may note with regret that so few of the traditional songs and folk tales of the Haitian peasantry have been or are being transcribed and preserved. This is all the more distressing since they are fast disappearing. Because most young people prefer to listen to transistor radios, and the *sambas*, or rural poets and story tellers, are dying out. If Créole is the language of the Haitian people, surely the treasury of their wit and wisdom deserves to be passed down to posterity.

Thomas Trezise

On Samuel Beckett's *Film*

Das Resultat ist nur darum dasselbe, was der Anfang, weil
der *Anfang Zweck* ist.

Hegel, *Phänomenologie des Geistes*

La fin est dans le commencement et cependant on continue.

Beckett, *Fin de partie*

In 1969, the director of Samuel Beckett's *Film*, Alan Schneider, wrote that
"all of [Beckett's] stage plays, radio and TV pieces, first get slammed, derided,
ignored. Then, five years later, they are hailed as classics. It's about time for that
to be happening to Beckett's *Film*."[1] However, almost 27 years after it was first
shot in Manhattan with Buster Keaton in the starring role, one can hardly say
that *Film* has been hailed as a classic. While millions have heard of *Waiting for
Godot*, relatively few people, even in intellectual circles, are aware that Beckett
ever made a film—and that it is called *Film*.

One of the main reasons for this is undoubtedly the poor marketability of
short experimental or avant-garde films. Yet it is also the case that, even among
students of Beckett's work, his cinematic accomplishment has received very
little attention and has certainly never elicited the kind of praise given the
theater and the mature prose. It is almost as though, having failed to achieve its
purported goal, namely, to represent in a convincing fashion what Beckett calls
a "search of non-being in flight from extraneous perception breaking down in
inescapability of self-perception,"[2] *Film* deserved no more than secondary
status in an *œuvre* whose major preoccupations are more successfully conveyed
through other media. Nevertheless, that *Film* was created by the man who once
claimed that "to be an artist is to fail,"[3] should restrain us from hastily endorsing
the judgment according to which, in its failure, it is of no more than minor
interest. Nor should we be misled by Beckett's own characterization of this
failure as simply "a problem of images which I cannot solve without technical
help" (12) and whose difficulty "I perhaps exaggerate . . . through technical
ignorance" (59). While it is a matter of indifference to me whether or not *Film*
is ever generally hailed as a classic, I shall argue here that it is precisely its

failure, the nature of which remains to be determined, that compels our attention, indeed that makes it a major work of Beckett's and a trenchant commentary on its medium.

Since I cannot show *Film* here, I will briefly describe it. It is in black and white, 22 minutes long, and divided into three parts respectively labeled, in the script, "The street," "The stairs," and "The room." There is no plot to speak of except, again, as Beckett states immediately under the Berkeleyan epigraph *"Esse est percipi"* ("To be is to be perceived"), a "search of non-being in flight from extraneous perception breaking down in inescapability of self-perception." As for the protagonist, he is "sundered into object (O) and eye (E)"—that is, into Keaton and camera—"the former in flight, the latter in pursuit." Beckett then adds: "It will not be clear until the end of film that pursuing perceiver is not extraneous, but self" (11). Finally, to conclude these general remarks: with three exceptions in the case of O and two in the case of secondary characters, the camera always approaches from behind and at an angle not exceeding 45 degrees. Whenever it exceeds this "angle of immunity," the character caught in its field experiences what Beckett calls an "anguish of perceivedness" (11) conveyed most often through a rather hyperbolic facial distortion.

Due to practical obstacles, the very first scene, a street panorama, was suppressed and replaced by a full-screen close-up of Buster Keaton's right eye, then by a simplified version of the street scene itself. Hugging the wall on his left and storming along in "comic foundered precipitancy" (12), O is wearing a long dark overcoat with the collar up, has his hat pulled down over his eyes, a briefcase in his left hand, and is shielding the exposed side of his face with his right hand. When E first encounters O, it is at an angle exceeding that of immunity, so that O stops and cringes toward the wall. Shortly thereafter, the camera respecting the angle of immunity, O literally runs into an elderly couple: when the man opens his mouth to curse, the woman utters the only sound of the entire film, namely, "sssh!" Having noticed the gaze of E, they look directly at it, gasp, then close their eyes and hurry away. In the meantime, O has moved down the street and is preparing to enter a doorway; E accelerates to catch up with him and, exceeding the angle of immunity in the vestibule, compels O once again to hide his face and to cringe toward the wall. Anew within the angle of immunity, O begins to climb the stairs, hears something, hastily redescends and crouches down so as not to be seen. At this point, an old flower-lady appears, unsteadily descending the stairway; when she sees E, her face assumes an expression of anguish before she faints and falls to the floor. O then hurries up the stairs and into the room.

The segment in the room consists of three parts. In the first, O is concerned with the suppression of all extraneous perception, animal, human, and divine: he accordingly draws the curtain over the window, covers the mirror with a rug, ejects—with some comic difficulty—the dog and the cat, destroys a print of

God the Father, and covers the parrot's cage and the fishbowl with a coat. In the second part, he is seated in a rocking chair whose headrest suggests a pair of eyes. From a folder, O removes seven photographs, all presumably of himself at different ages, which he inspects in chronological order and then, in reverse order, proceeds to tear up one by one. In the third part takes place what Beckett calls the "investment": after several tentative approaches, E confronts O full-face; O, still in the rocking chair and now awakening from his slumber, perceives E, begins to rise, stiffens and assumes the expression of anguish with which the elderly couple and the flower-lady have already familiarized us. The camera then cuts to E, that is, to itself, and shows Keaton's face, only with an expression, not of anguish, but of "acute *intentness*" (47). There follows a new cut to O, who closes his eyes, falls back into his chair, and covers his face with his hands; another cut to E, as before; yet another to O, bowed forward, head in hands, gently rocking; and a final cut to the same eye that was shown at the beginning of the film.

Even on a first viewing (or telling), it is clear that the "plot" of *Film* assumes the form of an ever greater internalization: the protagonist moves from the street to the stairway and finally to the room in which he systematically "reduces" all remaining sources of external or, as Beckett says, extraneous perception: the dog, the cat, the parrot, the goldfish, the window, the mirror, God the Father, the seven photographs of himself. If, as Beckett's quotation of Berkeley indicates, to be is here to be perceived, then the *telos* of this reduction, of this "search of non-being in flight from extraneous perception," would correspond to the literal disappearance of *Film*'s protagonist, just as, for example, the purported goal of the narrators of Beckett's trilogy of novels (*Molloy, Malone Dies, The Unnamable*) is to fall silent. On the face of it, however, the subsequent "breakdown" to which Beckett alludes in *Film* would not yield the same result as that which compels Moran, Molloy, Malone, and the Unnamable to continue speaking: whereas this very compulsion, produced by the perception of an intersubjective noise or static (variously thematized as a "voice," a "rumor," a "murmur," a "whisper," "screams," "pantings," "buzz-ing," "groans," "babble," etc.)[4] upon which the trilogy's narrators can impose the silence supposedly proper to them only by speaking and hence by renewing the dispossession of silence itself, endlessly reaffirms a non-self-identity more originary or fundamental than the integrity of selfhood, the "self-perception" in which the "search of non-being" purportedly "breaks down" would seem to promise, in *Film*, a fullness of being or self-possession grounded in the closure of specularity. Indeed, whatever its "negative" connotations may be, the "inescapability" of *self*-perception is clearly underscored by the fact that, of all the sources of perception in the room, only the mirror must be twice "reduced," that is, covered again when the rug that Keaton has placed over it slips to the ground. But the question then arises: Does *Film*, or rather *can* it, adequately represent this specularity? And if not, what does *this* breakdown or failure imply regarding not only the definition of the self but also its cinematic representation in Beckett?

To what, as we have seen, he characterizes as a technical problem, it may prove instructive to consider first of all the possible solutions that Beckett rejected. Referring to the "two independent sets of images" pertaining respectively, in the room sequence "up to the moment of O's falling asleep," to O and E, he says: "I feel that any attempt to express them in simultaneity (composite images, double frame, superimposition, etc.) must prove unsatisfactory. The presentation in a single image of O's perception of the print, for example, and E's perception of O perceiving it—no doubt feasible technically—would perhaps make impossible for the spectator a clear apprehension of either" (58). It is not merely a matter of this difficulty possibly encountered by the spectator, however; for a *single* image presenting both O's perception of the print (as opposed to O perceiving the print) and E's perception of O perceiving it is precisely *not* technically feasible, while the simple presentation of E's perception of O perceiving it (which is presumably, judging from the diagram I cannot reproduce here, what Beckett actually had in mind) obliterates the very difference to be emphasized. Yet the most important point to be made here is this: since the difference in question ultimately concerns the relation between O and E rather than between O's perception of the room and E's perception of O perceiving it, *any* comparison, whether simultaneous or successive, will remain uninformative if not also puzzling prior to the sequence of the "investment," that is, before the spectator learns that "pursuing perceiver is not extraneous, but self," that E *is* O. This explains why the solution suggested by Beckett, which the director in fact adopted and to which we now turn, proved equally unsatisfactory.

"The solution," Beckett continues, "might be in a succession of images of different *quality*, corresponding on the one hand to E's perception of O and on the other to O's perception of the room. This difference of quality might perhaps be sought in different degrees of development, the passage from the one to the other being from greater to lesser and lesser to greater definition or luminosity. The dissimilarity, however obtained, would have to be flagrant." He then offers another suggestion to which the director adhered: "Were this the solution adopted it might be desirable to establish, by means of brief sequences, the O quality in parts one and two" (58-59). Thus, as early as the encounter with the elderly couple in part one, we find, interspersed with the footage from E's perspective, a number of short takes corresponding, in their lesser definition, to O's perception. The reason for which Schneider felt, however, "that the two-vision thing never worked and that people would be puzzled (they were)" (90) is here again rather clear: as long as the spectator does not know that E and O are the same, their difference remains unintelligible.[5] Or more precisely: their difference remains unintelligible as long as E has not itself entered the field of sight and become in its turn subject to (or the object of) perception.

This leads us to a second puzzling component of *Film* and, finally, to the very heart of what Beckett recognizes as its "chief problem" (59). Each time that, prior to O's "investment," a character is confronted full-face by the camera (this happens in part one with the elderly couple and in part two with the flower-lady), the spectator can only wonder what exactly causes her or his expression of anguish. Is it O himself? While this is at least conceivable in the first case, it is ruled out in the second since the flower-lady never even glimpses him. Could it then be the character's own self? But this too is uncertain, for in none of these cases are we presented, through a sequence of shots, with the character's *own* perception of an investment analogous to O's. And to say that the expression of anguish is provoked by the camera is to miss the point entirely, since we assume that these characters are reacting to something or someone *within* at least a possible field of vision, whereas the camera is precisely its limit. Even in the case of O and even or perhaps especially when, subsequent to O's initial investment, E cuts to itself, the spectator cannot but feel perplexed; for although we have here proceeded a step beyond where we left the couple and the flower-lady, the perception of E by O substitutes terms of unequal value: the figure of Keaton within the visual field has replaced the organizing principle of the field itself, which is by definition invisible.[6] And conversely: E can only prove to have been O if O in turn becomes (another) E. With some luck, of course, the variation in photographic quality may at this point alert the spectator to the difference between O and E. Indeed, one might even be tempted to say that, if only for a moment, O has, by disappearing, brought to a successful conclusion his "search of non-being in flight from extraneous perception." Yet the problem has simply—and literally—been displaced inasmuch as the equation of O and camera is no less untenable an hypothesis, no less a fiction, than the equation of camera and E. The "problem" to which I have repeatedly referred may now be formulated as follows: the "self-perception" in which the "search of non-being" breaks down cannot it-self be perceived or represented unless an *apparently* self-identical subject (Keaton) is mistaken for an intersubjective relation (camera). In other words, and to the extent that E and O are in fact *not* the same, the "inescapability" that Beckett predicates of self-perception in *Film* pertains, strictly speaking, to the misperception of the self as an identity.

At the same time, however, it should be noted that this very misperception is undone by the "end" of *Film*. Indeed, even if we consider as technical failures in the banal sense of the term the two puzzling components to which I have just alluded, namely, the qualitative difference between E's and O's vision and the indeterminacy of the characters' source of anguish, as well as the misrepresentation of the self as an identity, they can all be viewed in the light of a more fundamental breakdown with which Beckett associates art itself and its "subject." This breakdown, too, is "technical," but in the more general sense in which *techne* means mastery or power. In the case of *Film*, such a failure corresponds to the Beckettian subject's inability to achieve the closure intrinsic to specularity. And closure is here understood at once temporally and spatially: the difference between E and O and the anguish of the characters both involve the perceptual exposure of an inside to an invisible outside and furthermore become intelligible only *nachträglich* or belatedly, that is, by virtue of a temporality (un)grounded in the non-self-identity of the instant or moment. As for the moment when O misperceives the source of his investment as a(nother) self (his "own"), it merely confirms the point: the movement of E into the visual field displaces the "outside" from E to O while triggering the series of cuts from one to the other that also testifies to their temporal non-self-coincidence. The "technical" impossibility of representing *in a single image* E's perception of O and O's perception of E *is* the impossibility of closure for the Beckettian subject or self, an impossibility to be understood in the etymological sense, as powerlessness—the powerlessness of its exposure to an impersonal outside. The irony of Beckett's *Film* resides in the fact that the "search of non-being in flight from extraneous perception" breaks down in a "self-perception" in which the self is discovered to be, itself, extraneous. And that, in a film in which to be is to be perceived, the non-self-identity of the subject, which makes the self-perceptual relation possible, is precisely what goes unnoticed.

Of course, Berkeley's proposition applies to *any* film, and this explains at least in part the generic title of Beckett's own as well as the general pertinence of its reflexivity. When we finally return to the same eye that was shown at the beginning, when the subject of perception has ostensibly become its own object, "we" in fact occupy relative to it the position that E occupied relative to O and that O occupied relative to the photographs of himself. Beckett thus inscribes, at the very end of *Film*, an abyssal structure that, in principle, has no end, and whose space is precisely that of the "medium"—*between* image and frame, statement and quotation, use and mention, film and *Film*.[7]

Notes

[1] Alan Schneider, "On Directing *Film*," in Samuel Beckett, *Film* (New York: Grove Press, 1969) 94.

[2] Samuel Beckett, *Film* (New York: Grove Press, 1969) 11. All further references to this script will be given in the text.

[3] Samuel Beckett and Georges Duthuit, "Three Dialogues," in *Samuel Beckett: A Collection of Critical Essays*, ed. Martin Esslin (Englewood Cliffs, NJ: Prentice-Hall, 1965) 21. Reprinted from *Transition forty-nine* 5 (1949).

[4] Samuel Beckett, *Three Novels* (New York: Grove Press, 1955; Grove Press Black Cat, 1965) 88, 10, 88, 40, 81, 206, 207, 335, 354.

[5] The same may be said, incidentally, of the difference between Moran and Molloy in the second half of *Molloy*, which I have examined at some length in *Into the Breach: Samuel Beckett and the Ends of Literature* (Princeton: Princeton UP, 1990).

[6] Susan Brison has drawn my attention to propositions 5.63-5.641 of Ludwig Wittgenstein's *Tractatus Logico-Philosophicus*, trans. C.K. Ogden (London: Routledge, 1922; 1981) 151-53, of remarkable pertinence to the "subject" of *Film* or simply of film. Here Wittgenstein says, among other things: "The subject does not belong to the world but it is a limit of the world. *Where in* the world is a metaphysical subject to be noted? You say that this case is altogether like that of the eye and the field of sight. But you do *not* really see the eye. And from nothing *in the field of sight* can it be concluded that it is seen from an eye."

[7] An earlier version of this article was read at the MLA convention in Chicago, December 29, 1990, as part of the session entitled "New Directions in French Studies: Literature and Film." I wish to thank my friends, Lynn Higgins, for inviting me to participate in the session, and Kimball Lockhart, for late night discussions that helped to clarify a number of issues raised by *Film*.

André Maman

Les Femmes dans une société d'inégalités: libertés et démocratie

La situation de la femme dans la société française a toujours été l'objet de controverses passionnées, où se mêlent accusations, indifférence, amertume, regrets et surtout doutes sur les intentions réelles de ceux qui pourraient amener des changements, c'est-à-dire les détenteurs du pouvoir dans le pays.

En effet, représentant 53% de la population, donc majoritaires, les femmes françaises n'ont jamais pu ni su s'organiser pour exiger des droits économiques, politiques, sociologiques qui soient égaux à ceux des hommes, puisqu'on leur a toujours dénié le pouvoir que, par leur nombre et leur importance, elles méritaient. C'est par une ordonnance du Général de Gaulle en 1944, à la fin de la Seconde guerre mondiale, que les femmes ont eu le droit de vote, droit qui aurait dû leur être accordé quand les hommes l'ont reçu, en 1875, à la naissance de la Troisième République. Il a fallu attendre 69 ans pour voir s'établir cette égalité, qui est capitale dans la démocratie.

Sous la Cinquième République, et surtout depuis la révolution de mai 1968, on a assisté à une accélération des changements légaux et sociaux, en faveur des femmes, mais à un ralentissement, sinon une régression, des droits politiques, qui ne débouchent toujours pas sur l'obtention d'un vrai pouvoir, du seul pouvoir qui permettrait d'arriver à l'égalité. Or, nous allons voir que des inégalités criantes continuent à exister, dans tous les domaines, d'autant plus que les mentalités masculines refusent de céder toute parcelle du pouvoir.

Il est certain que, depuis 1968, grâce aux prises de conscience suscitées par la révolution des étudiants, un véritable déluge de changements dans les divers Codes, mais surtout dans le Code Civil, a amélioré la situation de la femme, en la libérant des vieilles contraintes, nées au XIXe siècle. Les gouvernements du Président Georges Pompidou et du Président Valéry Giscard d'Estaing[1] ont rivalisé d'ardeur pour changer les lois civiles, si bien qu'à l'arrivée au pouvoir du Président François Mitterrand, en 1981, l'essentiel avait été fait.

On peut se poser la question de savoir si ces changements, que l'on suppose faits de bonne foi, sont vraiment bénéfiques pour les femmes, ou bien ne font-ils que renforcer le pouvoir et la domination des hommes. Anxieux de ne rien abandonner de leur pouvoir, ce que l'on voit très bien dans le domaine politique, les hommes, "les princes qui nous dirigent," ont voulu faire croire aux femmes, avec une bonne dose d'hypocrisie, que la victoire était en vue, qu'on leur avait octroyé les mêmes droits que les hommes et que maintenant, il ne fallait plus rien exiger.

En suivant le pamphlct, publié par le Centre National d'Information et de Documentation de Femmes et des Familles (CNIDFF), intitulé *Le Concubinage: vos droits,*[2] on examinera les changements capitaux, opérés dans le domaine des droits civils et sociaux de la femme, en essayant de percer derrière la surface et de faire ressortir les ambiguïtés de ces réformes, et leurs dangers.

Jusque dans les années soixante, le mariage légal, enregistré à la commune de sa résidence, était le seul reconnu, le seul entraînant des droits et des devoirs légaux, toute autre forme d'union n'avait aucune existence officielle. Le mariage légal était sanctifié par la République, il était la garantie de la force, de l'équilibre et de la survie de la société. La femme était soumise à son mari: en dehors du mariage, elle n'existait pas et il suffit de penser aux moqueries qui entouraient "la vieille fille" et à l'opprobre qui suivait "la fille-mère."

Aujourd'hui, le concubinage, ou la cohabitation, l'union libre, la vie maritale—quel que soit le nom qu'on lui donne—se trouve paré des mêmes droits et des mêmes conséquences que le mariage légal.

Cette cohabitation ne peut avoir d'organisation juridique, puisque ce serait en faire une institution, ce que ne veulent pas les personnes qui se sont unies de cette façon-là. Cependant, cette communauté de vie engendre des conséquences juridiques, qui n'ont fait qu'augmenter ces vingt dernières années, si bien qu'aux yeux de la loi, il n'existe pratiquement plus de différences entre ces divers modes de vie (CNIDFF 4).

Si le Code Civil ne reconnaît pas la cohabitation, par contre la jurisprudence a évolué dans un sens de plus en plus libéral et surtout plus pragmatique.

Ainsi, en droit fiscal, une loi de Finances récente a introduit la notion de "concubinage notoire," malheureusement sans en préciser la définition. Les services de la Sécurité Sociale qui, en France, couvrent les risques maladie, maternité, accidents du travail, qui allouent les prestations familiales et qui garantissent l'assurance vieillesse, prennent en considération la vie maritale et l'assimilent pratiquement au mariage, pour l'attribution de tous ces avantages. Si le Droit du travail ne laisse pas apparaître la notion de concubinage, c'est parce que c'est le salarié, ou dans notre cas la salariée que l'on considère, quelle que soit sa situation de famille (CNIDFF 5).

Le législateur a tout fait pour encourager la cohabitation et il paraît évident que c'est l'homme qui profite de cette situation de droit, largement plus que la femme, à qui on fait miroiter l'égalité complète avec l'homme. La cohabitation étant une situation de fait, elle peut être prouvée par tous moyens, témoignages, attestations, certificats, etc. Les mairies peuvent délivrer un certificat de concubinage, sur déclaration de témoins attestant que le couple vit en union libre. Rien n'est donc plus facile à établir que ce document, qui peut servir à obtenir certains avantages, en matière de logement ou de transports, par exemple (CNIDFF 8).

Si un enfant naît d'une union libre, son lien de filiation avec ses parents est établi par un acte volontaire de chacun de ses parents: c'est la reconnaissance, qui, étant divisible, peut n'être établie qu'à l'égard de l'un des parents (CNIDFF 8). La loi du 25 juin 1982 prévoit que le lien peut être établi par la possession d'état, quand il n'y a pas reconnaissance volontaire des parents. On devine que les cas de non-reconnaissance viennent surtout du père naturel, qui ne veut se créer aucune obligation légale envers l'enfant, laissant ainsi à la mère la responsabilité entière de la filiation.

Le nombre de mariages a chuté de 416.000, en 1972, à 273.000, en 1985, alors que la cohabitation est passée de 445.000 couples, en 1975, à 809.000 en 1982, soit 6,1% de l'ensemble des couples. Les naissances hors mariage qui, en 1960, constituaient 6% du total des naissances, étaient de 20% en 1984.[3] L'enfant naturel prend le nom de celui des parents qui l'a reconnu le premier, ce qui sera presque toujours la mère. Si les parents l'ont reconnu ensemble, il prendra le nom du père.

L'autorité parentale a vu ses règles modifiées par la loi du 22 juillet 1987. Désormais, les deux parents, et non plus seulement le père, peuvent exercer en commun l'autorité parentale. Ceci donne à la mère plus de pouvoirs, mais également plus de responsabilités. Le nombre de familles monoparentales a énormément augmenté en France depuis une vingtaine d'années et c'est dans l'immense majorité de cas, une mère seule qui volontairement ou non, élève ses enfants.

Sur une population féminine d'environ 28.200.000, en 1991, soit 53% de l'ensemble, mais 44% de la population active, on estime à 9,5 millions le nombre de femmes seules, âgées de plus de 15 ans. Elles se répartissent ainsi: célibataires: 5,3 millions; Veuves: 3,2 millions; Divorcées: 1 million.[4]

La sociologue Evelyne Sullerot appelle "solitaristes" les femmes qui choisissent de vivre seules. Selon elle, ce phénomène remonte au début des années 80. "La solitariste habite dans les grandes villes; elle a un niveau d'éducation élevé, un bon métier. Elle vit généralement 'en couple,' mais n'habite pas avec son compagnon, optant pour le co-concubinage."[5]

Evelyne Sullerot essaie de cerner la situation de ces "solitaristes": "La solitariste fait appartement à part. Beaucoup d'entre elles ont une liaison stable mais ne savent pas trop ce qu'il en adviendra. Certaines mères célibataires peuvent aussi être considérées comme des solitaristes. Toutes ces femmes ne sont pas égoïstes, comme certains le croient, mais individualistes" (CIEPD 26).

En ce qui concerne maintenant la question des biens, on va voir que là aussi, c'est la femme qui risque de faire les frais d'une ouverture et d'un libéralisme, qu'elle peut avoir à payer cher.

Comme c'est le cas pour une femme mariée, la concubine peut ouvrir un compte bancaire joint avec son compagnon. Les deux sont liés par une convention de solidarité—la responsabilité solidaire des co-titulaires est engagée en cas de solde débiteur. Contrairement aux gens mariés, chacun des co-titulaires peut, à tout moment, dénoncer le compte joint, et la solidarité prend fin (CNIDFF 10). Cette situation qui peut paraître pratique pour la femme est pleine d'aléas constants, dont l'homme, habitué à plus de mobilité, souffrira moins souvent. Une pratique de plus en plus courante se fait jour dans la signature de contrat devant notaire, de la part des concubins qui veulent ainsi indiquer la façon dont seront gérés leurs biens, pendant la cohabitation, et partagés en cas de rupture (CNIDFF 11). C'est, au fond, l'équivalent d'un contrat de mariage et quand on connaît le fort penchant des hommes de loi, notaires, conseils juridiques, avocats, à favoriser les hommes, on aperçoit là aussi les injustices envers les femmes, la solidarité masculine dépassant les barrières socio-professionnelles.

Depuis la loi des Finances de 1987, certains avantages fiscaux, dont bénéficiaient les concubins, ont été atténués, et l'on peut se demander si nous n'assistons pas à un durcissement progressif de la législation, dans le but de rendre la cohabitation moins intéressante et de privilégier le mariage légal pour essayer de lui redonner la place qu'il avait (CNIDFF 12).

En France, l'un des aspects capitaux de l'action du gouvernement et de son ingérence dans la vie privée est celui des droits sociaux, qui sont certainement les meilleurs au monde. Chaque gouvernement a voulu les améliorer, que ce soit les allocations familiales ou de chômage, ou bien la couverture des frais médicaux, ou encore les très substantielles retraites et pensions de vieillesse.

Depuis la loi No. 78-2 du 2 janvier 1978, les droits des concubins, au regard de l'assurance maladie et maternité, sont assimilés à ceux des époux (CNIDFF 14). Ceci veut dire que l'administration de la Sécurité sociale ne fait plus aucune différence, quelle que soit la situation de la mère, mère célibataire, mère concubine, ou mère mariée (CNIDFF 16).

La femme, qui ne bénéficie pas d'une couverture sociale à titre personnel, peut être ayant droit de son concubin, s'il est assuré social, et bénéficier des mêmes prestations en nature qu'une femme mariée, à condition d'être à la charge totale et permanente de l'assuré et de vivre sous son toit.

Là aussi, l'assimilation complète de deux situations de droit et de fait bien différentes ne peut jouer, nous semble-t-il, qu'en défaveur de la femme qui, au moment où les tensions et les difficultés surgiront, se trouvera du mauvais côté de la barrière sociale et juridique.

La loi du 5 juillet 1974 abaisse à 18 ans l'âge de la majorité, qui était jusque-là de 21 ans. Tout d'un coup, jeunes gens et jeunes filles sont considérés comme majeurs trois ans plus tôt. Le Président Giscard d'Estaing a voulu donner l'égalité aux garçons et aux filles, mais quand on connaît les conditions familiales prévalant en France, on voit que ce sont les jeunes filles qui souffriront de cette nouvelle liberté d'action. A propos de cette loi du 5 juillet 1974, Dominique Borne commente: "Cette décision traduit une transformation capitale: jusque-là la majorité (21 ans) correspondait non pas au moment de l'arrivée dans la vie active—la majorité des jeunes étaient depuis longtemps au travail à cet âge—mais au moment de *l'installation* quand le jeune homme ou la jeune fille quittait sa famille, s'établissait à son compte, fondait un autre foyer" (Borne 69-70).

Sous les présidences de Charles de Gaulle et de Georges Pompidou, on ne compte que trois grandes lois concernant les femmes: en 1965, la loi de réforme des régimes matrimoniaux; en décembre 1967, la loi sur les contraceptifs "modernes," dite loi Neuwirth; en 1972, la loi instaurant l'égalité des salaires masculin et féminin pour un travail égal. Ajoutons que cette loi n'a jamais été appliquée.

Dès son arrivée au pouvoir, Valéry Giscard d'Estaing a voulu améliorer la condition des femmes.[6] Il est le premier Président de la République à créer un Secrétariat d'Etat à la condition féminine, en 1974, qui deviendra ensuite un Ministère délégué, quatre ans plus tard, en 1978.

Entre 1974 et 1981, nous allons assister à une véritable explosion légale, conséquence des changements de mentalités survenues depuis la révolution de 1968, mais aussi volonté bien arrêtée d'un Président, que ni son passé, ni sa sensibilité ne semblaient préparer à une telle action.

En 1975, des droits égaux sont accordés au travailleur et à la travailleuse, notamment en interdisant toute discrimination à l'embauche. En ce qui concerne les droits civils, dorénavant la loi du 4 juin 1970 supprime la notion juridique de "chef de famille." L'article 213 du Code Civil stipule: "les époux assurent ensemble la direction morale et matérielle de la famille." L'autorité parentale a donc remplacé la notion d'autorité paternelle. L'article 372 du Code Civil ajoute: "Pendant le mariage, les père et mère exercent en commun leur autorité."

Depuis la loi du 4 juin 1970, la mère célibataire est titulaire de l'autorité parentale. Elle est également titulaire de l'administration légale des biens de son enfant mineur. On remet à la mère célibataire un livret de famille, et une circulaire ministérielle enjoint au personnel de l'administration de l'appeler "Madame" et non plus "Mademoiselle."

La femme, mariée ou non, a les mêmes droits que l'homme pour fixer le domicile conjugal.

La loi du 11 juillet 1975 a procédé à une importante réforme du divorce et de la séparation de corps et de biens.

"Jusqu'alors pour divorcer il fallait mettre en évidence des *torts*, on 'gagnait' ou on 'perdait' un divorce, et même quand les torts étaient 'partagés,' il ne pouvait y avoir séparation des conjoints sans qu'apparaisse la notion de *faute*" (Borne 70). Le divorce est automatique après une séparation de six années au moins. Ceci explique facilement que le nombre de divorces ait beaucoup augmenté. "En France, à l'heure actuelle, un mariage sur quatre se termine par un divorce. Le divorce, hier sanction d'une faute, est aujourd'hui banalisé" (Borne 87).

Il est surprenant de noter qu'au moment où la cohabitation augmente, que le nombre de mariages diminue, que la loi accorde beaucoup plus de droits à la femme, le nombre de divorces tend à atteindre les mêmes proportions qu'aux Etats-Unis et qu'en Suède.

Evelyne Sullerot fait remarquer que le refus du mariage s'est développé dans les pays les plus riches du monde: Suède, Suisse, Etats-Unis, Danemark, Angleterre, France.[7] Dans les sociétés pauvres, le mariage est d'abord une sécurité économique, "une assurance sur la vie" (Sullerot 66).

Elisabeth Badinter note les raisons du déclin du mariage: "Il y a à peine quelques décennies, le mariage était synonyme tout à la fois de sécurité, de respectabilité et de fécondité. Aujourd'hui, il a perdu ces trois caractères essentiels."[8]

La loi la plus importante, par les passions qu'elle a soulevées et les crises de conscience qu'elle a suscitées, est celle du 17 janvier 1975, loi temporaire promulguée pour cinq ans, et reconduite définitivement, le 31 décembre 1979, autorisant l'interruption volontaire de grossesse, jusqu'à la dixième semaine de grossesse. Madame Simone Veil, qui était ministre de la Santé, a voulu ainsi "réparer les échecs ou les erreurs de la contraception" (Borne 86). Elle a vu, dans cette loi "un moyen d'éviter les avortements clandestins pratiqués souvent dans des conditions déplorables" (Borne 86).

Le nombre d'IVG enregistrées est passé de 134.000, en 1976, à 157.000 en 1979 et 182.000, en 1983. Ce taux est de près de 25% par rapport aux naissances vivantes.

"Désormais, c'est la femme qui joue le rôle le plus important. Elle a conquis son indépendance par le travail, son pouvoir familial est renforcé, à elle la décision et la possibilité d'avoir ou de ne pas avoir d'enfant, de l'élever seule ou en couple" (Borne 88).

C'est là qu'on se rend compte des immenses libertés nouvelles qui ont été conférées aux femmes, souvent pour des raisons politiques, pour avoir leur vote, mais sans leur attribuer le corollaire du pouvoir économique, du pouvoir de la décision politique, de la vraie égalité avec les hommes. Il faudrait être aveugle pour ne pas voir les nouveaux défis que cela pose à la femme.

"Le plus important de tous les changements qui affectent notre civilisation à la veille du troisième millénaire, c'est la transformation irréversible des relations entre les hommes et les femmes," constate Antoinette Fourque, Présidente de l'Alliance des Femmes pour la Démocratisation, au moment de la Journée Internationale des Femmes, le 8 mars 1989.[9] "Et ce ne sont pas seulement les rapports entre hommes et femmes qui ne seront plus les mêmes, mais ceux de la triade humaine—femme-homme-enfant" (1989 - *Etats généraux des femmes* 11). Nous avons encore un long chemin à parcourir pour arriver à établir des relations plus harmonieuses.

Evelyne Sullerot, à qui on demandait d'expliquer le phénomène de société que constituent les "solitaristes," c'est-à-dire les femmes qui choisissent de vivre seules, a distingué les raisons suivantes: "Tout d'abord les femmes sont désormais maîtresses de la fécondité. . . . C'est la liberté de non-procréation" (CIEPD 26). Ensuite, Sullerot ajoute: "Elles ont également la liberté de se réaliser sexuellement et entendent goûter à cette liberté. . . . L'allongement du temps de vie—quatre-vingts ans pour les femmes—n'est pas étranger à ce phénomène. Les femmes, en effet, estiment qu'elles ont tout loisir de voir venir" (CIEPD 26). Evelyne Sullerot fait très justement remarquer: "Pour un grand nombre d'entre elles le travail a remplacé la famille. Auparavant, c'est le mariage qui conférait à la femme une identité sociale, maintenant c'est le travail" (CIEPD 26). On compte un ménage français sur quatre qui est composé d'une personne seule, veuve, divorcée ou célibataire. A Paris, on estime que la moitié des ménages sont constituées d'une personne seule (Borne 87).

Après avoir examiné l'aspect juridique et sociologique de la question, nous devons nous tourner vers l'aspect professionnel de la vie des femmes.

Dans un rapport fait au Ministre des Droits de la Femme, en 1982, intitulé "Les femmes en France dans une société d'inégalités," le chapitre I "Difficultés des femmes à concilier rôles professionnels, socio-politiques et familiaux" dit: "La croissance très forte de l'activité des femmes au cours de la dernière décennie n'a pas effacé le rôle prioritaire qui leur est attribué dans la société, pour la prise en charge des reponsabilités familiales et domestiques."[10] Les activités domestiques sont faites essentiellement pour les femmes, et 70% des femmes d'âge adulte ont un emploi en dehors de la maison. "Il y a là une double inégalité qui pèse lourdement sur toute la vie des femmes dans notre pays et qui permet d'expliquer leur infériorité dans tous les domaines" (La Documentation Française 24).

Dans le droit du travail, la notion de couple, qu'il soit légitime ou non, est inexistante. Un principe général de non discrimination, selon lequel il ne doit pas être tenu compte de la situation de famille dans la vie professionnelle de la salariée, règne dans ce domaine (CNIDFF 17). Trois lois importantes ont affirmé ce principe de non discrimination. La loi No. 75-625 du 11 juillet 1975 a introduit, à l'article 416 du Code pénal, le principe d'égalité en matière d'offre d'emploi, d'embauche et de licenciement. Toute discrimination, fondée entre autre sur la situation de famille est interdite, sauf motif légitime (CNIDFF 17). La loi du 4 août 1982, dite Loi Auroux, stipule qu'aucun(e) salarié(e) ne peut être sanctionné(e) ou licencié(e), en raison de son sexe, de son origine, de sa situation de famille.

Enfin, la troisième loi, No. 83-635 du 13 juillet 1983 définit l'égalité des droits dans la vie professionnelle des salariés. Nul ne peut mentionner ou faire mentionner le sexe ou la situation de famille du candidat recherché, dans une offre d'emploi ou dans toute autre forme de publicité relative à une embauche. De plus, nul ne peut refuser d'embaucher, refuser le renouvellement du contrat de travail, licencier pour des raisons tenant au sexe de la personne ou à sa situation de famille (CNIDFF 18).

C'est la première fois, en France, que l'on va si loin dans la complète égalité entre hommes et femmes, dans le monde du travail. Toutefois, les conditions d'emploi sont dures, avec un chômage chronique touchant 2.900.000 demandeurs et demandeuses d'emplois, soit près de 10% de la force du travail du pays. Sur les demandeurs d'emplois de moins de 25 ans, 53% sont des femmes. Ce sont elles qui sont licenciées les premières. Ajoutons que 75% des femmes salariées sont dans le secteur tertiaire et sur 455 professions recensées, 20 emploient 45% des femmes. On voit donc que la mixité des emplois est loin d'être une réalité et que, dans les conditions économiques actuelles, l'égalité des chances est loin d'être atteinte par les femmes. Les employeurs ont beau jeu pour imposer des conditions de salaire et d'emploi qui ne respectent pas la législation en vigueur. En moyenne, l'écart des salaires entre hommes et femmes dépasse 25%. Chez les cadres, ce chiffre atteint 30%. Certes, on peut encore constater que "les hommes conçoivent, fabriquent, dirigent, alors que les femmes exécutent, présentent, assistent."

En une vingtaine d'années, les mentalités françaises se sont libérées de préjugés aux racines profondes, si bien que sur le plan légal et sociologique, plus aucune discrimination ne devrait exister entre hommes et femmes, que celles-ci soient mariées ou non. Toutefois, on regrette de voir apparaître une sorte d'accord tacite entre les hommes possédant le pouvoir politique, le pouvoir économique, le pouvoir de décision et le monde féminin dans son ensemble: Vous avez, vous femmes, toute liberté de vous marier ou non, de procréer ou non, de travailler ou non, mais ne venez pas empiéter sur notre monde sacro-saint du pouvoir, que nous ne vous abandonnerons sous aucune condition. Gouvernements de droite et de gauche, hommes politiques de divers horizons ont essayé, ou fait semblant d'essayer de changer la situation, de façon à faire disparaître les inégalités et à mettre fin à la soumission des femmes.

Comment expliquer alors qu'à l'Assemblée Nationale, seules 33 femmes siègent parmi les 577 deputés que compte l'Assemblée et qu'au Sénat, sur 319 sénateurs nous n'ayons que 9 femmes?[11] La France se situe ainsi au 17e rang au classement européen des "femmes politiques."

Parmi les élues locales, sur 3694 conseillers généraux, on compte 154 femmes et pas plus de 1445 femmes sur les 36.441 maires de France. Au gouvernement actuel siègent 6 femmes sur les 39 Ministres et Secrétaires d'Etat (Kimmel 27). Alain Kimmel ajoute: "Ces chiffres permettent de faire un premier constat: la place des femmes dans la vie politique française est inversement proportionnelle aux innombrables discours, assortis de promesses prononcés ici et là depuis des décennies" (Kimmel 27). Sous la IVe République comme sous la Ve République, pendant les Présidences du Général de Gaulle et de Georges Pompidou, il n'y a jamais eu qu'une seule femme au gouvernement, sauf d'avril 1973 à février 1974, où il y en a eu deux.

Il serait trop facile de dire que cette situation de fait, qui s'est perpétuée depuis 1944, date du vote des femmes, est due au manque de qualités des femmes, à leur manque d'ambition et à leur peur de perdre leur féminité. La solidarité persistant entre hommes politiques, de quelque bord qu'ils soient, est une des constantes de la vie politique française. Quand on analyse les obstacles à la participation politique des femmes, on note que "certains sont inhérents aux mécanismes mêmes de la vie politique: nécessité du militantisme; mode de scrutin et concurrence pour le pouvoir, mode masculin de désignation des candidats . . . le cursus politique est discriminatoire, car il suppose une large disponibilité de temps et d'esprit" (La Documentation Française 161).

Louisette Blanquart dit: "Tous ceux qui écrivent sur les femmes et la politique constatent qu'elles adhèrent très peu aux partis politiques, y militent moins encore, ne les dirigent jamais."[12]

Dans la vie professionnelle, les mêmes différences existent et plus on monte dans l'échelle sociale, moins on trouve de femmes. Ainsi, en 1990, les femmes représentent 52% des effectifs contre 39,8% en 1960. Dans les Grandes Ecoles, leur pourcentage diminue: 20% à l'Ecole Nationale d'Administration et 7% à l'Ecole Polytechnique (CIEPD 22). Quelle que soit la profession considérée, jamais les femmes ne sont représentées aux échelons supérieurs dans la proportion qui refléterait leur nombre.

Dans les professions libérales, elles sont 24,6%. Entre 1962 et 1985, elle sont passées de 10,8% à 24,4% dans la fonction publique, de 12,8% à 23,4% chez les cadres administratifs et commerciaux et seulement de 3,7% à 6,3% chez les ingénieurs et cadres techniques d'entreprise (CIEPD 22). Les abandons des études supérieures par les femmes sont dûs à des erreurs d'orientation ou au mariage. Dans ce cas, "les enfants ou la carrière du mari stoppent les études." "Dès lors il n'est pas surprenant de voir les femmes occuper des postes de responsabilité inférieure" (CIEPD 22). Quand il arrive que, dans une profession, les femmes obtiennent la parité avec les hommes, ou même la dépassent, la raison en est la détérioration de cette profession qui présente moins d'attraits pour les hommes. C'est le cas du monde de l'enseignement, et ce sera bientôt le cas du monde de la justice et de celui de la médecine.

Il est flagrant que les femmes sont mal représentées dans les lieux de décision politique, sociale, économique et administrative. En 1989, on comptait 4 femmes ambassadeurs sur 150 et à l'administration centrale, 8% seulement des postes de responsabilité leur sont confiés. Les grandes entreprises ne sont confiées à des femmes que dans la proportion de 13%, et les Petites et Moyennes Entreprises (PME) dans la proportion de 12%.

Dans cet article, nous avons essayé de montrer les grands progrès réalisés ces vingt dernières années dans la situation juridique et sociologique des femmes. Cependant ces progrès sont ralentis, par ailleurs, leurs effets sont bloqués, les inégalités demeurent et elles sont criantes et d'autant plus injustes qu'elles privent le pays d'un potentiel de talents inexploités, au détriment de la communauté toute entière. Les pesanteurs restent nombreuses, et les femmes doivent se rendre compte que tout progrès, toute amélioration, toute victoire ne viendront que d'elles-mêmes. Elles n'obtiendront, non seulement l'égalité avec les hommes, mais surtout les places qu'elles méritent que quand elles auront pénétré dans les allées du pouvoir. Des espoirs se feront jour quand elles prendront carrément en mains leur propre destinée. On ne leur fera aucun cadeau, c'est leur courage et leur détermination qui décideront des résultats du combat.

Notes

[1] Valéry Giscard d'Estaing: "Je tiens à ce que mon mandat présidentiel soit marqué par la reconnaissance complète des droits et des responsabilités des femmes dans la société française." Déclaration du 3 octobre 1977 dans *Le Monde*, 3 octobre, 1977.

[2] Centre National d'Information et de Documentation des Femmes et des Familles (CNIDFF), *Le Concubinage: vos droits* (7, rue du Jura, Paris 75013, 1990).

[3] Dominique Borne, *Histoire de la société française depuis 1945* (Paris: Armand Colin, 1988) 87.

[4] Centre International d'Etudes Pédagogiques de Sèvres (CIEPD), *Echos: Portraits de femmes* (No. 58, 1990) 25.

[5] Evelyne Sullerot, entretien, réalisé par Françoise Lemoine, *Le Figaro*, 20 décembre 1988, dans *Echos: Portraits de femmes*, note 4.

[6] Valéry Giscard d'Estaing: "J'espère que, sur les dix ou douze lignes que les futurs manuels d'histoire réserveront à mon septennat, une ou deux seront consacrées à mes efforts pour améliorer la condition féminine." *Le Monde*, 5 octobre 1977.

[7] Evelyne Sullerot, *Pour le meilleur sans le pire* (Paris: Fayard, 1984) 67.

[8] Elisabeth Badinter, *L'Un est l'autre* (Paris: Odile Jacob, 1986) 241.

[9] *1989 - Etats généraux des femmes* (Paris: Des femmes, 1990) 11.

[10] La Documentation Française, *Les Femmes en France dans une société d'inégalités* (Paris: 1982) 21.

[11] Alain Kimmel, "Les femmes en politique," *Echos: Portraits de femmes*, note 4, 27.

[12] Louisette Blanquart, *Femmes: l'âge politique* (Paris: Editions Sociales, 1974) 97.

FRENCH FORUM MONOGRAPHS

Karolyn Waterson. *Molière et l'autorité. Structures sociales, structures comiques.* 1976.

Donna Kuizenga. *Narrative Strategies in* La Princesse de Clèves. 1976.

Ian J. Winter. *Montaigne's Self-Portrait and Its Influence in France, 1580-1630.* 1976.

Judith G. Miller. *Theater and Revolution in France since 1968.* 1977.

Raymond C. La Charité, ed. *O un amy! Essays on Montaigne in Honor of Donald M. Frame.* 1977.

Rupert T. Pickens. *The Welsh Knight. Paradoxicality in Chrétien's* Erec et Enide. 1977.

Carol Clark. *The Web of Metaphor. Studies in the Imagery of Montaigne's* Essais. 1978.

Donald Maddox. *Structure and Sacring. The Systematic Kingdom in Chrétien's* Erec et Enide. 1978.

Betty J. Davis. *The Storytellers in Marguerite de Navare's* Heptaméron. 1978.

Laurence M. Porter. *The Renaissance of the Lyric in French Romanticism. Elegy, "Poëme" and Ode.* 1978.

Bruce R. Leslie. *Ronsard's Successful Epic Venture. The Epyllion.* 1979.

Michelle A. Freeman. *The Poetics of* Translatio Studii *and* Conjointure. *Chrétien de Troyes's* Cligés. 1979.

Robert T. Corum, Jr. *Other Worlds and Other Seas. Art and Vision in Saint-Amant's Nature Poetry.* 1979.

Marcel Muller. *Préfiguration et structure romanesque dans* A la recherche du temps perdu *(avec un inédit de Marcel Proust).* 1979.

Ross Chambers. *Meaning and Meaningfulness. Studies in the Analysis and Interpretation of Texts.* 1979.

Lois Oppenheim. *Intentionality and Intersubjectivity. A Phenomenological Study of Butor's* La Modification. 1980.

Matilda T. Bruckner. *Narrative Invention in Twelfth-Century French Romance. The Convention of Hospitality (1160-1200).* 1980.

Gérard Defaux. *Molière, ou les métamorphoses du comique. De la comédie morale au triomphe de la folie.* 1980.

Raymond C. La Charité. *Recreation, Reflection and Re-Creation. Perspectives on Rabelais's* Pantagruel. 1980.

Jules Brody. *Du style à la pensée. Trois études sur les* Caractères *de La Bruyère*. 1980.

Lawrence D. Kritzman. *Destruction/Découverte. Le fonctionnement de la rhétorique dans les* Essais *de Montaigne*. 1980.

Minnette Grunmann-Gaudet and Robin F. Jones, eds. *The Nature of Medieval Narrative*. 1980.

J.A. Hiddleston. *Essai sur Laforgue et les* Derniers Vers *suivi de Laforgue et Baudelaire*. 1980.

Michael S. Koppisch. *The Dissolution of Character. Changing Perspectives in La Bruyère's* Caractères. 1981.

Hope H. Glidden. *The Storyteller as Humanist. The* Serées *of Guillaume Bouchet*. 1981.

Mary B. McKinley. *Words in a Corner. Studies in Montaigne's Latin Quotations*. 1981.

Donald M. Frame and Mary B. McKinley, eds. *Columbia Montaigne Conference Papers*. 1981.

Jean-Pierre Dens. *L'Honnête Homme et la critique du goût. Esthétique et société au XVIIe siècle*. 1981.

Vivian Kogan. *The Flowers of Fiction. Time and Space in Raymond Queneau's* Les Fleurs bleues. 1982.

Michael Issacharoff and Jean-Claude Vilquin, eds. *Sur tre et la mise en signe*. 1982.

James W. Mileham. *The Conspiracy Novel. Structure and Metaphor in Balzac's* Comédie humaine. 1982.

Andrew G. Suozzo. *The Comic Novels of Charles Sorel. A Study of Structure, Characterization and Disguise*. 1982.

Margaret Whitford. *Merleau-Ponty's Critique of Sartre's Philosophy*. 1982.

Gérard Defaux. *Le Curieux, le glorieux et la sagesse du monde dans la première moitié du XVIe siècle. L'exemple de Panurge (Ulysse, Démosthène, Empédocle)*. 1982.

Doranne Fenoaltea. *"Si haulte Architecture." The Design of Scève's* Délie. 1982.

Peter Bayley and Dorothy Gabe Coleman, eds. *The Equilibrium of Wit. Essays for Odette de Mourgues*. 1982.

Carol J. Murphy. *Alienation and Absence in the Novels of Marguerite Duras*. 1982.

Mary Ellen Birkett. *Lamartine and the Poetics of Landscape*. 1982.

Jules Brody. *Lectures de Montaigne*. 1982.

John D. Lyons. *The Listening Voice. An Essay on the Rhetoric of Saint-Amant*. 1982.

Edward C. Knox. *Patterns of Person. Studies in Style and Form from Corneille to Laclos*. 1983.

Marshall C. Olds. *Desire Seeking Expression. Mallarmé's "Prose pour des Esseintes."* 1983.

Ceri Crossley. *Edgar Quinet (1803-1875). A Study in Romantic Thought.* 1983.

Rupert T. Pickens, ed. *The Sower and His Seed. Essays on Chrétien de Troyes.* 1983.

Barbara C. Bowen. *Words and the Man in French Renaissance Literature.* 1983.

Clifton Cherpack. *Logos in Mythos. Ideas and Early French Narrative.* 1983.

Donald Stone, Jr. *Mellin de Saint-Gelais and Literary History.* 1983.

Louisa E. Jones. *Sad Clowns and Pale Pierrots. Literature and the Popular Comic Arts in 19th-Century France.* 1984.

JoAnn DellaNeva. *Song and Counter-Song. Scève's* Délie *and Petrarch's* Rime. 1983.

John D. Lyons and Nancy J. Vickers, eds. *The Dialectic of Discovery. Essays on the Teaching and Interpretation of Literature Presented to Lawrence E. Harvey.* 1984.

Warren F. Motte, Jr. *The Poetics of Experiment. A Study of the Work of Georges Perec.* 1984.

Jean R. Joseph. *Crébillon fils. Économie érotique et narrative.* 1984.

Carol A. Mossman. *The Narrative Matrix. Stendhal's* Le Rouge et le Noir. 1984.

Ora Avni. *Tics, tics et tics. Figures, syllogismes, récit dans* Les Chants de Maldoror. 1984.

Robert J. Morrissey. *La Rêverie jusqu'à Rousseau. Recherches sur un topos littéraire.* 1984.

Pauline M. Smith and I.D. McFarlane, eds. *Literature and the Arts in the Reign of Francis I. Essays Presented to C.A. Mayer.* 1985.

Jerry Nash, ed. *Pre-Pléiade Poetry.* 1985.

Jack Undank and Herbert Josephs, eds. *Diderot: Digression and Dispersion. A Bicentennial Tribute.* 1984.

Daniel S. Russell. *The Emblem and Device in France.* 1985.

Joan Dargan. *Balzac and the Drama of Perspective. The Narrator in Selected Works of* La Comédie humaine. 1985.

Emile J. Talbot. *Stendhal and Romantic Esthetics.* 1985.

Raymond C. La Charité, ed. *Rabelais's Incomparable Book. Essays on His Art.* 1986.

John Porter Houston. *Patterns of Thought in Rimbaud and Mallarmé.* 1986.

Mary Donaldson-Evans. *A Woman's Revenge. The Chronology of Dispossession in Maupassant's Fiction.* 1986.

Michèle Praeger. *Les Romans de Robert Pinget. Une écriture des possibles.* 1986.

Kari Lokke. *Gérard de Nerval. The Poet as Social Visionary.* 1987.

Virginia A. La Charité. *The Dynamics of Space. Mallarmé's* Un Coup de dés jamais n'abolira le hasard. 1987.

Anthony Pugh. *The Birth of* A la recherche du temps perdu. 1987.

Alain Toumayan. *La Littérature et la hantise du mal. Lectures de Barbey d'Aurevilly, Huysmans et Baudelaire.* 1987.

Robert Griffin. *Rape of the Lock. Flaubert's Mythic Realism.* 1988.

Michel Dassonville, ed. *Ronsard et Montaigne. Écrivains engagés?* 1989.

Lawrence D. Kritzman, ed. *Le Signe et le Texte. Études sur l'écriture au XVIᵉ siècle en France.* 1990.

Martine Motard-Noar. *Les Fictions d'Hélène Cixous. Une autre langue de femme.* 1991.

Barbara C. Bowen and Jerry C. Nash, eds. *Lapidary Inscriptions. Renaissance Essays for Donald A. Stone, Jr.* 1991.

Charles Krance. *L.-F. Céline. The I of the Storm.* 1992.

Maryann De Julio. *Rhetorical Landscapes: The Poetry and Art Criticism of Jacques Dupin.* 1992.

Raymond C. La Charité, ed. *Writing the Renaissance. Essays on Sixteenth-Century French Literature in Honor of Floyd Gray.* 1992.

Alain Toumayan, ed. *Literary Generations: A Festschrift in Honor of Edward D. Sullivan by His Friends, Colleagues, and Former Students.* 1992.